EUGENE TALMADGE

Eugene Talmadge, elected commissioner of agriculture, 1926, 1928, and 1930, and governor 1932, 1934, 1940, and 1946. (Photograph reprinted from the <u>Atlanta</u> <u>Constitution</u> by permission of that paper.)

EUGENE TALMADGE

Rhetoric and Response

Calvin McLeod Logue
Foreword by Bernard K. Duffy

Great American Orators, Number 3

Bernard K. Duffy and
Halford R. Ryan, Series Advisers

Greenwood Press
New York • Westport, Connecticut • London

Library of Congress Cataloging-in-Publication Data

Logue, Cal M. (Cal McLeod).
  Eugene Talmadge : rhetoric and response / Calvin McLeod Logue ;
foreword by Bernard K. Duffy.
    p. cm. — (Great American orators, ISSN 0898-8277 ; no. 3)
  "Speeches by Eugene Talmadge": p.
  Bibliography: p.
  Includes index.
  ISBN 0-313-25855-4 (lib. bdg. : alk. paper)
  1. Talmadge, Eugene, 1884-1946—Oratory. 2. Political oratory—
  Georgia. 3. Georgia—Politics and government—1865-1950.
I. Talmadge, Eugene, 1884-1946. Selections. 1989. II. Title.
III. Series.
F291.T3L64 1989
975.8'04'0924—dc 19   88-24748

British Library Cataloguing in Publication Data is available.

Library of Congress Catalog Card Number: 88-24748
ISBN: 0-313-25855-4
ISSN: 0898-8277

First published in 1989

Greenwood Press, Inc.
88 Post Road West, Westport, Connecticut 06881

Printed in the United States of America

The paper used in this book complies with the
Permanent Paper Standard issued by the National
Information Standards Organization (Z39.48-1984).

10 9 8 7 6 5 4 3 2 1

Dedication

To the newspaper reporters and editors who covered the political speaking of Eugene Talmadge and the responses generated by it. In their reports, some writers were prominently named, while others, on occasions, wrote anonymously, as in the <u>Cordele Dispatch</u>, <u>Covington News</u>, <u>Dalton Citizen</u>, <u>Dawson News</u>, <u>Lyons Citizen</u>, <u>Monroe Advertiser</u>, <u>Rome News-Tribune</u>, <u>Sandersville Progress</u>, <u>Middle Georgian</u>, <u>Elberton Star</u>, <u>Telfair Enterprise</u>, <u>Atlanta Daily World</u>, and <u>Augusta Chronicle</u>. Some writers backed Talmadge, even sitting on the speaker's platform with him to demonstrate their support, others opposed him, a couple shifted their loyalties, and a few primarily described what they saw and heard. But how does one remain dispassionate when tracking a tornado touching down in communities across the state! Most reporters seemed to enjoy their work. Unlike today, none complained of the "blandness" of their subject, but a few expressed concern about the future of democracy under Talmadge's leadership. While preoccupied personally with slick and dusty roads, train schedules, housing, food, refreshment, and meeting deadlines, professionally, the reporters contributed daily and weekly to the democratic process, providing valuable information and insights for citizens concerned with affairs of government. Representative of the many journalists at work in Georgia from 1920 to 1946 were Lovelace Eve, <u>Americus Times-Recorder</u>; J. B. Hardy, <u>Thomaston Times</u>; Bennett DeLoach, William H. Fields, and Thomas F. Coffey, Jr., <u>Savannah Morning News</u>; Dan McGill, <u>Athens Banner-Herald</u>; Ernest Camp, <u>Walton Tribune</u>; W. T. Anderson, John Chadwick, Henry Allen, and John W. Hammond, <u>Macon Telegraph and News</u>; Ben F. Meyer, Associated Press; Gladstone Williams, Paul Stevenson, L. A. Farrell, John Couric, Jim Furnis, M. L. St. John, Jack Spalding, Luke Green, Channing Cope, Ralph McGill, Jack Tarver, and Celestine Sibley, <u>Atlanta Constitution</u>.

Contents

viii   Contents

Series Foreword

The idea for a series of books on great American orators grew out of the recognition that there is a paucity of book-length studies on individual speakers and their craft. Apart from a few notable exceptions, the study of American public address has been pursued in scores of articles published in professional journals. Yet, no matter how insightful their intellectual forbears, each generation of rhetorical critics must reexamine its universe of discourse, expand the compass of its researches, and redefine its purpose and methods. To avoid intellectual torpor, scholars and students cannot be content simply to see through the eyes of those who have gone before them. As helpful as article-length studies have been, none has or can provide a complete analysis of a speaker's rhetoric. Book-length studies, such as those in this series, will help fill the void that has existed in the study of American public address. In books, more than in articles, the critic can explicate a speaker's persuasive discourse that ranges over politics and history, theology and sociology, communication and law. The comprehensive research and sustained reflection that books require will undoubtedly yield telling examinations and enduring insights for the nation's most important voices.

This series chronicles the role of public discourse in the United States. American speakers shaped the destiny of the colonies, the young republic, and the mature nation. During each stage of the intellectual, political, and religious development of the United States, great orators, standing at the rostrum, on the stump, and in the pulpit, persuaded their audiences with word and gesture. Usually striving for the noble, sometimes achieving the base, they urged their fellow citizens toward a more perfect Union.

Each book is organized to meet the needs of scholars and students who would evaluate the effects of American public address. Previously, if one desired to assess the impact of a speaker or a speech upon history, the path was, at best, not well marked and, at worst, littered with obstacles. To be sure, one might turn to biographies to learn about an orator, but for the public address scholar these sources often prove unhelpful. Rhetorical topics, such as speech invention, disposition, style, delivery, and persuasive effect, are often treated in passing, if at all. Authoritative speech texts are often difficult to locate and the problem of textual accuracy is frequently encountered. This is especially true for early figures, or for those whose persuasive role, though significant, was secondary to other leading lights of the age.

Part I is a critical analysis of the orator and his or her speeches. Within the format of a case study, one may expect considerable latitude. For instance, in a given chapter an author might explicate a single speech or a group of related speeches, or examine orations that comprise a genre of rhetoric such as forensic speaking. But the critic's focus remains on the rhetorical considerations of speaker and speech, purpose and effect.

Part II contains the texts of the important addresses that are discussed in the critical analysis that precedes it. To the extent possible, each author has endeavored to collect definitive speech texts, which have often been found through original research in historical materials. In a few instances, because of the extreme length of a speech, texts have been edited, but the authors have carefully deleted material that is least important to the speech, and these deletions have been held to a minimum.

Each book contains a chronology of major speeches that serves several purposes. Pragmatically, it lists all of the orator's known addresses. Places and dates of the speeches are also given, although this information is sometimes difficult to determine precisely. But in a wider sense, the chronology attests to the scope of rhetoric in the United States. Certainly in quantity, if not always in quality, Americans are historically talkers and listeners.

Because of the disparate nature of the speakers examined in the series, there is some latitude in the nature of the bibliographical materials that have been included in each book. But in every instance, authors have carefully described historical collections, and

have gathered primary and secondary sources that   bear
on the speaker and the oratory. By combining in   each
book critical chapters with bibliographical   materials
and speech texts, this   series notes that textual   and
research sources are interwoven in the act of rhetorical criticism.

  May the books in this   series serve as a   fitting
memorial to the nation's greatest orators as   students
and scholars study anew   the history and criticism   of
American public address.

Bernard K. Duffy
Halford R. Ryan

Foreword

This is the third book in the Great American Orators series. The first work discussed the oratory of Daniel Webster, and the second the speaking of Harry Emerson Fosdick. Professor Calvin Logue describes the rhetorical battles waged by Eugene Talmadge, who rose in Georgia politics by appealing to the geographical, social, and racial prejudices of his audiences. Talmadge was not, like Daniel Webster's Senatorial antagonists of the past century, a brilliant and fiery Southern statesman driven by principles derived from an identification with an aristocratic class. He was a politician who drew his power from an astute understanding of what the dirt farmers of rural Georgia expected in their politicians. They seemed first to want a person who could entertain them from the speaker's platform. There is little doubt that Talmadge's constituency delighted in his piercing attacks upon his political opponents, his repartee with the audience, his jokes, and political barbs. Talmadge was a consummate stump speaker who could manipulate an audience with an intuitive understanding of their emotions, a showman's timing, and the courage and tenacity of a bare-fisted boxer. Talmadge was an immensely colorful political persona. For Gene, as for his audiences, the issues of a campaign were not as important as the commanding presence of the man who was presenting them. There was no better name for his brand of politics than "Talmadgeism," for Talmadgeism was <u>sui</u> <u>generis</u>.

To classify Talmadge a demagogue, which he surely was, helps only partially to understand the man and his oratory. Professor Logue, a careful critic whose books and articles on Southern oratory have made him a leader in this field, has resisted pigeonholing

Talmadge.   Instead   he   helps   us   to   understand
Talmadge's unique approach   to the spoken   word as   an
instrument of immense political power.   But   Talmadge,
like the quintissential American demagogue, Huey Long,
Louisiana's "Kingfish," relied   upon his   considerable
ability to move his audiences with a torrent of highly
evocative   words.   To   a   large   extent   Talmadge's
politics   was   his   oratory.   Like   Long,   Talmadge
fulfilled some of his political promises.   In the end,
Talmadge fell prey   to hubris.   As   Logue remarks,   he
found it   personally impossible   to back   down from   a
fight,   even   when   he   was   losing   it,   and   his
ill-considered but pitched battle against the   Georgia
University System resulted   in a   loss of   face and   a
political defeat.
     This is   first of   all the   story of   a man   who,
sweat dripping from his   brow in the   heat of the   red
clay farmland, gave voice to the attitudes and   racial
biases of the many Georgians who identified with   him.
In an era of state   politics admittedly not known   for
its   sophistication   or   highmindedness,   Talmadge
nevertheless   managed   to   sound   new   depths   of
demagoguery.   Talmadge   made   his   red   galluses   the
trademark   of   his   rable-rousing   populism   that
characterized Georgia politics for decades.   This book
is also a carefully documented analysis of   Talmadge's
most significant political   and rhetorical   campaigns.
It attempts   to make   sense of   a style of   political
rhetoric that might be   dismissed as instinctive   were
it not for Logue's ability to perceive the contours of
Talmadge's rhetorical strategy and tactics.   Significantly, the   author has   expanded the   compass of   his
analysis to include   the response Talmadge's   rhetoric
elicited.   Another important   feature of   the book   is
its extensive   use   of   primary   documents,   including
audio   recordings,   films,   and   the   accounts   of
Talmadge's oratory in   small and prominent   newspapers
throughout Georgia.   Logue's access to these materials
and his   long experience   with Southern   oratory   have
made this an exceptional work.
     This   book   should   light   the   way   for   future
researchers of Eugene Talmadge's populist oratory.   It
should   also   help   guide   students   of   Talmadge's
biography, because what   is most   memorable about   the
Governor is his distinctive rhetoric.   This is a   book
about a bygone   era of Southern   state politics and   a
larger-than-life political personality who lives again
in these pages.

                              Bernard K. Duffy

Preface

In his book, <u>The</u> <u>Rhetoric</u>, Aristotle defined three
types of persuasive speaking: ceremonial, judicial,
and deliberative. Ceremonial speeches address issues
of honor and virtue, and include messages for special
occasions, such as eulogies and Fourth of July
orations when, for example, veterans are praised. In
Aristotle's view, judicial advocates debate questions
of justice and injustice, and judges and juries
render verdicts on deeds and decisions alleged to
have occurred in the past.

This book is about deliberative speaking.
Ideally deliberative discourse has citizens advising
each other individually and in public forums in forms
of expression that allow persons to make wise choices
and evolve worthy policies that govern their lives
equitably in arenas of ways and means, war and peace,
health and welfare, education, imports and exports,
legislation, and other communal interests.
Deliberative advocacy should have citizens exchanging
information and views within flexible parliamentary
procedures that encourage inventive and expansive
thought and positioning to determine binding
policies.

In the United States, courtroom (judicial)
discourse has largely replaced deliberative means as
the dominant method of reaching definitive decisions.
Deliberative discourse has atrophied to the point
that citizens now turn often to courtroom processes
for authoritative judgments in every branch of their
lives, including family, religion, education, media,
business, transportation, medicine, employment,
personal relationships, and entertainment. The
courts are handed issues because leaders and the
citizenry are unable to deliberate them meaningfully

and to formulate feasible policies in legislative and other public settings. Citizens too often are incapable of discussing significant issues to acceptable and productive conclusions. Citizens' choices are made, not in democratic debate, but within proceedings in courtrooms that severely restrict who may talk, how, when, and what they may say. In the United States in the 1980s deliberative discourse is stagnant and barren. Judicial procedures have inherited the substance of decisionmaking, leaving deliberative communicators preoccupied with showroom images of issues and personalities.

This decline in consequence of public speech has assigned potentially potent deliberations among elected officials in legislative bodies, members of civic clubs, religious groups, campus organizations, the business community, and families to the genre of the talk show. The decline in availability of occasions when serious discussion of issues is expected--more of a town meeting environment--has emerged, not primarily because of a conspiracy among liberal judges and lawyers bent on reinterpreting and creating new laws regulating contemporary life rather than mirrowing the intentions of the authors of the Constitution, but because citizens lack experience and education in the process of deliberative persuasion, and have forfeited their right to participate skillfully and responsibly in informed "speakings."

In his column in the Atlanta Constitution, on August 5, 1945, Channing Cope, lamenting the loss of neighbor Jim Rogers, illustrated the significance of salvaging arenas for deliberative discussions on issues vital to the well-being of the community. Cope argued that, with the death of Rogers,

> passed one of the old and important bulwarks
> of democracy, the forum of the country store.
> . . . A potbellied stove occupied the center
> of the store. Now, here was the important
> thing--the stove--for about it gathered the
> wise and the foolish, the noisy and the
> silent, each giving expression by one means
> of another to his views, or lack of them, on
> all important matters of the moment. It was
> around this stove that questions of real
> import were discussed, if not always settled.
> What variety of corn yields the best? Does
> the poisoning of cotton pay? What to do with
> an ailing calf? Does kudzu make good hay?
> Of course, politics came in for its share of

discussion--local politics, state-wide politics, and national politics. The congressman's
attitude on current questions was gone over
painstakingly. No one was in a hurry. There
was little or no oratory, for it was a forum
in which everybody who wanted to took part.
If an enthusiastic fellow-member got beyond
the reasonable stage in his arguments or became oratorical, his remarks were received
with heavy silence and the discussion ended
for the moment. The passing of such forums
as Jim Rogers' store is a tragedy of greater
importance than most of us realize. For the
great common sense of the great common people
is the factor which has made our country
great. Without the forum of the country store,
we become separated from each other. Without
the supporting indorsement of our neighbors we
lose confidence in our attributes and in our
views. Wedges are driven between us by special
pleaders. We come to lean on columnists and
radio personalities, and on Washington. We
permit our opinions to be manufactured for us.
Our own little community, being small and without voice, becomes even smaller and of less
importance in our thinking. In the end we doubt
ourselves and magnify the wisdom of others. The
individual grows less, the system grows greater.
. . . I hope some worthy successor to our old
neighbor, Jim Rogers, comes along and sets up in
our neighborhood on the Yellow river. [Reprint-
ed by permission of the Atlanta Constitution.]

Even   this   potbellied   democracy   had   its
limitations, as blacks were denied a seat at the
stove and women tolerated for a polite moment of
salutation. J. B. Hardy, editor and owner of the
Thomaston Times, after observing citizens' responses
to the public persuasion of Eugene Talmadge for five
years, wrote on August 14, 1931 a preamble to free
speech in contemporary political life, one that
contrasted sharply with the rhetorical conventions
governing a countrystore democracy: "Our people want
to be fooled and the candidate who is most successful
in this art will be winner . . . . This is the way
politics is played in Georgia." This rhetorical
theorem extends in the 1980s to a variety of forums,
including, for example, many viewers of thirty second
political and commercial advertisements on television, electronic preacher addicts, and some boosters
of collegiate athletics on and off campuses.

The immediate purpose of a political campaign is to win an election, not to create policies. However, Talmadge's twenty-six year career of campaigning and holding public office left an imprint on public life worth validating. In this book on rhetorical acts, one finds the seeds of a public discourse prominent today preoccupied with false appearances of issues and human virtues that would likely be met with "heavy silence" in a wood-stove democracy, with harnessing of participants accomplished through interactions among all persons present more than any prescriptive format like that dominating courtrooms. At the same time, in this book, in the accounts of individuals and groups responding to Talmadge's persuasive discourse, one identifies the potential for a more emphatic, responsible, and fruitful public initiation of substantive ideas and authentic convictions.

The author expresses appreciation to the following persons for encouragement and assistance: Dwight Freshley, Elise A. Hawkins, and Brenda Adams, University of Georgia; Jean Bowen; Michael J. Faherty, WSB Radio, Atlanta; Steven A. Gamble, Instructional Resources Center, University of Georgia; Sheryl B. Vogt and colleagues, Richard B. Russell Library, University of Georgia; Chris Paton and colleagues, Georgia State University Library; Dot P. Shackelford, Marie C. Ellis, Faye J. Dean, William R. Clayton, Jr., John L. Campbell, Max M. Gilstrap, Susan C. Field, Thomas E. Camden, Barbara B. Rystrom, and their colleagues, University of Georgia Library; Glenn McCutchen, <u>Atlanta Constitution</u>; University of Georgia Foundation; Herman Talmadge; Bran Parker; Bernard K. Duffy and Halford Ryan, Series Editors; Mildred Vasan and Teresa R. Metz, Editors, Greenwood Press; Mary Jo Logue, Michael Logue, and Andrew Logue.

Calvin M. Logue

I

A TURBULENT
RHETORIC

1

Threshold of
Political Power

From 1926 to 1946, Eugene Talmadge employed a volatile brand of politics in an attempt to win public
office and to rule Georgia. He worked to defeat
individual opponents and for personal interests
through the enforcement of his public personality.
Georgians came to know Talmadge by his public assaults upon individuals, issues, and institutions.
No friend or opponent was immune to his scurrilous
attacks. He attracted great interests in the press
by his public confrontations with issues and audiences. He attempted to overpower any person or group
who blocked his actions. When campaigning and while
holding office, Talmadge created a political persona
of a warrior fighting for the interests of abused
farmers and, later in his career, for the entire
working class. Talmadge talked energetically about
the problems faced by farmers, but ultimately did
little to solve them. In many elections, he won the
working class's votes by promising to rescue their
interests from the greed of wealthy capitalists. At
the same time, industrialists, bankers, and corporation executives helped finance Talmadge's campaigns
because he favored cutting taxes, reducing government
regulations of businesses, and constraining labor
unions. V. O. Key explained that Talmadge escaped
with this inconsistency in some elections between
stump claims and administrative policies because
there was no second political party in Georgia to
compete with him for followers.(1)
    By his uncompromising rhetoric, Talmadge con-
vinced Georgians to elect him Commisioner of Agriculture in 1926, 1928, and 1930, and governor in 1932,
1934, 1940, and 1946. Talmadge seduced voters who
were prostrate with a lack of education and job

skills, with little promise from his rhetoric of
entertainment for improving their lives. When
elected to public office, he was not reluctant to
abuse authority in order to implement personal
preferences over constitutionally reached policies.
Should established governmental procedures enable him
to achieve goals, he used them. If legal channels
became obstacles to his interests, he acted unilaterally. When he felt it was necessary and when allowed
to do so, he exercised his will over choices of
individuals and social and legal conventions. When
these improper or seemingly illegal acts received
significant opposition, in a trademark of his rhetorical behavior, Talmadge appealed directly to the mass
of Georgians to legitimize efforts he claimed were
made for them and to rescue him from what he portrayed as the evil opposition.

Certainly not all citizens appreciated
Talmadge's rhetoric of intimidation. He lost
state-wide elections in 1936, 1938, and 1942, in
part, because many voters were not pleased by his
strident posturing for self-interests and violation
of social and legal traditions. Critics came to
equate "Talmadgeism" with Nazism. Some journalists,
opposing candidates, students, and public officials
believed him to be a tyrant, and found the courage to
say so in public. Talmadge shouted defiantly that he
was tempestuous, but only as a means of aiding the
working class. Careful in public speeches to
circumvent the question of how his policies often
favored the wealthy, he won votes from many of the
working class by espousing lower taxes for farmers
and laborers, less government control over citizens,
increased pay for teachers, the prevention of "social
equality" for blacks, and better job opportunities
for white Georgians.

Early in life Talmadge demonstrated an interest
in learning to persuade audiences. In school he was
recognized for his ability to speak effectively.
Talmadge's teacher, W. D. Thurmond, recalled the
impression left by the young student who grew up on a
two-thousand-acre farm five miles outside of McRae,
Georgia, and rode to school on a Texas pony.
Thurmond indicated that the success with which
Talmadge campaigned in 1926 for the office of Commissioner of Agriculture against a powerful incumbent
came as no surprise to him. After all, at the age of
thirteen, when representing Hilliard Institute at a
"school meet" at Jackson, Georgia, Talmadge won a
medal in declamation. Proud that a former pupil was
elected Commissioner of Agriculture, Thurmon emphasized how, when a young student, Talmadge had been
faithful, ambitious, conscientious, respectful,
truthful, and honest. As a student at the University

of Georgia, Talmadge practiced debating skills in Phi Kappa and Euphradians forensics societies. He was selected "anniversariory" of Phi Kappa debating society. At the University Talmadge was a "leader" in forensics, winning the freshman debaters' medal and the sophomore declaimers' cup.(2)

Although caught up in the fervor of a local favorite winning the office of Commissioner of Agriculture, his teacher W. D. Thurmond hit upon a key to Talmadge's ability to persuade many Georgians. Thurmon believed Talmadge to have won the election because he spoke with a "ring of sincerity." After interviewing Thurmond, journalist W. K. Rhodes concluded: "From the above record it can now easily be seen how" Talmadge "out-classed" J. J. Brown in a debate for the office of Commissioner of Agriculture. Students who attended the University of Georgia with Talmadge agreed that he was an effective speaker. They told reporter Dan McGill that during their college days Talmadge was "some debater." After watching Talmadge defeat incumbent John J. Brown in debates in the 1926 race for Commisioner of Agriculture, Dan McGill concluded that the former champion collegiate debater was "still right there with the goods," but now his performance was "more finished."(3)

In refining his public speaking after college, Talmadge was influenced by veteran speakers who entertained and inspired audiences in south Georgia. According to Thurmond, Talmadge joined the Forsyth Baptist Church at the age of twelve, where he would have observed how preachers of the gospel established their own popularity, won converts, and collected funds. Indeed, when studying films of Talmadge's 1933 and 1935 Inaugural speeches, the author noted in the Governor's delivery a suggestion of the evangelistic preacher's sonorous vocal quality.(4) Talmadge also adopted speaking techniques employed by persuasive political orators. In 1920, the year Talmadge first campaiged for public office, Thomas W. Watson bolted the Democratic party and ran for the United States Senate. During that campaign, the "biggest crowd ever assembled in McRae," Talmadge's home town, waited to hear Tom Watson speak, only to learn that the visit was canceled, ostensibly because of his poor health.(5)

The day Watson canceled that speech in McRae, Georgians read that he had been placed in jail for using profanity in an address to an audience in which there were women present.(6) On a related issue, and one important for political campaigning in the 1920s and beyond, a few days after Tom Watson's use of profane language, citizens learned that Attorney

General R. A. Denny had informed Governor Hugh Dorsey that women in Georgia could vote in the 1920 campaign, providing a new constituency of supporters and opponents for Talmadge and other politicians.(7)

Talmadge liked Tom Watson's unrestrained manner of speaking in public, and adopted many of the more elderly Watson's belligerent podium manners. In the region where Talmadge was reared, he read a variety of stories about Tom Watson's speaking assaults on people and issues. In 1920, an editor reviewed the debate that took place between Watson and Tom W. Hardwick on August 6, 1910, one of the significant face-to-face political duels in Georgia preceding Talmadge's three debates with Commissioner Brown in 1926.(8) Talmadge said he modeled his political discourse after the elderly Watson's vehement speaking practices. Talmadge explained to a Thomson, Georgia audience how observing Watson's speeches influenced his own. "When I was a little boy, I . . . saw a man with red hair . . . and flashing eyes who talked to the people in large assemblages in language that brought them to their feet with wild cheers." Talmadge defended his own rowdy brand of public speaking and his concern for the common man and woman by comparing his rhetorical behavior with Watson's. In 1928, Talmadge promised to employ Watson's "language" in his own speeches for the "common people."(9)

During the early 1920s, Talmadge worked diligently to establish a political threshold upon which to manipulate audiences through explosive persuasive speeches. After being graduated from the University of Georgia in law and becoming dissatisfied with teaching, working in the (Albert) Howell, Heyman, and Bolding law firm in Atlanta, in his law offices in Ailey, Georgia and Telfair County, and farming full-time, Talmadge looked to local government as an entrance into politics. Because of the influence of his father, in 1918 Talmadge was appointed solicitor of the City Court in McRae, Georgia. In 1920, because of support he provided for J. C. Thrasher's successful candidacy for County Commissioner, Talmadge was appointed attorney for Telfair County.(10) That same year, at the age of thirty-six, Talmadge campaigned unsuccessfully for state representative. In that campaign, the Telfair Enterprise noted that Talmadge would speak in Lumber City on July 31, Jacksonville on August 3, and Powell School House on August 7.(11)

During that 1920 campaign, Talmadge demonstrated the self-confidence he achieved early in political life for confronting opponents extemporaneously before hostile audiences. Probably remembering his

own experiences in competitive disputations in
college and reading about the confrontations Tom
Watson had with Hardwick and others, Talmadge challenged opponent D. W. Phillips to "bring his friends"
and meet him in public debate.(12) When an underdog
in the 1926 campaign for Commissioner of Agriculture,
Talmadge repeated this early practice of challenging
his opponent and that candidate's supporters to
debate him.   In later campaigns, however, Talmadge
accepted the challenge from opponents to debate only
when it was to his advantage.   He lost the primary
election in 1920 by a vote of 756 to 1,187.   In 1922,
Talmadge campaigned in a three-county district for
state senator. He converted a number of citizens to
his camp, and won a majority of the popular vote.
Talmadge proved his ability to finesse support from
what should have been an unfriendly audience by
winning an endorsement from the Women's Christian
Temperance Union.(13) He lost the election because
his opponent won the county unit votes.

     The county unit system provided voters in rural
counties an inequitable share of power to elect
persons to public office. This explains why Talmadge
directed his public appeals to farmers and residents
of small towns rather than voters from the more
populated areas of Georgia.   Each county had twice as
many county unit votes as it had representatives in
the Georgia House of Representatives.   Eight counties
with the largest population had only six unit votes
each, thirty counties had four unit votes each, while
121 counties had two unit votes each.   The candidate
receiving a plurality of votes in a county won its
unit votes.   In the less populated counties, a few
well entrenched local office holders could swing an
election. A well placed sum of federal dollars could
do wonders for one's campaign, a factor motivating
Talmadge's conflict in the 1930s with the Roosevelt
Administration over who would control and distribute
federal Relief funds.   The political consequence was
that Talmadge could win an election by praising
farmers and attacking big business in Atlanta for
abusing agriculture.

     A split between rural and urban sections helped
flame Talmadge's rhetoric.   After Reconstruction,
Henry Grady and other New South spokesmen worked for
manufacturers and railroad interests at the expense
of agriculture.   It was to Talmadge's political
advantage, then, on the one hand, to soothe the
genuine hurt experienced by farmers and, on the
other, to implement policies in government that freed
the city capitalists to exploit the countryside.
Talmadge was supported by voters in the central and
southern sections of the state, along with persons

from "about ten counties in north Georgia." Of ninety-two counties "with no town over 2,500 only 12" consistently opposed Talmadge. Most of the workers in textiles and other manufactures lived in the north of the state, and opposed Talmadge.(14)

By 1924, although he had established considerable political visibility and support for his candidacy in home counties, Talmadge was unable to maneuver to a position of authority among the ring of Democrats controlling Telfair county. Because he could not win public office among neighbors, it appeared that Talmadge would suffer the same frustration in politics that he had experienced in teaching, law, and farming. With the speaking skills that he brought from college, one might have expected Talmadge to try a different line of work, possibly in sales or, with his ability to move southern audiences, in preaching of the Christian gospel for profit. Other than embellishing political messages with Biblical lyrics, Talmadge expressed publicly little commitment to organized religion. After he won the election in 1926 for Commissioner of the Department of Agriculture in Georgia, the Atlanta Constitution showered Talmadge with praise, reporting that his family were "staunch members of the First Baptist church of McRae" and how at least some of them showed an "active interest in church work."(15)

Talmadge found politics to be prescription enough for his soul. Politically Talmadge was not easily discouraged. Undaunted by losing campaigns in 1920 and 1922, he responded with the unpredictability and boldness that Georgians and others came to associate with the politician from Telfair County. In 1926 Talmadge surprised all observers, certainly the political rulers of Telfair and surrounding counties, by entering the state-wide campaign for Commissioner of Agriculture. Because the Commissioner of Agriculture exercised significant influence in Georgia politics, the Democratic party, and in affairs of state government, one can understand why Talmadge wanted that job but not why he thought he could win it.

Through his powers of public speaking, in 1926 Talmadge overcame what for most ambitious politicians would have been insurmountable odds, and won the election for Commissioner of Agriculture. Talmadge was re-elected relatively easily as Commissioner of Agriculture in 1928 and 1930. After establishing a large following of Georgia voters, he won elections for governor in 1932 and 1934. The contrast between Talmadge's political status in 1926 and 1936 was striking. In 1926, although unable to win public office at home, Talmadge campaigned successfully for

Talmadge addresses an outdoor rally broadcast by radio throughout the state. (Photograph reprinted from the <u>Atlanta Constitution</u> by permission of that paper.)

Commissioner of the Department of Agriculture.   By
the end of his second term as governor, in 1936, it
appeared unlikely that Talmadge could lose a
state-wide campaign. But in 1936 and 1938 he lost
elections for the United States Senate.   In later
campaigns for governor, Talmadge won in 1940, lost in
1942, and won in 1946, the year he died. How in 1926
could this novice and defeated politician have
unseated John J. Brown for Commissioner of Agriculture? In contrast, how in 1936, 1938, and 1942,
after achieving such great political popularity, did
this experienced and successful politician lose
elections?

The author analyzes the means by which Talmadge
converted citizens to his view of issues and events,
won votes, and justified his own controversial
political acts. The writer explores how, during his
political career, Talmadge employed rhetorical skills
learned in grade school, in college, when observing
veteran Georgia speakers, and while practicing law.
The author considers how the man made the citizenry
an extension of his own persuasive efforts for
self-interests. Talmadge tried to mobilize Georgians
as a giant audience for legitimizing his will in the
state. Although the book keeps Talmadge on center
stage, significant attention is given to the roles of
citizens and organizations responding publicly to
Talmadge's politics of intimidation. Thus the author
attempts to reconcile Talmadge's increasingly
demagogic rhetoric with democratic processes and
values that harbored it.

In Chapters 2 and 3, the author investigates
how, in the 1926 campaign for Commissioner of
Agriculture, Talmadge developed a prototype of
persuasive speaking for political occasions that
marked the man, the period, and the citizenry of
Georgia for twenty years, leaving its imprint upon
southern politics and state government well beyond
his death in 1946. Talmadge perfected a model of
political speaking conceived in rallies during June
and July of the 1926 campaign for Commisioner of
Agriculture, the subject of Chapter 2, and refined in
three debates with incumbent John J. Brown in August
of that election, the theme of Chapter 3.

Talmadge's success in politics depended upon the
citizens' willingness to join his political drives.
He transformed personal crusades for office and
self-interests into political theater, with voters
cast in a strong supporting role. Consequently he
developed a means of speaking that attracted attention of journalists, publicly enlisted large numbers
of Georgians to participate in his campaign for votes
during elections, and obtained endorsements of

controversial decisions while he was in office.   For
Talmadge's profane variety of persuasive speaking to
flourish, it required a convulsive social and political environment with a wounded antagonist on hand
willing to defend his record publicly.   Talmadge's
tempestuous public personality and his   arrogant
behavior usually assured the involvement of the mass
of Georgia voters and opponents in his private social
movements. He left opponents no choice; either they
came out to meet him in a public arena, or he relent-
lessly tracked them across the state. How successful
Talmadge was in winning an election or enforcing a
controversial or illegal decision depended also upon
the will, character, and effectiveness of persons and
organizations who opposed him.

In Chapters 4, 5, 6, and 7, the author analyzes
how Talmadge applied his prototype of political
persuasion in different social and political settings. The author evaluates how Talmadge forged and
adapted his mode of persuasive behavior as a means of
attempting to dominate discussions of issues and
determining and defending policies.   In each instance
he tried to impose his will upon that of other
interested parties. Of course, Talmadge shifted into
slang, rural speech when talking to farmers gathered
in the shade of oak trees still dusty from field
work, and formalized his address when responding to
questions from League of Women Voters meeting in a
University community. But no matter what the context, audience, opposition, support, cause, or event,
rather than merely adapting to changing scenes and
perceptions, Talmage stayed with the source of power
that was native to his political behavior, a <u>violent</u>
<u>rhetorical turbulence</u> that generated interest,
support, and opposition. When convulsive social and
political conditions existed to which his prototype
of persuasive speaking was indigeneous, Talmadgeism
often flourished. When a situation was less agitat-
ed, and he attempted to create social and political
disturbances artificially as a strategy for winning
his way, the results were mixed. No matter what the
mood and the moment, however, ultimately Talmadge
deployed a paradigm of public rowdiness as a last
line of defense. When an individual, issue, event,
or decision pleased him, Talmadge smiled and cajoled,
with the personal wrath smoldering constantly within
and predictably erupting the moment he was challenged
by supporter or opponent.

Because Talmadge expressed desires and preferences in public with such rhetorical abandonment, his
speeches revealed significant insight into the man,
his views, and his rhetorical methods. He was a
shrewd strategist, and said what he knew would win

him support. At the same time, when defending his
candidacy for office or a controversial act initiated
while holding office, because of his extemporaneous
and bombastic manner of presentation he was less able
to hold back, and storms of contempt expressed in
public speeches carried something of the man's
motivation and convictions. When responding to
speaking situations and audiences extemporaneously,
he was less able to monitor the content of his
preferences and prejudices; thus, as will be demonstrated in the case studies in this book, he found
himself calling neighbors' young sons and daughters
"bums and loafers" for participating in a federal
work program.

His public comments upon persons and issues
showed something of the values he esteemed. By his
freewheeling rhetoric Talmadge publicly committed
himself to claims and actions any fair-minded, or
even politically controlled person would later have
modified or retracted. To Talmadge, however, change
of mind meant weakness of heart and loss of votes.
He persisted in indefensible positions brought upon
himself by extravagant claims made extemporaneously
because of impassioned responses they provoked from
audiences, an exercise too often resulting in recip-
rocal rhetorical delusion between speaker and audience. As he won and lost elections, accumulated
political power, attacked "social equality" between
black and white citizens, and fed upon his own
exaggerated claims, Talmadge intensified his defiant
rhetoric, the prayer of his politics being, My will
be done!

Study of films of Talmadge's Inaugural speeches
of 1933 and 1935 reveals something of his magic
behind the political podium. Having just come in
from battle in gubernatorial campaigns where he made
hundreds of talks to large and vocal audiences
throughout Georgia, in the Inaugurals, he harnessed
the raucous stump rhetoric to celebrate victories
before a joint session of the legislature and guests
meeting in the House of Representatives chamber. In
these more formal settings, the governor dressed
conventionally and behaved decorously. For example
he wore a dark suit with flower in left lapel and
handerkchief in coat pocket, what critics called his
slicked down look for city audiences. Still he
communicated enthusiastically and with great confidence and conviction. Varying the inflection of his
voice somewhat in the idiom of a Baptist preacher,
unlike on occasions when talking to audiences gathered under oak trees and hanging out of courthouse
windows, he measured phrases deliberately, and
articulated words and thoughts with considerable

precision. His son, Herman Talmadge, informed the
author that, for his inaugural addresses and other
formal occasions, Eugene Talmadge prepared manu-
scripts. Although there was no indication on the
films that he referred to manuscipts when delivering
the Inaugurals, comparison of differences in texts
published in newspapers with passages from the films,
may indicate that he followed some prepared line of
thought. The texts published in newspapers appeared
to be taken from advanced copies made available to
the press. Filmed excerpts of the Inaugurals show
that he followed the text, but only in a general way.
Of course he had addressed the same topics in hundreds of campaign talks; so he needed no special
preparation for presenting the Inaugurals.(16)

Films of his two more formally presented Inaugurals reveal how at times he spoke with both hands
behind him, standing erect, and leaning back slightly
with an attitude of boldness, wiping his mouth with a
handkerchief. Then he leaned his left shoulder
toward the audience, clenched his right fist, extended the fingers of that hand, hitting the air for
emphasis. He chopped with both hands open and
fingers pointing straight ahead, as if hitting the
heels of both on a table. He spoke in standard
southern speech, using the accent of the region to
stress certain ideas. At one point he pronounced
every syllable of the word "government," in more
general American speech. Then, warming to the
occasion, to nail home a point, he talked of the cost
of "guv'm't" having to be cut. He said that during
his first term as governor, "we've been he'ah [here]
in the state busy." At times Talmadge leaned forward, extended his right hand high above his head,
and brought it down forcefully along his right side
in time with the vocal emphasis, shouting in the 1935
Inaugural: "With a savings in the highway department,
we have two million dollars . . . and are asking you
members of the General Assembly to . . . divert it
for the purpose of paying up the past due salaries of
school teachers and Confederate pensioners propor-
tionately [applause]."

In a silent film of Talmadge speaking outdoors,
at what appeared to be one of his more representative
political rallies, one sees in that setting that his
nonverbal delivery was far more animated than when
giving the two Inaugural addresses. Outdoors, before
a microphone on which hung the letters, WATJ, he
addressed a large crowd of attentive listeners, many
of them men wearing hats, some squatting, most
standing. In the opening of the film, one sees car
after car arriving for the speaking, as if stacked up
on a busy freeway, with small flags blowing from both

front fenders of one of the cars. Attractive young
women sat near him while he spoke, also facing the
throng. He spoke without coat, displaying the famous
suspenders over long sleeved shirt buttoned at the
wrists.

His facial expression matched the scorn with
which he routinely ridiculed opponents and their
views, as he sneered at the supportive and responsive
crowd. One is impressed by the intense seriousness
and high energy that he displayed physically to the
listeners. Talmadge also had a nice smile, and
enjoyed moments of persuasive humor with the crowd.
At one point in the speech, delivered among pine
trees prominent in Georgia, he gestured with both
arms, elbows bent, hands toward the sky. Loosening
the tie with his left hand, he extended the right arm
above the crowd, then pointed directly into the
audience to his right, in an intimidating fashion,
drilling home his point to the wellsatisfied audience. On the film, one sees supporters carry
Talmadge triumphantly from behind the microphone, not
on their shoulders, but high in their arms so as to
display him to the voters, with the spent speaker and
listeners smiling pleasurably back and forth.(17)

In a film recording of the 1933 Inaugural, one
hears the audience applaud Talmadge's prescription
for recovery from economic depression. He argued
that "We've got to cut the cost of this government.
The only way I know to do it is to abolish every
department that we can do without." Talmadge possessed perfect pitch for oratorical sounds. Just as
some persons perfect musical skills, Talmadge mastered many rhetorical notes. He borrowed speech
patterns from evangelists, but one would not confuse
him with a preacher speaking; his was an oratory of
politics and power. To emphasize key thoughts, he
placed special emphasis upon certain words, holding
them as a singer would a note, much like the cooing
of a dove. For example, in an audio recording of his
May 4, 1946, WSB radio speech, one hears Talmadge
praise the courage of World War II veterans "carried
out on to the seeeee's [seas]." In discussing
pensions for the elderly, he explained that the
funding approved was all he "could offf'aaaa [of-
fer]." Other words he savored, in this speech and in
a Columbus, Georgia, speech studied on audio recording, were "stream," "yard," "say," "watch out,"
"war," "ever saw," "at me," "take," "great," "engineers," "not afraid," and "enemy soil." At times, to
stress the great significance of a thought, he added
a slight quiver to his voice, when saying such words
as "dark" and "ponds."(18)

Periodically in his speeches he built to a

climax, ending in a higher pitch, as in the 1935
Inaugural when he said, "The only way to have an
honest guv'ment is to keep it poor [applause]. You
can't help people by give'n 'em some'um. You weaken
the soul, you weaken the heart, and you dry up the
muscles [applause]."   Dr. Dwight L. Freshley, an
authority on the speaking voice, using the words just
quoted, helped explained Talmadge's distinctive
speaking patterns. "In this passage, after shrieking
to the equivalent of the high musical note, 'A,' more
than one octave-and-a-half above Middle C, on the
word, 'You' in the phrase, '<u>You</u> kain't hep,' Talmage,
sounding like an Irish lyric tenor, drew out the
words, 's-o-u-l' and 'h-e-a-r-t.' He possessed a
remarkable pitch range of two octaves that enabled
him to achieve great dramatic effect at the stump.
For example, when acknowledging Mrs. Talmadge's
presence at an Inaugural speech, like a ring announcer introducing a boxer, he chanted: 'I present to you
Mrs. Eugene Talmadge, the first lady of the land'".

"Talmadge had a slightly nasal quality," continued Freshley, "but its resonance made the voice
project easily. Confronting large audiences outdoors, he tended to speak loud, and the louder he
spoke the higher the pitch. As is true of many
southerners, Talmadge did not pronounce the 'r' in
words such as 'merchants,' 'first,' and 'hear.' He
omitted the 'l' sound in 'help,' and the 'ng' in
'giving.' He said 'kaint' for 'can't.' Unlike many
southerners, in pronouncing most diphthongs, such as
'i,' 'ou,' and 'oi,' Talmadge pronounced both
sounds." For oratorical impact, Talmadge also ended
some sentences on a distinctively low pitch, once
again taking advantage of his unique vocal range. In
discussing the Supreme Court's decision in 1946
against racial segregation on interstate transportation, for example, he noted how that judgment was
"decided about four weeks <u>ago</u>," lowering his pitch
unexpectedly on the last word in an exaggerated
manner.

In several cases studied in this book, one finds
Talmadge defending recurring themes on cost of
government and race, but often in rhetorical performances less civil than those displayed in victory in
the 1933 and 1935 Inaugural addresses. In coming
chapters we find Talmadge hard at talk winning a
state-wide election for Commissioner of Agriculture,
invading a farm meeting in Macon, Georgia, campaigning for the first time for governor, losing a campaign for the United States Senate, seducing the
University System in Georgia, and ending his political career in victory.

But other important voices are heard. A number

of persons opposed the political demagoguery, including a president of the Macon Chamber of Commerce, a minority of the members of the Board of Regents, a Vice Chancellor, a former Chair of the Board of Regents, college president, University of Georgia alumni president, journalists, professor of English, professional organization, and college students. Several civic clubs and a radio station made available their forums for the public expression of opposing views, among them the Kiwanis Club of Griffin, the Lions, Rotary, and Civitan clubs of Atlanta, the Rotary Club of Decatur, the Kiwanis Club of Savannah, and WSB radio of Atlanta.

NOTES

1. V. O. Key, Jr., Southern Politics in State and Nation (New York: Vintage Books, 1949), pp. 116-117.
2. W. K. Rhodes' interview with W. D. Thurmond, Atlanta Constitution, September 12, 1926; Sarah McCulloh Lemmon, "The Public Career of Eugene Talmadge: 1926-1936," Ph.D. dissertation, Univ of North Carolina, Chapel Hill, 1952, pp. 3-4.
3. Dan McGill, Athens Banner-Herald, August 13, 1926.
4. January 10, 1933 and January 16, 1935 Inaugural Speeches, WSB Newsfilm Archives, Instructional Resources Center, University of Georgia, Record 40353, Tape Reel 0854.
5. Telfair Enterprise, August 26, 1920.
6. Eastman Times-Journal, August 26, 1920.
7. Telfair Enterprise, September 2, 1920; Eastman Times-Journal, August 12 and September 2, 1920.
8. Eastman Times-Journal, July 29, 1920.
9. Americus Times-Recorder, August 27, 1928; see Atlanta Constitution, July 15 and 22, September 10 and 16, 1932, and August 9, 1934.
10. Lemmon, "Public Career of Eugene Talmadge," pp. 3-12; William Anderson, The Wild Man from Sugar Creek: The Political Career of Eugene Talmadge (Baton Rouge: Louisiana State University Press, 1975), pp. 23-26.
11. Telfair Enterprise, July 29, 1920.
12. Telfair Enterprise, July 29, 1920.
13. Telfair Enterprise, August 3, 1922.
14. Key, Southern Politics in State and Nation, pp. 113, 117-119, 122.
15. Atlanta Constitution, September 10, 1926.
16. University of Georgia, Record 40353, Tape Reel 0854; Record 41261, Tape Reel 0888; Atlanta Constitution, January 11, 1933 and January 17, 1935.
17. Film of Eugene Talmadge speaking at a political rally. The date and locale of the speech are unknown; however, the model of the cars in the film

indicate that the speech was delivered after 1939.

18. Audio recording of WSB radio campaign speech, Atlanta, Georgia, May 4, 1946; audio recording of WSB radio speech, Columbus, Georgia, July 13, 1946. Both in Special Collections Department, Georgia State University, Atlanta.

2

Leading the Pack

Having lost political campaigns at home, and having been rejected by the powerful courthouse leadership in Telfair County, Talmadge looked for another avenue to authority in public office. He campaigned for Commissioner of the Department of Agriculture in Georgia. By criticizing Commissioner John J. Brown and promising to improve the plight of farmers, he defeated the incumbent in the election of 1926 for Commissioner of Agriculture, and was re-elected to that office in 1928 and 1930.

One can readily see why a man of Talmadge's uncanny ability to assess a situation for its potential political benefits looked to the arena of agriculture in which to seek personal political power. In the 1920s, agriculture dominated the economy of Georgia, and farmers were in need of assistance that Talmadge broadcast from stumps throughout the state. Most Georgians depended upon agriculture for income. In 1920 only 25.1 percent of Georgia's population was urban.(1) The county unit system of electing public officials favored the rural areas, a fact that Talmadge clearly understood and exploited.

The economic depression came to agriculture in Georgia "several years" prior to the crash of 1929. Between 1920 and 1925 the total value of farms in the state decreased nearly fifty percent, with the drop continuing until 1935. The cotton industries also suffered.(2) Numan Bartley reported that destruction caused by the boll weevil cut cotton production in 500-pound bales from 2,122,000 in 1918 to 588,000 in 1923. Even with the restoration of cotton production to near the higher level in the late 1920s, farmers continued to suffer from low market prices.

Consequently many farmers looked for work in the towns.(3)   The textile mills in the South increased, with 221 new mills and expansions in 1921, 480 in 1922, and 469 before the end of 1923.(4)   Persons remaining in agriculture experienced pressing problems.

In Georgia historically, economic issues have been closely tied to political interests. Since the Civil War economic and political competition existed between rural and urban citizens in Georgia, a conflict Talmadge exploited for political power. Individuals and groups advocated policies they claimed best represented the interests of farmers. After 1865 many southern whites lost their farms under a crop-lien system, bringing about the Populist protests of the 1880s and 1890s.   The Populists opposed an economic system they said enabled nonproducers such as merchants, bankers, and lawyers to earn profits at the expense of workers. Barton Shaw found that by 1889 the Southern Farmers' Alliance in Georgia had attracted 85,000 supporters. The rural, "wool hat" citizens formed the Georgia People's party in 1892.   The wool hat boys were noncity dwellers from the mountains, piney woods, coastal plain, and small towns. Although the young Tom Watson strived to organize and represent all members of the working class, regardless of their race, Populists in Georgia were mainly hostile to blacks.(5)

In political campaigns, Talmadge directed his appeals to residents of rural counties because they held the balance of power in elections.   To win a campaign one had to obtain a majority of county unit votes; thus, candidates were required to campaign throughout the state and win the support of local leaders who influenced their neighbors' votes. Talmadge profited from this system by praising farmers and chastizing the wealthy who resided in urban, "street car" communities. As explained in Chapter 1, Talmadge devised a mode of turbulent rhetorical behavior well suited for farmers and other workers who felt they had been denied equal opportunity for earning a fair income.

Talmadge's agitation of the rural/urban conflict came on the heels of others' attempts to organize the working class into a powerful voting bloc.   Tom Watson, a political personality with whom Talmadge identified in public speeches, served as a link between Populism and Progressivism, supporting child labor laws and the regulations of railroads. In 1906 Watson endorsed Hoke Smith's progressive administration in Georgia.(6)   For the most part, organizers placated the prejudices of whites by not extending promised benefits to blacks. In his later years, Tom

Watson employed blatantly racist appeals, a practice
that Talmadge emulated. Hoke Smith also was willing
to disfranchise blacks to accomplish progressive
reforms beneficial to whites. By 1910 literacy tests
and poll taxes were employed to keep blacks in their
subservient station and to lessen the political power
of poor whites. When those constraints failed, some
whites used various forms of coercive persuasion.
The Populists sought more equitable competition based
upon social and economic classes, but were defeated
by conservative Democrats. With the demise of the
Populists in 1910, Watson returned to the Democratic
party. T. Harry Williams stated that Progressivism
derived from "middle-class and urban" influences and
advocated "moderate reforms" in the economy, including the control of big corporations and support for
agricultural schools. Progressivism also failed to
meet the needs of the citizenry.(7)

When Populism ebbed, the elderly Tom Watson
adopted the racist rhetorical appeals popularized by
white politicians during Reconstruction, and be-
queathed them to Eugene Talmadge, who perfected and
stocked them for use as needed to agitate a particular situation.(8) Talmadge selected issues that were
ripe for exploiting rhetorically by his turbulent
form of behavior. He was far more interested in an
issue for the opportunity it provided to him for
gaining autonomous power than for its potential for
improving the lives of others.

Unlike some leaders who attempted to organize
voters around a substantive agenda, Talmadge offered
himself as the hope of the common man and woman. He
promised that his personal courage and skill in
speaking for farmers alone were prescription upon
which the working class could rely. His policies and
programs were forged primarily in arguments created
extemporaneously from behind the stump, taking the
form required to attract support for campaigns and
for controversial acts committed while in office.
Because rural voters controlled the county unit votes
required for winning public office, in his public
speeches Talmadge chose issues and treated them in a
manner often pleasing to them. He assured farmers
that cutting taxes and reducing the cost and influence of government were in their best interests. He
carefully avoided stating publicly how those policies
benefited wealthy capitalists, a charge articulated
forcefully by Richard B. Russell, Jr., in the campaign for the United States Senate in 1936. In
developing issues for their persuasive value, he
echoed Bourbon Democrats' opposition to high taxes
and expensive government services, Populists' promises to provide relief for rural persons, and

Progressives' efforts to regulate railroads and utilities.(9)

To win office and to defend policies, when necessary Talmadge shouted warnings of "race mixing," drawing upon a genre of racist rhetoric indigenous to southern politics. The topic of race was particularly potent in southern campaign discourse. Aside from the young Tom Watson's call for cooperation among poor whites and blacks for self-interests, in Georgia ultimately neither Populist nor Progressive forces seriously threatened the dominance of whites over blacks economically and politically. When he determined the strategy would win votes, Talmadge capitalized upon the fears and prejudices of whites by envisioning an arrangement of social equality that had little or no chance of taking place during his career, although the Supreme Court ruled against holding political primaries for whites only and against segregation in interstate transportation in time for his final, 1946 campaign for governor.

Having grown up on a farm in south Georgia and having listened to Tom Watson and other leaders proclaim the abuses suffered by farmers, Talmadge was better prepared than one might think to campaign for the office of Commissioner of Agriculture. He made this race a public battle against the evils committed by incumbent Commissioner J. J. Brown and corruption in the state agency. The Department of Agriculture in Georgia was created to provide services for farmers within a state where agriculture dominated the economy. The department inspected oil, gas, and fertilizer to ensure that products of high quality were available for consumers. Commissioner Brown appointed Heads within the Department of Agriculture for divisions such as Entomology, Pure Food, Veterinary, Drugs and Narcotics, Fertilizer, Oil, and Bureau of Markets. Brown appointed 191 inspectors who were distributed throughout all counties to monitor the quality of oil, gas, and fertilizer.

The Department of Agriculture apparently rivaled the Road Department in political influence and corruption. Having served as head of the department for nine years, Brown had his appointees well placed in jobs in Agriculture throughout the state. Inspectors were assigned to every county in Georgia, giving him a powerful political base and a potent channel of influence. Consequently, persons campaigning for public office in Georgia sought the support of the Department of Agriculture and its Commissioner. One favor was promised for another, and persons in powerful positions in farming, business, and government were soon in debt politically to Commissioner Brown.

Because the Department of Agriculture had been weakened by mismanagement, in 1926 it was political prey. Certainly the department was a formidable force for Brown; however, the sheer reach of the Commissioner, heads of divisions, inspectors, and staff rendered Agriculture difficult to manage. There existed a wide assumption in the Georgia press that Brown had fostered a permissiveness in the department that encouraged employees to exploit financial and political opportunities that occurred, with little concern for moral integrity or worry of being caught. The department appeared to be beyond the control of Commissioner Brown or even the state legislature. Brown had made too many political ap-pointments, a fact that Talmadge stressed in speeches throughout Georgia.

Because of its autonomous authority and political successes, the department exuded an institutional arrogance that Brown personified. This contentious spirit bred dissension in the department. During Brown's campaign for re-election in 1926, at least three of his employees turned against him and cited corrupt practices within the department as evidence that their former boss should be defeated. On June 26, 1926, the _Atlanta_ _Constitution_ editorialized that, because of the "unwholesome situation" in the Department of Agriculture, its "employees" ought to be placed "under a rigid civil services . . . system . . . divorced from poli-tics."(10)

To defeat Brown, a candidate would have to achieve two goals, specify clearly and forcefully in public the evils of the Department of Agriculture and its Commissioner and, secondly, convince voters that he had the courage and the ability to implement badly needed reforms. The 1926 race was crowded with candidates who claimed to meet those two criteria. Each of the five challengers jostled for the best position from which to attack Brown, to discredit the other four challengers, and to take over the powerful Department of Agriculture for himself.

This campaign transformed Eugene Talmadge from a political loser to a winner, from an individual rejected by persons in control of government in Telfair County to a public official with far-reaching powers. This analysis of the 1926 campaign for Commissioner of Agriculture in Georgia is in two parts. The initial stage, covered in this chapter, is an investigation of speeches given by Talmadge in Georgia during June and July of 1926, when he sparred with four other hopefuls to earn the chance to remain in the race and challenge Brown alone. The second phase of the investigation, presented in Chapter 3, focuses upon the three debates that took place in

August between Talmadge and Brown.

Five candidates joined the incumbent Brown in the race for Commissioner of the Department of Agriculture. Talmadge announced for the office first, on June 10, 1926.(11) Throughout the campaign he reminded voters that registering first for the race was evidence of his sincerity in wanting to cleanse Agriculture of its political corruption. Soon the race was packed with persons challenging Brown. Two weeks after Talmadge announced his candidacy, the Department of Agriculture exploded with dissension. The Atlanta Constitution perceived that a "bomb ruptured" the solidarity within the department when James H. Mills, an appointee of Brown's, entered the race, dividing the Commissioner's "forces." Two other employees of the department, Fred T. Bridges and J. B. Jackson, announced publicly their support for Mills.(12) This challenge to Brown from within his own department revealed three factors important for the campaign, that Mills and colleagues were ambitious to gain the power they knew their Commissioner possessed, that these men were aware first-hand of wrong-doings with which Brown could be associated, and that the dissidents believed their employer could be defeated.

Reporter Paul Stevenson predicted that confrontations among the candidates would "rival some of the historic campaigns by the sensational bitterness." In addition to Brown, Talmadge, and Mills, the list of candidates included Charles E. Stewart, John R. Irwin, and J. Shettlesworth. During the first stage of the campaign, in June and July, the five challengers attacked Brown and bargained for recognition and advantage among themselves. During this period, the dominant concern was who would survive the fight to oppose Commissioner Brown. Reports to the press the last of June had Charles E. Stewart and John R. Irwin meeting in Atlanta to decide upon one candidate who could defeat Brown.(13) Irwin, observing how scurrilous the speeches and statements to the press were becoming, advised that he would remain in the race, but would "conduct" his campaign in "a dignified and elevated" manner.(14) Considering Talmadge's will to win and the voters' rapture with his rhetoric, Irwin's plan of political civility may have been a sure formula for failure. On July 17, James H. Mills, the person who resigned from Agriculture to challenge his former employer, Commissioner Brown, sensing that he was being linked closely to corruption in the department, withdrew from the race.(15) Within the week, in a speech in Newnan, Georgia, pushing his bandwagon prematurely, Talmadge claimed to have "received word from many

Talmadge in an intimidating posture on the stump. (Photograph reprinted from the <u>Atlanta Constitution</u> by permission of that paper.)

strong friends of Mr. Mills that they will support
me. . . . I am a certain winner by a big
majority."(16) Within a few days, John R. Irwin,
deciding his decorous rhetoric had run its course,
pledged to support Talmadge.(17)

Looking back at the 1926 campaign, one tends to
carry perceptions of Talmadge acquired from reading
about the "Wild" man's entire twenty-year career. It
is worth noting that Irwin, a person who committed
himself publicly to a responsible form of campaigning, in 1926 supported Talmadge. Regardless of
Irwin's motivation for choosing Talmadge over Brown,
and all of the challengers wanted any person but the
incumbent to win, one should remember that, in 1926,
Talmadge had not been elected to public office and
had not developed a state-wide reputation for bullying people. What public persona Talmadge created in
the state was conceived in June and July of this
campaign, and fully developed during the McRae,
Dawson, and Elberton debates.

Daily Talmadge constructed his public
credibility with Georgia audiences, in person and
through the busy and biased press. The <u>Atlanta
Constitution</u> reported some pressure upon Talmadge to
retire in support of Charles Stewart. One learns
from this incident something of Talmadge's personal
motivation and drive for running for public office.
On July 25, candidate J. Shettlesworth published a
letter in which he asked Talmadge to withdraw from
the race, reminding readers that the man from McRae
pledged that he believed it was more important that
Brown be defeated by someone than to win himself!(18)
Talmadge must have chuckled privately with pleasure
over the politically naive advice offered publicly by
some of his opponents. Irwin had made his choice to
withdraw from the race rather than campaign unethi-
cally, but Talmadge chose a different strategy. He
stayed in the campaign and employed what tactics were
required to win. Shettlesworth, after observing the
public response to two of Talmadge's debates with
Brown,(19) and Charles E. Stewart, after considering
the results of all three debates,(20) surrendered to
Talmadge. There was certainly a bandwagon load of
candidates joining Talmadge's camp now.

Before considering how Talmadge survived the cut
of challengers, one should know the status and
activities of incumbent John J. Brown. When the
campaign began, Commissioner Brown appeared in public
meetings with the confidence expected of a well
entrenched official. On June 29, this sense of
security was bolstered by a published report that
seventy-five employees in the Department of Agriculture expressed their support for Brown; however, one
wonders why the other employees in the agency did not

support him publicly.(21)   As of July 13, the politically smug Brown demeaned other candidates by lumping
them vaguely into an insignificant opposition so as
not to legitimize their candidacies with names, a
favorite ploy of many politicians.(22)

Observing Brown's public statements during June
and July, before the debates, one senses that after
reviewing the credentials of the challengers the
commissioner decided that he could be easily
re-elected for a third term.   Consequently, he
lowered his guard a bit, a strategy that proved to be
a fatal mistake. Brown was particularly pleased that
five persons were opposing him, for this diluted each
candidate's attack. Reporters covering the campaign
could devote only a certain amount of space to each
of the challengers. When Brown read in the press
that some candidates were convening to choose a
representative who would continue against him, he
became concerned, and said that any one who withdrew
from the race wore a "streak of yellow coward-
ice."(23) This potent language lowered the tone of
the campaign to a level that delighted the tempestuous Talmadge.

Brown announced an "auto tour" to "every county
or section" of Georgia. In speeches early in the
campaign, he made a special effort to exude the
appearance of a commissioner secure in office and
discussing issues of great concern to farmers.
Listening to his speeches, one would not have known
that he managed a state agency of agriculture that
was licentious and about to be tried in campaign
debate and rendered guilty at the polls. On July 8
in Athens, Georgia, Brown talked in a statesman-like
posture about the successful eradication of the
"cotton hopper" (Texas Flea).(24) Continuing to play
the role of a Commissioner on guard for agriculture
in Georgia, on July 22, Brown explained to a Dawson
audience the subject of marketing, positioning his
candidacy above the withering fire coming from the
challengers.(25) Dawson would be the locale of the
second of three debates Brown had with Talmadge,
studied in the next chapter. Sensitive that he first
came to the commissioner's office from the Armour
Fertilizer Company, a business whose product inspectors in the Department of Agriculture would have
examined, in the Athens speech, Brown made a special
point to emphasize that he was well qualified to lead
the department.(26)   Unlike the other candidates,
Brown feigned, <u>he</u> was a "dirt farmer."

By early July, Brown felt obliged to react to
the mounting criticism the other candidates directed
at him. In a speech at Rome, Georgia on July 16,
Brown developed arguments he repeated throughout the

campaign. To refute criticism of abuses existing in
his department, Brown reminded audiences that a state
auditor declared that Agriculture had been "properly
administered." As for the number of persons he had
appointed, Brown said it was his legal responsibility
to hire "200 employees."   When attempting to refute
critics' claims that he hired members of his family
and friends, Brown replied candidly and haughtily
that he hired only friends and supporters; "no enemy
need apply," a confession that Talmadge effectively
attacked.

As for the qualifications of candidates opposing
him, Brown said they were "respectable men and
lawyers, but not farmers."   Brown angrily attacked
the treasonous audacity displayed by a former employee who dared criticize his administration. Referring
to James H. Mills' resignation and challenge to his
candidacy, Brown stated that he had been "stabbed in
the back by a traitor." As criticism of him accelerated, Brown became less professorial and more strident. Demonstrating the great authority to which he
had become accustomed, Brown labeled the head of the
National Farmers' Union a "pussy-footer and
side-stepper."(27) This strong language further
established an unruly environment in which
Talmadgeism could flourish.   Sensing the potency of
Talmadge's charges against him, Brown abandoned any
remnants of a conciliatory style for an aggressive
rhetoric of one placed on the defensive.

Early in the campaign, Brown expressed no
particular worry about Talmadge's candidacy.
Certainly it pleased Brown to hear from oil and
fertilizer inspectors in Telfair County that Talmadge
had lost elections in his own home town. By July 24,
however, Brown felt it necessary to respond to the
persistent and damaging attacks made by Talmadge upon
his department.   Feeling that his reputation was
being abused, and growing impatient with the
opposition, the overconfident Brown assaulted
Talmadge's personal credibility.   Looking back, one
knows that at this point in the campaign Brown should
have refrained from awakening the "little giant" from
Scotland, Georgia.   Commissioner Brown would soon
regret the day that he picked a public fight by
characterizing Talmadge as "a lawyer, but not of the
best repute, and . . . not a practical farmer."(28)
The campaign was heating up. Increasingly the debate
was primarily between incumbent Brown and underdog
Talmadge. Unfortunately for Brown, he, the fox, had
cornered the hound! One can see in Brown's
questioning of Talmadge's credibility the origins of
a strategy the incumbent used in the first debate in
McRae in August, another decision he would regret.

Talmadge defeated Brown because he effectively
criticized the corruption and inefficiency in Agriculture and convinced audiences on the stump and
readers of the press that he had the courage and
ability to implement urgently needed reforms for the
good of farmers and others. He explained to many
thousands of Georgians precisely and confidently the
alleged corruption of the Department of Agriculture
and its commissioner. Instinctively Talmadge recognized that the department and its administration were
in a politicially precarious state. Reading the
newspaper coverage of events during this period, one
finds that many persons knew that the department was
bloated with personnel and stagnated by political
nepotism. Certainly Talmadge and the four other
challengers knew that it was advantageous to criticize the department. But Talmadge was particularly
incisive and provocative when attacking a state
agency weakened by political intrigue and a lack of
managerial discipline. Basically Talmadge highlight-
ed what many citizens knew, but in stump narrative
others failed to match and audiences liked to hear.
Capitalizing upon an opportunity to establish an area
of agreement between himself and a Newnan, Georgia,
audience, for example, Talmadge assured them that
"every man and woman in Georgia knows the story by
this time." The task remaining for him was to "take
the stump" and "present the facts to the people."(29)
    The Fourth of July barbecues brought the
campaign into "full activity."(30) During June and
July of the 1926 campaign, prior to the three
debates, Talmadge issued a number of "charges" on the
stump that caused the commissioner to abandon his
statesman-like discussions of cotton hoppers and
marketing practices. From behind hundreds of stumps
in small towns Talmadge managed to elevate campaign
claims to metaphysical principles. Under Brown's
leadership the department had evolved into a powerful
political organization, Talmadge said, that threatened democratic government itself. In a published
statement Talmadge asserted that when viewed in
relation to powers granted to other agencies and
branches of government, the authority usurped by
Agriculture created a "dangerous balance of power."
He made "a caustic attack" upon the Brown administration for turning the department "into a political
machine the like of which the state has never known
before."(31) By appointing "relatives of legislative
leaders" as inspectors of oil and fertilizer throughout the state, the Commissioner had built a "system"
that could "almost control legislation in Georgia at
will."(32) Indeed Talmadge said the legislature had
become "a ratifying body" of Brown's wishes.

Building a vision in the campaign of Brown being a sultan of corruption, Talmadge entertained crowds with metaphors manufactured at the stump from images of military domination, religious tyranny, and royal majesty. Brown, for example, had transformed "agricultural science" into an "army . . . for his own political causes." In 1924 alone, Talmadge argued, the personnel in the department spent $9,789 on telegram and telephone messages "for building up political forces." The result was a "shrine at which every aspirant to political office . . . must worship."(33) Talmadge anointed Brown "King John" of Georgia politics.(34)

Although Talmadge entertained audiences by ridiculing Brown, he knew privately that many voters assumed that the commissioner could not be defeated. Neighbors warned Talmadge not to enter this race because of the power of incumbency. Brown had been in office nine years, more than long enough to barricade Agriculture with hand-picked employees. Talmadge appreciated the seriousness of advisors' convictions, but he sensed what political laymen and leaders could not see. There was a rip in the mask of the commissioner's impenetrableness. In numerous speeches in June and July, he strived to convince voters that the commissioner was vulnerable. The Department of Agriculture was a barn about to fall of neglect. To convince voters that Brown could be defeated at the polls, Talmadge disrobed him publicly of commissioner accoutrements. In Talmadge's speeches, the Head of an important state agency became a political buffoon, "King Jay Jay." Talmadge tore away Brown's false respectability. Personalizing his appeals as few could do, he derided the Commissioner's mode of speaking, labelling it as mere "Brown talk." Constructing a similie from outdoor scenes native to Georgia, Talmadge reduced the politically pompous Brown to a low station. Brown's speeches were "like that of the bull frogs. When you listen to them at night it sounds like a great roar, but in the day you'll find two or three little frogs blinking on the banks."(35)

When James H. Mills resigned from the Department of Agriculture to oppose Brown, one assumed that Mills would be a formidable candidate. The act of a Brown employee turning against him in public caused a great stir in the press. Had Talmadge been in Mills' position, no doubt, because of his rhetorical skills, he would have turned the notoriety to political advantage. This situation dramatized how politically alert and astute a relatively inexperienced Talmadge was to capitalize on fast changing conditions in the 1926 campaign. The man who jumped the most hurdles

would win. Talmadge stopped Mills' candidacy in its
tracks, equating Mills and Brown as one evil candidacy. In Talmadge's speeches, Brown and Mills became
co-architects of a fallen state agency. With Mills
announcing for office, that meant more candidates in
the race, but Talmadge explained to the voters that
they still had but two choices. They could vote for
Brown or Mill, both "insiders" in a partnership of
wickedness, or they could vote for "Talmadge," an
"outsider" capable of instituting reforms.(36)   "The
whole fight," Talmadge maintained, is between the
"continuation of the machine" and "its complete
destruction."   Talmadge promised the   "complete
annihilation" of the Brown-Mills-Jackson machine. He
characterized the angry charges and denials exchanged
between insiders Brown and Mills as proof of impro-
prieties that threatened the "political honor and
public welfare" of Georgia. Speaking in the Biblical
language that Georgians appreciated, Talmadge alluded
to the squabble between Brown and Mills as a "house
arrayed against itself." He quoted an "old proverb"
as a way of prophesying his election. It was des-
tined that Talmadge and the voters would soon have
their time at the trough: "When thieves fall out,
honest men get their due."(37)
     Talmadge blamed Agriculture for serving the
personal whims of its employees at the expense of
farmers. He criticized the department for ignoring
the problems of farmers and other citizens. Developing a martial analogy, Talmadge told a Sandersville
audience that the department served, not the "interests of the people," but their own "army of political
employees." Talmadge asked persuasively: "Is Georgia
going to stand for this?" In the heat of the Deep
South, farmers were accustomed to fighting off
infestations of several kinds, and with his election
Talmadge guaranteed an administration that would
"kill this swarm of politicians . . . the deadliest
swarm of boll weevils in the state."(38)
     Employing the colorfully critical language that
drew thousands of Georgians to his public meetings
for two decades, Talmadge indicted Brown for hiring
relatives and friends. Citizens were well aware of
having to deal with the "bureau" of this and the
"bureau" of that in Georgia; so Talmadge entertained
them with a new branch of government. Attacking the
agency of Agriculture, Talmadge ridiculed Brown's
conversion of the "department for the farming people"
to a "bureau of family employment." In a truly
devastating mortar attack upon Brown's personal
integrity, Talmadge itemized for citizens, many of
whom were financially distraught, the family members
hired by Brown and their salaries: a son at $2,400;

second son at $1,200; third son at $2,400;
half-brother at $2,400; nephew at $3,000; second
nephew at $1,200; third nephew at $1,500.(39)

Talmadge oppugned Brown from the stump for
offering jobs to potential employees in Agriculture
in exchange for political loyalty. When James H.
Mills quit the department to run against Brown, and
Fred T. Bridges and J. B. Jackson resigned to support
him, their jobs became vacant. In many speeches,
Talmadge explained this development as evidence of
Brown's bartering jobs for political support.
Referring to the vacancies left by Mills and supporters, Talmadge ridiculed Brown for "leading a bunch of
jackasses around Georgia with a bundle of fodder."
Talmadge accused Brown of assessing employees a
specified percent of their annual salaries as "fees
for a campaign fund." Realizing that statistics at
the stump put audiences to sleep, Talmadge shrouded
speeches in pathos with which Georgians empathized.
Brown was so base as to exploit Cobb Holland, "a
one-legged world war veteran." Brown made Holland
"contribute" to a fund for "fixing the legislature."
When Talmadge was elected, this "traffic in state
jobs . . . for private political gain" would
stop!(40)

Talmadge reminded farmers that the Department of
Agriculture was created to assist them. Under
Brown's leadership, that agency had become wasteful
and inefficient. He told a Newnan audience that
state Auditor Sam J. Slate found that the department
spent approximately a million dollars a year.
Because of an "obsolete system" of keeping records,
Brown did not have to account for expenditures.(41)
The department employed 340 workers to do what twenty
"efficient" persons could accomplish.(42) Georgia
hired 191 friends of Brown, Talmadge continued, just
to inspect gas brought into Georgia, while Florida
required only six. Even with that inflated number of
inspectors, Georgia was a "dumping ground" for
"inferior gas." The poor quality gas slipped by
inspectors because Georgia used a "gravity test that
proves nothing of commercial worth of gas." As
commissioner, Talmadge would use the more reliable
"distillation test." Georgians were also paying far
too much for the inspection of fertilizer. Talmadge
bitterly complained to a Sandersville audience that,
"we pay into the coffers of [the department] 30 cents
on every ton of fertilizer sold." Brown's ineptness
was "costing you about $300 to have one ton of
fertilizer inspected."(43)

Talmadge elevated the corruption in Agriculture
to a crisis in southern values. The campaign for
Commissioner of Agriculture became a debate on the

destiny of Georgia.   Talmadge told   voters that   the
results of this one election would leave an indelible
stamp on the quality of life in the state.   This race
"overshadows" all   others "put   before" Georgians   in
the past   twenty-five   years.   In   an   apostrophe   to
egotism,   one   that   ironically   held   some   truth,
Talmadge forewarned   that   the "economic,   moral   and
political welfare"   of   Georgia for   the   next   fifty
years "depends absolutely on the outcome of the . . .
race   for   commissioner   of   agriculture."(44)   The
"functions" of the   department influence "every   man,
woman and child."(45)

Rather than   maintain the   swamp of   corruption,
Talmadge envisioned, the   Department of   Agriculture,
after the September 8 election, could be   transformed
into a bastion for values that southerners   esteemed.
In the genre of the post-war orations of General John
Gordon, Confederate hero, Talmadge said that "we   are
the greatest people, but   we must assert our   pioneer
stock and pull back to   the old original lines."   In
Talmadge's speeches, farming became the foundation of
southern principle.   Echoing Henry Grady's pronouncements, Talmadge advised that Old South values   could,
in the proper hands, accommodate New South   prosperity.   Under   Brown's management,   Talmadge warned   the
League of Women Voters,   Agriculture "is not   helping
our great industry of farming, on which all civilization and all progress rests."   The department must be
made to function properly or be "abolished."(46)

Talmadge went after   the newly approved   women's
votes.   Candidates at the time assumed that the   most
effective means of adapting to women as voters was to
offer them   a special   invitation to   attend   outdoor
"speakings," provide   seats (with   the   men   in   the
audience standing),   comment   on   how   "lovely"   they
looked,   talk   about   refraining   from using   crude
language,   and   discuss   ethical   standards   in   the
community.   Following   these rhetorical   conventions,
Talmadge attempted to   convince the   League of   Women
Voters in Athens that, because Brown's administration
was "handling matters"   outside of its   jurisdiction,
that department was   "exercising bad moral   influences."

When the race   for Commissioner began,   Talmadge
was as far behind as one   could be.   He was not   well
known   throughout   the   state.   Before   the   August
debates in   1926, Talmadge   contested for   audiences.
For example, on June 24,   Talmadge and John R.   Irwin
spoke in Sandersville,   and "all   that were   expected
did not attend."(47)   When candidates first   entered
the race for Commisioner of Agriculture, the   <u>Atlanta
Constitution</u> only knew to report that Talmadge was   a
"farmer and   lawyer of   McRae."(48)   Clark   Howell,

editor of that newspaper, and brother of Albert
Howell, for whose law firm Talmadge was earlier
employed in Atlanta, opposed Brown's re-election,
supported Talmadge at times during his career and,
finally, in 1941, turned against the "wild" politician raised on the banks of Sugar Creek. W. T.
Anderson, editor of the <u>Macon</u> <u>Telegraph</u> <u>and</u> <u>News</u>
changed his loyalties in the same way, supporting
Talmadge in 1926, turning against him, then praising
his candidacy.

In June and July of 1926, before the debates
with Brown brought notoriety to Talmadge that few
persons in the South attained, he faced the very
difficult task of convincing audiences that he was a
viable candidate. On stumps across the state, he
fought his way out of the pack of challengers to
become a front runner with Brown. "It will take all
summer to tell the story of this remarkable stifling
of the people's will," he stated. "But I intend to"
do just that.(49) Talmadge used issues and citizens'
personalities to fuel his interests. In the early
months of the campaign, Talmadge conceived the
prototype of persuasive speaking that powered his
politics, both when seeking public office and when
governing Georgia. Because of total confidence that
he could persuade audiences, Talmadge attempted to
achieve his will in and out of government on the
backs of the citizens of Georgia. He explained to a
Newnan, Georgia, audience the theorem of persuasion
that fueled his political demagoguery for twenty
years: "<u>I am going over the heads of the petty
politicians and making my appeal to the people
themselves</u>."(50) In Talmadge's conception of social
and political hierarchy, there were only two branches
of government, his will be done and the potential of
voters for mobilization for his causes. All other
factors--elected officials, government offices,
official channels, accepted procedures, social
conventions, and laws--were inconveniences to be
avoided, ridiculed, intimidated, or exploited.
Having his will adopted by citizens meeting in mass
on the hustings was Talmadge's way of preventing
judicious examination of his policies and acts by
knowledgeable persons in positions of authority.

If Talmadge was hyperbolic about Agriculture's
mission of restoring cherished values to Georgia, he
was concrete about his candidacy being a remedy for
corruption and inefficiency in state government. The
"crucial situation reached a stage," he admonished,
"where it is squarely up to the voters." Because
Brown claimed he was unqualified to be Commissioner
because he was a lawyer, Talmadge expounded upon his
practical experience in agriculture. In this race,

the candidates quarrelled about which person was
actually a farmer. Candidates ranked each other on
the bases of where a farm was located, to what extent
each was committed to farming, the number of years
one lived on a farm, and kind of work each had done.
Talmadge effectively defended his experience in
agriculture, claiming to be the "only 'dirt' farmer
in the race."(51) Unlike Brown, he was a "real
farmer." He resided "on a farm five miles from
McRae."(52) Talmadge reminded voters that he had
been farming for fifteen years, and was now "busy,
like other Georgians, trying to work out the many
difficult problems that confront farmers."(53)

Talmadge's "platform" was "to reorganize" the
department for the "benefit of the farmers."(54) As
commissioner, he would restructure the agency as a
means of avoiding "duplication of work."(55)
Talmadge made a special effort to portray himself as
a man of action, a candidate who could finish a job.
He promised a Newnan audience to "work night and day"
to make the department more responsive to needs of
farmers.(56) Reorganization alone, however, would
not solve the problem of payrolls burgeoning with
political appointees. The number of oil and fertilizer inspectors had to "be cut down."(57) When
elected, he would ensure no persons jobs as inspectors, since individuals he would fire would not be
replaced.

Talmadge held the attention of listeners and won
votes because he talked to crowds in a way they could
understand. He reduced the complex issues of agriculture, economics, and employment to a personal
choice with which voters could identify. "The issue
is simple," he said, Georgians could "keep the Brown
political machine or . . . clean house." "I am the
only man in the race who [can] beat Brown." Like
David anticipating the confrontation with Goliath,
"somebody has got to start the fight." With Talmadge
leading the charge, voters could "wipe out" Brown's
"machine with one blow." The Department of Agriculture would be freed of "professional political
control."(58) "Political manipulation" would be
reduced to a "minimum," giving the department a
"chance to function." For reforms to be implemented
the voters only had to "elect a man" who could manage
the agency "in the interests of farmers." When
elected he would not "for one moment" be influenced
by the "arrogant dictation" of Brown's policies.(59)
"What" are "the people of Georgia . . . going to do
about it," he shouted, answering that the voters
would give Brown and the inspectors "a long rest in
private life." If "I don't make good" on promises,
Talmadge boasted, "kick me out."

Aware that he was running an aggressive race, and concerned that he might alienate voters by speaking so stridently, Talmadge supplemented criticism of Brown with a page from Irwin's wellbehaved campaign. As an afterthought, he cooed that "abuse and vilification have no part in the fight" with the commissioner. "I could talk here for five hours, throwing mud and billingsgate, but it would have nothing to do with the real issue in this race." During this first state-wide campaign, once he moved ahead of other challengers in the race, Talmadge reined in his rhetoric on occasions when he determined that a more constructive persona was required. If elected, for example, he "pledged" to the Newnan audience to "cooperate to the fullest" with legislators in the "constructive" reconstruction of Agriculture. In later campaigns and in speeches while in office, Talmadge insisted that talk of cooperation and constructive behavior was the vocabulary of sissy college professors and weakly losers. In the 1926 campaign, in some instances, he left the impression of one presenting relatively accurate accounts of corruption in Agriculture in a colorful, clear, and documentary fashion. In his Sandersville speech on June 24, 1926, according to one journalist, he "cited figures" and provided "proof to back up every statement."(60)

At the same time, in the 1926 race, Talmadge perfected the rowdy demeanor that characterized his entire career in and out of public office. When supporters yelled at him from the audience to "go to it," he abandoned any consideration of conciliatory debate, and attacked issues and personalities in a fluent, articulate, and merciless manner. Journalists who watched Talmadge during June and July of 1926, described his public speaking as follows: "waxes facetious,"(61) "strong speech," "full of fire in his attack,"(62) "interesting speech," "eloquent orator of the old school,"(63) and "caustic."(64) Samples of language Talmadge employed during the first stage of the campaign demonstrate the scathing and colorful stump personality he was cultivating. Talmadge used the following terms when criticizing the Department of Agriculture and Commisioner Brown, language taken from speeches quoted in this chapter: "political farmers," "solid phalanx," "patronage," "arrogant dictation," "pernicious," "corrupt," "pile up salaried jobs," "extravagance," "shameful," "curse," "waste," "political machine," "deadly menace," "incompetency," "degeneracy," "perpetuate its political ring," "lax," "inefficient," "expensive," "sweet orgy of robbery," "bacchanalia of spending," "perfidy," "evils," "family pay roll," "private political machine," "nefarious political machine," "corrupt distribution of patronage," "excess," "profit-sharing henchmen," "bribery," "dishonor," and "robbery."

The June and July stage of the campaign for Commissioner of Agriculture ended with Talmadge having received the support of several other campaigners and leading the pack of challengers. Talmadge had so convinced Georgians of the abuses in the Brown administration of Agriculture, that the commissioner shifted from the stance of a confident incumbent to a posture of an accused placed on the defensive. In the process, Talmadge forged a prototype of public discourse characterized by relentless attack upon issues and opponents in language that was increasingly harsh and uncompromising.

NOTES

1. Dewey W. Grantham, Southern Progressivism: The Reconciliation of Progess and Tradition (Knoxville: Univer of Tennessee Press, 1983), p. 6.

2, Michael Stephen Holmes, "New Deal in Georgia: An Administrative History," Ph.D. dissertation, Univer of Wisconsin, 1969, pp. 9-15, 36.

3. Numan V. Bartley, Creation of Modern Georgia (Athens: Univer of Georgia Press, 1983), pp. 169-170, 173.

4. George Brown Tindall, Emergence of the New South, 1913-1945 (Baton Rouge: Louisiana State Univer Press, 1967,) p. 75.

5. Barton C. Shaw, Wool-Hat Boys Georgia's Populist Party (Baton Rouge: Louisiana State University Press, 1984), pp. 1-3, 23.

6. Shaw, Wool-Hat Boys, pp. 208-209.

7. T. Harry Williams, Romance and Realism in Southern Politics (Athens: University of Georgia Press, 1961), pp. 58-59.

8. Calvin M. Logue, "Rhetorical Ridicule of Reconstruction Blacks," Quarterly Journal of Speech, 62 (1976), 400-409; Logue, "Rhetorical Appeals of Whites to Blacks During Reconstruction," Communication Monographs, 44 (1977), 241-251.

9. Sarah McCulloh Lemmon, "The Ideology of Eugene Talmadge," Georgia Historical Quarterly, 38 (1954), 226-227.

10. Atlanta Constitution, June 26, 1926.

11. Qualifying statement, Atlanta Constitution, June 11, 1926.

12. Atlanta Constitution, June 24, 1926.

13. Atlanta Constitution, June 30 and July 1, 1926.

14. Statement to press, Atlanta Constitution, July 6, 1926.

15. Atlanta Constitution, July 18, 1926.

16. Atlanta Constitution, July 23, 1926.
17. Atlanta Constitution, July 21, 1926.
18. Letter in Atlanta Constitution, July 25, 1926.
19. Atlanta Constitution, August 8, 1926.
20. Atlanta Constitution, August 22, 1926.
21. Atlanta Constitution, June 29, 1926.
22. Quoted in Rome News-Tribune, July 14, 1926.
23. Quoted in Rome News-Tribune, July 15, 1926.
24. Atlanta Constitution, July 9, 1926.
25. Atlanta Constitution, July 23, 1926.
26. Atlanta Constitution, July 23, 1926.
27. Atlanta Constitution, July 17, 1926.
28. Statement to press, Atlanta Constitution,   July
25, 1926.
29. Atlanta Constitution, July 23, 1926.
30. Atlanta Constitution, June 27, 1926.
31. Qualifying Statement, Atlanta Constitution,
June 11, 1926.
32. Sandersville speech, Atlanta Constitution, July
25, 1926.
33. Qualifying statement, Atlanta Constitution,
June 11, 1926.
34. Quoted in Atlanta Constitution, July 4 and 25,
1926.
35. Statement to press, Atlanta Constitution,   July
4, 1926.
36. Quoted in Atlanta Constitution, June 30 and
July 1, 1926.
37. Quoted in Atlanta Constitution, July 7, 1926.
38. Sandersville speech, Atlanta Constitution, June
25, 1926.
39. Quoted in Atlanta Constitution, July 25, 1926.
40. Newnan speech, Atlanta Constitution, July 23,
1926.
41. Atlanta Constitution, July 23, 1926.
42. Qualifying statement, Atlanta Constitution,
June 11, 1926.
43. Atlanta Constitution, June 25, 1926.
44. Statement to press, Atlanta Constitution,   July
4, 1926.
45. Sandersville speech, Atlanta Constitution, June
25, 1926.
46. July 27, 1926 speech reported in   Athens
Banner-Herald, July 30, 1926.
47. Sandersville speech of June 24, 1926, reported
in Sandersville Progress, June 30, 1926.
48. Qualifying statement, Atlanta Constitution,
June 11, 1926.
49. Statement to press, Atlanta Constitution,   July
4, 1926.
50. Atlanta Constitution, July 23, 1926; emphasis
added.
51. Sandersville speech of June 24, 1926, in

Sandersville _Progress_, June 30, 1926.
    52. Quoted in _Atlanta Constitution_, July 1, 1926.
    53. Statement to press, _Atlanta Constitution_,   July 4, 1926.
    54. Statement to press, _Atlanta Constitution_,   July 4, 1926.
    55. Quoted in _Atlanta Constitution_, July 1, 1926.
    56. Newnan speech, _Atlanta Constitution_, July 23, 1926.
    57. League of Women Voters speech, Athens, July 27, 1926, _Athens Banner-Herald_, July 30, 1926.
    58. Quoted in _Atlanta Constitution_, July 1, 1926.
    59. Statement to Press, _Atlanta Constitution_,   July 4, 1926.
    60. _Sandersville Progress_, June 30, 1926.
    61. _Atlanta Constitution_, July 18, 1926.
    62. _Atlanta Constitution_, July 23, 1926.
    63. _Sandersville Progress_, June 30, 1926.
    64. _Atlanta Constitution_, July 4, 1926.

3

Talmadgeism Born in Campaign Debate

Because of his persistent and effective criticism of Commissioner John J. Brown during June and July of 1926, Talmadge entered the last weeks of the campaign the front-runner among the challengers. Ironically, in addition to Talmadge's skill in persuasive speaking, a decision by Brown contributed substantially to Talmadge's success. In a surprising move, Brown challenged Talmadge to debate. Initially Brown declined an invitation to debate Charles E. Stewart, indicating that he would debate only persons who were "really candidates."[1] Probably because of overconfidence in his experience in campaigning and his knowledge of the Department of Agriculture, Brown believed he could defeat all the challengers. He even "expressed doubt" publicly that any of the opponents would meet him in debate.[2]

In a decision that launched Talmadge's twenty-year career in politics, the naive Brown "publicly challenged" Talmadge to debate before their home-town audiences in McRae and Elberton. Brown probably invited Talmadge to debate for two reasons. Having read in the press of Talmadge's criticism of Agriculture and his administration, and having had the impact of the challenger's speeches corroborated by his employees, Brown felt a need to answer the charges. Secondly, Brown knew that Talmadge lost two elections in his home region and, while serving as attorney of that county, was investigated by a grand jury for acts allegedly committed while in that office. Thus, Brown assumed that Talmadge was vulnerable to attack even in his home town. Brown outlined the issues he would raise in the debates, giving the persuasively talented Talmadge adequate time to formulate rebuttals. Brown threatened to make Talmadge "answer" for his work "as attorney for board of roads and revenues and court record . . . in the presence of your own people." He would argue that Georgians could not "trust" Talmadge with the "affairs" of Agriculture because he was an unreliable lawyer. Brown said he would convince Talmadge's neighbors that the challenger was not "a practical farmer." In addition, he promised to "answer any charge" Talmadge made against his administration, a formidable task indeed.(3)

Had Brown been aware of what Talmadge's former classmates at the University of Georgia knew about their friend's forensics talents, he may have had second thoughts about risking his office as Commissioner in public confrontations. Did Brown's oil and fertilizer inspectors in and around Telfair county not know of Talmadge's formidable debating skills! Perhaps Brown, even with some knowledge of Talmadge's talents in disputation, had confidence in his own experience before audiences. After all, unlike Talmadge, he had won state-wide elections. Brown believed that his knowledge of Agriculture provided a significant advantage when debating farm issues.

Talmadge had worked in the Howell, Heyman, and Bolding law office in Atlanta, practiced law in Ailey, Georgia, and farmed and practiced law in Telfair County, but apparently few persons throughout the state had witnessed him in public debate, providing an advantage of surprise attack. Talmadge knew his potential for persuading the mass of voters; certainly he was anxious to try. Brown could not have anticipated the devastating impact that the three public debates would have upon his campaign. In a way, Brown received what he requested, for he helped set the emotionally antagonistic tone of the debates by attacking Talmadge's personal credibility.

Talmadge teemed with anticipation over this unexpected opportunity to attack the commissioner face-to-face before friendly and hostile audiences. He recognized the political implications of the debates and took full advantage of the initiative handed to him by Brown. Brown's invitation to debate placed him in the campaign spotlight with the incumbent. In the view of the state newspapers and the voters, the debates established Talmadge as the one serious contender to Brown. In a letter to Brown accepting the challenge to debate, published in the press, Talmadge interpreted the political significance of the invitation: "By your challenge . . . you admit that I am a formidable candidate . . . and that I have made charges of a vital nature. . . . I will give you an opportunity to prove" the "charges" you made against me.(4) Turning to the Georgia electorate, Talmadge announced accurately that, by challenging "me," Brown has "eliminated the other candidates."(5)

With the three debates, for the first time in his political career Talmadge had a forum in which to exhibit skills in debating an opponent before a state-wide audience, a means through which to establish his persona as a courageous fighter for farmers and to win public office. After his successes in public speaking as a college student, he had been searching for a scene in which to stand before a large audience and convince voters that he was a person they could trust to represent their interests. Talmadge knew, when given the appropriate arena, he would win the support of Georgia voters and establish for himself a powerful place in state government.

The pending debates between the tough speaking Talmadge and "King J. J." Brown became the talk of the entire state. The press heightened the anticipation by Georgians for the championship debates by publishing numerous articles and predictions. To hold its readers' attention, the Atlanta Constitution promised they could expect the two candidates to "cross verbal swords," the result being that "fur will fly" between the "doughty opponents."(6) Characteristically, Talmadge played the politically charged drama as would John Carson the fiddle in his later campaigns for governor. He fed the hungry press hyperbolic claims and charges that many published throughout the state and beyond. After accepting Brown's challenge to meet before audiences in McRae and Elberton, Talmadge re-gained the offensive by daring the Commissioner to extend the debates "to all the congressional districts of the state."(7) To out-dare his opponent, as the athletically inclined Talmadge learned to do on playgrounds in south Georgia, he invited "as many members" of the state legislature and Brown's inspector corps to attend the McRae debate as possible.(8) To dramatize the debates, Talmadge re-accepted Brown's invitation to debate each day before a different audience. In a speech in Tifton on August 31, for example, he promoted the debates and his candidacy: "I unconditionally accept Mr. Brown's challenge. . . . The people are interested in this matter. Let's accommodate them. The people are entitled to the light. . . . I want every one that possibly can to come to the speakings, friends and foes alike. . . . The members of the general assembly who voted for the distillation test and to reduce the oil inspectors to six, are also especially invited. You lit the torch that I am now carrying on."(9)

For two reasons Talmadge offered a special

invitation to women. Women could vote in the election, and Talmadge favored any person who would vote for him. Secondly, as a source told author William Anderson anonymously, during Talmadge's campaign for the state senate in 1922, "courthouse lawyers" charged before a grand jury that Talmadge had "intercourse with his plowing mule," a situation that caused considerable discussion at the time.(10) Because Brown had said publicly he would discuss charges brought against Talmadge in the past, Talmadge wanted women present in the audience as a means of forcing Brown to censor his own criticisms. Talmadge knew that if Brown mentioned the alleged mule incident to an audience in which there were women, he risked the fate of Tom Watson when he committed a similiar act of rhetorical indiscretion six years earlier.(11) Consequently, Talmadge announced to his Tifton audience that, "Ladies are especially invited. I will see that these debates are kept on a courteous and dignified basis."

THE MCRAE DEBATE

The first debate took place in Talmadge's home town of McRae on August 3, the second in Dawson on August 4, and the third in Brown's home town of Elberton on August 12. The first debate created great interest throughout the state. W. T. Anderson, editor of the Macon Telegraph, a strong supporter of Talmadge in 1926, wrote that from four to five thousand persons were expected in the south Georgia town. The "hotels announced" they had "ample facilities to care for a large registration," but "most" persons would "come by auto" and not "stay the night." Although barbecue rallies were popular at this time, there was no free "public dinner" for this occasion.(12) When Talmadge spoke at Sandersville on June 24, at a time when he was relatively unknown among voters of Georgia, supporters provided a "big barbecue" to attract a "large audience." For the well publicized "wordy warfare" expected at McRae, organizers felt that food was not needed to attract a crowd. Alert venders took advantage of the crowd's need for nourishment. In some ways, the atmosphere was like that at one of the court's hangings. Watermelons were piled for sale at the "outskirts of the crowd" and, in the oppressive heat, the "demand was heavy."(13) The "Woman's Club" sold "sandwiches and drinks" for "the speaking."(14)

Conditions for the debate were perfect for a final testing of Talmadge's prototype of public speaking power. Conditions at McRae well satisfied the rhetorical elements prerequisite for Talmadge's rancorous persuasive temperament. A political storm

was building in Georgia over the corrupt and inefficient state of the Department of Agriculture, a force
that helped Talmadge propel himself into the lead in
the race. Secondly, an antagonist in the personality
of Brown had volunteered to have himself sacrificed
on a stump altar. The extensive advanced publicity,
warm weather, sizeable crowd of persons packed
together with all standing, mood of the audience, and
presence of a perfect target in Commissioner Brown,
guaranteed a confrontational atmosphere in which
Talmadgeism could excel.

The speaking was held "under a broiling South
Georgia sun"(15) at Windsor Park, "in a pine grove
across the street from the Telfair county courthouse,
where a temporary stand had been erected for the
speakers." Journalists from a "half-dozen or more
daily newspapers" in the state were in McRae to cover
the kill. The Atlanta Journal estimated the crowd to
be between 1,500 and 2,000, fewer than some had
predicted.(16) Maybe Talmadge's neighbors should
have provided barbecue to bait more supporters and
potential converts. Perhaps some voters from Telfair
and surrounding counties who had rejected Talmadge
twice before in elections had doubts about the home
challenger's ability to stand up to a powerful
incumbent and stayed home. The Telfair Enterprise,
Talmadge's supportive home town paper, reported that
between 2,000 and 3,000 "almost" filled Windsor Park.
The Atlanta Constitution, also opposed to Brown,
estimated the crowd to be "more than" 2,000 persons
who, "long before the debate," gathered for the
speeches.(17)

The Atlanta Constitution reporter wrote that
"farmers with their wives and children from hinter-
land" arrived in transportation ranging "from mule
cart to limousine." Talmadge was successful in
recruiting women enough to curtail Brown's criticism
of him. Some women wore "sunbonnets and homespun,"
while others were dressed in the "latest fashions of
Parisian boulevards." Children waved "red, green and
yellow baloons and [munched] stick candy." "Aged and
bearded patriarchs edged close to the speakers'
stand," drawing on "clay pipes and corn cobs."

Lovelace Eve covered the debates for the
Americus Times-Recorder and eventually cast his
support with Talmadge. Eve provided another view of
the scene, describing how "the little town" of McRae
"filled with automobiles from every point in South
Georgia. Men and women with a scattering of children
are streaming into the pine grove, most of them
crowded as near the platform as possible and all
standing." The audience was "coatless," with dress
ranging from "hickory shirt" to "overalls."(18) A

reporter corroborrated a "number of women in the crowd," and that they "stood throughout the speaking."(19) That two reporters mentioned women were required to stand perhaps indicates how unconventional was the practice of not providing these new voters seats. Having the entire audience stand facilitated collective responses from persons "massed around" the platform, an arrangement that favored Talmadge.(20)

The crowd cheered when the two speakers "mounted" the stand, with one reporter determining somehow, as when golfers are greeted to a green, that Talmadge received the "bulk of applause."(21) The debate was scheduled to begin at 11:00 A.M., but started "shortly after" that hour.(22) Brown and Talmadge paced "back and forth on the stand," measuring the mood of the people crowding in around them, and making last-minute adjustments in strategies they employed on stumps throughout Georgia in June and July prior to this debate.(23) Even at this late hour, Brown probably still believed that, because of Talmadge's past public record, the home town challenger would not be well received by many in the audience. Both speakers would have noted the presence of women and children, with Brown concerned that he would be unable to use the mule incident as an example of Talmadge's questionable character.

A significant rhetorical variable in this debate was the attitude of the audience toward the candidates prior to the speeches. Was Brown correct in assuming that Talmadge's credibility was vulnerable in Telfair county? Clearly that was his motivation for recommending the debates and beginning them in McRae. Brown's knowledge that Talmadge had lost two campaigns at home also determined the strategy he had previewed in the press, to expose his opponent's questionable record of public service and to criticize Talmadge's personal reputation. Based on previous campaigns he conducted in the region, Talmadge would have assessed the attitude of the crowd reliably. He was aware of significant variables in his former campaigns that Brown probably missed. For example, between the time of the 1920 and 1922 races, he converted a significant number of voters to his camp. Indeed, in the 1922 race, Talmadge won the popular vote, losing the county unit vote. One important factor that may have puzzled both candidates was the question of how many persons attended this first debate undecided as to the candidate they would support?

The size of the audience may help explain the attitudes of the persons waiting anxiously to hear the two candidates. Because approximately 2,000 persons attended the first debate, rather than the

4,000 to 5,000 predicted by the <u>Macon</u> <u>Telegraph</u>, one might infer that most of them were from the three-county area in which Talmadge had campaigned early in the 1920s, as McRae would have been more accessible to them.(24)   The number of persons voting in the 1922 campaign was comparable to the apparent size of the audience attending the McRae debate.   In his 1922 campaign, a total of 1,943 persons voted, with 1,187 of them choosing Talmadge.   One must be cautious, however, in inferring that the same persons voting in 1922 formed the bulk of the audience for the first debate in 1926, for persons were present who resided outside the Telfair region.   For example, W. T. Anderson's <u>Macon</u> <u>Telegraph</u> <u>and</u> <u>News</u>, a newspaper opposed to Brown, observed that 2,000 persons attended the debate "from 20 South Georgia counties."(25) One does not know what percentage of the 2,000 or more persons in the audience resided in or near Telfair county, but probably many of them lived within that area.   And citizens from the twenty South Georgia counties identified more with neighbor Talmadge than outsider Brown.

Probably a significant favorite son factor operated during this debate, and Talmadge could expect a warm response.   To the degree that the <u>Telfair</u> <u>Enterprise</u> represented the attitudes of the people of the county at the time of the first debate, it is interesting to note that this newspaper was brazenly biased for Talmadge.(26)   Knowing Talmadge's astuteness for analyzing audiences' perceptions and adapting to them, he must have realized the danger in which Brown had placed his political future by sponsoring this debate.   Lovelace Eve, editor of the <u>Americus</u> <u>Times-Recorder</u>, an influential newspaper in the region, closely observed this debate, and reported evidence of the crowd's mood.   Eventually during the campaign, Eve endorsed Talmadge's candidacy, even introducing Talmadge to an Americus audience.   While it is important to realize that Eve was not a fan of Brown's, he covered the speeches in a relatively responsible way and provided important details of what happened at the scene of the first debate.

Observing the people as they arrived in Windsor Park for the McRae debate, Lovelace Eve concluded that "Talmadge's home folks have come out en mass to back their champion."   Although during June and July, Talmadge had moved out in front of the other challengers, one finds Eve's assessment that Brown, in this debate, was "fighting for his political life" a bit overstated.   It could be, however, that, because Eve witnessed first-hand many of Talmadge's speeches, that he measured the relative status of the candidates reliably.   In retrospect, Eve's judgment was correct; however, it was probably Talmadge's effective performance in this first debate that put Brown's campaign for re-election as Commissioner of Agriculture in jeopardy. Probably Lovelace Eve, a keen observer of the scene, traveling with Talmadge at the time and observing the speeches and the crowds' responses, accurately sensed that, unless Brown produced a miracle during the debates, he would be unable to derail the challenger.

Standing in the crowd close to the speakers, Lovelace Eve recorded testimonial evidence of the audience's motivations, preferences, and expectations. One learns from Eve's report what brought Georgians to a Talmadge speaking. Eve reported what an "old woman" in "polk bonnet" predicted would be the outcome of the debate. The woman "whispered" to her "aged husband, 'that's Eugene, he's smart; jest watch him skin Brown'," and her partner nodded in agreement.(27) One can speculate whether her opinion was representative of the expectations of members of the audience, but this rare glimpse of the private thoughts of the elderly couple demonstrates the political charisma Talmadge was cultivating in the minds and hearts of many Georgians. The whispered judgment by the elderly woman indicated why Talmadge's campaign had been successful. Watching the two candidates crisscross the stage, she recognized which person was Talmadge. The first requirement of a politician, certainly for one so little known as Talmadge, is to achieve a high state of visibility among the voters. Of course, Talmadge was speaking at home; however, the woman felt a need to identify Talmadge for her partner. The woman may have attended a previous public meeting at which Talmadge spoke, read reports in the press about Talmadge's campaign persuasion, or talked to her neighbors about his performances on the stump. Talmadge's effective campaign of speaking during June and July brought him a wide audience personified in the woman's response. Persons walked and drove long distances to witness for themselves Talmadge's stump magic.

The elderly couple represented a second important factor of the campaign. They attended the debate. They wanted to watch Talmadge perform. The woman came expecting to see an unusual and interesting occurence, a public brawl. She desired to see Talmadge "skin" Brown in public, in much the fashion that residents of south Georgia skinned a deer hung head down from a limb. She was excited about the aggressive and effective manner in which she knew Talmadge would attack and finish off an opponent. Important also was the fact that the woman

told another person about Talmadge's reputation for
fighting in public.   Through word of mouth, radio,
and the press, Talmadge acquired notoriety for
destroying political victims.

One can envision the elderly woman watching
Brown as he paced about, smiling and shaking her
head, wondering why any person holding office would
risk his political hide unnecessarily.   Brown was
caught in a trap of his own creation; however, the
fracas provided voters an opportunity to judge the
candidates for themselves. Referring to the meeting
at McRae, reporter Dan McGill concluded that, "The
political debate is the best means of determining
what a man has to offer the people."(28) It was just
after eleven o'clock in the morning, and more than
2,000 persons in McRae were about to have an opportunity to judge the speaking performances of Brown and
Talmadge. One can say with certainity that there
were three persons present who believed that Talmadge
would bludgeon Brown into political obscurity. Those
three were the elderly couple and Talmadge.

The McRae planners placed few restrictions upon
the two speakers, a decision that greatly favored the
rumbustious rhetoric of Talmadge. Although increasingly strident in his defense against criticism made
upon the Department of Agriculture and himself, Brown
had attempted to retain some semblance of civility
expected of a nine-year incumbent.   In contrast,
Talmadge primaily made colorful assaults in full
throttle. Because so few guidelines were established
by the sponsors and moderator of the event, the McRae
debate would be a Donnybrook.   The day prior to the
debate no one had even determined how long the
speakers would talk. A newsman reported that the
meeting would begin at 11:00 A.M. and "last 'indefi-
nitely'."(29) In a fight with few restrictions,
Brown would lose. Talmadge had said he was willing
to debate the commissioner before a convention of
Brown's own fertilizer inspectors!

Brown was either unaware or he totally misjudged
the nature of the debate he had inspired in McRae.
Information reported concerning how ground rules were
adopted for the first debate, even by newspapers
largely opposed to the commissioner, demonstrated
convincingly that Brown was uninformed of the kind of
warfare Talmadge would wage.   Talmadge wanted a
free-for-all among himself, Brown, and the audience,
and the speaking situation was evolving into that
permissive state. Again, to be fair to Brown, few
persons had watched Talmadge debate. Apparently oil
and fertilizer inspectors in the commissioner's
department knew little about Talmadge's aptitude for
oratorical disputation. How could the elderly woman

quoted by Lovelace Eve, however, have known clearly what Brown did not suspect, that the commissioner was about to be stripped publicly of his personal dignity. Perhaps it was characteristic of a Talmadge campaign that men and women from the cotton fields of Georgia sensed the nature and effectiveness of his candidacy better than a Commissioner shielded by governmental bureaucracy. Brown entered the debate blind to the reality of Talmadge's rhetorical superiority.

Unbelievably, to one looking back at the McRae meeting, after having studied all three debates, the principals held merely "a short conference"(30) on the speaker's stand in front of the restless crowd, just before the fight, to determine any rules under which the speakers would be allowed to attack. The only regulations imposed were the order of speaking and length of the speeches. Commissioner Brown would speak first for one hour, followed by Talmadge, who would talk for one and one-half hours, ending with Brown's rebuttal of twenty minutes.(31) Although Brown was uninformed or naive about the gravity of the danger in which he had placed his candidacy, the casual and impromptu procedure by which the speakers decided rules of debate indicated both candidates' remarkable confidence in their abilities to adapt to the difficult task at hand. Both men had the stump experience required for such a challenge, but probably neither candidate had confronted a scene in which the stakes were so high. Brown risked his office by challenging Talmadge to debate. Talmadge risked nothing, and realized that the meeting provided him the public forum he had been seeking since 1920 and before.

Fortunately for Talmadge, Max L. McRae, the Mayor of McRae, presided over the debate. He was referred to in the press as "Judge McRae." The Mayor would need all of his judicial skills to moderate this confrontation. Mayor McRae presided about as fairly as one could, considering that few rules had been established and announced to the crowd. The listeners were free to behave as their biases and rhetorical skills dictated. The preliminaries over, the Mayor excited an already anxious audience with the observation that, "This is the most important event in Georgia politics." As an afterthought, by a person who owed his office to many of the Talmadge supporters standing before him, Mayor McRae unwittingly revealed the identity of the candidate he felt the crowd favored by asking that they give <u>Brown</u> "a quiet and courteous hearing." The Mayor assumed the south Georgians would do no harm to Talmadge's speech.(32) Mayor McRae introduced Brown to the crowd.

Even the pro-Talmadge _Telfair_ _Enterprise_ reported that, in "his opening remarks," Brown "created a deep impression."(33) The _Atlanta_ _Constitution_, also opposed to Brown, admitted that, during his first hour of speaking, Brown put up a "stormy fight."(34) Probably concerned about Talmadge's growing reputation for rendering effective and uninhibited attacks upon his candidacy, Brown stated that he would not "deal in personalities" and didn't "want any mudslinging" from either candidate.(35) To the extent that was true, Brown challenged the wrong opponent; he should have invited John R. Irwin to a polite forum, before that candidate retreated from the campaign rather than behave rowdily. The more civil the debate the better for Brown. Yet, in a strategy that mistakenly assumed Talmadge was vulnerable in his own community, Brown attacked Talmadge's lack of trustworthiness, citing a series of incidents as proof that Talmadge would be an unreliable Commissioner of Agriculture.

Ignoring signs that the crowd favored his opponent, Brown portrayed Talmadge to be an unscrupulous candidate. The Commissioner reminded many in the audience that, while serving as Telfair attorney, Talmadge persuaded the county commissioners to purchase "a tract" of his land for "almshouse" at thirty dollars per acre, when it was not worth more than ten. A grand jury of the county recommended that the sale be revoked. This questionable dealing with public funds was used by Brown as evidence that Talmadge could not be "entrusted" with the affairs of Agriculture.(36)

Brown gave other instances of Talmadge's alleged swindles. Each of Brown's examples carried the conclusion that Talmadge was out to capitalize personally upon the public's trust. Brown accused Talmadge of "buying up cattle," and shipping them to Atlanta and "charging the farmers a commission." Brown proclaimed proudly that the bureau of markets, an agency of the Department of Agriculture, "put a stop to that."(37) In another questionable deal, Talmadge was a "middleman for Shippey Brothers of Atlanta in the sale of hogs." Talmadge used $150 of the county's money for a "trip to Atlanta to defeat a local bill," thereby influencing the official decisions of state legislators. Brown questioned Talmadge's loyalty to the Democratic party for, when it was advantageous to his interest, Talmadge "bolted" to run as an independent.(38) Probably noting the presence of women in the audience, Brown apparently did not cite the grand jury probe of Talmadge and his mule. While criticizing Talmadge, Brown experienced some interruptions by members of the audience. For example, "a keen voice somewhere on the outskirts" of the crowd proclaimed "every few minutes that your sins will find you out," a practice Talmadge loyalists routinized at public appearances.(39)

As Talmadge first "arose" to begin his one-hour and twenty-minute speech, the crowd gave him "a great ovation."(40) He "walked calmly to the center of the stage."(41) His supportive home town newspaper asserted that any "lead" initially "gained" by Brown in his opening speech was soon "relinquished."(42) Talmadge turned to the examples Brown employed to poison his credibility. The way in which Talmadge disposed of these charges demonstrated well the adeptness he employed in choosing the ground upon which to confront an opponent. He ignored Brown's charges of questionable dealings with cattle, hogs, and travel to Atlanta. As for abandoning the Democratic party, a practice that was suicidal for Georgia politicians, Talmadge employed sarcasm as a means of deflecting the audience's attention to Brown's own divided loyalties. Talmadge was a master craftsman at sidestepping substantive attacks and turning the thrusts back upon an opponent in a form of ridicule that pleased many in the audience. He yelled: "You, Mr. Brown, once was a bull-mooser."(43)

Because Brown directed several charges at him at once, Talmadge was able to let some pass by, while fielding the one he could exploit best before a friendly crowd. He isolated the "land deal" as the most potent issue on which to feed the 2,000. Talmadge used the land issue as a means of refuting most of Brown's charges. In the process, he inspired a supportive audience to an emotional peak and enhanced his image as a charismatic and credible leader. Looking out over the large crowd, Talmadge amused the neighborly gathering: "Mr. Brown tried to hit me with that land deal." Talmadge represented Brown as an outsider trying to tell south Georgians how to handle their business, a powerful instrument of disputation among southerners long impatient with the intervention of carpetbaggers of every kind. As the quotation below illustrates, from time-to-time during the debate Talmadge approached Brown physically, confronting him face-to-face on the speaker's stand as a way of showing dominance. "Turning to Brown," Talmadge charged him with outside interference: "You came down here to pick up our family row and make it a state issue." Talmadge reminded the south Georgia audience that the land issue had been resolved by their grand jury.(44)

Prior to the debate, Brown warned that he would

exhume Talmadge's act of selling property to the
county for profit; thus the accused was well prepared
to answer the charge.   One of Talmadge's great
strengths in public debate was to clarify an issue
for his advantage.   He cast issues in a sense that
was common to citizens.   "There is no law which says
a man can't sell land to Telfair county," he explained.(45)   "The county commissioners wanted to buy
some land out where I happened to own some," he
continued.   "I sold it to them for $30 an acre. . . .
When the new commissioners came in . . . I bought it
back [for] $30 an acre." The court "held that" there
"wan't anything illegal."(46)   One can envision the
elderly woman described by Lovelace Eve, turning to
her partner and both nodding agreement.
    Talmadge employed the audience as a form of
support for his candidacy.   Indeed, because so few
rules restricted the speakers, Talmadge involved all
the actors, including Mayor McRae, Commissioner
Brown, the general audience, and handpicked members
of the crowd.   The debate was characterized in the
press as "quick repartee and spirited rejoinders on
heated questions of the moment, interrupted at
intervals by shouts from the people and frequent
applause."(47) Although Talmadge was skillful in
involving an audience impromptu, he also had persons
planted in the crowd to provide corroborative and
extemporaneous testimonies on his behalf.   In this
first debate, Talmadge may not have rehearsed crowd
members' responses, for he apparently judged that he
could assume the presence of a supportive crowd.   He
prompted most of the audience's reactions from the
speaker's stand.
    By involving the audience, Talmadge demonstrated
confidence in his ability to think quickly and to
remain in command.   He also created immense interest
in his candidacy.   After all the elderly woman and
the multitude came to see him "skin" a commissioner
alive, not to be put to sleep by a boring lecture on
agriculture and economics.   With Talmadge, the
content of an issue was far less significant than its
potential for exploitation for desired audience
response.   For example, little needed to be said
about the land Talmadge sold to the county.   But
Talmadge employed that well worn topic as a means by
which to galvanize the crowd around his candidacy.
    In the idiom of rural south Georgians, Talmadge
drew the attention of the audience to the attitudes
of county commissioners present: "Why, all these
county commissioners are for me.   Ain't you boys?"
Several from the crowd "answered, 'yes'."(48)
Watching the behavior of the Commissioners carefully,
and encouraged by the initial response, Talmadge, as

if prodding Lazarus, "called members of the county commission 'to arise' and state that the deal on his land was fair."(49) Heightening the rhetorical drama, he asked a county commissioner if "Talmadge" had "done anything" he "shouldn't," and the man replied "No." By this point in the platform dialogue, Talmadge had the man entrapped; there was no way this person would risk the wrath of the crowd and loss of their votes in coming elections by disagreeing with any of Talmadge's directives. "You are for me, aren't you?," Talmadge shouted. "You bet I am," the politically powerful recruit from the courthouse gang responded. Unwilling to let this peak of excitement subside, keeping perfect time, Talmadge turned to the crowd and nailed his point home. That county commissioner is with me, he said, just as are the "majority" of Georgians.(50)

Talmadge had come a long way politically in Telfair county, for in elections in 1920 and 1922 the courthouse bosses opposed him. In quite a reversal, Talmadge now had County Commissioners dancing by his tune at a political rally. At times during the debate audience applause was "sustained until" Talmadge was "forced to plead for silence so that he might proceed."(51) Talmadge so refuted Brown's criticism of the land deal that the audience "laughed at this charge."(52)

Brown held that, because Talmadge was not a genuine farmer, he was not qualified to be Commissioner of Agriculture. To ridicule Talmadge's lack of experience in any one profession, Brown referred disparagingly to his opponent as "Colonel Talmadge." Distinguishing between a person who worked with his hands and one who merely visited the farm, Brown insisted that Talmadge was not a "dirt farmer."(53) Brown told the audience that Talmadge was a county attorney, but not a practical man of the earth.(54)

To try to convince a hostile crowd that Talmadge was not a farmer, Brown referred to an agricultural directory, and pointed out that Talmadge's name was not listed among the roll of farmers. Many in the audience knew that Talmadge lived on a large farm in Telfair county. Although this was a political era in which each candidate tried to out-document the other in the most dramatic fashion possible, it is doubtful that many among the two thousand were concerned whether Talmadge was named in a published directory. Brown's quoting from a directory was somewhat like the Baptist fellow who preached from a prepared manuscript, in contrast to Talmadge who conceived the truth intuitively. To further document his point, Brown said that Talmadge's name was included in an American law directory but, in the commissioner's

opinion, he did not "rank any too high as a lawyer."
Thus Brown maintained that, because Talmadge's name
was in a published directory, he was not a farmer
but, in spite of being included in a second directory, he was not a respected lawyer.(55) Finally Brown
argued that "Talmadge knows but little about the
department of agriculture and this is shown by the
charges he made."(56)

Brown failed to grasp accurately the nature of
Talmadge's reputation in and around Telfair county,
and he was unable to convince the listeners that the
home candidate was not a farmer but an incompetent
lawyer. Even if half of the indictment were accurate, many in the crowd refused to agree with it.
The Telfair Enterprise was too biased to be believed
fully, but its editorial probably echoed the senti-
ments of many in the crowd: "Mr. Brown was given a
respectable hearing and was roundly cheered in his
opening speech, but at the conclusion of his rejoinder of twenty minutes, wherein he attempted to bring
in new charges he was hissed by the crowd for his
continuous attempt to prove Talmadge was not a
farmer."(57)

Because he lived just five miles outside of
McRae on a large farm, Talmadge enjoyed considerable
advantage in defending his familiarity with agriculture. In the debate, Brown's close analysis of the
content of a written document lost out to Talmadge's
colorful characterizations and lively exchanges with
members of the crowd. "Turning to Brown" tempestu-
ously, Talmadge admonished: So "you still charge I am
not a dirt farmer."(58) During the next hour and
twenty minutes, Talmadge probably won the 1926
campaign for Commissioner of Agriculture. He also
perfected the prototype of rhetorical behavior that
came to be known as "Talmadgeism." He orchestrated
Windsor park as only a master of crowd psychology and
effective public speaker could do. Talmadge expertly
employed a favorite tactic of the public persuader,
involving the audience in a series of overt responses.

He provoked audience reaction favorable to his
candidacy. Talmadge refined the "good 'ole boy"
syndrome to a persuasive art form. In this manner,
he solidified thousands of rural-thinking Georgians
into a formidable force for his cause. He created a
cultural and regional bond with many Georgians by
forging a political kinship with them. "Is this
charge that I am not a dirt farmer false, boys?," he
cajoled. "The crowd yelled 'yes'." "Is the charge
that I am not a good lawyer, false? 'You bet it is,'
came the cry from the crowd." This was a campaign
call rehearsed by Georgia audiences at Talmadge's

meetings in 1926 and beyond.   They learned their
parts well.
       One of his audiences' favorite responses was,
"Go to it."   Talmadge led the McRae throng to a
crescendo of support.   "Mr. Brown says I am not a
dirt farmer. How many of you people here have ever
seen me farming?," Talmadge urged.   "Hundreds of
hands went up in all parts of the crowd."   He
conditioned the crowd to respond favorably through a
second series of questions.   "'How many of you have
ever seen me plowing? How many of you have ever seen
me putting out fertilizer? How many of you have ever
farmed with me?'   Cries of 'I have' came from all
parts of the crowd while many called, 'Go to it,
Talmadge'." Lovelace Eve noted that "Mr. Brown sat
calmly in his chair, his expression never changing."(59) Brown was probably looking out over the
crowd for the missing fertilizer inspector who
advised him to debate Talmadge in his home town! The
audience continued its affirmation: "'I've plowed
mules with you,' one man shouted.   'I've seen you
bale hay,' said another.   'I've helped you curb a
well,' said a third man."(60)
       Beyond involving the audience, Talmadge seduced
poor Mayor Max L. McRae on to his side. The hapless
Judge was trying to preside over this raucous exchange in as nonpartisan a manner as an elected
official of McRae could. Talmadge called on Brown to
ask Judge McRae if he were not a dirt farmer, disregarding any protocol of even a public political
meeting. Mayor McRae, probably torn between embar-
rassment for having been asked to depart from his
responsibility as moderator and a chance to solidify
his own political strength with thousands of local
voters, did some sidestepping of his own. He said
that Talmadge "was a dirt farmer" and "practiced law
to a certain extent,"(61) confirming some of both
candidates' claims without angering local voters.
       To refute Brown's insistence that he was a
lawyer of ill repute, Talmadge inducted the entire
legal community of Telfair county to substantiate his
good character. He "called on the lawyers, judges
and his clients" to tell the crowd that he had "never
violated the ethics of the law profession."(62)   Two
newspapers, both supportive of Talmadge, recorded
that, in all, fifty individuals testified that
Talmadge "plows in his fields, strews guano through a
bugle, chops cotton, and pulls fodder."(63) Now they
were learning just how well Talmadge could trumpet
words in political debate! To cap the argument that
he was a successful farmer, Talmadge invited "Mr.
Brown and all of these newspaper men out to see my
crops and you can take away as many watermelons as

you wish."(64) With "thrust after thrust," Talmadge
kept Brown "constantly on the defensive."(65) In a
threat that Talmadge repeated on stumps throughout
Georgia, he promised to climb "up" Brown's "collar"
and stay there until the September 8 election.(66)
Tasting victory, Talmadge accelerated his attack upon
the Commissioner. In a relatively insensitive
comment, even for Talmadge in a politically heated
debate, Talmadge told the audience they could expect
to see Brown "cry" right there in public, as he often
did when informing persons that their relatives would
not get the jobs in the Department of Agriculture
first promised them.(67) Talmadge followed a
similiarly personal line of argument when he
criticized Brown for being disloyal to Tom Watson, a
legend in Georgia politics. According to Talmadge,
Brown only "stuck to Tom Watson" while that patriot
was living. "As soon as he died," Brown "forgot all
about him," actually firing a Mr. Davenport from the
position of oil inspector for which Watson had
recommended him.(68) To supplement his personal
attacks upon Brown's administration of Agriculture,
Talmadge satisfied an important rhetorical convention
of that period by presenting stump facts, producing
affidavit after affidavit, and citing "acts of
law."(69)

     Talmadge attacked the Department of Agriculture
and Comissioner Brown's management of that state
agency. He argued that the department no longer
provided the services for which it was created.
Brown's own "record" in the department would "do the
indicting." Through "bad judgment" the commissioner
hired too many inspectors, a total of 191, when there
was a need for merely six. Talmadge insisted that
those inspectors "don't work six hours a day."(70)
The performance of the inspectors was "lax" and
"inefficient." "Inferior oils and gasoline" were
being "dumped" in Georgia. Brown's department failed
to respond to inquiries made by farmers. Talmadge
insisted that, "I have talked to 40,000 people in
Georgia and in each speech have asked if any one of
them ever received a message from the agricultural
department about farm matters, and not one has
answered in the affirmative." Relating his claims to
the crowd's experience at the pump, Talmadge described how the poor quality gasoline "clogs up and
ruins engines with carbon." About that time in his
speech, "an automobile passed by making a lot of
noise. 'There goes a machine now talking for
Talmadge,' the speaker said, and the crowd
cheered."(71)

     By comparing the language employed by Talmadge
in the debate at McRae with the words he used when
speaking to the League of Women Voters in the

university town of Athens, one learns how he adapted
stylistically for different settings. When talking
to the 2,000 at McRae, Talmadge couched his comments
in language such as "messed up" and "ain't."(72)   To
the League of Women Voters, however, on July 27,
1926, Talmadge employed more formal terms, for
example, the words "medium," "overlapped the functions," and "highly scientific matter." To the
League of Women Voters, Talmadge also offered more
technical explanations of chemical processes. He
said: "The inspection of gas for the specific
gravity proves nothing as to its commercial worth.
Under the distillation tests it shows the absence of
highly volatile materials . . . which are combusti-
ble, which do not burn up, and those materials form
in your engine."(73) Unlike Brown, Talmadge adapted
stylistically to different audiences. Talmadge
pleased the League of Women Voters because he spoke
formally, like Brown. In contrast, Brown was less
able to talk colloquially like Talmadge when addressing the crowd at McRae.

Talmadge maintained that Brown's Department of
Agriculture was not only inefficient, but also
corrupt. He charged Brown with several counts of
political and financial abuse of the public trust.
To dramatize the inappropriateness of Brown's appointments, Talmadge labeled the 191 oil, gas, and
fertilizer inspectors as "oily boys." In the McRae
debate, Talmadge examined Brown as if addressing a
jury of 2,000. Turning to Brown and back to the
crowd, Talmadge interrogated his opponent concerning
relatives he had appointed: "Who did you appoint, Mr.
Brown?," asked Talmadge. "Pope Brown," replied
Brown. "Who is Pope Brown?," continued Talmadge.
"My Son," answered Brown. One wonders why Brown
cooperated in this selfincriminating dialogue;
however, Talmadge was able to intimidate persons
publicly to behave to his advantage.(74) Brown was
fearful of negative crowd response and loss of
credibility to be bought by a failure to reply to
Talmadge's initiatives.

Talmadge hit hard at Brown's alleged practice of
collecting fees from departmental employees for
personal political advantage. "Through the inspection system," Brown was "conducting a banking department." In other words, after inspectors collected
fees, they retained them longer than the law allowed
as a means of having funds on hand accumulating
interest and influence for the holder. The law
required that inspectors collect fees, explained
Talmadge, deduct their own income, and forward the
remainder to the Commissioner of Agriculture. At
this point, Brown interrupted Talmadge with a

correction: The fees are forwarded to the "State treasurer." Talmadge fired back: But you know they are "credited to your department." In a genre of argumentation popular at that time, Talmadge documented his claim dramatically with a 1925 auditor's report showing that $62,000 had "not been paid in by inspectors."(75)

Talmadge called Brown "the blankest man on this earth" for claiming not to know that money was being collected from employees to fund his campaigns and to influence the legislature.(76) Talmadge provided the crowd with a "complete and itemized list of contributions to Brown's campaign funds for 1922 and 1924" by inspectors and other employees of the department. A total of $7,993 was contributed in 1922. Talmadge displayed affidavits indicating that Fred T. Bridges, former assistant Commissioner of Agriculture, collected $40 from Tye Holland, the veteran.(77) Talmadge maintained that the fees collected from employees were used by Brown to manipulate the state legislature. Contrasting Brown's personal elitism with his own portrayed image as one of the "good 'ole boys" of Georgia, Talmadge envisioned: "Imagine this monarch, this king, this man who boasts that he controls Georgia through the senate, who makes and unmakes men."(78) Funds had been collected from employees by which to "fix the legislature of 1925," Talmadge argued, resulting in the pouring of "bad gasoline of the world" upon Georgia.(79) "Senator Morgan" reported that Brown accomplished this goal by persuading the "Senate committee" to "kill the distillation test bill."(80)

Fighting back, Brown defended the work of the Department of Agriculture, labeling Talmadge's criticism "poppycock." Brown "reviewed" divisions within the department, and "praised various heads." The fertilizer inspectors served "like police" to protect the "interest of farmers," he said. With another jab at his opponent's credibility, Brown maintained that this was the "most criticial time in the history of agriculture since the Civil War," and changing Comissioners would do "injury" to the farmers.(81) Brown followed with a number of initiatives. Talmadge's assertion that funds in the department were short was false, he argued. The finding of a 1923 committee appointed by Governor Hugh Dorsey to investigate Brown concluded that the "charges against the department were worthless."(82) The department made a "profit each year," continued Brown, of $600,000 "from inspection fees." Mayor Max L. McRae, trying to referee the debate fairly, found himself again batted between the candidates. When asked by Brown if he didn't receive "a rebate on fertilizer," Mayor McRae answered "yes," demonstating that the Department of Agriculture did respond responsibly to the needs of citizens. Trying desperately to relate to a crowd whose temperament he had so badly misjudged, Brown mentioned other Telfair county farmers who had been served well by the department.(83)

During his term at the podium, Talmadge played the audience with a hand poll, a strategy he ritualized during his political career. Confident now that the crowd was with him, he asked that "all those who believed he should get out of the race" to "raise their hands" but, according to the bias press, "not a hand was raised." Then he asked persons who believed Brown should retire from the campaign, and "every hand . . . went up" amidst "great whooping and yelling."(84) To prolong the impact of the public vote, Talmadge "shouted for" the audience to "hold" their hands "up there for a minute" and, turning "dramatically to Mr. Brown," said: "There is your verdict."(85) A newspaper supportive of Brown gave a different account of the hand vote. The reporter from that paper, who had been sitting "within arm's length of Mr. Talmadge" when the debate ended, wrote that "several delegations of Brown supporters . . . did not raise their hands" when Talmadge asked if Brown should retire from the race.(86)

The debate ended with the clock in the "court house tower" striking two o'clock.(87) Both speakers finished "in good humor." The audience had taken in "every word," with the _Atlanta Constitution_, a paper supportive of Talmadge, concluding that the "crowd was overwhelmingly in favor of Talmadge."(88) W. T. Anderson, outspoken supporter of Talmadge, wrote in his _Macon Telegraph and News_ that, in the beginning of the speeches Brown's "admirers and friends" were "much in evidence"; yet, as the speeches progressed, "they faded like dew in the sun."(89)

Brown had supporters in the audience, but they found much during the debate about which to be concerned in the remainder of the campaign. Lovelace Eve, maybe reflecting his pleasure in the strong showing of Talmadge, noted the "extreme courtesy of the two debaters to each other and the fairness of the crowd to Mr. Brown," ignoring some of Talmadge's more strident assaults and the audience's cooperation with the challenger. Eve reported that "the crowd pressed about" Talmadge and "slapped him on the back," carrying him off on their shoulders, a ritual that was carefully planned. "It was a Talmadge day and Talmadge crowd." The "firey little" Talmadge, continued Eve, "put Mr. Brown in a hole."(90) The _Atlanta Journal_ observed that "hours after" the

Mayor Max L. McRae (left) greets Talmadge. (Photograph reprinted from the Atlanta Constitution by permission of that paper.)

debate "there were groups about the streets discussing the points made by the two speakers."(91) The results of the debate had a rippling effect in other Georgia campaigns. Politicians for other state offices accelerated their attacks upon the commissioner, hoping to mount the Talmadge bandwagon to victory. L. G. Hardman, for example, candidate for governor, predicted that the John N. "Holder/Brown political machine would be smashed."(92)

Not all observers agreed with newspapers that reported Talmadge winning the McRae debate decisively. For example, a writer for the Middle Georgian contended that Talmadge's unprofessional manner of debate cost him votes. That writer argued that "the heckling to which Mr. Brown was subjected . . . hurt Talmadge. It was inexcusable . . . roudyism." In contrast, "the manner in which" Brown "kept his head and . . . poise . . . denotes bigness and superiority. Brown's chances for re-election are even better than they were before that debate." This newspaper critic also provided considerable insight into how

Talmadge provoked response from a friendly audience. The critic distinguished between the spontaneous reaction by supporters of Talmadge and the reasoned vote that he predicted from a majority of Georgians:

> For quickness and agility in repartee, for abaility [sic] on the instant to capitalize on a shouted exclamation . . . from the audience and to turn to his own purpose and adverse reply . . . Mr. Talmadge had Mr. Brown worsted. In appoint of appeal to prejudice on the part of the voters, he had all the b[e]st of the "argument". In point of forensic pyrotechnics, bombast and vituperation, he had the more sedate Commissioner . . . "backed off the boards," and that sort of substitute for argument seemed abundantly to satisfy the majority of the crowd. . . . Mr. Brown made . . . charges against Mr. Talmadge. Mr. Talmadge did not convincingly dispose of a single one of them--unless flat denial, heckling, [and] counter charges . . . [are] accepted by the voter as satisfactory disposal. . . . But was it an answer that will . . . have any weight with the voters?

The critic for the <u>Middle Georgian</u> contrasted what he perceived to be Commissioner Brown's statesman-like performance with the barbaric behavior of Talmadge. "Mr. Brown was cool, dignified, [and] courteous. . . . He had documentary evidence. . . . He indulged in no manner of . . . character assassination. He was argumentative. He talked like a business man. . . . He was dressed in a black business suit, and despite the torrid heat, spoke with bared head and kept his coat on. No water had been provided for him . . . during this hour-long speech."

The <u>Middle Georgian</u> critic described Talmadge's churlish podium behavior. In contrast to Brown, Talmadge "wore a light gray suit. Soon after he started speaking he dramatically doffed his coat, and slung it to a table. . . . Then he put on his straw hat, saying that the sun made his head hot, and kept it on during the rest of his speech. McRae friends kept him supplied with water." The critic complained vociferously about an obscene story told by Talmadge in the presence of women: "An anecdote he told . . . of . . . why Len Jackson quit the department of agriculture was shocking to all the sense of decency . . . for it was an audience of Georgia men and women . . . boys and girls. It was a vulgar story." The "smutly yarn" would "cost Talmadge votes."(93)

The complaint by the writer about Talmadge
relating an obscene story characterized perfectly the
twenty-year career of Talmadge in and out of public
office. Even in public performances, he was totally
uninhibited, employing any means he felt would win
votes. Talmadge involved himself in public confrontations about controversial topics. This was the
essence of his turbulent rhetorical strategy. In
some elections voters accepted his brazenness. Other
times he repulsed enough persons to lose an election
or cause. Regardless of the outcome, he refused to
vary his behavior. Somehow, in the 1926 election and
on other occasions in and out of office, many citizens considered his political vulgarity to be in
character and, for him, acceptable stump behavior.
Had the more stately Brown attempted to exploit the
wellknown charge of Talmadge's intercourse with a
mule, the McRae crowd would probably have been even
less tolerant of him than they were.

THE DAWSON DEBATE

Talmadge and Brown debated a second time in
Dawson on August 4. They had agreed to a debate at
Atlanta, but canceled it. The scene in Dawson was
entirely different than the setting at McRae.
Because the second debate occurred the day after the
first, there was no time for Talmadge, his supporters, and the press to create the storm of expectation
experienced in McRae. There were several additional
reasons why the impact of the Dawson meeting was
deadened. The press announced that the debate had
been canceled. Because of the shock of the treatment
received at McRae, Brown did not want to debate
Talmadge again in south Georgia. He desired that the
second confrontation be called off. The Mayor of
Dawson announced through the press that there would
be no debate because Brown would be speaking to a
gathering of the Georgia State Agricultural Society,
a "nonpolitical organization."(94) After McRae,
Brown wanted as nonpolitical an occasion at which to
speak as he could find, maybe an audience of oil
inspectors!

Characteristically, Talmadge simply traveled to
Dawson and forced a debate with Brown in an impromptu
arrangement. Persons "jammed" into the court house
to hear the second debate. The audience was estimated to be between 600 and 2,000.(95) No mention was
made of what percentage of the audience was made up
of members of the Georgia State Agricultural Society,
but biased pressmen indicated that the listeners gave
Talmadge a warm reception. Both speakers appeared
tired. Talmadge had spoken three times since the
McRae debate the day before, an indication of the

pace he set in the campaign.(96)

Because of the unsettling experience in McRae, Brown was a changed candidate. He needed no fertilizer spy to advise him on what to expect in the second debate. The Commissioner was now keenly aware of Talmadge's enormous talent for manipulating a crowd. He was shell-shocked from the first battle. During his term at the podium, Brown complained that, although informed that the second "debate was off," Talmadge "came . . . without invitation from anybody."   Brown's   reluctance   to   meet   Talmadge face-to-face in Dawson was not the act of a confident person.   Once again Talmadge had entrapped the commissioner within a rhetorical dilemma. For Brown to deny Talmadge a chance to talk might prove more costly in the press and in votes than to lose a second debate to him.

Because he could not stop Talmadge from speaking, unlike at McRae, Brown took specific steps to obstruct his opponent. Again Brown was scheduled to speak first but, to disrupt the dramatic climax to which he knew Talmadge would build the audience, the commissioner gave twenty minutes of his first hour to L. G. Hardman, candidate for governor.(97) In a way, Talmadge was being forced to debate two men, odds he could use to build the courageous and fighting image he sought. But Talmadge's effectiveness depended in part too upon his ability to control the audience, manipulate the order of business, and create a boisterous occasion.   To defang Talmadge, Hardman attempted to establish an atmosphere in the court house more sacred than political. Hardman began the evening with prayer, saying he did not "care to bring in personalities."   Each time Hardman stopped and asked "if his time is up," Brown insisted, "go on, take your time."   Brown was happy having Hardman protect him from Talmadge! At the end of the debate, Brown cut his twenty minute rejoinder short, ostensibly because the hour was nearly 1:00 A.M.(98)

The press viewed the Dawson debate as "a summing up" of the speeches at McRae;(99) however, their performances provided significant insights into the candidates' persuasive choices and public personalities. In speeches and statements prior to the first debate, Brown was bold and, as it turned out, overly confident. He thought that his status as commissioner plus the considerable resources of the Department of Agriculture would enable him to fend off any challenge by the five opponents.   Rattled by the demolition debate at McRae and realizing that he could not out-maul Talmadge, at Dawson Brown returned to an argumentative stance of a statesman-like incumbent. He retreated to a public posture with which he was more familiar and secure.

In his speaking style at Dawson, Brown became more controlled and even contrite. Ineffective matching Talmadge's platform unruliness, Brown shifted from assailant to businessman. Brown hoped that voters, when contrasting Talmadge's boisterousness with his renewed stump dignity, would perceive him to be the more credible candidate. Samples from Brown's forty-minute speech at Dawson illustrate this rhetorical transformation to a more judicious argumentation. Having apparently listened carefully while surrogate Hardman spoke of promises of "righteousness, justice, truth, and honesty," when he finally had to speak, Brown said:(100) "It makes no difference to me who is elected as long as truth and virtue prevail."(101) Possibly in some campaigns against other candidates, this elevated strategy would have worked, but Talmadge interpreted Brown's new stance as proof of political weakness.

The reporter for the <u>Americus Times-Recorder</u> provided a full account of the events at Dawson. Talmadge had forced Brown into a defensive attitude from which it was difficult to argue. Brown was in the awkward position of defending his inability to manage the Department of Agriculture. To answer Talmadge's charge that employees in the department were collecting fees for mere political purposes, Brown knew only to say: "There are 75 people in my department in the capital and I must trust my heads of departments to overlook [supervise] things. . . . It was impossible for any one man to look after so large a number of employees." Brown made other concessions pleasing to Talmadge. Because of a false claim he made at McRae, Brown found himself admitting the mistake in Dawson, an act that seems admirable enough, but one Talmadge interpreted to be a sign of a mortally wounded candidate.

Throughout his twenty years in Georgia politics, Talmadge refused to compromise or seriously confess a mistake. Brown, however, corrected the "error" he made in McRae when he criticized Lawson Stapleton for work alleged to have been done while an employee of the Department of Agriculture. This mistake dramatized Brown's unfamiliarity with employees in his department, because Lawson was never hired by Agriculture. Brown retracted the mistake also because Stapleton had corroborrated Brown's error in the press, and now was sitting in the audience in Dawson ready to testify for Talmadge. Brown clarified that Stapleton had not been an employee, but was "a disgruntled applicant for oil inspector" over a six-year period. In correcting the mistake, Brown so jumbled the explanation that he misrepresented

Stapleton's status a second time and, as he took his seat, persons present amended overtly what he obviously had tried to say. By this time, Brown must have been badly shaken.

Although placed on the defensive by his mistakes, by Talmadge's persuasive tenacity, and by hostile audience responses, at Dawson Brown managed to counter effectively. Obviously having been prompted by a knowledgeable source on the subject of employment in his department, Brown exhumed a witness he, like Talmadge, should have been able to call upon spontaneously during the McRae debate. Having observed or read in the press about their boss's losses at McRae, and greatly concerned about the stability of their own jobs, employees in Brown's department from across the state rushed to him documentary examples to be used in the debates at Dawson and Elberton. To convince the Dawson audience that he supervised the department with integrity, he quoted the man who presided over the debate in McRae, but a day late: "Why Judge Max L. McRae . . . asked me to appoint his brother" as an inspector "and I refused."

Contrasting Talmadge's persuasive behavior under conditions that beset the Dawson debate with his uninhibited speaking in the less restricted McRae confrontation provides a clearer understanding of the public personality and persuasive activity Talmadge employed in politics for two decades. Observing Talmadge's public behavior in the Dawson debate, where the rhetorical elements were more disjointed and less subject to his impromptu control, one discovers that he was more insecure rhetorically and less able to ravage a situation and an opponent. The delaying tactics by Brown at Dawson, the extra speaker run in at the last moment, the lateness of the hour, the indoor setting, and the weariness of the debaters disrupted the denouement of forensic conflict that Talmadge prospered upon at McRae. Even at Dawson, a biased press decided that Talmadge "won the hour," but he was kept off balance when trying to reload his speech.

Pleased with the results of the planned disruption of Talmadge's persuasive performance, at times in Dawson Brown mounted a recovery of his own. For example, when Talmadge "turned to Brown" and inquired about how much "wild-cat gas he has found in the state," Brown was better fortified than he had been at McRae, answering authoritatively: "8,000,000 gallons," knocking Talmadge off balance with a quick and precise reply. Having no agricultural directory of his own from which to refute Brown's figures reliably, Talmadge attempted to intimidate the

commissioner: "You know that ain't true."   Refusing
any longer to remain a stationary target, Brown
countered assertively: "It is true."   Unable to
disprove Brown's supporting evidence and worried that
listeners might see behind his mask of infalibility,
Talmadge tried to rescue himself with a bluff.   This
example illustrates how Talmadge's strategy of
tormentation depended completely upon his audacity
and effectivness in holding a posture of rhetorical
intimidation. This bully behavior left little room
for rhetorical blunders.   Once Talmadge committed
himself to a public career of rhetorical turbulance
there was no turning back. To recover from Brown's
well supported reply, Talmadge blustered: "You wait,
I'll tell you.   You are dogging the issue, and you
know it."
     At McRae, the publicity in the press prior to
the debate, the congregating outdoors of an anxious
crowd crushed around the platform, and the
unregulated format that allowed unlimited crowd
participation created an explosive setting in which
Talmadge's turbulent rhetoric increased.   Due to
Brown's decisive actions in disorganizing the meeting
at Dawson, however, the persuasive volatility
necessary for Talmadge's rowdyism was largely missing
in the second debate.   Within a setting less
conducive to the kinetic rhetoric he displayed in the
first debate, at Dawson Talmadge resorted more to a
public contempt for his opponent, a variation on his
theme of vituperation. For example, Brown contended
that the "audit of 1926 of funds collected in 1924"
would show that the Department of Agriculture owed
"no man a cent," and "shook his finger" at his
opponent. The Americus Times-Recorder described how
Talmadge answered with a rhetorical threat employed
to provoke a crowd reaction to drown out Brown's
documentation.   Ignoring Brown's citation of the
audit, Talmadge said: "Don't worry about what I don't
know; I'm going to tell you in a few minutes," and
the "crowd went wild again."

THE ELBERTON DEBATE

     The two candidates debated for a third time on
August 12 in Brown's home town of Elberton. After
the confrontations at McRae and Dawson, interest in
the third debate heightened with each passing day.
The political plot unfolding in Elberton created
enormous intrigue concerning the final debate.   To
the media, the voters, and the two candidates, the
main mystery remaining in the campaign was how
comparatively effective Talmadge and Brown would
perform in Brown's home town. After the McRae and
Dawson debates, the principals had more than a week

in which to tout the significance of the pending meeting in Elberton, with each camp negotiating for advantage in the media and among the voters. The "leaders" in Brown's campaign contended that their candidate would "even" the "score" in Elberton. This prediction of victory, however, carried the admission that Brown had lost the other debates and was behind in the campaign.(102)

In a sense Brown faced a difficult assignment in Elberton, for citizens expected him to win decisively before a home audience. The results of the first two debates could not have strengthened his confidence, although he now had a more realistic assessment of the challenge that awaited him in Elberton. A weak showing in the third debate would likely end any chances Brown had of winning the election. Editor W. T. Anderson, outspoken supporter of Talmadge, anticipating a winning performance by his candidate, used the Macon Telegraph and News to set Brown up for a final fall. Anderson reminded readers that certainly Brown should be well received since he was speaking "on home ground and surrounded by . . . friends."(103) The Elberton Star was more confident of Brown's abilities and hopeful that he could regain the lead in the campaign. The editor of the Star predicted that Brown's speaking performance before a friendly audience would provide the voters a more reliable indication of his excellent leadership qualities than the speeches he had delivered under extremely hostile conditions in south Georgia. The Star explained that Brown "will be in his home county and Mr. Talmadge will have the same odds against him here that Mr. Brown had to contend with in McRae and at Dawson."(104)

His confidence pumped up by successful speaking engagements during June and July, and particularly because of his success in the McRae debate, Talmadge liked the odds facing him in the third confrontation. At Elberton he would be the underdog debater. Talmadge welcomed the opportunity to dispute with Brown in the Commissioner's back yard only because it was necessary if a challenger was to defeat an incumbent. As will be shown in analysis of future elections, Talmadge only debated when the exposure was to his political advantage. At Elberton, the risk would be high but the potential returns were great. In contrast to Brown's mere adequate response to hostile conditions at McRae, if Talmadge could defeat the incumbent decisively in the commissioner's home town, the election would be his.

At Elberton once again the rabbit was thrown into the briar patch. The more rhetorically energized the occasion, media, issues, audience, and

speakers for the third debate the better Talmadge
liked his chances of winning the day and the
campaign. Talmadge was ecstatic about the feverish
pitch of the Elberton debate. He could hardly wait
to take on Brown and the more hostile crowd. Because
he experienced at McRae what it was like to
intoxicate an audience and himself, the record shows
that for the Elberton debate and for future campaigns
and causes, Talmadge attempted to recreate conditions
required for repeating that experience.

For Talmadge's tumultuous persuasive techniques
to work effectively, however, certain prerequisites
had to be met, some that he could manage more than
others. The scene in Elberton the day of the debate
satisfied the requirements of another Talmadge
shoot-out. Because most observers seemed to believe
Talmadge was winning the race, increasing numbers of
persons boarded his campaign wagon. Although endors-
ing Brown, the Elberton Star noted that, "Many
friends of Mr. Talmadge from McRae and elsewhere . .
. were present" for the third debate. Unlike the
Dawson event, the meeting at Elberton was held
outdoors in the "sweltering heat," beginning at 11:21
A.M. before a crowd numbering about the same as that
of McRae.

The editor of Brown's home-town newspaper estimated the size of the audience to range between 1,800
and 3,000.(105) An editor for Talmadge judged the
number to be 2,500.(106) Most persons observed the
debate from the courthouse lawn under the "scorching
sun," seeking shade beneath the "big oaks and elms."
"Hundreds" watched from "windows and porches on the
first and second floors of the court house, and at
windows on three floors of the Piedmont Hotel." The
meeting at Elberton had the makings of a second
hanging. Unlike arrangements at McRae, supporters of
the more dignified Brown provided "many seats" for
"older men and for the ladies, many of whom were
present." The "great majority" of the audience stood
for three hours.(107)

Brown preferred addressing a staid occasion like
that at Dawson more than the unrestrained setting at
McRae. Brown's actions during the Dawson debate,
when he shared speaking time with a candidate for
governor and ended his speech early, demonstrated
that he recognized he was no match for Talmadge under
conditions that permitted an oratorical ruction.
Unfortunately for Brown, the politically charged
atmosphere that characterized the McRae debate was
forecast for the meeting at Elberton. Brown and
supporters knew from contrasting experiences of the
first two debates that some means had to be found by
which to tame Talmadge in Elberton. If Talmadge were

allowed to speak full bore, Brown would be shot down
before his turn to speak, as Talmadge was to lead off
with an hour's talk. If allowed to speak unmolested,
Talmadge would so inflame many in the crowd that
Brown would never recover.

In the first debate, Mayor McRae had earnestly
tried to preside in a fair way, but was eventually
dragged into the debate.   In the session at Dawson,
the participants were somewhat left to their own
disgraces. To Brown's credit, he managed the con-
fused format at Dawson to a relative rhetorical
advantage. Of course no one in the Brown camp could
be optimistic about a candidate who was more effective against an opponent not speaking than speaking!
Brown and supporters sought some means of preventing
the incumbent from having to exchange direct blows
with a powerful challenger before a rowdy crowd.

The challenge for Brown and supporters was to
find a debating format for Elberton that enabled
Brown to speak without having him harassed into
submission. Wisely, persons in Brown's home town
established a format designed to constrain Talmadge's
podium talents. Organizers were careful to see that
the third debate was supervised much more strictly
than the first. As he astutely demonstrated during
the Dawson debate, if given a choice, Brown would not
confront Talmadge on the challenger's own terms.
Brown needed none of his oil inspectors to tell him
that "goose-grease" Talmadge would be difficult to
handle, even on home ground. The only chance Brown
had of achieving even a draw in the final debate was
to partially neutralize Talmadge's oratorical skills.
Supporters of Brown planned the format of the debates
to favor the more business-like speaking delivery of
Brown. They established rules that disallowed the
audience response on which Talmadge depended to
create the free-for-all that so pleased many in the
crowd at McRae. In this fashion the Elberton promot-
ers hoped to partially subdue Talmadge.

To enforce the more restrictive guidelines, the
Elberton planners selected a no-nonsense moderator,
Judge Raymond Stapleton of Elberton, one decisive
enough to prevent a stump killing. The stern Judge
announced to the speakers and to the audience tight
rules under which the debate would proceed. Clearly,
supporters of Brown in Elberton had carefully constructed an order of business that favored the
professorial demeanor to which Brown was returning.
Judge Stapleton told the crowd that interruptions of
the speakers by any member of the audience would only
be tolerated upon the "consent" of the person speaking, a measure designed to protect Brown, since
Talmadge would make every effort to establish a

boisterous banter with the listeners. Realizing that
supporters of Talmadge would be planted in the
audience for the purpose of disrupting his speeches,
Brown was depending upon Judge Stapleton's gavel to
protect him.

The performance of Judge Stapleton was one of
the few topics on which newspapers for opposing
candidates agreed.   The Macon Telegraph and News,
supportive of Talmadge, observed that Judge Stapleton
presided over the debate "right rigidly."(108)   The
Elberton Star, promoting Brown, praised the Judge for
preserving "excellent order," claiming that the third
meeting was "more orderly" than the melee in McRae
and that the audience listened "attentively and
courteously."(109)   During the speeches, Judge
Stapleton "sometimes" called "hecklers" and others to
order.(110) But Talmadgeism was not easily con-
strained! Better control of the behavior of the
speakers and the crowd should have been a significant
advantage for Brown; however, the Judge was unable to
stop all partisan responses by the crowd for, because
of "interruptions and some heckling of both candidates," the speeches lasted "well over three
hours."(111)

The Brown camp was somewhat desperate to stay
Talmadge's momentum in the campaign. The Elberton
debate probably was Brown's final chance to regain
the advantage he apparently had in June. After the
McRae and Dawson debates, Brown's campaign needed
help. He received more public support, in part
because persons knew that he was now losing the campaign. Brown was not the only person threatened with
a loss. Because most persons in the Department of
Agriculture owed their employment to Brown, their
jobs were also in jeopardy.   It was in their interests and that of many business persons and politicians that dealt with the department to rescue Brown
from Talmadge. No one was surprised when the workers
in the Brown campaign, then, brought in supporters
for the third debate. Brown's "chief oil inspector"
and other employees "from the department" came from
Atlanta to see for themselves if press reports of
their boss's demise were accurate. Because a number
of the influential newspapers in Georgia were highly
criticial of policies and practices in the Department
of Agriculture and of the commissioner, Brown sought
endorsements and favorable coverage of his campaign
from the Georgia press. The Elberton Star attempted
to create a more positive perception of Brown's
candidacy.

A letter published in the Elberton Star
attempted to refuel Brown's campaign. Reminding
readers that Talmadge had been defeated in elections

in his home region, the writer portrayed Talmadge as
a "loser."   The writer also contended that the
"charges" made by Talmadge could not be supported,
and that Brown would be re-elected because there was
"no better man running against him." Brown had "made
mistakes," the letter continued, but he was being
"persecuted" unjustly.   Brown had his candidacy
identified with Tom Watson, an individual many
Georgians admired.   Taking a page from Talmadge's
campaign strategy, Brown had Mrs. Julia Watson
Cliatt, the "only living sister" of the late Thomas
E. Watson, tell the Elberton Star that "my brother
counted" Brown "as one of his best .   .   .
friends."(112)

Reversing the order followed at McRae, Talmadge
spoke first. Generally Talmadge repeated the charges
made during June, July, and in the first two debates,
that the Department of Agriculture was inefficient,
politically corrupt, and beyond Brown's managerial
control. To satisfy the insatiable appetite that
listeners and readers had acquired for Talmadgeism,
however, he increased the dosage of strident discourse.   The Elberton Star, defender of Brown,
admitted that Talmadge "refused to take the defensive
side," even in "the rebuttal," and stayed "on the
aggressive throughout."(113)

Talmadge had a perfect ear for stump music, and
by August had talked so many times without manuscript
that his phrases were well rehearsed. But there was
more; he was unusually effective forging visions
extemporaneously from scenes familiar to rural
audiences.   At Elberton he spoke in a campaign
vocabulary that held the attention of the crowd,
quenched their thirst for political hyperbole, and
caused most of them to admire him. For example, in
words that engined a rhetorical figure familiar to
farmers and most Georgians, Talmadge took aim at the
crowd of employees in the Commissioner's department
"sucking a teat under Brown."   Talmadge advised
cutting "off some of the teats."(114)

In earlier speeches, Talmadge tried to give the
appearances of factualizing his indictment of Brown's
deportment. Indeed, prior to the final debate, parts
of the candidates' speeches seemed more suitable for
a courtroom than a political campaign, with Talmadge
in particular introducing numerous "charges" and
written "affidavits."   The absurdity to which
Talmadge carried the rhetoric of documentation was
found in his amusing but sharp distinction in
Elberton between a charge and a near-charge: "I do
not make it as a charge, but I have been informed
that besides the 191 oil inspectors, he has a number
of men who work on split fees thus doubling the
number." In contrast, more assured of the

reliability of other information given to him, he did
charge that not one of the inspectors "works more
than six hours a month."(115)

In the Elberton debate, Talmadge supplemented
documentary materials with argumentation of human
interest. He replaced statistics found in audits
with more emotional concerns drawn from the experience of the crowd. He portrayed Brown listening "to
the buzz of political self-seekers until his ears
were deafened to the cries of his people."(116)
Talmadge was particularly skillful painting a scene
of suffering white southerners, an argument with deep
roots in the region. He warned listeners that, after
nine years in office, Brown could no longer "hear the
cry of barefooted white women and children in the
fields, whom he claims to love so well."(117) Not to
be out-done by Brown recruiting Tom Watson's sister
to his camp, even the Elberton Star was impressed by
the "interest" Talmadge created when he read from "a
letter said to have been written by Walter Brown, son
of" Commissioner Brown!(118) The letter showed that
"Oil Inspector J. A. Pearson of Alma owed the department $702 in fees which had not been paid."(119)

Talmadge pleased audiences by overly simplifying
subjects and procedures in a way that any one could
"understand." In this manner, Talmadge disposed of a
significant issue to his advantage, while Brown
offered a technical explanation more suitable for a
written pamphlet to be studied by a technician.
Throughout the campaign, Talmadge promised to disman-
tle the bloated Department of Agriculture, redistrib-
ute personnel in divisions, and decrease the number
of inspectors from 191 to six. When debating at
Elberton, Talmadge reduced that recurring argument to
a routine within reach of every Georgia family.
After he reformed the Department of Agriculture,
"your boys and girls can analyze fertilizer on your
back porch."(120) While this kind of rhetorical
boast lowered much of Talmadge's discussion of issues
to a level of absurdity, many voters swallowed the
superficial lure.

Talmadge portrayed himself as the only person
tough enough to fight the battles of the common man
and skilfull enough to win. He promised not to
retract a single charge. Responding to the warning
that the commissioner was being "slandered" about
payment of fees, Talmadge, in the genre of the
elderly Tom Watson, insisted that the criticism "was
true and they might send him to jail for making it,
and sue him for libel all they wanted to," but the
charges would continue.(121) Talmadge indicated that
he could manage Agriculture "unhampered."(122)

Following Talmadge's speech, Brown talked for one hour and twenty minutes. According to a paper supportive of Talmadge, Brown was "given a cordial reception." Probably intended as a disparaging greeting by a Talmadge supporter, "one man cried 'Hurrah for the bee inspector'!"(123) Nervous from the public meetings at McRae and Dawson, Brown hoped that the Elberton debate would retain some semblance of civility. But Brown was dowsing for votes. Unwilling to depend solely upon Judge Stapleton's presiding skills for advantage, as he had done in Dawson, Brown attempted to stabilize the meeting by acts of his own. He announced that he would become involved in "no personal fight" with Talmadge.(124) Hoping to disarm Talmadge, Brown said he "was the friend of his opponent" and wanted to discuss the "issues with him fairly," a desperate attempt to establish a mood favoring his more decorous appeals for votes.(125) Most significantly, as a means of smothering the response ignited by Talmadge's speech, Brown adopted an entirely new speaking delivery, one he hoped would so contrast with Talmadgeism that it would win him converts. He actually read a segment of his speech, a practice that in this era was normally considered out of place in a heated political debate.

Brown knew, however, that this was not your typical predicament. Understandably, Brown resorted to reading some of his speech because of an insecurity he acquired on the stump in McRae. A paper supportive of Talmadge stated that Brown "departed . . . from his unbroken custom of past ten years in all the hundreds of speeches he has made extemporaneously by reading the main point of his talk from a prepared typewritten sheet." Brown needed some means by which to overcome a significant handicap in matching Talmadge's entertaining delivery. He decided to employ a business-like approach.

Another motivation Brown had for reading portions of his speech was to improve the accuracy by which the hostile press had been reporting the debates. Brown explained to the audience that he would "break a rule and read a part" of his speech so that the press could "get some of the main points in my speech." After he finished the speech, he would "hand" copies "to the press."(126) The editor of the Elberton Star interpreted Brown's new delivery favorably, saying that he "was in fine form and made one of the best speeches of his life. Part of it was read . . . but the greater and better part of his speech was not included in this."

Brown attempted to answer charges made by Talmadge against the Department of Agriculture.

Explicating a complex subject to a crowd set mentally
and emotionally to be entertained was difficult, but
Brown employed the strategy about as well as one
could.   He "explained" that farmers were paying
thirty cents a ton for inspection of fertilizers
because the "price was charged them by the manufacturers. . . .   The manufacturers were getting the
extra 20 cents per ton."(127)

Brown mounted an attack of his own. A newspaper
opposed to Brown observed that the commissioner
"changed his line of" argument to associate "sinister
politicians" with Talmadge. Brown insisted that, if
elected, Talmadge would serve as a pawn for a "hired
opposition," rather than a representative of the
people's interests. The commissioner argued that
Talmadge was nothing more than a "stalking horse" for
Clarke Howell, editor of the _Atlanta_ _Constitution_,
his brother, Albert Howell with whom "Talmadge" was
"formerly connected" in a "law office in Atlanta,"
and W. I. Anderson, editor of the _Macon_ _Telegraph_ _and_
News.(128)   Brown warned that through Talmadge's
election the Howells and Anderson planned to control
agriculture. Brown claimed that Clark Howell was
"angry" with him because he refused to use influence
as commissioner to have Howell "re-elected National
Democratic Committeeman from Georgia."   Brown said
that Editor Anderson hated him "because I don't take
his advice and dictation."   On Talmadge's back,
Anderson "would" become "a political Mussolini in
Georgia." The Howells and Anderson, continued Brown,
would use Talmadge's election to "force a state bond
mortgage on this state."(129)

To place Talmadge off-balance and to occupy his
final twenty-minute rejoinder, Brown read a number of
questions that he challenged Talmadge to answer.
This was the kind of rhetorical ploy Brown devised at
Dawson to disrupt the continuity of the second
debate.(130) Talmadge answered, "Let's see them
questions."(131) Wisely for his cause, Talmadge
informed the audience that time did not remain for
answering the questions in the Elberton debate, but
that he would respond to them later, which he did in
Lovelace Eve's _Americus_ _Times-Recorder_ on August 16,
1926.

Although Brown did better in the third debate
than one might have expected, he decided not to
confront Talmadge face-to-face again. Earlier Brown
had agreed to debate Talmadge in Atlanta, but in a
"dramatic climax" of the Elberton debate, he announced that campaign advisors convinced him he would
not have time for additional debates. Talmadge told
the crowd that he and Brown "both" had "been invited
to go to Macon on Labor day. Well, I don't know

whether Brown will be there, but Talmadge will."
Continuing an aggressive offensive, Talmadge challenged Brown to debate in every congressional district.   Unable to tempt Brown to debate again,
Talmadge promised to maintain the attack until the
day of the election. Brown must have breathed a sigh
of relief that he would not be facing Talmadge again
in Atlanta, Macon, or any of the congressional
districts. As for Talmadge's feelings about the
final debate, he told a Washington, Georgia, audience
the next day about the "little fun we had for three
hours" in Elberton.(132)

EPILOGUE

        After the debates, Talmadge assumed a posture on
the stump of a winning candidate. The momentum had
shifted to his camp.   The Lyons Progress editorialized that it had "not declared" for any candidate,
but did "oppose" Brown because the Department of
Agriculture was "spending a quarter of a million
dollars without getting value received for the
citizens." The editor argued that Brown had not
"successfully refuted" charges made against him. "We
think a great deal of Eugene Talmadge," he continued.
Talmadge could be "no worse" than Brown.(133)   After
listening to Talmadge speak to "farmers and business
men of Newton County," the editor of the Covington
News explained that the candidate's "plain statements
. . . appeal to the people who hear him."(134)   Not
all persons listening to Talmadge's speeches approved
of what they heard. The Gwinett Journal disliked his
"snipping" at individual agencies. Georgians should
not "interrupt" the "successful work" of Agriculture
for the "political ambitions of any man."(135)
        Delivering three or four addresses each day
after the McRae debate, Talmadge intensified his
criticism of Brown.   In a Newton County speech, he
called the commissioner a "political
scandalmonger."(136) At Dalton, after shaking hands
with "most everybody in town," he promised to "bury
bossism under a landslide." The editor found him to
be "a likeable fellow, full of . . . pep," a man who
"knows exactly what he is doing."(137) At Winder he
was "aggressive in speaking" about his
"accomplishments."(138) Lovelace Eve introduced
Talmadge to an audience of between 200 and 300
"representative farmers and merchants" at Americus.
        Although "tired and worn, with husky voice," at
Americus, he reminisced persuasively about how he
"wore" his "first pair of long pants here" at the age
of fifteen, when calling "on one of your most beautiful girls." Responding to Brown's persistant claim
that he courted the support of powerful men like W.

T. Anderson, Clark Howell, and Albert Howell,
Talmadge outlined a favorite political strategy: "I
want the support of Anderson and Howell, and every Ku
Klux and every Jew and every Catholic in Georgia,
because it takes votes to make a commisioner of
agriculture." Tasting victory, Talmadge broadened
his base of support with promises not found in
earlier speeches in the 1926 race. Talmadge complained that the "railroads, power lines and other
industries are protected by government . . . at the
expense of the farmer." On a second subject saved
for the final days of campaigning, he expressed
interest in using money wasted on Brown's inspectors
to meet the needs of school teachers. "Amidst
laughter," Talmadge told how Brown hired "inspectors
of everything from bees to fertilizer," employees who
had "hands like those of a lady." When Talmadge "cut
'em down to a working basis," they would not "have
time to play politics."(139)

Concerned that his militant image would be
repugnant to some voters, he assured a Fayetteville
audience that he was "attacking" the "system," not
Brown personally. Talmadge asked that the audience
ignore rumors spread about his "campaign thunder."
He ran "more along constructive than critical
lines."(140) The day of the election, Talmadge
blamed Brown for his own intemperate speaking,
asserting that the Commissioner shifted "voters'
attention" from "his own public record by assailing
my character," a claim that had some merit. Talmadge
said that Brown tried to "pull" him "into a campaign
of personal abuse." But Talmadgeism required no
encouragement! Unable to restrain a combative
rhetoric conditioned by three months of usage,
Talmadge, referring to Brown, promised to "banish
forever this tyrant who is seeking to fasten on the
people of Georgia his yoke of political slavery."
The voters would decide whether Georgians would live
"free" or "take their orders" from Brown. Georgians
"in whose veins flows the same bright blood that fed
the hearts of" Stonewall Jackson and Robert E. Lee,
shall not "take orders from any man."(141)

Georgians went to the polls on September 8,
1926, a "good day to vote" because of the "fair
weather," to elect a Commissioner of Agriculture.
That same day the Atlanta Constitution decided that
it was "impossible" to obtain "figures concerning the
probable vote because of the recent enfranchisement
of women." This was the "first state-wide election
in which women have participated in large numbers."(142) Talmadge won the election 123,115 to
66,569, receiving sixty-five percent of the vote.
Talmadge received 362 county unit votes, and Brown

fifty-two. Talmadge won in 139 counties, and Brown
in twenty-one. In the eight counties each having six
unit votes, Talmadge won in six.   In the thirty
counties each having four unit votes, Talmadge won in
twenty-nine. In the 121 counties each having two
unit votes, Talmadge won in approximately 104.

In Telfair county, Talmadge's home base and the
locale of the first debate, he received 1,221 votes
and Brown 139, ninety percent of the votes.   In
Brown's home county, Elbert, locale of the third
debate, Talmadge won 1,317 to 860, receiving sixty
percent of the votes.(143)   The Telfair Enterprise
editorialized that "Telfair county did herself
proud." After winning the election, Talmadge arrived
in McRae "on a Southern Railway train from Atlanta at
7:30" P.M.   The "town of Scotland, 5 miles below
McRae," Talmadge's "hometown," provided a "mammoth
fish fry and picnic."(144) The Atlanta Constitution
added that the "business houses" in Scotland closed
for the homecoming of its "first citizen."   Editor
Clark Howell wrote that, because Talmadge won the
campaign, he had become a "lawyer of no mean ability"
and a "most progressive and successful farmer."

Editor Howell, asserting that the Atlanta
Constitution "gave every candidate a fair deal,"
lived to regret his false prophecy that, with the
victory of Eugene Talmadge over John J. Brown,
Georgia would know "a better day" devoid of "petty
politics." Having "swept all sections of the state,
both rural and urban," Talmadge declared a desire to
"cooperate with the state legislature" and "complete"
the reorganization of the agriculture department."(145) Two years later, Commissioner Talmadge
admitted in a Covington speech that the "past seven
or eight years had been lean years with us dirt farmers."(146) To further establish empathy with rural
voters who lived a difficult life, during his first
term in office, Talmadge reminded them of the sacrifice he had made to become Commissioner.   "The
campaign which we waged two years ago cost me more
money than I was able to spend. I am owing a little
over one thousand dollars of it now." Those funds
were "dug out of the ground, it was farm money."(147)

For the Covington audience, Talmadge forecast
for his second term as Commissioner of Agriculture a
"sun peeping over the eastern horizon . . .
bring[ing] about a new day. The banking and
industrial interest already have seen that the old
hen which laid the golden eggs had stopped laying."
He instructed listeners to learn the "value of
fertilizer." Commissioner Talmadge advised farmers
"not to give away their cotton seed," for it was
"worth $30 a ton to you as fertilizer." Remembering

his criticism of Brown, Talmadge boasted that he had "worked for the establishment of the distillation test in the inspection of gasoline." Alluding to the improved efficiency with which he claimed the Department of Agriculture was now being administered, he said the agency had "received 13,000 fertilizer samples and . . . sent back 10,000 reports on these samples." "The time has come," the commissioner proclaimed to an Augusta audience, "to make the farm attractive and to draw to the farms the bright young men and women."(148) Lovelace Eve, editor and publisher of the <u>Americus</u> <u>Daily</u> <u>Times-Recorder</u>, "traveling at" his "own expense" with Talmadge's re-election campaign, in two years had come to view the new Commissioner as "the little giant," a leader "like David" who "had pulled his sling and entered a combat with a Goliath."(149)

In 1928, G. C. Adams of Newton county opposed Talmadge's bid for re-election as Commisioner of Agriculture. He called Talmadge a "fifth-rate lawyer posing as a dirt farmer," a claim that, when he read it in the press, must have made former Commissioner Brown wince. Adams argued that Georgia needed a "constructive department of agriculture instead of" Talmadge's "Punch and Judy show." The challenger "charged" Talmadge with "building a machine" rather than "serving" farmers.(150) De-emotionalizing the debate to his advantage, Talmadge swamped his opponent in official statistics. Talmadge contended that, because of his recommendation to the governor and General Assembly, there had occurred a reduction in the number of employees in the department "from 200 to 6." Under his leadership the department, over a six-month period increased the number of analyses of samples of fertilizer by 2,800, from 3,700 in 1927, to 6,500 in 1928. At the same time, the cost to Georgians was reduced from $11.03 per sample to $4.74.(151)

Talmadge published in the press a remarkably detailed "Statement by the Commissioner of Agriculture," that was comparable to an address by a governor to the General Assembly. In it he ranged from the elimination of the cattle tick to the inspection of fruit. Talmadge boasted of Georgia's increased productions of tobacco, peaches, peanuts, corn, oats, sweet potatoes, watermelons, apples, pecans, and sugar cane.(152) To an audience in Athens, home of the University of Georgia, Talmadge recommended "diversification and better freight rates" as a means of avoiding "over-production of cotton" and "violent fluctuations" in the market.(153)

In 1928, Talmadge was re-elected over Adams for

Commissioner of Agriculture by a vote of 129,868   to 98,631, receiving fifty-seven percent of the   votes. Talmadge received 289 county unit votes, and   Adams 125.   Talmadge won 113 1/2 counties, and G. C.   Adams 47 1/2.(154) Talmadge won a third term as   Commissioner in 1930, defeating the man he debated   three times in 1926, former Commissioner John J. Brown. In that election, Talmadge received 148,150 votes   to Brown's 57,219, or seventy-two percent. He won   406 county unit votes to Brown's eight. Talmadge won   in 158 counties, and Brown three.(155)

In the 1926 campaign, Talmadge developed a mode of persuasive speaking that characterized his public career until his death in 1946. In grade school, at college, and during the early stage of his career, Talmadge learned to measure the attitude of many audiences and, in some settings, to adapt to them effectively. Certainly during the 1926 campaign he adjusted shrewdly to a variety of occasions and audiences. He could even change colors when speaking to the League of Women Voters, and tell obscene stories to mixed audiences. Later, after winning the race for Commissioner of Agriculture and experiencing power in state government, Talmadge came to crave political authority and situations he could exploit persuasively.

Eventually Talmadge acquired an addiction for power that caused him to attempt to manufacture synthetically issues and events he could inflame rhetorically for self-interests, as the author will show in studies of cases in coming chapters. By his stump behavior in the 1926 campaign, Talmadge committed himself to a tempestuous style of leadership that molded his entire career in and out of state government. In a "Statement to the People of Georgia" in 1926, Talmadge explained the satisfaction he felt about his own public performances in the campaign for Commissioner of Agriculture: "Every speaking engagement that I have had has touched a warm spot in my heart. I have told you the truth in my talks."(156)

NOTES

    1. Quoted in <u>Newnan Herald</u>, July 16, 1926.
    2. Quoted in <u>Rome News-Tribune</u>, July 15, 1926.
    3. Quoted in <u>Atlanta Constitution</u>, July 25, 1926.
    4. Letter in <u>Athens Banner-Herald</u>, July 27, 1926.
    5. Quoted in <u>Atlanta Constitution</u>, August 1, 1926.
    6. <u>Atlanta Constitution</u>, August 1, 1926.
    7. <u>Atlanta Constitution</u>, July 27 and 28, 1926.
    8. <u>Atlanta Constitution</u>, July 28, 1926.
    9. <u>Atlanta Constitution</u>, August 1, 1926.
   10. William Anderson, <u>Wild Man From Sugar Creek:
The Political Career of Eugene Talmadge</u> (Baton

Rouge: Louisiana State Univer Press, 1975), p. 31.
    11. Eastman Times-Journal, August 26, 1920.
    12. Macon Telegraph and News, August 3, 1926.
    13. Atlanta   Constitution, June   25 and   August   4,
1926.
    14. Macon Telegraph and News, August 3, 1926.
    15. Monroe Advertiser, Forsyth, August 4, 1926.
    16. Atlanta Journal, August 4, 1926.
    17. Atlanta Constitution, August 4, 1926.
    18. Americus Times-Recorder, August 4, 1926.
    19. Atlanta Journal, August 4, 1926.
    20. Macon Telegraph and News, August 4, 1926.
    21. Atlanta Constitution, August 4, 1926.
    22. Macon Telegraph and News, August 4, 1926.
    23. Atlanta Constitution, August 4, 1926.
    24. Macon Telegraph and News, August 3, 1926.
    25. Macon Telegraph and News, August 4, 1926.
    26. Telfair Enterprise, August 5, 1926.
    27. Americus Times-Recorder, August 4, 1926.
    28. Athens Banner-Herald, August 13, 1926.
    29. Atlanta Constitution, August 3, 1926.
    30. Atlanta Constitution, August 4, 1926.
    31. Macon Telegraph and News, August 4, 1926.
    32. Americus Times-Recorder, August 4, 1926.
    33. Telfair Enterprise, August 5, 1926.
    34. Atlanta Constitution, August 4, 1926.
    35. Telfair Enterprise, August 5, 1926.
    36. Macon Telegraph and News, August 4, 1926.
    37. Atlanta Constitution, August 4, 1926.
    38. Macon Telegraph and News, August 4, 1926.
    39. Americus Times-Recorder, August 4, 1926.
    40. Atlanta Constitution, August 4, 1926.
    41. Americus Times-Recorder, August 4, 1926.
    42. Telfair Enterprise, August 5, 1926.
    43. Americus Times-Recorder, August 4, 1926.
    44. Macon   Telegraph   and News   quoted   in   Atlanta
Constitution, August 4, 1926.
    45. Macon   Telegraph   and News   quoted   in   Atlanta
Constitution, August 4, 1926.
    46. Macon Telegraph and News, August 4, 1926.
    47. Telfair Enterprise, August 5, 1926.
    48. Macon   Telegraph   and News   quoted   in   Atlanta
Constitution, August 4, 1926.
    49. Atlanta Constitution, August 4, 1926.
    50. Macon Telegraph and News, August 4, 1926.
    51. Macon   Telegraph   and   News,   August   4,   1926;
Telfair Enterprise, August 5, 1926.
    52. Atlanta Constitution, August 4, 1926.
    53. Macon   Telegraph   and   News,   August   4,   1926;
emphasis added.
    54. Monroe Advertiser, August 4, 1926.
    55. Americus Times-Recorder, August 4, 1926.

56. <u>Macon</u> <u>Telegraph</u> <u>and</u> <u>News</u> quoted in <u>Atlanta Constitution</u>, August 4, 1926.

57. <u>Telfair</u> <u>Enterprise</u>, August 5, 1926.

58. <u>Atlanta</u> <u>Constitution</u>, August 4, 1926.

59. <u>Americus</u> <u>Times-Recorder</u>, August 4, 1926; emphasis added.

60. <u>Atlanta</u> <u>Constitution</u>, August 4, 1926.

61. <u>Atlanta</u> <u>Constitution</u>, August 4, 1926.

62. <u>Macon</u> <u>Telegraph</u> <u>and</u> <u>News</u>, August 4, 1926.

63. <u>Telfair</u> <u>Enterprise</u>, August 5, 1926; <u>Macon Telegraph</u>, <u>and</u> <u>News</u>, August 5, 1926.

64. <u>Americus</u> <u>Times-Recorder</u>, August 4, 1926.

65. <u>Atlanta</u> <u>Constitution</u>, August 4, 1926.

66. <u>Americus</u> <u>Times-Recorder</u>, August 4, 1926.

67. <u>Macon</u> <u>Telegraph</u> <u>and</u> <u>News</u>, August 5, 1926.

68. <u>Macon</u> <u>Telegraph</u> <u>and</u> <u>News</u>, August 4, 1926.

69. <u>Telfair</u> <u>Enterprise</u>, August 5, 1926.

70. <u>Macon</u> <u>Telegraph</u> <u>and</u> <u>News</u>, August 5, 1926.

71. <u>Atlanta</u> <u>Constitution</u>, August 4, 1926.

72. <u>Macon</u> <u>Telegraph</u> <u>and</u> <u>News</u>, August 4, 1926.

73. <u>Athens</u> <u>Banner-Herald</u>, July 30, 1926.

74. <u>Macon</u> <u>Telegraph</u> <u>and</u> <u>News</u>, August 4, 1926.

75. <u>Macon</u> <u>Telegraph</u> <u>and</u> <u>News</u>, August 4, 1926.

76. <u>Americus</u> <u>Times-Recorder</u>, August 4, 1926.

77. <u>Atlanta</u> <u>Constitution</u>, August 4, 1926.

78. <u>Macon</u> <u>Telegraph</u> <u>and</u> <u>News</u>, August 5, 1926.

79. <u>Atlanta</u> <u>Constitution</u>, August 4, 1926.

80. <u>Macon</u> <u>Telegraph</u> <u>and</u> <u>News</u>, August 4, 1926.

81. <u>Telfair</u> <u>Enterprise</u>, August 5, 1926.

82. <u>Macon</u> <u>Telegraph</u> <u>and</u> <u>News</u>, August 4, 1926.

83. <u>Macon</u> <u>Telegraph</u> <u>and</u> <u>News</u>, August 4, 1926.

84. <u>Monroe</u> <u>Advertiser</u>, August 4, 1926.

85. <u>Macon</u> <u>Telegraph</u> <u>and</u> <u>News</u>, August 5, 1926.

86. <u>Middle</u> <u>Georgian</u> quoted in <u>Elberton</u> <u>Star</u>, August 10, 1926.

87. <u>Telfair</u> <u>Enterprise</u>, August 5, 1926.

88. <u>Atlanta</u> <u>Constitution</u>, August 4, 1926.

89. <u>Macon</u> <u>Telegraph</u> <u>and</u> <u>News</u>, August 5, 1926.

90. <u>Americus</u> <u>Times-Recorder</u>, August 4 and 5, 1926.

91. <u>Atlanta</u> <u>Journal</u>, August 4, 1926.

92. <u>Atlanta</u> <u>Constitution</u>, August 19, 1926.

93. <u>Middle</u> <u>Georgian</u> quoted in <u>Elberton</u> <u>Star</u>, August 10, 1926.

94. <u>Dawson</u> <u>News</u>, August 3, 1926.

95. <u>Dawson</u> <u>News</u>, August 10, 1926.

96. <u>Americus</u> <u>Times-Recorder</u>, August 5, 1926.

97. <u>Macon</u> <u>Telegraph</u> <u>and</u> <u>News</u>, August 5, 1926.

98. <u>Americus</u> <u>Times-Recorder</u>, August 5, 1926.

99. <u>Atlanta</u> <u>Constitution</u>, August 5, 1926.

100. <u>Atlanta</u> <u>Constitution</u>, August 5, 1926.

101. <u>Americus</u> <u>Times-Recorder</u>, August 5, 1926.

102. <u>Atlanta</u> <u>Constitution</u>, August 12, 1926.

103. <u>Macon</u> <u>Telegraph</u> <u>and</u> <u>News</u>, August 13, 1926.

104. Elberton Star, August 10, 1926.
105. Elberton Star, August 13, 1926.
106. Macon Telegraph and News, August 23, 1926.
107. Elberton Star, August 13, 1926.
108. Macon Telegraph and News, August 13, 1926.
109. Elberton Star, August 13, 1926.
110. Atlanta Constitution, August 13, 1926.
111. Americus Times-Recorder, August 13, 1926.
112. Elberton Star, August 10, 1926.
113. Elberton Star, August 13, 1926.
114. Atlanta Constitution, August 13, 1926.
115. Macon Telegraph and News, August 13, 1926;
emphasis added.
116. Atlanta Constitution, August 13, 1926.
117. Macon Telegraph and News, August 13, 1926.
118. Elberton Star, August 13, 1926.
119. Atlanta Constitution, August 13, 1926.
120. Atlanta Constitution, August 13, 1926.
121. Elberton Star, August 13, 1926.
122. Atlanta Constitution, August 13, 1926.
123. Atlanta Constitution, August 13, 1926.
124. Macon Telegraph and News, August 13, 1926.
125. Atlanta Constitution, August 13, 1926.
126. Macon Telegraph and News, August 13, 1926.
127. Elberton Star, August 13, 1926.
128. Atlanta Constitution, August 13, 1926.
129. Macon Telegraph and News, August 13, 1926.
130. Atlanta Constitution, August 13 and 15, 1926.
131. Atlanta Constitution, August 13, 1926;
Macon Telegraph and News, August 13, 1926.
132. Atlanta Constitution, August 14, 1926.
133. Lyons Progress, August 12, 1926.
134. Covington News, August 27, 1926.
135. Lawrenceville speech, Gwinett Journal,
August 25, 1926.
136. Atlanta Constitution, August 25 and 27, 1926.
137. Dalton Citizen, August 12, 1926.
138. Atlanta Constitution, August 19, 1926.
139. Americus speech, Americus Times-Recorder,
August 23, 1926; Atlanta Constitution, August 22,
1926.
140. Atlanta Constitution, August 10, 1926.
141. Atlanta Constitution, September 8, 1926.
142. Atlanta Constitution, September 8, 1926.
143. Georgia's Official Register, 1926, pp. 308,
327, 329.
144. Telfair Enterprise, September 9, 1926.
145. Atlanta Constitution, September 10 and 12,
1926.
146. Covington speech, Americus Times-Recorder,
August 27, 1928.
147. Advertisement in Americus Times-Recorder,
August 11, 1928.

148. Augusta speech, _Atlanta Constitution_,
August 17, 1928.
    149. _Americus Daily Times-Recorder_, August 17, 1928.
    150. _Atlanta Constitution_, July 29, 1928.
    151. _Telfair Enterprise_, August 9, 1928.
    152. _Atlanta Constitution_, June 14, 1928.
    153. Athens speech, _Telfair Enterprise_, January 27,
1928.
    154. _Georgia's Official Register_, 1929, pp. 381,
395.
    155. _Georgia's Official Register_, 1931, pp. 636,
666.
    156. _Telfair Enterprise_, September 2, 1926.

4

Prohibition of Cotton and Demagoguery

If John J. Brown's lax management led to inefficiency and corruption in the Department of Agriculture, Eugene Talmadge used that state agency as a platform from which to agitate issues that enhanced his political stature with the rural voters. The Great Depression of the 1930s affected most Georgians adversely, but brought "crushing economic disaster" to agriculture. Federal programs brought some relief to larger landowners, but life was "desperate for small farmers, tenants, and laborers."(1) In 1930, when Talmadge began his third term as Commissioner of Agriculture, 67.9 percent of the South's population was rural, with 42.8 percent of its work force employed on farms at a monthly per capita income of $189 in contrast to $484 for nonfarm employees. Between 1927 and 1932 "forced sales of Southern farms rose from 21 to 46 per thousand." That same year dry weather and the depression combined to "unsettle the entire economy and credit system of the rural South."(2)

Because of a depressed economy and because more than half the farmers were having to abandon agriculture, Talmadge decided that conditions were perfect for increasing his stock in Georgia politics by publicly notarizing the suffering of families on farms. This strategy bolstered his credibility significantly as he prepared to run for governor in 1932. Rather than planning programs for the long-range benefit of Georgians who turned to him for help, Commissioner Talmadge attempted to radicalize the debate on agricultural needs to solidify his own political authority.

By 1931, Talmadge had convulsed affairs in Georgia about as much as a Commissioner of

Agriculture could.   He attempted to recreate on a state-wide level the raucous scene he and supporters produced during the McRae debate in 1926.   Talmadge so exploited the <u>Market Bulletin</u>, a publication sponsored by the Department of Agriculture for the benefit of farmers, that the General   Assembly "killed" his editorials.   In response,   Talmadge threatened to "publish his own newspaper." He later used the <u>Statesman</u> as a source with which to supplement opinions he communicated in public speeches and in statements to the press.(3)

In 1931, the General Assembly, considering the possibility of impeachment proceedings, investigated the "dangerous" way in which Talmadge conducted affairs of his office. He was charged with a series of wrong doings.   State Auditor Tom Wisdom charged that the Department of Agriculture kept an "inactive account" in a bank in Ailey, where the Talmadges had lived, that the department had not turned in all fertilizer fees to the state treasury, and that Talmadge spent $10,000 of unauthorized funds to attempt to improve the price of hogs in Georgia.[4]   A Senate committee examined Talmadge's payment of $40,000 for salaries and expenses for himself and his family.   It did not appear to worry Talmadge politically that he was being accused of repeating the corruptive practices of J. J. Brown.   Characteristically, while holding public office, Talmadge behaved as if immune to ethical and legal constraints.

As always, Talmadge defended each controversial action by taking his case to the jury of voters. Talmadge's hog rhetoric illustrates perfectly his preference of selecting an issue for its public relations value rather than devoting the   time, thought, and coordination required for developing programs beneficial to farmers. As to why he peddled pigs, he argued that "raising the price of hogs" was better than "hiring extra help."(5) The outlaw sale, he alleged, boosted the price of hogs by "one and one-half cents above the Chicago market."(6)   He claimed to have sold the hogs in Chicago as a means of increasing the price farmers would receive, a highly novel and visible ploy many farmers applauded. In their minds, at least the commissioner was doing something!(7)

Because of his unbridled behavior, Talmage was forever explaining particular controversial acts, often by using them as evidence of his political independence, concern for the working class, and willingness to take action.   He charged the state $12.35 per day while on an alleged fact-finding trip to the Kentucky Derby. Ridiculing persons who criticized him, Talmadge bragged: "If I, a red-blooded

man, had not gone to that derby--that horse race--I
ought to be impeached."   He said he   attended the
Kentucky Derby to address southern commissioners of
Agriculture.(8)   No matter what the   accusation,
Talmadge refused to admit any wrong-doing.   He used
what many perceived to have been misdeeds to build
his image as a leader beyond the control of a political and business establishment that had   abused
farmers.   When pushed by an investigating Senate
committee as to whether he visited "Magnolia Gardens
in the interest of tariffs" at state   expense,
"Talmadge, with the committee and the   gallery,
smiled."(9)
     When explaining how he and stepson John A.
Peterson wrecked cars paid for by the state, he said
that they were "unavoidable accidents." The stepson's car wreck was caused by consumption of alcohol,
but Peterson was behaving "just like most young
fellows who come to the city from the country."(10)
When defending the employment of stepson Peterson as
fertilizer inspector at $200 per month, Talmadge
ridiculed the investigative procedure with   the
admission that $50 of that salary went to Mrs.
Talmadge "to teach the boy," at age twenty-five, "to
save money."   Increasingly Talmadge came to defy
constitutional authority.   He went beyond the
good-old-boy tactic used in the 1926 campaign to
actually "challenge" the legislative   committee's
"authority" to investigate him.(11)
     Talmadge seldom backed down from a challenge.
Even when forced to do so, he retreated as if in
victory for the common man. His stump behavior in
the 1926 campaign committed him to a rhetorical genre
of recalcitrance. He built a public image of personal infallibility, of a man who would not concede to
opposition. Through exaggerated claims he assured
farmers that they too were undefeatable, and many
appreciated having a man independent and courageous
enough to speak for them.
     Confident of his ability to defend controversial
actions before what was too often the uncritical eye
of the public, Talmadge transgressed authority until
he was convinced that his position of power was
threatened, the one possession he valued more highly
than rhetorical effectiveness. When confronted by
persons armed with the courage, power, and skill to
threaten his base of authority, he   skillfully
side-stepped so as not to reveal to his public army
of voters any change of stance. On occasions, when
confronted by a person or group armed with parliamentary, institutional, or constitutional   powers,
fortitude, and skill enough to use them, Talmadge
found a face-saving means by which to ease out of the

line of fire. For example, initially he refused to appear before the committee of the General Assembly to answer charges, bragging publicly that his allegiance was solely to the people.

Talmadge personalized every discussion. He even portrayed charges of constitutional wrong-doings as personal attacks upon his efforts to bring relief to farmers. Talmadge explained to a Cordele audience that he refused to appear before the legislative committee, not because of the "legal issue," but because of "the senate probers' attitude toward him."(12) When the processing of impeachment proceedings against him were begun, in an attempt to conceal his retreat, he admitted in a letter, but not on the stump, that he "was in error" for not appearing before the investigating committee, but not for actions committed that fell well within the jurisdiction of his office. The committee accepted his veiled apology and dropped the contempt charges.(13) Throughout his political career Talmadge carried his challenges to conventional and constitutional procedures to the limit allowed, circumventing a person or organization only when made to do so.

Because of Talmadge's enormous popularity with voters in the 1930s, his rancorous temperament, and his willingness to fight in public--when opponents were often too embarrassed to join in the exhibition--many individuals and office holders were reluctant to confront the man in public debate. Ralph McGill of the Atlanta Constitution, after observing the political behavior of Talmadge and other politicans for a number of years, asked, "Where have the . . . 'good people' been?" Those persons "kept aloof" from the "struggle," creating a "vacuum" which "extremists" filled.(14) In winning three elections for Commissioner of Agriculture, Talmadge achieved great political power. In 1931, when most Georgia voters looked upon him increasingly as the new champion of forgotten workers, it took considerable courage to oppose him. But other journalists warned citizens of the dangers of Talmadge's discursive recklessness and personal dominance.

After observing Talmadge's political posturing, J. B. Hardy, editor and owner of the Thomaston Times, blamed the deteriorating state of affairs in politics in Georgia upon a susceptible citizenry. Hardy was "amused" by how "gullible are the voters . . . to swallow all the propaganda" mouthed by Talmadge, for he was now copying John J. Brown's practices of mishandling state funds and "hiring his kinfolks" at "extravagant salaries." Disgusted with what he saw happening in public life, Hardy wrote a provocative preamble for all democracies strong enough to harbor

political demagoguery: "Our people want to be fooled
and the candidate who is most successful in this   art
will be winner. . . .   This is   the way politics   is
played in Georgia."(15)

As Commissioner of   Agriculture, Talmadge   chose
cotton to be the staple   element in his campaign   for
expanded influence   in   the   state   and   to   aid   the
farmer.   By 1931 "King Cotton was   sick,   and   the
disease infected . . . manufacturing as well as
farming."   A number   of cures   had been   recommended.
Traditionally southerners supported low tariffs.   But
when trade agreements   threatened southerners'   profits, twenty-five percent of southern   representatives
voted for the Smoot-Hawley tariff.   In 1929 Talmadge
also switched his support to higher tariffs.(16)   In
the Market Bulletin on April 19, 1931, Talmadge wrote
that it was   "un-American for any   man to advocate   a
policy of   reduction of   acreage of   any   staple
crop."(17)

After attending   an All   Southern Conference   in
New Orleans, Talmadge returned to Georgia   advocating
variations of Huey Long's plan to raise the price   of
cotton by not planting that crop in 1932.   To
Talmadge, what was   a patriotic policy   and what   was
not, depended solely upon what he said on a   particular occasion.(18)   The Dawson News editorialized   why
farmers were   losing money   on cotton.   It "cost   14
cents per pound to produce" cotton   that will   "sell
for 9."(19)   Other efforts to control cotton   production, in 1915, 1921, and 1927, were unsuccessful.(20)
Tindall explained that, although   the Huey Long   plan
for 1932 also failed, the efforts by Long,   Talmadge,
and others to have   it implemented prepared   citizens
for more "meaningful" programs   for the reduction   of
cotton under the   New Deal.(21)   Ironically but   not
surprisingly, as illustrated in Chapter 6,   the
politically motivated Talmadge   opposed   Roosevelt's
plan to curtail cotton   production, claiming that   it
violated biblical teachings.

Rather than negotiate   with Governor Richard B.
Russell, Jr., members   of the   General Assembly,   and
other office holders, Talmadge, true to his prescription of "people over   petty politicians," toured   the
state for confirmation of   the Long/Talmadge plan   of
not picking   cotton   in   the fields   in 1931   and   not
planting the crop   in 1932. He   sought support   from
farmers of the   state because he   knew that   Governor
Russell and   the General   Assembly were   unlikely   to
agree to   such a   radical plan   as prohibiting   the
planting of a staple crop upon which much of the
state   economy   was   based.   Repeatedly during   his
career in and out of public office, Talmadge
attempted to mobilize people to do his will.

On his stump trip in Georgia for the prohibition
of cotton, Talmadge confronted two different types of
audiences, those supportive or undecided about his
plan to end cotton production for a year and, secondly, those opposed to his view. In speaking to all of
these persons, he assumed that he was an infallible
source and attempted to disallow opposition to his
cause. On some occasions, then, no one questioned or
challenged Talmadge's plan for abolishing cotton,
either because listeners agreed with him or were too
intimidated to offer a minority opinion. One should
not assume that Talmadge achieved his goal on these
occasions simply because all persons agreed with his
plan before listening to him speak. Many farmers
believed some action was needed, but a number of
plans were under consideration. Talmadge attempted
to convince them that his plan was worth any sacrifice that ceasing to plant cotton might bring. Even
with this first form of rhetorical agitation, when
little or no opposition was expressed, Talmadge had
to dominate a public meeting by the power of his
rhetoric.

Two of Talmadge's speeches illustrate how he
performed before supportive audiences. When he urged
a "large and representative crowd of Upson County
farmers" in Thomaston to "abandon" or "very strin-
gently curtail" the growing of cotton, they reportedly "seemed in accord" with his plan.(22) Talmadge
also delivered a speech in Cordele to "farmers and
citizens of Crisp and adjoining counties," a meeting
at which there was no vocal opposition. At Cordele,
after giving "side lights on the huge" meeting he
attended in New Orleans, Talmadge "unfold[ed] the
details" of the plan to curtail cotton production for
a year.

While other proposals were being discussed
nationally and regionally, typically Talmadge wanted
no consideration of a compromise. He insisted that
his policy "alone was the one practical . . . proposition for the farmer." He explained that all
southern states were being asked to "withhold sale"
of the 1931 crop and to have legislatures make it
illegal to grow cotton in 1932. Having been investigated because of his controversial actions as commissioner of Agriculture, he was defensive about advocating such a controversial measure as abolishing
cotton in a farm region. Anticipating criticism, he
justified the constitutionality of the proposal under
the heading of a "quarantine measure." Avoiding his
earlier admonitions that ceasing the planting of a
staple crop would be un-American and would violate
biblical teachings, the "psychological effect" of the
action, he envisioned, "would be tremendous." He

"predicted" an "immediate rise" in the price of
cotton. A price of 25 cents per pound was "not
beyond reason."

A reporter observed the instant impact of the
speeches in Cordele by Talmadge and others present.
The audience "voted unamimously" to support a policy
of reducing or ending cotton production for a year.
"Nearly 500" persons signed the resolution calling
for a special session of the General Assembly to pass
a law disallowing cotton. "Private telegrams and
letters" were "pouring out of this city to Atlanta"
urging the special session. The editor of the
Cordele Dispatch described the impact of Talmadge's
speech. "Until we heard" Talmadge "this morning, we
wondered whether the Long plan was feasible." The
"fiery commissioner of agriculture . . . spoke for
one hour." "One can easily see the interest he
holds" for the farmer "is real and if any one doubts
the intensity of his views he has but to hear the
commissioner talk." He has "put across the plan . .
. wherever he has been."(23)

On some occasions when Talmadge spoke, persons
spoke out against his recommendation not to plant
cotton for a year. To oppose the authoritatively
behaving Talmadge required great personal courage.
Talmadge's invasion of a farm meeting in Macon in
1931 illustrates how he attempted to dominate persons
who disagreed with him publicly. "Almost 1,000
cotton farmers, bankers and business men" gathered in
Macon to compare plans for assisting the farmer.
Ironically, W. T. Anderson, editor of the Macon
Telegraph and News, opposed Talmadge's plan. During
the 1926 debate in McRae, Anderson sat on the speaking platform in support of Talmadge. Throughout that
campaign for commissioner, Brown accused Talmadge of
obeying Anderson's political dictations. In a
"keynote address" at this Macon conference, five
years after the McRae debate, Anderson opposed
Talmadge and defended United States Senator Walter F.
George's proposal making loans "contingent on the
farmers' contracting to cut their cotton acreage 50
percent." Anderson warned that "we have been regulating ourselves by laws for the last 50 years, and
not paying any attention to them."(24)

Representative E. E. Cox of Camilla also opposed
the Talmadge/Long policy, warning that "abandonment
of cotton farming in the southern states for a year
would so stimulate cotton culture in foreign countries as to afford ruinous competition." Cox
insisted that any "rise in cotton prices" would be
"accompanied by a drop in food crop prices," when
65,000,000 acres "devoted to cotton farming" were
"turned at one time to production of other crops." A

Talmadge drives home a point. (Photograph from
Herman E. Talmadge Collection, Richard B. Russell
Memorial Library, University of Georgia Libraries,
Athens, Georgia. Reprinted by permission.)

constructive and informative debate upon vital
implications of the various proposals continued among
participants attending the farm meeting. Seeking a
compromise decision, H. W. Davis of Jefferson spoke
for the "George plan . . . to be followed by the Long
plan as soon as obtainable." "Strongly advocating"
the Long/Talmadge measure, Tom L. Graham of Dodge
county complained that "life has brought us down to a
condition lower than the slavery under which our
Negroes worked." Congress had protected "other
industry and left the farmers to be robbed."

A reporter covering the convention for the <u>Macon</u> <u>Telegraph</u>, including the participation by his employer, Editor W. T. Anderson, wrote his perception of what occurred when Commissioner Talmadge arrived for the meeting "during the lunch recess." This was not a typical Talmadge campaign rally. In contrast, this was a formal farm meeting in which successful businessmen, bankers, and farmers were seriously negotiating what policy was best for agriculture in Georgia. Albert Menard, president of the Macon Chamber of Commerce, introduced Talmadge to the large audience. Talmadge behaved as if addressing supporters in the first McRae debate in 1926. By his performance, Talmadge showed the great gall with which he approached an audience. Rather than adapt rhetorically to the business-like tone of the meeting, Talmadge tried to topple the conference. "The meeting, which had progressed in an orderly manner," reported the journalist, "verged on complete disorder when Mr. Talmadge arrived . . . and began a continuous and violent attack on any plan but that of Governor Long for relief of the cotton farmer."

Talmadge addressed conference participants in a discourse of disrespect. "Such invectives as 'brother jackass' and 'hand-picked politicians' flew from his lips at other participants in the meeting." Referring to his 1926 campaign, Talmadge said that Senator George's plan for farmers "required as many inspectors as J. J. Brown and I put together ever had." Unlike his proposal, George's plan was "impractical" and "unconstitutional." In an argument he broadened in later years to include President Franklin D. Roosevelt, the New Deal, Richard B. Russell, and Walter F. George, Talmadge attacked the failure of the federal government to assist the farmer. Ignoring Georgia Senator George's proposal, he warned that the "cotton industry" should "not expect one scintilla of aid" from the federal Congress. Indeed, the "policy of our government of encouraging our farmers to borrow has brought about this crisis. The tariff policy of this country in protecting all manufactured products has ruined" farmers "too."

To allay fears that the Long/Talmadge proposal would increase competition from abroad, he said that Great Britian, India, and China could not grow cotton. "The climate in India isn't suited" for growing it, and "Egypt is growing all she can." Only Russia could compete, and that country "will not submit to an increase of more than 1,000,000 bales." Using a favorite tactic, Talmadge tried to close the sale of his proposal by threatening Georgians with being left out of an attractive deal. He attempted to stampede persons attending the Macon meeting to support his plan without further consideration of its merits. "The farmers of Georgia want the Long plan. The farmers of Louisiana want it, and the farmers of Texas want it." Talmadge urged the members of the audience to "let the governor and legislators know they want an extraordinary session of the legislature to pass" a law forbidding the growing of cotton for a year. Showing his disgust for opponents and demonstrating a recurring strategy of advocating that only his will be done, he boasted that with or without the endorsement of the Macon conference, "we'll have it." In contrast to the other policies advocated at the convention, he continued, only "this" one "is the answer to those crying children, tired women and dispairing [sic] men." Because of his skill in winning audiences, Talmadge received "much applause as he finished."

To this point in the debates the reporter, favoring his editor, Anderson, was disturbed by Talmadge's vituperation; however, Commissioner Talmadge basically was defending the Long/Talmadge proposal for increasing the farmers' income. He did use uncompromising language with which to smother views of other participants; but, after all, it was his turn to speak. Editor J. B. Hardy's maxim that political propagandists prevail because citizens "want to be fooled" did not apply well to this conference. Unlike many of the rallies ruled by Talmadge, a number of persons attending the Macon session participated in the decision-making debates. An editor, a teacher of vocational agriculture, a Representative in the General Assembly of Georgia, president of a Chamber of Commerce, Commisioner of Agriculture, and others stood and defended various points of view. In addition, there were cotton farmers, bankers, and businessmen listening to and weighing suggestions on how to aid agriculture.

What occurred next, however, revealed the unbending wrath that motivated Gene Talmadge, the recurring means by which he sought to muffle opposing views and to enforce his will upon opponents. After listening to the arguments and interpretations expressed on the conference floor, a committee reported its "resolutions" to the members. This meeting was run under parliamentary guidelines, entirely different from the campaign rally chaired with few rules by Mayor McRae in the first 1926 debate. The resolutions brought before the Macon meeting in 1931 "contained features from a number of plans which had been submitted." At the "direction" of presider Menard, M. C. Edwards of Dawson, home of the second 1926 debate, "began to read the recommendations of the committeee, of which there were nine." At this point, Talmadge "advocated discarding the whole series of resolutions," and substituting the Huey Long plan. Ironically, the Long plan was the ninth recommendation Edwards would report out of committee, and thus would have been among those Talmadge attempted to discard.

Talmadge tried to bully the convention into ending its parliamentary consideration of several proposals and immediately adopting his and Long's measure. In this instance the citizens were not being bamboozled because they were too gullible to know what Talmadge was doing, as Editor Hardy conjectured. Some of the members had spoken on proposed plans. Most listened to informed debates of the issues. They were well prepared to choose from among the several proposals being reported out of committee. The vital decision facing the one thousand delegates and the presider of the meeting was whether Talmadge would be allowed to force his will upon the conference. He had every right to advocate the Long plan but, in doing so, he would also demand that his edict be substituted for the parliamentary decision-making process under which the meeting was established. Many in the audience agreed with the Long/Talmadge plan; however, the stands taken by speakers on the floor of the conference corroborated that a number of persons present opposed it. Would opposing views continue to be represented, evaluated, and voted upon? Would democratic processes win out over demagogic tactics?

Talmadge began his defense of the curtailment of planting of cotton and his assault upon the integrity of free discussion being practiced at the Macon meeting. At this point, Talmadge's public conduct approached the boundary between effective oratory and demagogic dominance. Political demagoguery occurs when a person employs persuasive means that deny others the free expression that allowed him or her to speak, when individual appetite swallows collective will. To block consideration of the committee's recommendations, Talmadge vented personal hostility through parliamentary machinery. He learned how to manipulate parliamentary bodies in the Phi Kappa Literary Society and the Euphradians forensics society at the University of Georgia, student organizations where he could have practiced debating, handling motions and amendments, and outwitting opponents through parliamentary maneuvers.

Referring to the nine amendments reported out of committee, and seemingly to the entire judicious process of going through a parliamentary committee, Talmadge said: "Every bit of this recommendation is slop." His barnyard language indicated the contempt he had for participants in the conference, for it

certainly violated the business-like tone of the
meeting. He displayed utter disrespect for democratic processes that interfered with attempts to have
his will dominate that of others. He was willing to
challenge the fundamental procedure by which the
conference reached decisions. Equally significant,
one of the nine resolutions to be read, discussed,
and voted upon supported his Long plan. He only had
to wait until that plan was brought properly to the
floor, and he could have defended it with his usual
skill. That he opposed consideration of the nine
recommendations indicated clearly his desire to end
open discussion within a parliamentary format.

Talmadge insisted: "I offer as a substitute the
Long plan!" Ridiculing the regulations under which
the conference was governed, and exuding the meanness
that lay at the heart of his penchant for rhetorical
insolence, Talmadge again called upon his followers,
a sizeable corps of Georgians who became increasingly
raucous with the passing of years, to protect him
from open challenges by persons who disagreed with
him. In still another variation of the good-old-boy
axiom for crushing an opposition, developed on the
campaign stump, he called for an end to what he
portrayed as a useless discussion. After introducing
his amendment as a substitute for the committee's
nine resolutions, he said: "Now second it, boys!"
The second came in the form of "yells and applause"
whose purpose was to intimidate more decorously
behaving delegates.

In a further effort to terminate consideration
of issues covered during the convention speeches,
many of which Talmadge was not on hand to hear, the
commissioner personally attacked those with whom he
disagreed. The essence of his broadsides was to
label an editor, a teacher of vocational agriculture,
and the others as "hand-picked politicians" who want
to "run things" their way, an ironic claim coming
from his mouth. The truth is that, on occasions,
Talmadge did not want persons having opinions different from his own to have a voice in making a decision, in and out of government, a stance that clearly
marked him as a political demagogue. Totally insensitive to the feelings of the persons serving on the
Resolutions Committee, and probably unaware of its
membership, he maintained that those individuals,
because they dared consider proposals other than his
own and relied on parliamentary processes rather than
his dictation, were "unfit." He deprecated the
process of citizenship-involvement itself, damning
the parliamentary framework through which the committees contributed to the decisions of the conference.
He threatened the Macon meeting of farmers and

supporters with the prayer of his politics, that his
will be done, not the conference's: "What does it
mean for us to resolute? . . . Not a thing!"

What mattered to Talmadge was the success of his
attempt to ramrod a plan for farmers down the throat
of the Macon convention, motivated by a strategy of
using that endorsement to pressure Governor Richard
B. Russell, Jr., to call a special session of the
legislature that would be given no choice but to pass
without amendment the Long/Talmadge plan to terminate
the planting of cotton for a year. Talmadge's
persuasive behavior at the Macon meeting showed
clearly why he continuously turned to the "people"
over the state's leadership, excluding politicians,
farmers, businessmen, educators, government officials, extension service employees, and all others
opposing him. In his language, he "trusted" the
people to be gullible or cowardly enough to be
threatened into submission. In other words, the
meetings at Macon and at other towns he toured in
1931, were not for reconciling the differences of
citizens into a farm policy best for Georgia agriculture. He told why he toured the state: "'We're
putting the fire on the governor's back,' he cried,
'and on the legislature's back'." Impatient to
stampede the conference to endorse his whim, Talmadge
"cried," "Let's have him call it Monday morning."

Understandably Albert Menard, presider over the
farm meeting, "appeared somewhat ruffled" by
Talmadge's brazen responses. At first presider
Menard appeared to be establishing a parliamentary
permissive mood for the remainder of the meeting
comparable to that allowed by Mayor Max McRae during
the first 1926 debate between Talmadge and John J.
Brown. Feeling the conflicting pressures of bringing
the meeting under control and allowing the powerful
commissioner of Agriculture Talmadge to have his way,
presider Menard advised: "We must govern ourselves
according to parliamentary rule to an extent, but as
this is a farmers' meeting, I believe as many as
possible should be heard." Obviously the issue was
not whether Talmadge would be heard, but whether the
official committee of the conference would finish its
report and have its recommendations acted upon,
whether the majority of members' views would be
voiced! At many farm meetings in the South,
Menard's relaxation of parliamentary prescriptions
would be justifiable and productive, but not with the
involvement of a political demagogue like Talmadge.
Former Commissioner of Agriculture John J. Brown
could have advised Menard wisely on how to chair a
meeting that Talmadge attempted to plunder.

The session in Macon continued under Menard's

leadership. After one participant spoke for the Long/Talmadge plan, another individual "said something" for the George plan, and Talmadge "arose once more." Editor W. T. Anderson, Talmadge's supporter during the 1926 campaign, "shouted apparently at the top of his voice, 'Mr. Chairman, have you completely laid aside parliamentary rule?'" Presider Menard, who probably had considerable experience chairing a meeting, being the president of the chamber of commerce, reassured Anderson that discussion would continue under parliamentary procedure. Editor Anderson attacked Talmadge's credibility and abuse of official rules. Significantly Anderson reminded the convention of their parliamentary authority, a courageous act and a direct challenge to Talmadge's efforts to disrupt official proceedings for self-gain. Anderson advised the conference: "Anybody . . . knows you have to give 10 days' notice for an extraordinary session of the legislature. Here you would have as a leader [Talmadge] a man who has misled you on two occasions this afternoon. His substitute is out of order. We have first to dispose of the whole series of recommendations which you have voted unanimously to have read for your consideration and action." Talmadge demeaned the product of the conference's discussions, implying that his way be followed. Unwilling to discuss the substance of the various proposals, Talmadge resorted to shallow and emotional generalizations. He said that, "To adopt this resolution is not worth the paper its written on."

Even Thomaston Times Editor J. B. Hardy would have been proud of presider Albert Menard, for this Chamber man brought Talmadge's demagogic behavior under control, an accomplishment that the investigating committee of the entire Georgia General Assembly had only achieved by the threat of impeachment. Mounting his opposition within parliamentary rules, Talmadge bellowed: "A substitute is in order." After further discussion, the presider "decided that it was not." Then "Mr. Edwards began again to read his committe's recommendations." During the debates on resolutions, to prevent constant outbursts by Talmadge and possibly others, "someone introduced a motion that the same person not be allowed the floor more than 12 times before everybody else in the meeting had spoken!" After the first eight recommendations had been debated and resolved, in proper order under presider Menard's strong leadership, the conference considered the ninth resolution, the one advocating the Talmadge/Long plan. Believing that the resolution on the Long policy was not "strong enough," Talmadge and two colleagues wrote a substitute. His motion "passed with less than a half dozen dissenting votes," placing the convention on record for the Long plan, and urging the Governor to "immediately convene" the legislature for consideration of legislation prohibiting the planting of cotton in Georgia for the year 1932.

At the Macon farm meeting, Talmadge once again won his way. Importantly for democratic processes and for citizenry involvement, however, this powerful and beligerent commissioner of Agriculture was prevented from bluffing the convention into forfeiting its collective authority. The case study of the Macon convention illustrated well the process of democracy winning over demagoguery. Because J. E. Newby of Dublin, C. F. Richards of Camilla, E. E. Cox of Camilla, H. W. Davis of Jefferson, Tom L. Graham of Dodge County, J. M. Lee of Hawkinsville, and B. F. Horn of Dodge County were willing to address the one thousand participants, the convention was informed of strengths and weaknesses of several plans for helping farmers. Because M. C. Edwards of Dawson was willing to chair the Resolutions Committee and to read each recommendation in the face of open hostility from the politically powerful Talmadge, the conference's adopted process for making decisions was preserved. Because Editor W. T. Anderson opposed Talmadge's threat to the operations of the assembly publicly, directly, and effectively, the Commissioner's continued efforts to muffle the meeting were blunted and participatory democracy preserved.

Macon Chamber of Commerce president and presider Albert Menard, although momentarily knocked off balance by Commissioner Talmadge's aggressive behavior, recovered courageously, and judiciously enforced parliamentary laws governing the debates and committee reports. Because of Menard's decisive leadership, Talmadge was guaranteed equal opportunity for advocating a plan for assisting farmers but denied the power of prohibiting free discussion by persons holding opposing views. The courageous acts of these several participants ensured that decisions in the farm meeting were made through the free expression of opposing views and not by the dictation of Talmadge. Apparently Talmadge convinced many delegates to support his plan for farmers.

NOTES

1. Numan V. Bartley, <u>Creation of Modern Georgia</u> (Athens: Univer of Georgia Press, 1983), pp. 172-173.
2. George Brown Tindall, <u>Emergence of the New South, 1913-1945</u> (Baton Rouge: Louisiana State Univer Press, 1967), pp. 111, 365.
3. <u>Atlanta Constitution</u>, August 4, 1931; <u>Cordele</u>

Dispatch, August 26, 1931.

4. Sarah McCulloh Lemmon, "The Public Career of Eugene Talmadge: 1926-1936," Ph.D. dissertation, Univer of North Carolina, Chapel Hill, 1952, pp. 87-88.

5. *Atlanta Constitution*, July 21, 1931.

6. *Atlanta Constitution*, July 31, 1931.

7. *Atlanta Constitution*, July 17 and 21, 1931.

8. *Macon Telegraph and News*, August 20, 1932.

9. *Atlanta Constitution*, August 12, 1931.

10. Quoted in *Atlanta Constitution*, July 31, 1931.

11. Quoted in *Atlanta Constitution*, August 5, 1931.

12. *Cordele Dispatch*, August 11, 1931.

13. Quoted in *Atlanta Constitution*, August 5 and 8, 1931.

14. Ralph McGill, "DePaul University Commencement Address," June 9, 1965, in Calvin McLeod Logue, editor, *Ralph McGill Editor and Publisher*, vol. I (Durham, North Carolina: Moore Publishing Co., 1969), p. 366.

15. *Thomaston Times*, August 14, 1931; emphasis added.

16. Tindall, *Emergence of the New South*, pp. 361, 358.

17. Quoted in Lemmon, "Public Career of Eugene Talmadge," p. 76.

18. *Dawson News*, August 27, 1931; *Coffee County Progress*, Douglas, August 27, 1931.

19. *Dawson News*, August 6, 1931.

20. Michael Stephen Holmes, "New Deal in Georgia: An Administrative History," Ph.D. dissertation, Univer of Wisconsin, 1969, p. 37.

21. Tindall, *Emergence of the New South*, pp. 357-358.

22. *Thomaston Times*, August 28, 1931.

23. *Cordele Dispatch*, August 28, 1931; emphasis added.

24. *Macon Telegraph and News*, August 28, 1931.

5

Campaigning for Governor in High Gear

In 1926 Talmadge, an unknown candidate, fought his way out of a pack of five challengers, out-debated incumbent John J. Brown, and became commisioner of the Department of Agriculture. He won by convincing the voters that Brown and his department were politically corrupt and were not serving the interests of Georgians. Talmadge persuaded voters that he was fighter enough to correct the problems in Agriculture. When that campaign began, no one expected Talmadge to win. In 1932 Talmadge and nine other persons ran for governor of Georgia. Having won campaigns for re-election as commissioner of Agriculture in 1928 and 1930, in 1932 few persons expected Talmadge to lose the campaign for governor. Certainly the candidacy of former Governor Thomas W. Hardwick received significant attention. Abit Nix of Athens ran a strong race. But Talmadge's rhetorical assertiveness had made his a household name. Near the end of the campaign, in Good Hope, Georgia, a teacher emulating the ritual Talmadge performed at the conclusion of his stump speeches, took a hand-poll of her fifth grade class. She asked thirty-six children if they knew who was running for president. One pupil said, "Mr. Roosevelt." When she asked them who was running for governor, thirty-six "little sunburned hands went up and they all sung out, 'Mr. Talmadge'."(1)

In his campaign for governor in 1932, Talmadge carried forward themes introduced in the latter stages of his 1926 race for commissioner of Agriculture, advocating a cut in taxes, decrease in government services, and curtailment of government interference in the affairs of men and women, policies that also pleased wealthy businessmen. George

Tindall provided insight into the context in which Talmadge forged his political platform from behind the stump. Tindall indicated that in the 1920s the "progressive urge" for "'good government' and public services remained strong." Business progressivism extended "themes of public services and efficiency," "good roads and schools," "cries for economy, but . . . elimination of waste rather than the reduction of services." The Great Depression "halted the expansive impulse of business progressivism, but . . . spurred action for efficiency, centralization, and new revenues." Richard B. Russell, Jr., was elected governor of Georgia in 1930 on promises of economy and efficiency. "The period of business progressivism afforded a brief interlude in plebeian politics between its earlier heyday and the new era of Huey Long, Eugene Talmadge, and later Bilbo."(2) Bass and DeVries maintained that, unlike Huey Long, who opposed corporations and provided free textbooks and medical care for the poor, Talmadge won the votes of "poverty-stricken rural" citizens "primarily through racist appeals" and the support of wealthy businessmen in Atlanta by taking a "conservative" stance on the role of government in society, low taxes, few government services, and even opposition to the New Deal."(3) Certainly Talmadge had no patience with those who called for new revenues.

When he thought the strategy would work or was needed, Talmadge employed racist appeals to win elections and to defend policies. Talmadge selected an issue that he judged to be most potent for winning votes and support for causes. Because he devised public discourses more for their voter appeal than from any set personal beliefs or plans for improving the economy, his attitudes and stances shifted as the occasions changed. In 1931, he emphasized the need to raise the price paid to Georgia farmers for cotton by curtailing the harvesting and planting of that crop. In 1941, to justify his political interference in the administration of the University System of Georgia, and in 1942, when campaigning for governor, he turned to raw racist appeals, and in both situations they failed to rescue him politically. In 1946, after the Supreme Court ruled that blacks could vote in "white primary" elections and abolished segregated seating in interstate transportation, his direct appeals to racial prejudice elected him to the governor's office.

In 1932, from behind the stump in his first campaign for governor, Talmadge created a platform that borrowed some populist and progressive teachings while opposing others. From his campaign rhetoric in the 1932 election, one can distill the following positions. He continued to be somewhat defensive about his wild rhetorical performances, insisting that he was fearless in fighting for the needs of farmers, but was no "demagogue." When elected governor, he would see that the Highway Department was managed efficiently and without corruption; reduce the cost of automobile tags to a flat fee of three dollars; adopt policies that no longer favored the wealthy and would enable the working class to earn a living; cut the cost of government; reduce the working man's taxes; increase taxes on wealthy persons' investments; support urban citizens as well as farmers; cut freight rates to stimulate business; implement higher tariffs as a way of providing increased incomes for farmers; improve rural schools; provide medical care; and satisfy the needs of veterans.

In the 1932 campaign, Talmadge spoke often and to supportive audiences. Because Talmadge performed largely before friendly crowds, the campaign brought into high relief the man's persuasive craftsmanship. He rehearsed attacks he would make upon expensive and bloated government in future political battles. Talmadge paid special tribute to each town in a way that linked the residents with his candidacy. In Sparta he talked for one and one-half hours, and "drew much applause" when praising and identifying his candidacy with favorite son W. J. Northen as the "last" governor in the state who was a friend of the farmer.(4) Sandersville was the home town of opponent and former Governor Thomas W. Hardwick, and Talmadge thanked the "large crowd" for braving "the heat to turn out for his speech."(5) In reply to criticism that his political behavior was disgraceful, Talmadge said Georgia needed more leaders like "Talmadge." He was "happy to be" in Crawfordville, home of Alexander Stephens"; "I pay tribute to his honesty, courage and patriotism, qualities claimed for his own leadership. We need more men of his type" who are "willing . . . to fight fearlessly . . . and yet be free from demagogy."(6)

By July 24 in the 1932 campaign, Talmadge had made twenty-five speeches. In an interview about those talks, he said that he was pleased "with the large crowds." Rested after a "week-end on his McRae farm . . . eating watermelon, looking over the crops and talking with the tenants," Talmadge returned to the race. His "speaking itinerary" for the next week was published in the press: Monday morning, Dalton; Tuesday morning, Lyons; Tuesday afternoon, Baxley; Wednesday morning, Eatonton; Wednesday afternoon, Greensboro; Thursday morning, Waycross; Thursday afternoon, Douglas; Friday morning, Lakeland; Friday afternoon, Quitman; Saturday morning, Edison; Saturday afternoon, Leesburg.(7)   He continued that rigorous speaking schedule throughout the race. Talmadge delivered the first speech of the campaign in McRae on July 4. In Leesburg, on July 30, he gave his thirty-seventh address.(8) By September 11, a reporter estimated that he had delivered "over 100 speeches to approximately 175,000 people."(9)

Talmadge argued that the size of his audiences was proof of his great popularity among the voters. Talmadge and the other candidates used the sizes of the turn-out of listeners to prove the success of their campaigns. Each man bragged that his crowds were larger than others'. A reporter maintained that on a number of occasions Talmadge "trailed some of his opponents into the same town by a day," but was able on those occasions to "more than triple the numbers of those who heard his adversary."(10) Because the courthouses could not hold the crowds, he usually spoke outdoors, repeatedly boasting that no indoor facility could hold his large audiences.(11) To be heard by the large crowds, on some occasions Talmadge used a "loud speaking apparatus."(12) He also reached a much wider audience by means of radio, speaking over that medium on July 7, August 22, 28, and 29, 1932. In Lyons he talked to an audience that overflowed the Toombs County courthouse. This was a scene in which Talmadge could excel; the larger and more vocal the audience the better for his brand of oratory. "All of the seats in the building were filled and scores of persons stood in the aisles and in the rear of the hall."(13) At Greensboro, Talmadge addressed "one of the largest crowds ever assembled in Greene county for a political speaking," a recurring claim in political campaigns that is difficult to verify. Demonstrating the importance placed at the time upon political "speakings," Judge J. B. Park "adjourned court while the speaking went on." Talmadge "estimated" the audience to exceed 2,500.(14)

Candidates debated which person attracted the largest audiences. Although hostile toward Talmadge, H. B. Edwards explained to a Barnesville audience something of the war going on behind the scenes of the campaign. Adding an Old Testament flavor to his attacks, and anticipating the way that advertising agencies and media specialists would later dominate political communication, candidate Edwards complained that "Talmadge's paid henchmen" were "infesting Georgia in almost as great numbers as frogs and locusts in Egypt, making bandstand efforts to drum him up crowds." Talmadge's "paid employees" were "failing miserably to get the crowds, but his paid publicity experts" had "vivid imaginations" and were exaggerating sizes of crowds "accordingly." In a doubtful claim, he concluded that Talmadge "seldom" attracted a "crowd as large as Edwards'."(15)

The candidates used other rhetorical variables to convince voters that they were best qualified to govern Georgia, a practice due in part to Talmadge's great success before crowds at the stump. The number of speeches a candidate delivered was represented to be indicative of a candidate's committment to causes and to his progress toward winning the election. I. S. Peebles, Jr., Thomas W. Hardwick's campaign manager, boasted that "we have on file . . . two hundred and fifty requests for" the former Governor "to make speeches."(16) Enthusiasm generated by a speaker's performance was another measure of a man's worth. After observing the great reaction Talmadge received from the one thousand persons gathered in Griffin, a reporter interpreted the implication of that and other audiences' response for potential victory. Talmadge was "interrupted by cheers in all places and in two instances" was carried about by audiences on their shoulders, a common practice carefully planned at his rallies. When "translated into political terms," continued the reporter, that "enthusiasm" meant that, "in the minds of the people," Talmadge was in the lead.(17)

Talmadge was so effective in marshaling overt crowd support that opponents began to criticize the method by which he achieved that response. Some reporters argued curiously that Talmadge's success in motivating audiences was a reliable sign that he would lose the campaign. Dan McGill, Managing Editor of the Athens Banner-Herald, worker in Abit Nix's campaign during this race, and the journalist who praised Talmadge's debating skills during the 1926 campaign, by 1932 had turned against the McRae native. On August 21, desiring to aid Nix's efforts, Dan McGill predicted wishfully that Talmadge's "skillfully ballyhooed political campaign" was on the verge of "collapse." The sound defeat of Talmadge's campaign would result from "its inherent weakness" and to the daily "attack" by "newspapers and individuals." Initially, McGill continued, the "loud-mouthed" supporters "caused people" to believe he would "be elected." McGill portrayed Talmadge as a "wild" politician who "thrived" on "crowds, the circus atmosphere . . . much noise, hat throwing and a general hullabaloo." But the "crowds" were recruited by "workers," many of whom "some say" were employed by the state. McGill was correct when he indicated that persons came to "see the show"; however, in 1932, the best entertainer was also collecting the most votes.(18)

The press contributed to the public's perception of the relative rhetorical stature of each candidate. In 1926 many Georgia newspapers supported Talmadge over incumbent J. J. Brown, including the formidable Macon Telegraph and News and Atlanta Constitution. By 1931, when Talmadge tried unsuccessfully to disrupt the farm meeting at Macon, the Macon Telegraph and News and its editor, W. T. Anderson, had withdrawn support. In 1932 and later, a number of editors severely criticized Talmadge's arrogant rhetorical behavior. Talmadge complained to a Thomson audience about the unfair coverage he and Tom Watson, former resident and venerated legend of that community, received in the press. Talmadge argued that "freedom of the press" had come to include "suppressing true accounts in news columns." Just "day before yesterday," he protested, the headlines claimed that "a big crowd" attended an opponent's speech, when there were "not more than 40 or 50 people." When "I spoke" in Griffin to a crowd that "overflowed the courthouse square and blocked traffic . . . not a word was carried in the daily press about the size of the crowd." He charged that the same prejudiced omissions were made in press coverage of speeches at Tifton, Cairo, Ellaville, Newnan, Franklin, and Danielsville.(19) In Hartwell, Talmadge boasted that opponents' "whispering campaign of slander" had "fallen flat," as confirmed by the size of his audiences.(20) Curiously, on other occasions Talmadge relied upon the press to do his bidding as extensions of his own speeches. He advised a Douglas audience to "read the papers on Saturday morning," because in speeches at Lakeland and Quitman, he would discuss the "terrible danger" facing the "rural schools of Georgia."(21)

When Talmadge had been the underdog in 1926, he attacked J. J. Brown ferociously. That open fighting stance became the substance of his message. Having won three consecutive state-wide campaigns for Commissioner of Agriculture, however, in 1932 Talmadge carried the advantage of incumbency, although racing for a new office. Therefore, he could measure a particular subject, audience, and occasion carefully, and plan campaign strategies to best serve his cause. In 1920 and 1926, Talmadge was such an unknown candidate that he challenged opponents to debate as a means of increasing the visibility of his candidacy. Indeed, Talmadge was so convincing in challenging opponents that the author of this book was convinced that he would debate any person any time, regardless of his relative position in a race for public office. As coverage of his campaigns revealed, however, Talmadge was as cunning and expedient as he was fearless. His challenges to opposing candidates to debate in 1920 and 1926 were sheer political weaponry. When winning a campaign depended upon him debating an opponent, he was first to the stump, challenging all other candidates to bring their supporters and meet him in a public brawl on unfriendly territory. Certainly he possessed the rhetorical tools, if not always the mature judgment, for hammering a front-runner into political obscurity. Commissioner J. J. Brown could attest to that.

But when a public debate endangered his position at the head of a race, Talmadge refused to meet challengers. In the 1932 campaign for governor, John I. Kelley of Lawrenceville, employing a Talmadge-like strategy, challenged front-runner Talmadge to a "joint debate at Greensboro." For bait, he indicated that refusal by Talmadge would be an admission that "facts" of wrong-doings were "so damning" that he was "unwilling to defend them." Kelley criticized Commissioner Talmadge for "spending large sums" of the state's public funds for personal "traveling expenses."(22) Talmadge was proud that he and family attended the Kentucky Derby each year, and said so publicly. Unlike the politically naive and somewhat rhetorically inept "King J. J." Brown, Talmadge refused to take the hook. The far more cunning Talmadge said he declined to debate because "the people" did not consider Kelley to be "a serious contender," and he "joined them in this opinion."(23) Few persons could out-maneuver Gene Talmadge for political advantage in a campaign, as would Richard B. Russell, Jr., and Ellis Arnold in 1936 and 1942.

He complained that "the other candidates were trying to "follow him around," as he did with J. J. Brown in 1926 when, as an underdog, he so desperately needed the visibility associated with incumbency. "I know some of the other candidates are having trouble getting crowds," he ridiculed, "and are watching my speaking dates and coming along right after me in the hope of drawing some of the people who came to hear Talmadge." Responding to Kelley's challenge to debate, Talmadge answered: "I understand" he "has decided to speak in Greensboro at 2:30, although it has been advertised that I will speak there at 1:30. I can't really blame the boys," he cajoled. "One of them spoke at Thomson last week to a crowd numbering exactly 57 by actual count," he scorned. "They had to stand in the aisles when I spoke there a day or two later."(24) In a never-ending attempt to top the performance of competitors, Talmadge ridiculed the notion of campaign debates. He suggested a political spectacle with him cast in a role larger than David's

of old. He would "meet all nine" challengers "at any
time and any place provided all nine of you are there
on the stage with me."(25) The rhetorically astute
Talmadge knew that such a scene would bring him
notoriety in the press equal to that created by his
1926 debates.

Because of his bulldog tenacity, Kelley did
manage to draw front-runner Talmadge into a press
debate. Kelley persisted that Talmadge lacked the
"moral courage to face the people" on his
"record."(26) At Ashburn, Kelley challenged Talmadge
to "meet" him "on the stump anywhere in Georgia."(27)
Talmadge chastised the upstart Kelley for attempting
to "butt in" on "his meeting," and "charged that" he
"represented the co-ops and 'horse doctors'."   When
Talmadge spoke in Greensboro, Kelley was in the
audience ready to debate. After all, Talmadge had
needed no invitation to debate Brown in Dawson in
1926! In his speech at Greensboro, Talmadge ridiculed Kelley, but refused to debate him face-to-face.
To his credit, however, Kelley had brought the wily
Talmadge into a debate in the Georgia press.   Trying
to win the press debate, Talmadge said he was ready
to fight nine foolish politicians at the same time,
but not one John I. Kelley.

When Talmadge finished speaking at Greensboro,
"a large part of the crowd followed" him to the "drug
store for a cold drink," leaving Kelley to address a
"diminished audience." Talmadge claimed that Kelley
had fifty-seven people hear him speak at Thomson, and
seventy-nine at Jackson, "by actual count."   These
judgments come from the Atlanta Constitution, whose
editor, Clark Howell, supported Talmadge during the
1926 campaign.   However, in the 1932 gubernatorial
campaign, that newspaper provided relatively balanced
coverage.(28) Kelley threatened that, unless there
were two debates, he would "trail" Talmadge and speak
after he finished speaking.(29) A third candidate,
H. B. Edwards, accused Kelley and Talmadge of "staging fictitious debates, a "stage play" by which
Kelley was doing the "bidding" of "his boss."(30)

Candidate and former Governor Thomas W. Hardwick
called Talmadge "a dangerous and shameless demagogue."   At Barnesville, attempting to frighten
Georgians not to vote for an extremist, Hardwick
warned that each Georgian had better make up "his
mind, or her mind" that the choice was between
Talmadge and himself.(31) In the final days of the
campaign, probably sensing that he was losing,
Hardwick challenged Talmadge to debate him in
Macon.(32) Remembering the importance of the debates
in his campaign against J. J. Brown in 1926, Talmadge
must have breathed with relief that ahead of him in

the 1932 race were merely stump appearances before
friendly forces. And, unlike the farm meeting in
Macon in 1931, there would be no parliamentary
constraints and no Albert Menard with Chamber-of-
Commerce experience to control his dominating outbursts from the stump.

Because of strong support from the electorate,
Talmadge was able to stump the state at times in high
gear. He was relatively secure in winning this
campaign. Persons from the audience asked him to
"pull off your coat and roll up your sleeves," and he
obliged in the dramatic manner to which all came to
expect and demand.(33) With his biting "quips," he
"kept" the crowd in Atlanta in "constant uproar."(34)
He used special effects mastered in 1926. The M. S.
Bishop family, for example, drove for thirty-five
miles to watch Talmadge speak in Lexington, Georgia.
Bishop wanted his children to watch Talmadgeism at
work. Bishop desired "the next governor of Georgia
to see" his twelve year old "afflicted" boy, transported in a "specially constructed Ford car." In a
"touching" and rhetorically potent act, candidate
Talmadge walked "over to" the car and "shook hands
with the little fellow," expressed appreciation for
the "deep loyalty" of the family, and once again
out-flanked opponents for press coverage of his
campaign. The message left from this memorable act
was that only Talmadge in the governor's office could
heal the common man's afflictions. Having mastered
the art of documenting the avariciousness of office
holders in the 1926 campaign, in 1932 he brought down
his wrath upon the Georgia Highway Commission.
Building the stump drama, Talmadge exhibited "original" letters and affidavits to link Thomas W.
Hardwick, John N. Holder, and Frank Holder with
"highway contracts obtained by" the R. J. Davidson
company.(35)

Because he was favored to win the election, at
times Talmadge transfigured personal political meanness to stump hyperbole. Films of his speeches show
a determined and stern man, contrasted with the "fun"
of one favored to win in 1932. His wife had managed
the farm outside of McRae the five years he served as
commissioner of Agriculture. When elected, he told a
Talbotton crowd, he would "take the best woman farmer
in the state and put her in the governor's man-
sion."(36) Talmadge would "knock the bark off the
politicians who have been knocking the bark off of
you." From his safe position at the front of the
race, Talmadge toyed with the opposition. He "poured
scorn" on the many adversaries as a "baseball nine"
attempting unsuccessfully "to put him out" at the
stump.(37) Talmadge was masterful in trivializ-

Prompted by the crowd, Talmadge removes his coat, displaying the famous red suspenders. (Photograph from Herman E. Talmadge Collection, Richard B. Russell Memorial Library, University of Georgia, Athens, Georgia. Reprinted by permission.)

ing serious criticism made against him. Turning charges back upon an opponent, Talmadge used criticism that he abused the agricultural commissioner's "expense account" as proof of his statesmanship. The money was spent to enable him to render efficient service to citizens. To keep engagements punctually, he reminded citizens of Fort Valley that he did travel first-class by automobiles, train, and airplane. This was a "modern age" and he should "be congratulated" for arriving punctually for meetings at "such a low rate."(38)

At Statesboro, the commissioner portrayed opponents Thomas W. Hardwick and John N. Holder as "Siamese twins."(39) Compared to his public attack upon university officials in 1941, a situation studied in Chapter 7 of this book, and his racist rhetoric during the 1946 campaign for governor, reviewed in Chapter 8, little discussion of race was reported in the press in the 1932 election. The white primary was in place, black voters were no threat to white dominance of state government, and Talmadge was the frontrunner; thus, there was less need for him to employ the "racial equality" argument. As will be demonstrated in the analysis of the 1936 campaign for the United States Senate, in Chapter 6, Talmadge used that form of attack the moment he judged it to be to his advantage. Even in the 1932 campaign, ever alert for means of adding a racist twist to a persuasive appeal, in a speech at Blairsville, Talmadge contended that Hardwick's tax exemption plan, when implemented in Telfair county, would "allow two negroes to pay their taxes and would exempt approximately 65 per cent of the white citizens."(40)

Turning to the second of the campaign twins, Talmadge hit hard at the candidacy of John N. Holder, former chairman of the Highway Commission, a position with political clout comparable to the agricultural commissioner's post held by John J. Brown during the 1926 race. At Lyons, Talmadge accused Holder of receiving funds unlawfully. "Holder is quibbling about receiving a check, but I ask him now, did he receive any money from J. W. Gwin."(41) He charged at Greensboro that funds appropriated for roads were being misused. Talmadge promised to rescue the highway department from political corruption. Talmadge would end the lingering "influence" of Holder from the highway department. He was astute in manufacturing campaign issues that Georgia voters could easily visualize. Although Georgians had "poured $130,000,000 in cash into the highway system," Talmadge accused, there was "not a single east-and-west cross-state highway to the sea."

Insisting that better services could be provided for less money, he pledged to the Greensboro audience to "move more dirt, grade more roads and lay more concrete miles than has heretofore been done in any preceding year."(42) Talmadge urged voters to "wake up to the fact" that public funds were "not reaching the roadbed." As governor, Talmadge would require that "every legitimate businessman, material man and contractor" be given the "absolute right" of negotiating with the highway department. "Contracts" were to be "let to the lowest reliable bidder without Holder dictation." That promise is remarkably different from the procedure Talmadge employed while he was governor. William Anderson described how Talmadge allocated nine million dollars in highway funds during his second term as governor. The "major road contractors and their suppliers . . . assembled in a large room . . . and a huge map of Georgia was

tacked on the wall. . . . Each contractor went
before the big map and marked where he wanted a road
built."(43)

Leading the race in 1932, Talmadge exhumed
issues that served his interest. He claimed his
campaign was "pitched on a high plane" in which
"issues" were confronted rather than "men." In one
of the more over-stated observations made in the
history of political oratory, Talmadge claimed that
he dealt with "principles and not personalities."(44)
Instead of a "King J. J. Brown," Talmadge warned of a
new dragon in Georgia to be slayed. He attacked
economic policies that were discriminatory for the
working class. This task, he alerted, required a
"God-fearing man in the governor's chair." There was
no evidence, however, that even a Source of that
authority could monitor Talmadgeism. Unlike Moses,
who was drafted, Talmadge graciously volunteered to
"lead the people of Georgia in this great undertak-
ing."(45) He insisted that his plan for economic
recovery was "in line with the tracks" he made while
serving as commissioner of Agriculture. As commissioner, he reduced the number of oil inspectors from
"more than 200 to 6," enforced the "fertilizer
inspection laws," and "reduced expenses."(46)

Talmadge covered the same topics in speeches
throughout Georgia, but added segments to heighten
local interest. A reporter following Talmadge from
town-to-town noted on July 29, September 6, and
September 13 that he gave "his usual address."(47)
When speaking in one town, Talmadge created excitement about speeches he would be giving later in other
communities. He revealed to a Douglas audience that,
"I have already spoken more than one hour, and it is
impossible to cover the ground in any one speech."
He alerted the listeners that "tomorrow" speeches at
Lakeland and Quitman would be "devoted" entirely to
the "terrible danger" now confronting the "rural
schools of Georgia." His revelations would "be in
the nature of a sensation."(48) Attracted by Talmage
coming to town with sensatational news, the Lakeland
audience was too large to accommodate in the courthouse.(49)

Talmadge campaigned for governor in this 1932
election on a "platform" of enjoying an "honest
living," "educating our children," and building "good
roads." He assured a McRae crowd that an honest
income was only possible if both government costs and
citizens' taxes were decreased.(50) To restore
fiscal responsibility, Talmadge promised at Talbotton
to cut the costs of the state government "just as
your incomes have been reduced."(51) As governor,
Richard B. Russell, Jr., restructured the state "from

112 departments to 19," complained Talmadge, but merely reorganizing agencies failed to lower expenses. Under his administration, "useless bureaus and boards" would be abolished. To save the farmers' income, state "appropriations" were to be slashed.(52)

Previewing his vicious personal attack upon President Franklin D. Roosevelt and the New Deal in his campaign for the United States Senate in 1936, a confrontation studied in Chapter 6, Talmadge detailed how government bureaus favored the upper socioeconomic class at the expense of farmers and workers. He argued that the Reconstruction Finance Corporation (RFC) for one was a "colossal failure." Attempting to shore up the corporate and financial structure, Herbert Hoover had supported the creation of the RFC, an agency chartered in January 1932 to issue loans to corporations.(53) In Washington, Georgia, Talmadge complained that the RFC had lent billions to "broke millionaries in the vain hope that some of it" would "sift down to the masses." The "working man" was not helped when "bankrupt stock brokers" and "railroad presidents" were allowed "to liquidate their gambling debts with government money."(54) In LaGrange, Talmadge made a "vitrolic attack upon the federal farm board," urging that "it be abolished."(55)

Talmadge argued that equal in importance to economic policies that treated the working class equitably was the election of a governor obstinate enough to implement those plans. To retrench public agencies and to cut government expenditures that contributed to wealthy persons' profits would require a person strong enough to withstand counter-attacks. Talmadge reminded audiences that he was a veteran of battles initiated for farmers and workers. He claimed that, as commissioner of Agriculture, like Tom Watson, he had been "persecuted and muzzled" for "telling the truth" about "special interests and certain corporations."(56)

Transforming criticisms to rhetorical assets, he admitted to being tempestuous in the sense that no one could "dictate" to him. He was "wild," Talmadge argued, to be armed with the "power of the governor's chair" so he could "reduce the length of the bread line" and the "sales of homes for taxes."(57) In an appeal that frightened many observers, he requested authority that placed him beyond reach of constitutional constraints.(58) He asked his "countrymen," a word with which the politically popular Tom Watson was identified, to secure for him a "position" in which "they cannot law me."(59) Later, in the Atlanta Constitution on July 5, 1934, when defending his actions as governor, Talmadge admitted that "possibly I have been a little different. . . . Possibly I have not been so timid, or a little brash in carrying out my campaign pledges."

In 1932, farmers and most Georgia workers were suffering under a depressed economy, and Talmadge hoped his request for unrestrained political authority would be perceived by the mass of voters as proof of his commitment to their cause. "No man or corporation has a bridle on me," he told a Swainsboro audience. "I acknowledge allegiance to no special group or class." He would work for the "welfare of the masses of the people."(60) Sensitive to opponents' claims that, unlike Talmadge, they would "govern Georgia 'smoothly and without distrubance'," he pledged in Dalton "to risk a row for his principles."(61) Talmadge wanted to extend personal immunity from controls to protection from constitutional constraints.

Few persons doubted Talmadge's willingness to say and do what he determined was best for his public record. "Let" the giant interests "howl," he advised listeners at Conyers. Georgians "will be better off with . . . a governor who will agitate."(62) In response to critics' contentions that he favored farmers over city dwellers, Talmadge assured audiences he prized the labor vote. Referring to a "central Georgia" newspaper editorial that the "only way to beat Talmadge is for the city people" to cooperate in voting for one of his opponents, ironically, he accused the writer of pitting "one class against another."(63) At Sandersville, trying to win the labor vote, he "interruped his address" to say that the state should not "interfere" with the "right" of laborers "to bargain collectively or individually."(64) "Until the farmers are better organized and represented in high places in" government, he advised a Sparta audience, "we cannot hope for a return to anything like prosperity."(65)

Talmadge contended that retrenchment in state government had to be accompanied by a reduction of taxes. Indeed to decrease the expense of government, Georgia had to reduce taxes. "The remedy lies," he explained to a Washington, Georgia audience, "in reduced taxation made possible by a radical reduction in government expenses."(66) Just as the "blood of our fathers" freed citizens from the "yoke of taxation," so should Georgians "again assert ourselves free of . . . taxation to the point of starvation." That "taxes are too high" was the "basic principle on which all issues must rest." High taxes were "stiffling business" and "confiscating property."(67) Promoting an image of an official courageous enough to battle the establishment, Talmadge reminded voters that "the budget law placed a red pencil in the hands of the governor, and I ask you to send a man there with nerve enough to use it."(68)   In a photograph taken of Talmadge stump speaking, housed in the Richard B. Russell Library, Athens, Georgia, there is a pencil the size of a baseball bat by him, probably employed as a visual aid to dramatize his willingness to cut taxes.

Talmadge was highly effective in illustrating for voters the "unreasonableness" of tax policies. In Georgia, "every acre of land, every house, every mule, every store and stock of merchandise," he told a Gainesville audience, was heavily taxed.(69)   Any druggist can name "25 to 50 different taxes which he pays daily."(70)   Talmadge serialized the taxes paid on transportation with the same devastating effectiveness that he listed family members employed by "King J. J. Brown" in 1926. The sheer repetition of the dreaded "tax" was enough to bring people to their feet. Georgia "levies a tax of six cents" on each "gallon of gasoline" you buy. "The state and county" levy "an ad valorem tax on your automobile. The federal government levies a tax" on gas you purchase, "in addition to the state tax and a tax on the oil that you pour into your motor." Then "you must buy a tag from the state." The "cheapest of these tags is $11.25."

Building to his stump remedy to oppressive government, Talmadge promised "to cut the cost of automobile tags" to a "flat rate of $3," saving Georgians $3,250,000. The promise of a three-dollar tag was another of Talmadge's issues with which voters could readily identify, and one with which he was long associated and remembered. That was state income, he continued, that "should not be replaced." Even when he established a $3 fee for tags, he said, "God knows you would" still pay "enough tax on automobiles." For campaigns for public office and for personal causes, Talmadge created potent maxims voters could easily remember. In 1932, the "3 dollar tag" became the slogan with which he rallied listeners to vote for him and to support a policy of slashing government expenses.(71) The lower price for tags also pleased businessmen dependent upon large trucks for hauling their products.

Talmadge argued that if the cost of government and citizens' taxes would be lowered, more equitable policies had to be implemented.(72) He would "lay a part of the expense of government on that great mass of wealth" that had been "exempt from taxes." When "invisible wealth in the form of stocks and bonds" were properly taxed, "the present rate of taxes on farms, houses and business" could be "cut in half."

Because farm commodities were "back to rock-bottom
prices, this would surely be enough tax to pay."(73)
He pledged in Cairo, Georgia to expose "millions of
dollars" worth of tax-exempt securities.(74)   The
"noonday nap of the coupon clippers" would be disturbed.(75) Armed by a mandate from the people, the
governor would "go into the dark vaults and safe
deposit boxes and bring it out."(76)

Extending a theme developed during the 1926
campaign, Talmadge claimed to speak for farmers and
other workers forgotten by "petty politicians" and
held down by discriminatory policies. Many of his
comments in the 1932 campaign carried the connotation
of conflict between members of advantaged and disad-
vantaged socioeconomic classes. To reenforce his
intention to remedy the disparaging inequities
between entrepreneurs and workers, he promised to
redecorate government offices in a style more receptive to the working class. If a cheap automobile tag
symbolized the need of the average farmer and laborer
for lower taxes and less oppressive government,
expensive furniture represented the extravagance and
exploitation of workers by the wealthy. He promised
"if elected" to "darken some of the rooms in the
basement of the capitol and pile 'a lot of those
pretty mahogany desks in it'."(77)

After hearing Talmadge's speech in Griffin, a
reporter for the Marietta Journal wrote how "the
fighting farmer-lawyer" had "spoken in ringing,
understandable terms of the condition of the state
government."(78) Contributing to and exploiting the
adversarial relationship between socioeconomic
classes, Talmadge ridiculed financially prosperous
persons before a Washington, Georgia, audience for
being as bloated individually as was the Department
of Agriculture prior to his election in 1926.
Curiously, Talmadge argued that the wealthy contributed little to the economy. In a raw style of
demeaning prosperous citizens that many working men
and women found entertaining, he argued that wealthy
persons did not contribute to the whole economy by
spending their inflated incomes. He asserted that
"rich men don't work hard enough to wear out many
clothes and shoes, and they don't eat any more than
we do. Not as much, because most of them have got
dyspepsia anyway."

In contrast, Talmadge praised farmers and other
workers for the vital contributions they made to the
economy. A reporter wrote how Talmadge explained
in a "vernacular that is familiar to the wire grass"
resident how the "farmer and the small-salaried
man, who constitute the market of the world, are
not" benefiting from funds distributed by the

Reconstruction Finance Corporation. "Prosperity" in
the state and nation "would not return until this
market is re-established." In a genre of persuasion
that was a forerunner of the contemporary television
beer commercial, Talmadge advised the Washington
audience that "the basis of the buying power of this
country is in the wallet of the man behind the plow;
the man who lays brick, drives spikes or operates a
lathe."

Exhibiting a keen familiarity with the life
cycle of the majority of families in the South,
Talmadge sketched a clear and vivid picture of
investments made by working men and women in the
nation's economy. In a remarkable display of stump
poetry for a Washington, Georgia, audience, Talmadge
captured the scene of the working men and women on
the job for America. In this passage, one sees how
Talmadge won the loyalty of many Georgia voters
suffering for clothing, shelter, and daily bread.
From the stump in 1932, because he talked in the
specialized vocabulary of the farm and work place, he
was able to arouse most Georgians to fight, laugh,
cry, and vote by explaining the basic principles of
fire-side economics. In the Washington speech, he
inspired: "When a man gets money in his pockets the
first thing he spends it for is food, and then he
pays the rent and last year's doctor bill. Then he
buys Mary a dress and himself some overalls. If
there is any left he is sure to buy an automobile or
some new tires, and maybe some fresh curtains for the
living room and a chair or two. Then he looks
around, and about the time that hole in the roof gets
big enough to throw a chicken through, he will buy a
roll of ruberoid roofing and patch it."(79)

Talmadge maintained that for farmers and the
railroads to prosper and contribute to a stable
economy, freight rates had to be decreased. High
freight rates brought "depreciated revenues with a
consequent spread of unemployment." The "remedy" lay
in a "general reduction of the present 'war time and
over-war time' freight rates."(80) Dropping the
rates, he continued, would increase the "traffic
volume" on the railroads. The railroads could
"afford to cut rates" to correlate with the "decline
in revenues of other businesses." Reduced freight
rates would make it "profitable for the farmer to
ship" cotton, watermelons, and peaches. The increase
in business would put "idle cars and engines back
into use," provide jobs for persons "laid off," and
earn "profit for the railroads."(81)

So that farmers could haul crops to markets
profitably, and "business people and bankers" could
experience "prosperity," not only would taxes on

railroad freight be reduced, but taxes on trucks and
buses would be increased. Farm crops were "decaying
in the fields" because farmers could not "profitably"
transport them "to market." Talmadge described the
vicious cycle in which all segments of the market
were trapped. Farmers had no "buying power"; thus,
there was "no freight to be hauled from factory and
city to the country." With reduced rates, farmers
could move their commodities "to the cities," the
farmers' purchasing power would be "restored," the
traffic on railroads would increase, and "thousands
of men . . . laid off" would be "re-employed." At
the same time, the "truck and bus lines" owned by
"railroad companies" were "destroying the highways .
. . built with the people's money." Those vehicles
"should be taxed off the highways, and the business
that they are handling should be hauled on the
railroads."(82) At Lakeland, Talmadge said: "I have
stated in more than 25 speeches . . . that the size,
length and tonnage of commercial trucks and busses
must be regulated and must be required to pay taxes
in the various counties."(83)

Talmadge advocated higher tariffs as a means of
assisting agriculture. In speeches at Tifton and
Cairo, he warned that farmers were "headed for a
system of peonage unless unfair tariffs and unequal
taxation" were corrected.(84) The cost of "hardware
and automobiles" was "fixed" in the United States,
but "the prices of raw agricultural products" were
not. They were set in "the orient, where 20 cents a
day is high wage and people live in grass houses and
go half naked."(85) Talmadge said that the market
for the South's cotton crop also should be protected.
For example, a tariff should be imposed on jute for
it was used "extensively as wrapping for bales of
cotton and in manufacture of tapestries," replacing
"approximately 3,000,000 bales of cotton in the
United States." Protective measures were also
required for coconuts, peanuts, soybeans, and other
vegetable oils, the advantage for farmers being
"greatly increased prices for dairy products."(86)
Talmadge promised "relief for the dairymen who
suffered from "powdered milk importation." To "make
a cow worth something," he wanted "strict regulations" on "milk trade."(87)

Talmadge promised to help rural schools, improve
medical care, and provide for veterans, while slash-
ing the cost of government. He said that funding
rural education in Georgia was another expression of
his support for working class citizens. Declaring
that education had been "kicked about as a 'political
football'," he quoted State Superintendent of Schools
M. L. Duggan as predicting that "three-fourths of the

rural schools of Georgia" would be unable to operate
the "full term" because of "vast indebtedness."   This
did not include the "big city system[s]" in Atlanta,
Augusta, Macon, Savannah, and Columbus, he complained. He warned a Lakeland audience that the
threat is to "your" schools, to the "rural schools."
Charging that inequities existed between rural and
urban schools, Talmadge argued that this was "discrimination of the worst possible sort."   Shifting
from the Old to the New Testament, he prophesied: "I
tell you this thing must not come to pass."   Because
of his concern for the "country boys and girls," he
stated categorically "that the rural schools of
Georgia shall not close if I am elected governor."(88) As for the Board of Regents that Governor
Russell had recently created, in a volley that would
not hit its mark until 1941, and studied in Chapter 7
of this book, Talmadge offered the new agency "a fair
opportunity to show that they can improve our university system."(89)

Talmadge was much more supportive of the State
Board of Health than of other agencies, promising to
restore it to the high level of performance by which
it was administered prior to Governor Richard B.
Russell's "re-organization" of that body. The "time"
had come "for the business of caring for the sick and
maimed to be taken out of politics," he declared to a
Griffin audience.(90) The state had a "duty" to
"furnish" blind persons an "opportunity to secure an
education and to learn a trade."(91)   Talmadge
pledged his allegiance to the veterans of America.
When elected, he would "see that" the salaries of
veterans of the Confederacy and of "1917-1918" would
be "paid just as promptly as the governor's salary."(92)

Talmadge envisioned the way life would be after
he was elected governor. The nation's economy would
be resurrected from its depressed state. He promised
to put people back to work. Even hoboes would be
able to pay their own way: "It won't be long then
before the factory wheels will begin to turn again;
the thousands of men who now ride freight trains free
will buy tickets or drive their own cars, and the
merchants will have to give up their checker games;
lawyers will blow the dust from their books and the
stream of commerce will once more flow in unobstruct-
ed channels."(93)

When the votes for governor were counted in
1932, the Dalton Citizen headlined that the "'Wild
Man of Soil' Plows to Victory."(94)   Talmadge re-
ceived 116,381 (fourty-three percent) popular votes,
Abit Nix, 78,588 (twenty-nine percent), Thomas W.
Hardwick, 35,252 (thirteen percent), John N. Holder,

10,697 (four percent), H. B. Edwards, 12,897 (five percent), John I. Kelly, who attempted to debate Talmadge through the press, 12,115 (five percent), Hoke O'Kelly, 1,823 (one percent), and F. B. Summers, 197 (.001 percent). Talmadge received 264 county unit votes, Nix 94, Hardwick 30, Holder 10, Edwards 8, Kelly 4, O'Kelly 0, and Summers 0.(95) Of the eight counties with largest populations, each having six unit votes, Talmadge won in only one, and in the thirty counties each having four unit votes, he won in sixteen and split the four votes in one. Of the 121 counties each having two unit votes, the more rural areas of the state, Talmadge won in ninety-six.

The race produced various judgments about the nature and quality of participants' performances. "From the bottom of" his heart, at McRae, Talmadge thanked "the people of Georgia who so loyally supported" him. "I hope that as governor of Georgia I can help the state I love so much." He expressed appreciation to Hugh Howell, prominent Atlanta attorney, who "worked 14 hours every day and half of every night to elect me governor."(96) A number of Georgians voted for Abit Nix of Athens, a candidate in the mold of John R. Irwin who dropped out of the 1926 campaign because his decorous rhetoric was ineffective. Nix dealt largely in issues and not personalities, but lost the election. On August 2 in Ringgold, Nix had predicted for the audience that the "average man does not want to hear denunciation from the platform."(97)

The editor of the Savannah Evening Press interpreted the meaning of this "heated and acrimonious state party campaign." The candidates "mystified" and "beclouded" issues for the citizenry. Voters "of intelligence," the editor continued, were "puzzled to understand what to believe." The issues of "past years . . . degenerated into personal abuse, villification, [and] malicious charges." The campaign began during the "general depression," and candidates promised "more jobs than there are jobs in the state government." The editor wrote that the 1932 campaign was "an era of wild and extravagant lure dangled in the face" of citizens. Participants "revel in the fleshpots at the expense of the uninitiated."(98) During the race, candidate Thomas W. Hardwick "characterized" Talmadge as "a man impatient of any restraint and contemptuous of law." Hardwick quoted Talmadge as saying that he desired "to be governor" because in that office, unlike the Commissioner of Agriculture, one could be "above the law." Having served as governor, Hardwick insisted that a person in that office was "not above the law. He should be as 'submissive to law as a vestal

virgin'."99
      V. O. Key explained that Talmadge introduced
into Georgia's one-party politics "elements of
stability and form" absent before. With his election
as governor in 1932, "multifactionalism declined"
because voters coalesced around his leadership. He
forged a "cohesive, personal faction" of followers.
At the same time, Talmadge's turbulent dominance
caused opponents to "unite against him." As governor, after the 1932 election, Talmadge once again
attempted to exercise his will in state government.
Because the public service commissioners were elected
to their postions and functioned independently of the
governor's authority, Talmadge "dramatically ousted"
them by calling upon the National Guard. In this
manner he fulfilled his promise to lower utility
rates and to work beyond the reach of the law.
      The highway department also had some authority
beyond that of the governor. Thus, to reduce the
cost of an automobile tag, Talmadge waited until the
General Assembly had adjourned, fired some of the
members of the highway board, and implemented the
three-dollar fee unilaterally.(100) Largely by
executive order, then, Talmadge lowered utility
rates, economized in managing the government, and
approved the lowering of the ad valorem tax, an act
that became an issue in the 1936 campaign against
Richard B. Russell, Jr., for the United States
Senate, covered in Chapter 6. Governor Talmadge paid
the teachers, in part from surplus funds in the
highway department, and reduced the state debt.(101)
While Talmadge was winning his first campaign for
governor in 1932, Franklin D. Roosevelt was being
elected to the presidency.
      When campaigning for reelection in 1934,
Talmadge admitted that as governor he had been "a
little brash."(102) In that election, Judge Claude
C. Pittman challenged Talmadge to meet him in "joint
debate," but the Governor refused.(103) Pittman
criticized Talmadge for not cooperating with the
Roosevelt Administration and accused him of "political tyranny."(104) Pittman reminded Georgians that
Talmadge had reportedly called the young persons from
Georgia participating in the Citizens Conservation
Corps "bums and loafers."(105) Shifting its allegiance, the Atlanta Constitution warned that "history
is filled with instances where seeds of race hatred,
sown by dictators, have reaped the whirlwind of
revolution and destruction."(106) W. T. Anderson,
editor of the Macon Telegraph and News, returned to
Talmadge's side, and "severly scored" the governor's
critics for "the tactics they" used "against
him."(107) In a telling speech over WSB radio in

Atlanta, Talmadge complained that the "opposition" did not challenge the action he took during his first term, but "only criticize[d] the method in which it was done."(108)

In the 1934 campaign for re-election as governor, Talmadge spoke effectively before boisterous, supportive, and large audiences. During his speech at Waycross, Talmadge was "halted time and again by shouting supporters, some of them requesting an attack upon his opponents." "The crowd shouted madly," and the governor had to "halt the cheering in order that he might complete his speech."(109) He promised a Louisville, Georgia, audience that he only wanted to serve as governor two additional years, and would not campaign against Richard B. Russell, Jr., for the United States Senate in 1936. After his second term as governor, he would "retire to" his "wire grass farm and fish and hunt and work the rest of my days."(110)

Reporter L. A. Farrell noted that in the 1934 campaign Talmadge displayed his flaming red suspenders, wiped his forehead with red bandanna handkerchief, bristled with "enthusiasm," and sparkled with "wit" that brought him "more hearers in two years than any other public speaker the state has ever had."(111) Talmadge reminded voters that during his first term he had fulfilled promises made in 1932, pending ratification of those unilaterial actions by the General Assembly. He continued to oppose "exorbitant taxes."(112) Attempting to expand his base of support, Talmadge emphasized his concern for labor. "I resent anyone on earth saying that they are closer to labor. I am a laborer myself."(113) Having won the allegiance of rural citizens, he went after city votes.

In 1934, he predicted to a Columbus, Georgia, audience that, "We did not carry a county where the street cars run two years ago, but when the vote is counted this year, I'm sure that Muscogee [County] will" have voted for "Talmadge."(114) In Muscogee County, Talmadge won with 2,119 (sixty-six percent) of the votes, giving him the six unit votes. Of the eight counties with largest population, each having six unit votes, Talmadge won in six, five more than in 1932. Talmadge received 178,409 votes (sixty-six percent), Claude Pittman, 87,049, and Ed Gilliam 5,073. Talmadge won 394 county unit votes, Pittman 16, and Gilliam 0.(115) Reporter Farrell accurately assessed the dominant theme in 1934, concluding that "there is only one major issue with the voters and that is Talmadge. They either like him or they do not."(116)

NOTES

1. Quoted in Atlanta Constitution, September   10, 1932.
2. George   Brown   Tindall, Emergence of the New South, 1913-1945 (Baton Rouge: Louisiana State Univer Press, 1967), pp. 219, 224, 368, 233.
3. Jack Bass and Walter DeVries, Transformation of Southern Politicis: Social Change and Political Consequence Since 1945 (New York: New American Library, 1977), pp. 136-137.
4. Atlanta Constitution, July 22, 1932.
5. Atlanta Constitution, July 23, 1932.
6. Atlanta Constitution, September 8, 1932.
7. Interview in Atlanta Constitution, July 25, 1932.
8. Atlanta Constitution, July 31, 1932.
9. Atlanta Constitution, September 11, 1932.
10. Covering Griffin speech, Marietta Journal, July 21, 1932.
11. Atlanta Constitution, September 11, 1932.
12. Atlanta Constitution, September 9, 1932.
13. Atlanta Constitution, July 27, 1932.
14. Atlanta Constitution, July 28, 1932.
15. Atlanta Constitution, July 27, 1932.
16. Atlanta Constitution, August 5, 1932.
17. Marietta Journal, July 21, 1932.
18. Quoted in Macon Telegraph and News, August 21, 1932.
19. Atlanta Constitution, July 22, 1932.
20. Atlanta Constitution, September 3, 1932.
21. Atlanta Constitution, July 29, 1932.
22. Atlanta Constitution, July 25, 1932.
23. Quoted in Atlanta Constitution, July 26, 1932.
24. Interview in Atlanta Constitution, July 25, 1932.
25. Quoted in Atlanta Constitution, July 26, 1932.
26. Quoted in Atlanta Constitution, July 27, 1932.
27. Atlanta Constitution, August 4, 1932.
28. Greensboro speech, Atlanta Constitution, July 28, 1932.
29. Atlanta Constitution, August 16, 1932.
30. Covington speech, Atlanta Constitution, July 30, 1932.
31. Atlanta Constitution, August 12, 1932.
32. Atlanta Constitution, September 7, 1932.
33. Elberton speech, Atlanta Constitution, August 28, 1932; Nahunta speech, Atlanta   Constitution, September 6, 1932.
34. Atlanta Constitution, September 9, 1932.
35. Atlanta Constitution, August 20, 1932.
36. Atlanta Constitution, July 15, 1932.
37. Blairsville speech, Atlanta Constitution, July 16, 1932; Statesboro speech, Macon Telegraph and

News, July 10, 1932.
   38. Atlanta Constitution, July 19, 1932.
   39. Statesboro speech, Macon Telegraph and News,
July 10, 1932.
   40. Atlanta Constitution, July 16, 1932.
   41. Lyons speech, Atlanta Constitution, July 27,
1932.
   42. Atlanta Constitution, July 28, 1932.
   43. William Anderson, The Wild Man from Sugar
Creek: The Political Career of Eugene Talmadge (Baton
Rouge: Louisiana State University Press, 1975), pp.
116-117.
   44. Leesburgh speech, Atlanta Constitution, July
31, 1932; Dawsonville speech, Atlanta Constitution,
August 3, 1932; Winder speech, Atlanta Constitution,
August 5, 1932.
   45. McRae speech, Atlanta Constitution, July 5,
1932.
   46. Franklin speech, Atlanta Constitution, July 17,
1932.
   47. Nahunta speech, Atlanta Constitution, September
6, 1932; Madison speech, Atlanta Constitution,
September 13, 1932.
   48. Douglas speech, Atlanta Constitution, July 29,
1932.
   49. Atlanta Constitution, July 30, 1932.
   50. Atlanta Constitution, July 5, 1932.
   51. Atlanta Constitution, July 15, 1932.
   52. Editorial in Macon Telegraph and News, July 16,
1932.
   53. Tindall, Emergence of the New South, pp.
373-374.
   54. Atlanta Constitution, July 21, 1932.
   55. Atlanta Constitution, July 17, 1932.
   56. LaGrange speech, Atlanta Constitution, July 17,
1932; Talbotton speech, Atlanta Constitution, July
15, 1932; Fort Valley speech, Atlanta Constitution,
July 19, 1932.
   57. Atlanta speech, September 9, 1932.
   58. Quoted in Atlanta Constitution, August 10 and
11, 1932.
   59. Atlanta Constitution, August 12, 1932; emphasis
added.
   60. Atlanta Constitution, July 23, 1932.
   61. Atlanta Constitution, July 26, 1932.
   62. Atlanta Constitution, August 9, 1932.
   63. Swainsboro speech, Atlanta Constitution, July
23, 1932.
   64. Atlanta Constitution, July 23, 1932.
   65. Atlanta Constitution, July 22, 1932.
   66. Atlanta Constitution, July 21, 1932.
   67. McRae speech, Atlanta Constitution, July 5,
1932.

68. Talbotton speech, _Atlanta Constitution_, July 15, 1932.

69. _Atlanta Constitution_, August 7, 1932.

70. Dallas, Georgia speech, _Atlanta Constitution_, August 10, 1932.

71. Thomson speech, _Atlanta Constitution_, July 22, 1932; Fort Valley speech, _Atlanta Constitution_, July 19, 1932.

72. LaGrange speech, _Atlanta Constitution_, July 17, 1932.

73. Thomson speech, _Atlanta Constitution_, July 22, 1932.

74. Cairo speech, _Atlanta Constitution_, July 13, 1932.

75. Crawfordville speech, _Atlanta Constitution_, September 8, 1932.

76. Macon speech, _Macon Telegraph and News_, August 28, 1932.

77. Talbotton speech, _Atlanta Constitution_, July 15, 1932.

78. _Marietta Journal_, July 21, 1932.

79. _Atlanta Constitution_, July 21, 1932.

80. Washington, Georgia speech, _Atlanta Constitution_, July 21, 1932; Tocca speech, _Atlanta Constitution_, August 5, 1932.

81. Sandersville speech, _Atlanta Constitution_, July 23, 1932.

82. Blairsville speech, _Atlanta Constitution_, July 16, 1932; Waycross speech, _Atlanta Constitution_, July 29, 1932.

83. _Atlanta Constitution_, July 30, 1932.

84. _Atlanta Constitution_, July 13, 1932.

85. Fort Valley speech, _Atlanta Constitution_, July 19, 1932.

86. Washington, Georgia, speech, _Atlanta Constitution_, July 21, 1932.

87. Blairsville speech, _Atlanta Constitution_, July 16, 1932; Fort Valley speech, _Atlanta Constitution_, July 19, 1932.

88. Lakeland speech, _Atlanta Constitution_, July 30, 1932; Leesburg speech, _Atlanta Constitution_, July 31, 1932.

89. Carrollton speech, _Atlanta Constitution_, August 11, 1932.

90. Griffin speech, _Atlanta Constitution_, July 20, 1932, and _Marietta Journal_, July 21, 1932.

91. Thomasville speech, _Atlanta Constitution_, August 13, 1932.

92. Sparta speech, _Atlanta Constitution_, July 22, 1932; Clarkesville speech, _Atlanta Constitution_, August 6, 1932.

93. Washington, Georgia speech, _Atlanta, Constitution_, July 21, 1932.

94. <u>Dalton</u> <u>Citizen</u>, September 15, 1932.

95. <u>Georgia's</u> <u>Official</u> <u>Register</u>, 1933-1935-1937, pp. 542-545.

96. <u>Atlanta</u> <u>Constitution</u>, September 16, 1932.

97. <u>Dalton</u> <u>Citizen</u>, August 4, 1932.

98. <u>Savannah</u> <u>Evening</u> <u>Press</u>, September 10, 1932.

99. Royston speech, <u>Atlanta</u> <u>Constitution</u>, August 21, 1932; see editorial, <u>Macon</u> <u>Telegraph</u>, August 21, 1932.

100. V. O. Key, Jr., <u>Southern</u> <u>Politics</u> <u>in</u> <u>State</u> <u>and</u> <u>Nation</u> (New York: Vintage Books, 1949), pp. 106-108; Numan V. Bartley, <u>Creation</u> <u>of</u> <u>Modern</u> <u>Georgia</u> (Athens: Univer of Georgia Press, 1983), pp. 175-176, 179.

101. Mary Glass Crooks, "Platform Pledges of Governor Eugene Talmadge and Resulting Statutes," M.A. thesis, Univer of Georgia, 1953, p. 59.

102. Bainbridge speech, <u>Atlanta</u> <u>Constitution</u>, July 5, 1934.

103. Thomaston speech, <u>Atlanta</u> <u>Constitution</u>, September 6, 1934.

104. Warm Springs speech, <u>Atlanta</u> <u>Constitution</u>, July 5, 1934.

105. Douglasville speech, <u>Atlanta</u> <u>Constitution</u>, August 22, 1934.

106. <u>Atlanta</u> <u>Constitution</u>, July 5, 1934.

107. On the occasion of Talmadge's Macon speech, <u>Atlanta</u> <u>Constitution</u>, September 4, 1934.

108. <u>Atlanta</u> <u>Constitution</u>, September 12, 1934.

109. <u>Atlanta</u> <u>Constitution</u>, August 31, 1934.

110. <u>Atlanta</u> <u>Constitution</u>, July 13, 1934.

111. <u>Atlanta</u> <u>Constitution</u>, July 5, 1934.

112. Bainbridge speech, <u>Atlanta</u> <u>Constitution</u>, July 5, 1934.

113. A North Georgia speech, <u>Atlanta</u> <u>Constitution</u>, August 5, 1934.

114. <u>Atlanta</u> <u>Constitution</u>, September 6, 1934.

115. <u>Georgia's</u> <u>Official</u> <u>Register</u>, 1933-1935-1937, pp. 542-545.

116. <u>Atlanta</u> <u>Constitution</u>, September 9, 1934.

6

Talmadgeism Sidetracked

In 1936, Georgians waited anxiously for Gene Talmadge to announce which public office he would seek. Having won elections for Commissioner of Agriculture in 1926, 1928, and 1930, and campaigns for Governor in 1932 and 1934, Talmadge appeared to be undefeatable, regardless of the public office he sought. Talmadge began campaigning for office in April of 1935. That month he toured the South and beyond, speaking in Oklahoma and Texas, a trip observers interpreted to demonstrate the governor's "excursion into national politics."(1) Realizing the interest he created by delaying announcement of his political future, Talmadge flirted with several interests. He expressed "ambition" to be Secretary of Agriculture of the United States, an office he felt would be a natural extension of his experience as Commissioner of Agriculture.(2) When interviewed in New York City about a higher position in government, Talmadge replied that, "Any man who wouldn't run for president if he thought he could be elected is a damn fool."(3) Some persons expected him to run for Governor. Although state law disallowed him to campaign for re-election, he had talked of having that statute changed.

A reporter noted that observers listened with "unusual interest" to Talmadge's July 4, 1935, speech in Canton, Georgia to determine how the crowd reacted to "his attacks on the New Deal" and to note hints to his political plans. In his speech to the "Grass Roots" Convention in Macon on January 29, 1936, he charged that the "federal government is working consistently to tear down states' rights." Northern industrialists and wealthy southerners funded the convention, an arrangement that incumbent Senator

Richard B. Russell, Jr., exploited for re-election. Talmadge insisted that President Roosevelt "had enacted laws" telling "manufacturers, store keepers, hotels and shops what to pay their labor." Talmadge boasted that as governor he did not allow the New-Deal to cram bills "through the legislature, providing for thousands of federal jobs in the state of Georgia at the expense of the state."(4) The "Grass Roots" Convention to which Talmadge spoke was attended by representatives from many states to oppose Franklin D. Roosevelt's New-Deal policies. By July 1, 1936, people "on every street corner and in every hotel lobby" in Georgia were predicting which office Talmadge would seek.(5)

Wearing shirt sleeves, tie, and the famous red suspenders he displayed as a badge of political independence and means of identifying with farmers, in a speech over WSB radio at McRae on July 4, 1936, Talmadge announced he would oppose incumbent Richard B. Russell, Jr., for the United States Senate. He also supported Charles Redwine for Governor against E. D. Rivers. In the General Assembly, Rivers opposed Talmadge and worked to bring New-Deal programs to Georgia. In this speech, Talmadge reviewed his record as Commissioner of Agriculture and as Governor, claiming that cutting the number of inspectors and improving the "fertilizer laws" had been more difficult than he anticipated, and impossible during his first term as Commissioner. He boasted that "we finally got it across." He faced impeachment charges for "raising the price of hogs," but once again the people, he argued, rescued him from evil hands. Talmadge said that he was able to keep his office only because "the people . . . rallied to" his cause.(6) In her study, Sarah McCulloch Lemmon concluded that as Commissioner of Agriculture, Talmadge improved laws governing inspection of oil and fertilizers, decreased the number of inspectors, provided more efficient service to farmers, and inspected more fertilizer, drugs, and food. She also found that Talmadge "tended to seize upon panaceas, such as the protective tariff or the cotton holiday plan, and waste his leadership . . . on these impractical or even harmful ideas."(7)

After serving as Commissioner of Agriculture, Talmadge proclaimed at McRae that the farmers "called on" him to "get a little bigger job," that of Governor, where the critics and public officials and policies could "not law" him. As governor, after the "legislature went home," by skirting legal channels, he fired the Public Service Commission and proudly "put in five men" of his own. They cut the freight and utilities rates as he directed. While the

legislature was not in session, he reduced the cost
of automobile tags to three dollars, he reminded,
resulting in an increase in motor vehicles on the
road and in gasoline taxes collected. In addition,
he argued at McRae, the state owed "not a dime" in
debt. Now he asked Georgians to elect him to the
United States Senate.

    Voters, he insisted at Columbus, Georgia, should
elect a candidate with courage to "speak out."(8)
Only he would fight the battles of the people.   He
pledged to extend the purposeful political turbulence
beyond the boundaries of Georgia. "If they won't
listen to me," I will "rock this old country."(9)
Upon hearing that Talmadge pledged to disturb the
entire country, incumbent United States Senator
Richard B. Russell, Jr., laughed, perhaps a little
nervously, with his Marietta audience: "That's a
mighty big job for a little man like Gene."(10)

    In the McRae speech Talmadge promised that, as
Senator he would cut the national budget, and amend
the Constitution so that the federal government could
not carry debt "beyond the fiscal or calendar year,
except in time of war." Federal funds would be
distributed to the states "according to the population." Government would not compete with private
industry. Sponsorship of tax-exempt government bonds
would be stopped, unless adopted by the states.
Under his leadership, only the Congress would levy
taxes, not any "board or bureau."   In a promise he
said was "sort of" like the three-dollar tag, the
postage stamp would be cut "from 3 cents back to 2
cents." To defeat incumbent Russell, Talmadge
searched for an issue he could exploit in the manner
that he attacked "King J. J. Brown" and a corrupt
Department of Agriculture in 1926. He decided to
assault Franklin D. Roosevelt and Russell as virtual
co-authors of expensive and wasteful New-Deal programs. W. T. Anderson, editor of the Macon Telegraph, supported Talmadge in 1926, opposed him during
the Macon farm meeting in 1931, and reboarded his
campaign wagon in 1936. Revealing more about his own
fickle political commitments than the Senator's
character, Anderson called Russell a "cheap politician" who had not worked for "a dime by the sweat of
his brow."(11)

    In Monroe Talmadge ridiculed Russell personally,
calling him "Junior."(12) Russell, son of a prominent chief justice of the Georgia Supreme Court,
answered by playing to southerners' loyalty to
family: "I never knew it was wrong for a boy to be
named for his daddy."(13)   A member of the audience
at Jasper yelled to speaker Russell, "You got a good
daddy and you're all right."(14)   Talmadge chided

Russell's "war record" as being limited to service in a military camp in Athens.(15) Russell replied that he served as "they told me."(16) He asked pointedly, "Where was Gene in the war?," a question the Governor failed to answer.(17) During the national Democratic convention in Philadelpia, Talmadge insisted that Russell "ran out under fire" because he was "afraid to speak," pretending that his brother was "seriously hurt" in a car wreck.(18) Unruffled by Talmadge's public abuse, Russell answered calmly that "family ties" were important, and that he went to his brother's bed and found him to be "a mighty sick man." He returned to the convention to find Talmadge missing.(19)

Talmadge argued at Cartersville that, because of an "inferiority complex," Russell surrendered to Roosevelt's policies at the expense of Georgia farmers. He "robbed" workers without "regard" for the "poor."(20) Talmadge forecast at LaGrange that Georgians would choose between a "rubber stamp" for New-Deal extravagence and a fighter for their interests.(21) Talmadge contended that Russell as governor, when negotiating a contract for children's school texts, "sold out to [a] book trust."(22)

Talmadge also castigated President Roosevelt. He ridiculed Roosevelt's physical handicap as a cause of wasteful government spending. As early as April 1935, Talmadge claimed that the nation faced a great "calamity" because a president governed who "can't walk around and hunt up people to talk to." Thus Roosevelt was advised only by the "gimme crowd." Attempting to identify with interests of workers, Talmadge assured rural audiences that the "next president" would be someone who was well enough to "work in the sun 14 hours a day," a person able to walk "a two by four plank."(23) Because of Talmadge's mean treatment of Roosevelt, one can understand why Gunnar Myrdal called Talmadge "one of the most vicious demagogues of the South."(24) Reassuring the nation that Georgia would not "secede" this time, Talmadge predicted that Roosevelt would be "defeated" by Republicans or a third Party, for the "real American people" wanted "less interference with business" and an end to "this crazy orgy of spending."(25) Talmadge warned that if "radical" Roosevelt won re-election, a "national calamity" would occur.(26) As a remedy to New Deal abuses southerners would "revive Jeffersonian doctrines."(27)

Talmadge's ridicule of Roosevelt lost him votes. Dewey Grantham noted that southerners liked President Roosevelt because he understood the "agrarian traditions" of their region, espoused "Jeffersonian

principles," exhuded "personal   charm," and   "identified" with the South.(28)   Roosevelt was a   part-time
Georgian, a   person with   whom the   citizens of   that
state were   familiar   and proud.   Roosevelt   visited
Warm Springs, Georgia, for treatment after his   polio
attack, establishing the   Warm Springs Foundation   in
1926 and building a cottage there in 1932.

George Tindall   explained   how   the   president's
"cordial   relationships   with   Southerners   proved
indispensable on Capitol Hill" because, by 1933, nine
of fourteen   major Senate   committees and   twelve   of
seventeen   in the House of Representatives were headed
by persons from the South.   Tindall wrote that in the
crisis atmosphere   of the   Hundred Days,   legislation
passed with little influence of congressional leadership.   Eventually,   however,   "Roosevelt's   New   Deal
would shake the social   and economic power   structure
of the"   South, generating   considerable   opposition.
Southern whites supported the "New Deal of stabiliza-
tion and recovery"   but not the   "second New Deal   of
reform and social democracy."(29)   Indeed eventually,
believing that some New-Deal programs threatened   the
segregation   of   blacks   and   whites   in   the   South,
Russell weighed each   proposed federal program   carefully to determine whether to advocate or oppose it.

Talmadge disliked   the Roosevelt   Administration
because officials   managing federal   agencies   denied
him the autonomous authority to spend New-Deal   funds
he desired   after   being elected   Governor   in   1932.
Michael   Holmes   described   how   New-Deal   officials
attempted to   thwart Governor Talmadge's efforts   to
take over the management and distribution of   federal
funds in Georgia.   The   Federal Emergency Relief   Act
was passed   in 1933,   the second   year of   Talmadge's
tenure as governor,   and was managed   by the   Federal
Emergency   Relief   Administration   (FERA).   Harry
Hopkins directed the FERA.   Georgia would apply for a
grant, with   the   federal   government   providing   one
dollar and the state matching it with three.   Hopkins
approved   requests   for   grants.   In   Georgia,   Gay
Shepperson, an experienced and competent administrator, managed the   distribution of   FERA grants.   She
was appointed by Hopkins but with Talmadge's   approval.   Talmadge   opposed her   because she   was   honest,
politically nonpartisan, a woman, and not subject   to
intimidation by the governor.   Talmadge insisted upon
signing all checks   for relief going   to counties   in
Georgia.

Because   the   county   unit   system   of   electing
persons to public office gave small courthouse   gangs
great   influence,   Talmadge   wanted   to   control   and
distribute   federal   funds   to   serve   his   political
interest.   At   one point   he refused   to sign   salary

checks for some persons, attempting to exercise his
dominance over the administration of a federal
program in the same manner that he, as Commissioner
of Agriculture, tried to intimidate delegates attending the farm meeting in Macon and, as Governor,
over-powered state officials. Flexing his own
authority, Hopkins ousted the Georgia Relief Administration, took control of the GERA, and placed
Shepperson in charge of distributing funds to the
counties. In a curiously creative means of retalia-
tion, the persistently obstinate Talmadge threatened
to "refuse all federal money."

Talmadge also experienced conflict with the
Public Works Administration (PWA), headed by Harold
L. Ickes, Secretary of the Interior. The PWA administered federal funds to states for major construc-
tion projects, paying thirty percent of labor and
cost of materials. The PWA pay scale was $1 per hour
for skilled labor and fourty cents per hour for un-
skilled labor. Talmadge complained on the stump that
these wages were payed regardless of race. Talmadge
placed restrictions on Georgia's ability to borrow
funds, but did receive funds in 1933-1934. At one
point Secretary Ickes purged state offices and
withheld federal money from road programs. Talmadge
ageed to increase the efficiency by which the funds
were administered by reorganizing the staff. Ickes
released the federal funds, and 225 highway and
bridge projects in 122 counties were completed in
Georgia.(30)

When he found that he could not bully federal
officials, Talmadge denounced members of Roosevelt's
administration. He called Roosevelt's associates
"brain trusters" for creating New-Deal waste,(31)
"relievers" for adopting lavish relief plans for
citizens, and "destroyers" for "burning cotton" for
farmers.(32) He directed a "withering fire" upon
Henry A. Wallace, Secretary of Agriculture, and
Harold L. Ickes.(33) Talmadge would "make" Wallace
"ashamed of himself" and demand that he "put your
money down here."(34) That Henry Wallace was speaking in Georgia on Thomas Jefferson's birthday,
Talmadge admonished, was a "mockery."(35)

Continuing to drive a wedge between the working
and entrepreneurial classes, he contended that the
only "farmers" to attend Wallace's speech were "those
that have offices in big buildings."(36) Snubbing
New-Deal programs for agriculture, Governor Talmadge
did not attend Wallace's Atlanta speech, boasting
that he was going "to Telfair county" to earn "a
living out of the farm."(37) He made a "vitriolic
attack" upon Harry L. Hopkins, insisting that he
"resign" as administrator of relief. Hopkins had

denied a federal grant requested by Talmadge. In "bitter tones," Talmadge called Hopkins a "publicity seeker," insisting that he "go back to being a charity broker" and stop "dishing out" money that belonged to "the people." In response, Hopkins tagged the governor a "yapper."(38) Talmadge made "biting comments" about Frances Perkins, Secretary of Labor, for apparently referring to the "shoeless people of the south."(39)

Because of his personal antagonism with federal officials, he was willing to stop New-Deal programs from helping poorly clothed, housed, and fed Georgians. If elected to the Senate, Talmadge promised to oppose Roosevelt's policies. Declaring his political independence from the Roosevelt Administration, Talmadge indicated that he "don't look down on" any person, and he "don't look up" to any individual. He would "follow" Roosevelt when "he's right" and "fight him" when "I think he's wrong."(40) Proud that he claimed to have intimidated a President, Talmadge bragged that Roosevelt "did what I told him to do." In a speech in Macon on a "national hook-up," he had demanded that Roosevelt "repeal" the Bankhead Bill and the Agricultural Adjustment Act.(41)

In 1936, Richard B. Russell, Jr., campaigned aggressively for re-election to the United States Senate. He had been a popular and effective governor, credited with reorganizing state government and creating a Board of Regents to administer higher education in Georgia less within the reach of political interference. One familiar with the professorial style of leadership practiced by Russell during the latter years of his service in the Senate would suspect him to have carried that stately rhetorical bearing into the 1936 campaign. In running for re-election, Russell could have stayed above the fray, dodging Talmadge's barbs as J. J. Brown had done in June and July of 1926, assuming a statesman-like posture appropriate for a United States Senator. The astute Russell refused to stand still for Talmadge's abuse.

Russell was no J. J. Brown. He was a wise political strategist and skilled public speaker. Whereas Talmadge was reckless and unpredictable, Russell was judicious and guarded. A reporter mentioned how Russell spoke "slowly . . . deliberating before every phrase."(42) Aroused by Talmadge's charges, the Senator proved to be fearless and extremely effective under pressure of a volatile campaign. Rather than stand aloof, Russell carried the fight to Talmadge, launching a "strenous speaking campaign" of his own.(43) A reporter noted at

Kingsland that the "fiery young junior senator bore
in on his opponent" and his "record" with "telling
blows."(44) In a Fitzgerald speech, Russell "tore
into the Governor with fists flying."(45) Speaking
over WSB radio in Atlanta, Russell issued a "devastating fire" on Governor Talmadge and "his platform."(46) Russell recommended to an Adel crowd that
this time the voters "leave" Talmadge "at home" to
learn "how poor folks feel."(47)

Russell was well received throughout the campaign. Large crowds came to his rallies. On August
14, reportedly the "greatest crowd ever gathered" at
a political meeting in Georgia heard Russell speak in
Tom Watson's hometown of Thomson.(48) Fifteen to
twenty thousand attended his speech in Commerce.(49)
In Clarkesville, an audience of "mostly farmers . . .
listened intently, nodding acquiescent heads." At
the end of Russell's speech, there came a "great
roar" and people "crowded about for an hour, hugging
him and shaking his hands."(50)

Talmadge's recurring strategy of creating a
rhetorical turbulence to suffocate opponents functioned most effectively when either he was in a
highly dominant position of authority, as when he was
governor, or the opposition was defenseless prey, as
was "King J. J." Brown in 1926. In challenging
incumbent Russell, Talmadge enjoyed neither of those
advantages. He was left to defend his candidacy on
far more even terms than in former elections. In
aiming at Russell, he misjudged his quarry. The 1936
campaign was a battle between two well conditioned
and fearless political gladiators. Talmadge had met
his match and on more neutral political grounds.
Talmadge was unable to stampede the press and the
voters into a frenzy of opposition against the
incumbent as he had done in 1926.

Russell attacked Talmadge's candidacy effectively as no opponent had done. Because of the injudi-
cious manner in which Talmadge talked in public and
the unruly, and seemingly illegal, way he behaved as
governor, he was vulnerable to criticism rendered
competently. Between 1926 and 1936, Talmadge was
able to market his tumultuous candidacy as a political novelty, representing himself as a man of the
soil, one courageous and independent enough to help
farmers. Because of the great popularity he enjoyed,
Talmadge's self-made image of political warrior for
the common people remained largely untarnished. In
his own bullish way, at times bypassing the state
legislature, he had cut the cost of automobile tags,
freight rates, and utility rates, and diverted
highway funds to other needs, policies many working
people seemingly supported.

Russell scathed Talmadge's credibility, preventing the "wild" man from achieving the initial rhetorical advantage upon which his turbulent persuasive
strategy depended.   Russell   disrobed   the   south
Georgia Robinhood to expose an evil and dangerous
politician. He argued that Talmadgeism was a "campaign of destruction"(51) run on "downright falsehoods"(52) and "appeals to prejudice."(53)   Russell
said he battled "deception, deceit and rule by
bayonet." On September 9, the Senator predicted in
Trion that he would liberate Georgians from a "ruthless and unscrupulous political machine."(54)   At
Griffin Russell insisted that Talmadge "arrested"
officials "without trial" and "held them without
bond."(55) On some issues, such as liquor, the
Senator continued, Talmadge "let the people decide."
On other subjects, such as the old age pension,
Talmadge claimed to be "greater than the state."
Following the example of Italy, contended Russell at
Swainsboro, Talmadge would not allow citizens to
vote.(56)

Russell reprehended Talmadge for his public
behavior, charging that there was no limit to what
Talmadge would do to dominate Georgians. Following
are criticisms Russell made of Talmadge at Douglas,
Columbus, Hinesville, Royston, and Dublin.   Talmadge
used state employees to "scatter" 1,000,000 copies of
his "political paper The Statesman" throughout the
state to "mislead the people" on New-Deal programs.(57) To win the 1936 race, Governor Talmadge
mobilized employees in the Highway Department, Fish
and Game Department, and other government agencies.
"Certain persons" were trying to "coerce" employees
to vote for Talmadge. Those bullies, insisted
Russell, "can't buy the votes of Georgia."(58)
Threatening a leverage that Talmadge's former opponents largely avoided, Russell would "give some of
those boys" several years in jail for "buying
votes."(59) Based upon the way he made other decisions, Russell warned, if Talmadge could manage it,
he would simply "declare himself United States
Senator."(60) Russell reminded voters that a senator
could not intimidate the United States Senate.   "You
don't get legislation" by "making faces," scaring
Congress, and "cursing the President," warned Russell. Huey Long had tried it and failed.(61)

In and out of office, by his pronouncements and
personal actions Talmadge established an atmosphere
of militancy and conflict that encouraged supporters
to take the law into their own hands. Near the close
of the race against Russell, five of Talmadge's
bodyguards were placed in the Whitefield County jail
on charges of assault and battery for allegedly

beating and kicking persons who booed the governor "loudly."(62) Talmadge fell into a pattern of relying upon soldiers for protection. In a state-wide rally at Canton on July 4, 1935, opening the 1936 Presidential preference campaign and dedicating a bridge over the Etowah river, a reporter noted that 50,000 "national guard police" would be used to control the crowd.(63) Russell rebuked Talmadge for using the National Guard to support his interests, building an image of the Governor as a militant dictator. Talmadge was a "petty tyrant" who governed by "domination and intimidation."(64)

Russell contended that Governor Talmadge employed the "bayonet" to enforce firings of "officers elected by the people." He used "his army" as a means by which to "herd" crowds, behaving as if voters had given "him a deed" to Georgia.(65) Talmadge "called out the army to get two old men out of the highway department," Russell ridiculed, when one "lady stenographer" could have accomplished the task. "More money" was wasted stopping a "no[n]-insurrection" in one year than had been been spent by all former governors on social unrest.(66) Russell compared Talmadge to a "French King" who favored "bayonets and machine guns" over "the ballot."(67)

Others criticized Talmadge. Labor in particular was opposed to Talmadge's use of force to control strikers. The Brotherhood of Railroad Trainmen complained that Talmadge enforced his "personal will at the point of bayonets."(68) Labor unions in the South had experienced "feeble growth" prior to the 1930s.(69) While Talmadge was governor, however, in 1934, the United Textile Workers sponsored a strike in which three-fourths of Georgia's textile workers walked off the job. Talmadge ended the strike by sending four thousand National Guardsmen throughout the state, arresting participants and imprisoning persons in a barbed-wire internment camp near Atlanta.(70) He had other confrontations with labor.

Placed on the defensive by mounting charges that he opposed labor, when asked in Rome, Georgia, "about the troops," Talmadge responded: "I hated to send troops to Rome for that foundry strike." He did so to protect "property and lives."(71) In an unsuccessful effort to win back the support of labor, Talmadge emphasized workers' "right to strike."(72) He promised to provide more jobs for Americans through high tariffs.(73) Russell, on the other hand, told a Columbus audience that he backed the national Democratic platform on labor, and pledged to assist the "average" worker.(74) Because labor deemed Russell's policy to be "fair and just," it

Talmadge braves the hot Georgia sun during a campaign
rally. (Photograph from Herman E. Talmadge   Collection, Richard B. Russell Memorial Library, University
of Georgia Libraries, Athens, Georgia. Reprinted by
permission.)

supported his re-election in 1936.(75)   Russell   told
voters that if elected to the Senate, Talmadge would
be an official "without an army."(76) The "voters"
would not allow Talmadge to take his "state militia
to Washington."(77)
    Other observers criticized Talmadge's coercive
methods. Ernest Camp, editor of the <u>Walton</u>   <u>Tribune</u>,
expressed "outrage" at the presence of the National
Guard, concluding Talmadge "knew" he "would   be
treated civilly" in Monroe.   Upon hearing   that
opponents would throw eggs at him during a rally   in
Monroe, Talmadge had National Guardsmen rope off   an
area in front of the courthouse where he would speak.
A "special squadron" stood guard while he opposed
Russell and the New-Deal. Camp predicted accurately
that in this 1936 election the county would "give
Talmadge   thunder"   at   the   polls.(78)   In   Walton

County, Russell received 1,980 votes (and all four unit votes), and Talmadge 953. In gubernatorial races in 1932 and 1934, in Walton County, Talmadge won both in popular and unit votes. A veteran of the Confederacy assured persons at Dalton in 1936 that "bayonets" did not "intimidate us" in the 1860s either.(79) The Atlanta Constitution, long-time supporter of Talmadge, shifting its loyalty, charged that Governor Talmadge's legislative floor leaders had been told to block any appropriations bill so he could "run the state."(80)

Russell effectively contrasted his constructive approach to government with Talmadge's disruptive behavior, employing humor as a powerful instrument of persuasion. To compete for attention in political rallies in Georgia, one had to entertain audiences. Russell had an ear for phrasing issues in a way that enhanced his image. Ridiculing Talmadge's dependence upon armed guards, Russell said: "If he's afraid, I'll send some of my friends with him so he won't be afraid of the people of Georgia."(81) At his rallies, Russell contrasted "Gene's soldiers" with his own "body guard," consisting of the "Winder Girls' Drum and Trumpet Corps."(82) During "a New Deal appreciation barbecue" at Fort Valley, the girls' corps entertained Russell's audience metaphorically with "Who's Afraid of the Big Bad Wolf." While Russell was speaking in Milledgeville, the girls' corps stood guard, and a citizen walked in with "dummy rifles, escorting a man made up to resemble" Talmadge.(83)

Russell condemned Talmadge's penchant for unilaterial hog-dealings carried on beyond the limits of the law at the public's expense. The governor had padded pockets with "reckless waste of public money in wild goose chase schemes to 'stabilize hog' markets." Russell told a Macon audience that Talmadge practiced "nepotism" by adding $50 to his "son's salary."(84) Talmadge was subject to political seduction, continued Russell, as indicated by his acceptance of $4,000 for addressing a grassroots convention at Macon that was openly hostile to the Demoratic party.(85)

As the race heated up, Russell ridiculed the "ballyhoo" by which Talmadge tried to deceive audiences.(86) He noted how the Governor relied upon "stooges" to prompt him from the audience.(87) He transported a "large gentleman" from town to town, explained Russell, to carry him from the platform after each speech, making it appear to the crowd and to the press that his speech was well received.(88) Supporters who refused to speak out for Talmadge at his rallies were severely rebuked. In contrast,

Russell assured voters at Omega that no person in his
camp would "lose his job" by not making "noise" at
rallies.(89) The anti-Roosevelt meeting in Macon
where Gene was paid to speak, Russell ridiculed, was
nothing but a "nut grass roots convention."(90)
Russell claimed that his frontal attacks upon
Talmadge had given the governor "a bad case of the
jitters."(91) Talmadge had "lost his temper" and
become "desperate."(92) Talmadge jumped "from plank
to plank" as his McRae platform failed him.(93) Even
his supporters wore a "dazed look."(94)

Russell charged that Talmadge acted cowardly
when he refused to answer the questions the Senator
fastened to the speaker's platform in Griffin immediately before the governor spoke. The Telfair candidate would be "buried" at the polls, predicted
Russell, "under an avalanche of resentment."(95)
Talmadge's "balloon" was "punctured" and falling in
"Sugar Creek."(96) Russell even attacked backers of
his opponent. W. T. Anderson was the editor of a
"cesspool" and the "high priest of the house of
Talmadge." After Russell's speech, 15,000 persons
"marched" on Anderson's Macon Telegraph and News
office, "shouting, clapping and tramping their feet,"
with cowbells "pealing" and a band playing "Hail,
Hail the Gang's All Here."(97)

Russell challenged Talmadge's traditional base
of political support, arguing that the governor
represented the wealthy rather than the working
class. The senator indicated that Talmadge founded a
public career "on the good faith" of working men and
women, but he "strayed off."(98) He "moved up town."
Talmadge wanted to protect wealthy Republicans from
paying taxes. In many of his speeches, Russell
accused Talmadge of being the favorite of John J.
Raskob, Renee du Pont, and Alf Landon.(99) Russell
told a Richland audience that the "mantel of Thomas
E. Watson would fall around Gene Talmadge like a
circus tent around a flea."(100) He "betrayed" the
farmers.(101) The farmers were "not leaving
Talmadge"; he was "leaving them." Russell tormented
Talmadge for creating a platform for this 1936
campaign that failed to even mention the farmer.(102)

Russell maintained that Talmadge could no longer
"hear the feeble voice" of the elderly, the cry of
children "for education," and the request of "farm
wives" for electrically powered ice boxes and
lights.(103) Russell complained to a Milledgeville
crowd that Talmadge was quick to decrease the pay of
state workers without reducing his "own pay one
cent."(104) As governor, Russell had cut his own
salary, but Talmadge, while in public office, had
accumulated farm lands and fish ponds. Russell asked

Fort Valley listeners why he wanted to "keep other" farmers "from   getting   something."(105)   Russell criticized Talmadge for asking poor farmers for donations to support his candidacy.(106)   Actually both candidates received donations, often in public as part of the ritual of a speaking rally in the form of bales of cotton to be auctioned.(107)

On occasions Russell equalled Talmadge's poetic stump narratives when verbalizing the hardships of workers. For Marietta listeners he contrasted the miserable life of citizens attempting to recover from an economic depression with the new conditions brought about by New-Deal programs. "Four years ago . . . conditions were different. . . . No farm house had a coat of paint, there were no repairs. We saw the women and children of this state working in the sun picking cotton and yet they were not able to get enough for it to buy clothes to wear. . . . A few men had collected into their hands most of the wealth . . . and the people decided to have a change.   That election in 1932 was a revolution," but, unlike Talmadegism, "a peaceful revolution." Russell said that Georgians could decide if cotton selling in 1936 at twelve cents a pound was preferable to the five cents received before. The Congress and the presi- dent had "broken" the "back of the depression," and Russell was "proud" of his "part in it."(108)

In speeches at Trion, Richland, Wrightsville, Marietta, Royston, Macon, and Fitzgerald, Russell portrayed the governor as a "traitor" to Demo- crats.(109)   After winning office on Roosevelt's "coat-tail," chided Russell, Talmadge decided that the "New Deal" was "communistic."(110)   When, as governor, he could not control federal relief money going to Georgia, Talmadge "began to hate the admin- istration."(111) Inspiring a large crowd of farmers to "a roar," Russell warned that Talmadge would "scuttle" the Democratic party "from within."(112) The "stamp of republicanism" was upon his "back with those red suspenders."(113)   "The waters of Sugar Creek," ridiculed Russell, would be "polluted" when the Republican "stain" was washed from his candidacy. Talmadge attempted to "blindfold" Georgians into Alf Landon's camp.(114)   The Republicans supporting Talmadge brought Georgians "breaking banks," "bread- lines, and four cent cotton."(115)

In speeches at Dublin, Dalton, Richland, Eatonton, and Hinesville, Russell contrasted his loyalty to the Democratic party with Talmadge's political traitorousness. The voters elected Russell "a Democrat" and he "remained one; they elected Talmadge a Democrat and he "got city ways and wan- dered off" into the "arms of the Republicans."(116)

When Russell mentioned that Talmadge spoke in Spring-
field, Illinois, at the tomb of Lincoln, the Dalton
audience "waxed vociferous and militant."(117) "I am
willing to admit Lincoln was a great man," argued
Russell, "but as long as there is a Confederate left
I will not say as a democrat" that he was the "greatest man that ever lived."(118) When Russell repeated
at Eatonton that the governor had prayed on the
occasion of Lincoln's birthday, A. J. Wommack,
elderly Confederate veteran, "grew grim and shook his
head sorrowfully" and, while the audience looked on,
glanced "at the stone stature of the young Confederate soldier" near   the   speaker's   platform.(119)
Speaking from a stand in a large pinetree, Russell
told a Hinesville audience that one can't "pretend"
loyalty to Democrats and, at the same time, "subma-
rine the party."(120)
     Talmadge was knocked off balance by Russell's
barage of criticism. Because Talmadge expounded
recklessly on the stump on so many different topics,
he found himself trying to clarify or refute those
controversial claims from an unfamiliar defensive
posture. Thus far in his career, after 1926, his
frontrunning status meant that he felt no need to be
accountable for his wild assertions. Often when
speaking, as in Austell, he "fitted" the content of
his message to the "shouted suggestions" from the
crowd, stengthening the bond with the audience but
providing himself less self-control of the content
and interpretations of assertions.(121)
     By entertaining and intimidating crowds into
submission, Talmadge planned to win approval without
having his conclusions critically examined. Many
audiences applauded more the extravagence of his
stump hyperbole than the substance of arguments. To
win a roar of approval from a crowd at Royston, he
criticized Roosevelt, Russell, and the New-Deal, and
said he had done "more for the common" person than
the entire United States Senate had achieved "for a
half century."(122)
     Because Russell clearly, forcefully, and repeat-
edly criticized Talmadge's extravagant statements,
increasing numbers of voters were not seduced by the
governor's generalizations. Citizens ate Talmadge's
barbecue and voted for Russell. Because of his
unbridled rhetoric, Talmadge was required to devote
considerable effort explaining and defending past
acts.(123) For example, he was forced to deny T. F.
Graham's accusation that he told a Rotary Club in
Macon that persons who "accepted farm benefits" from
the government were nothing but "shiftless" people.(124) Talmadge invested significant portions of
speeches answering criticism for saying that working

Georgians were not "worth more than $1 a day."   At
Austell he tried to refute accusations by contending
that, "I'm not long out of overalls myself."(125)
Talmadge assumed his authority to be so great and the
reach of his influence so far that no one could
require him to answer for claims, no matter how
extravagant and strident they became. He wanted to
be Governor, and now Senator, so that no one could
challenge his public acts and rhetorical edicts.   He
conducted himself as if his public pronouncements
were invincible and unalterable.

Responding to Russell's indictment that he had
abandoned the working man and woman, he reminded
auditors that he knew how it was "to labor in the sun
for 14 hours" without a profit.(126) When he asked a
LaGrange audience if he had broken any promises, many
cried "no, no."(127)   In speeches at Monroe and
Griffin, Talmadge defended his kinship with farmers
and laborers.   Rather than wealthy Republicans
funding his campaign, as Russell had argued, Talmadge
told voters that the "millionaries" were "fighting"
him.(128) It was not the "Raskobs and du Ponts" who
sponsored his campaign, but the "horny-handed sons of
toil" with their dimes, quarters, and half dollars.
Placing himself in high cotton, Talmadge said he wept
over the "widows' mites" given to him.(129) Talmadge
was forced to answer other charges. Russell made the
governor explain why he waited until the General
Assembly was not in session and then went outside
constitutional channels to reduce the cost of an
automobile tag to three dollars, lower utility rates,
replace the Public Service Commission, and change the
Highway Board membership by "executive order."

Demonstrating his belief in the political maxim
that ends justified means, Talmadge complained to a
Royston audience that Russell and other critics were
focusing merely upon "the way" he behaved rather than
what he achieved.(130)   There was no compromise in
his public justifications for demagogic behavior. If
Talmadge wanted something done, to him that was
rationale enough for doing it. To Talmadge, inflated
claims he made from behind the stump in a rollicking
campaign were equal in authority to decisions argued
in a courtroom and policies reached through deliberative discourse over time in a legislative assembly.
He stood behind claims he made extemporaneously
before hundreds of audiences no matter how cruel,
exaggerated, or devastating were the assertions.

When defending statements he made publicly or
acts done while in office, Talmadge often ignored the
substance of criticism and resorted to humorous
analogies to provoke uncritical and supportive
reaction. He excused his removal of "state officers"

elected by the people by comparing that method of
enforcing his will with the "calling" of pigs and
hogs "out of the garden." "I would like to have got
them out with a melodious voice," but they wouldn't
come.(131) Increasingly he devoted a significant
percentage of stump time answering Russell. In
Swainsboro, reacting to a charge that he employed
National Guardsmen to control citizens, he boasted
arrogantly that the only soldiers present at this
rally were those who would "vote for" him. Criticized for having employees of the Highway Department
build his speaking platform in Swainsboro,(132) he
assured a LaGrange audience that "the platform and
radio time" were contributed by supporters from Troup
County.(133) His private fish pond had cost $350,
and not the $10,000 claimed by Russell, and was built
by "hands" on his place.(134) Talmadge had to
respond to "whispers" circulating that the schools
would close if he were elected. He assured a
Cedartown audience that this rumor was "a sample of
the false reports" made about him.(135)

In response to Russell's charge that he abandoned the Democratic party, Talmadge maintained that
he was criticizing Roosevelt's expensive New-Deal
policies and Russell's blind support of them.
Talmadge stated that he had "always voted" for
Democratic candidates.(136) The Democratic party to
him, however, was "a badge" and not a "chain."(137)
There was "nothing Democratic" about the Administration in Washington. "Despite" what Russell said, the
"only real Democratic" policy was found in Talmadge's
McRae platform.(138) Unlike Russell, he would
"abolish" a government position rather than vote to
fill it with Roosevelt's Republican nominees.(139)
Russell had approved "three republicans" for the
Roosevelt administration, Wallace, Ickes, and
Perkins.(140)

In speeches at Carrollton, LaFayette, and
Savannah, Talmadge criticized Russell's support of
expensive programs, and defended his speech to
celebrate Lincoln's birthday. Russell "rubber
stamped" New-Deal policies no matter how expensive or
inefficient.(141) Russell betrayed his promise of
1932 to back a Democratic platform of "economy in
government," parroting Roosevelt's "orgy of spending."(142) Because Talmadge was a master at perform-
ing symbolic political acts that enhanced his reputation as a defender of southerners, one wonders what
motivated him to speak on the occasion of Lincoln's
birthday. Because Russell kept this ceremonial
speech before the voters, Talmadge was forced to
reply that he was "proud" to have been the "main
speaker" at the former President's tomb on that

occasion.(143)

Throughout the campaign, Talmadge and Russell maintained a running debate on several issues. They skirmished over benefits for veterans and laborers. The governor declared he was "for the soldiers."(144) Talmadge accused Russell of cutting military personnel's pay while increasing his own salary.(145) Russell answered that he was a "friend" of veterans, and voted for their bonus.(146) Talmadge insisted that Russell only voted for the soldiers' bonus after he, as Governor, advocated it.(147) To symbolize his patriotism, Russell gave Confederate veterans a prominent role at his rallies, recruiting them to escort him to the platform. As a slap at Talmadge's Republican leanings, Russell reminded a Dublin audience that the "hearts" of the Confederate veterans "beat as Democratic today as they did in the sixties."(148) It was ironic that Russell, the Senator who would play such a key role in bolstering the national defense during World War II and beyond, promised at Dallas, Georgia, that "none of our boys" would be sent overseas to "fight" someone "else's war."(149)

Because he was losing the campaign to Russell, Talmadge introduced the subject of race. The debate over race was vital to the two candidates because of its potential historically in southern politics for helping or destroying a candidate. In speeches Talmadge delivered between 1926 to the early 1930s, as reported in the press, relatively few references were made to race. In these instances, Talmadge echoed the stock response of most whites speaking in public, ranging from a paternalistic attitude toward blacks to that of extreme hostility. Talmadge opposed any hint of social, economic, and political equality and opportunities for blacks.

Talmadge sensed the need for a theme that would create the rhetorical turbulence upon which his brand of politics depended. He introduced race as a way of creating interest among white voters, calling attention to his campaign, angering whites, discrediting Russell, and enhancing his own candidacy. Unlike in 1926, when political corruption actually existed in the Department of Agriculture, in 1936 there was no "threat" of significant political advances by blacks. Because of gross discrimination and abuse experienced in all segments of society, blacks were no challenge to whites politically or economically. Certainly Talmadge was not answering any moderate statements made by Russell on race, for the senator agreed that blacks must be forced to remain in the subservient station to which they were assigned. In this campaign, Russell assured voters that, "This is a white

man's country" and "we are going to keep it that
way."(150) Talmadge manufactured the "issue" of race
synthetically for one reason, to provide a rhetorical
advantage over a tough, effective, and respected
incumbent. The more decorous and reasonable a
campaign, the less chance Talmadge had of winning it,
and Russell, in the context of that period, was
running a relatively informed and effective race.

Talmadge's strategy was to argue race in a way
that triggered whites' racist attitudes and transformed entrenched emotions of frustration, fear, and
anger into votes for him. Because of confidence in
his ability to make Georgia whites believe what he
asserted, Talmadge forged the theme of race, a topic
with which he was intimately familiar and comfortable
on the stump. He had a perfect pitch for stump
appeals, whether chastising "King J. J.," advocating
the three-dollar tag, or making unfounded racist
charges. Assuming that shouting various forms of the
topic of race would strengthen his campaign, Talmadge
made no effort to monitor the relevancy or validity
of his assertions.

Talmadge assumed that the wilder his exaggera-
tion on race the better the statements would be
received by most white voters. At Lincolntown, in an
apostrophe to self-deception, Talmadge echoed the
words of hundreds of politicians in the South and
beyond who for many years had constructed arguments
that only made sense when translated through racist
perception. Here is an example: "I protect the negro
in his rights. I have [black] friends. . . . I have
been amongst them as they labored on my farms. But I
don't believe in social equality."(151) To increase
his own political stock, Talmadge "complimented"
whites of Harris county for "chasing" a black man
"out of the state" for working for the "interest of
negro farmers."(152) A black instructor had been
sent to Harris county to assist with a "resettlement
project." When he entered a "drug store to eat a
sandwich and get a drink," the residents "made him
take bush bond." Talmadge searched far and wide for
examples of blacks and whites associating equally,
and employed those instances to inflame white crowds.
Up North was fertile and safe ground from which to
draw illustrations, so he attacked the staging of the
New York play, "Turpentine," for having a racially
mixed cast, saying it accused "white men of atrocities upon negro men and women" in southern turpentine
camps.(153) By his own statement on the subject, one
sees that whether atrocities were committed was of
less concern to Talmadge than the number of voters he
converted to his camp.

In the 1936 campaign, Talmadge strained to fit

race into the debate. Of all topics available to him
in the region, he linked race to pensions for the
elderly. This rhetorical choice was peculiar because
many older Georgians helped form the hard working
class for whom Talmadge promised to fight.   Because
he usually attacked individuals and groups that were
easy prey, apparently Talmadge decided that the
elderly were the most vulnerable segment of society
available for exploitation.   Certainly Talmadge had
no quarrel with older citizens. His campaign was in
trouble, however, and he would sacrifice blacks, the
elderly, friends, supporting editors, any other
group, and his own credibility to win an election.
     Talmadge argued that white Georgians should vote
for him because Russell supported a pension for
elderly citizens that older blacks would share.   The
"white folks" would "pay" for the pension, Talmadge
warned an Arlington audience, "and ninety percent of
it" would go to blacks. "Everybody should" not be
"heavily taxed" to "give" blacks this "huge pension,"
he inflamed.(154)   Talmadge concluded that 75,000
blacks over the   age of   sixty-five would   get
$13,000,000, while a mere ten percent of 112,000
whites were receiving $168,750. When hearing Russell
praise benefits derived from the Social Security Act,
stated Talmadge, voters should guard against "siren
music of lotus eaters" that "would destroy the supply
of negro labor."(155)   Talmadge promised that, when
elected to the Senate, he would "undo what Russell
has done."(156) He would "fight against [racially]
mixed bureaus."(157)
     In responding to Talmadge's argument that whites
would pay for a pension plan primarily benefiting
blacks, Russell, for the era of 1936, faced a difficult rhetorical balancing act.   On the subject of
race, Talmadge hoped to force incumbent Russell into
a defensive posture to which he had backed J. J.
Brown and others. Once again Talmadge underestimated
Russell's tenacity for asserting his argument offen-
sively and effectively.   Even when addressing the
explosive subject of race, Russell came out swinging.
At the same time, this public exploitation of blacks
for political gain, by Talmadge and Russell, demonstrated well the low level to which southern discourse dropped when the rhetoric turned racist.
     The speeches by Talmadge and Russell showed
clearly that racist attitudes among whites in 1936
were so well entrenched that politicians felt secure
in baiting voters with incorrect, crude, irrevelant,
and unethical forms of racist rhetoric. In talks at
Royston and Eatonton, Russell warned that, "You can
always depend" on Talmadge to shout "nigger, nigger,
nigger", argued Russell. But Whites would not "be

deceived" by that ploy. Then Russell answered
Talmadge's assertion that whites would lose pension
checks to blacks, shifting to the needs of older
citizens and others. Russell argued that there was a
compelling need for social security. Poverty-strick-
en parents, crippled children, the blind, and the
elderly who "helped build this country" would receive
social security benefits. When hearing this promise,
citizens of Royston "stopped" Russell's speech with
their supportive "roar," and a citizen referring to
Talmadge yelled, "we are fooled once but never
again."(158)

Russell demonstrated the faulty attack made by
Talmadge upon the distribution of social security
benefits. In 1936 and long after, white southern
politicians opposed equitable distribution of government funds among blacks and whites. Russell followed
a line of reasoning more acceptable rhetorically to
white voters in 1936, one that carried the ring of
common sense and a promise of services for whites.
Talmadge claimed that "old negroes will get the
pension." In an extremely guarded argument at
Cartersville, Russell demonstrated the absurdity of
Talmadge's claim. That was like saying, Russell
continued at Cartersville, that we "won't build any
highways because a negro might ride on one. It's an
old trick and it won't work."(159) Russell lofted a
second volley against Talmadge's peculiar claim,
reminding voters at Douglas that as governor Talmadge
used state funds to purchase school books for children, and "about half of it" went for "books for
negro children."(160) Then Russell nailed his point
home: "If the negro gets a little bit of pension
money," that is better than keeping payments from
"old people."(161) Russell presented data at
Milledgeville to refute Talmadge's assertion that
blacks would primarily benefit from programs for the
elderly. "I have here in my hand federal statistics"
indicating that only 35,000 blacks sixty-five and
older in Georgia would receive payments in contrast
to 75,000 whites.(162)

Talmadge made the role of government in the
lives of citizens a dominant issue in the 1936
campaign. As he had nominated the Department of
Agriculture as the protector of southern values in
1926, in Murphy, North Carolina, Talmadge forecast
the 1936 campaign for Senate to be a battle for basic
values. Rather than a New-Deal, Georgians should
return to the "fundamentals" of "country church and
brick school houses."(163) For a Canton audience,
Talmadge portrayed the New-Deal to be an encroachment
upon southern culture and "State rights."(164) He
concluded at Monroe that only Georgians should

"control" local "politics."(165)

Talmadge attacked a bloated federal government. He cast arguments against Franklin Roosevelt, the New-Deal, and Russell's endorsement of costly federal programs in stump maxims that citizens attended, remembered, and understood. "Wet nursing" was not "a proper function of government," he proclaimed.(166) Georgia voters should not be "bought with" their "own money."(167) "Bureaucracy" was the "enemy of" the farmers because working men and women would be made to "pay, pay, pay." These burdensome costs would "dwarf the souls of the American people."(168) Talmadge complained that even Huey P. Long, initially acceptable as a kind of "Paul Revere" for the nation, through his policy of "Sharing-the-Wealth" was "out-Rooseveliting Roosevelt."(169) Talmadge said that Russell also fell prey to "boondogglers" who funded their extravaganzas with "dimes and quarters" from the "pockets" of the poor, soldiers, and little businessmen.(170) When Russell ran for the Senate in 1932, he complained about the "orgy of extravagence" in the federal government, reminded Talmadge. When elected, he voted for a $4,880,000,000 relief bill.(171) By voting for "wasteful expenditures," Russell robbed Georgians.(172)

Talmadge seasoned speeches with examples of waste and inequity inherent to New-Deal programs paid for by working citizens. Answering a question from the audience in Monroe about the Agricultural Adjustment Administration benefits received by New Yorkers, Talmadge answered that they got "$1,000,000 to delouse human beings."(173) Talmadge ridiculed the funding of research projects he said did not promote the nation's "prosperity." He scorned the government's paying for the surveying of the Mediterranean and Caribbean Seas.(174) He criticized those who used public funds for "aesthetic dancing and ballet etiquette."(175) At Blairsville Talmadge accused Secretary Ickes of using the tax payers' money to brew liquor in the Virgin Islands at twenty-five cents a gallon, and sell it in the United States for $7.50 a gallon.(176) Russell was "out-Hoovering Hoover."(177) The senator approved a thirty-percent sales tax "on people."(178) Russell and Roosevelt placed the "highest sales tax in the world on cotton." Russell voted for a tax of seventy-five cents per hundred pounds on "all Irish potatoes."(179) He supported a 33 1/2 percent sales tax on "food-stuff."(180)

In speeches at Cartersville, Swainsboro, and Austell, Talmadge emphasized the harm done by the Roosevelt Administration's agricultural policies to Georgia farmers and businessmen. The National

Recovery Act backed by Russell took millions of dollars out of the state and "bankrupted thousands of little saw mills" and "put little people out of work." Russell hurt the farmer by supporting increasing importation of jute, cotton, cottonseed, corn, wheat, and hogs.(181) Researcher Michael Holmes judged the National Recovery Administration to have been the "least successful of New Deal programs." The NRA was created primarily to help industrial states by increasing the wages of workers, a policy that did not aid southern farmers.(182) Angry that foreign imports harmed southern markets, Talmadge said, when elected he would fight for tariff protections. In Swainsboro, he "called for a baseball," and someone in the audience, who just happened to be near the speaker's stand, tossed one to him. He glowered at it, threw it "into the audience," and shouted, "Look at it," it says on it, "Made in Japan."(183) In Austell he exhibited handkerchiefs and a baby's slip made in Japan, concluding that importations of products cost Americans thousands of jobs.(184)

Talmadge even opposed a program introduced by the Roosevelt Administration that was similiar to one he advocated in 1931. As discussed in Chapter 4, Talmadge supported a Huey Long plan in the South for increasing the demand and price of cotton by leaving that crop in the field in 1931 and growing none in 1932. The Agricultural Adjustment Act (AAA) was created in May of 1933, and was directed by Henry A. Wallace, one of Talmadge's favorite targets, and administered in the states by county agents in the Agricultural Extension Service. Tindall observed that the AAA included "every major device that had been advanced for farm relief." Farmers who voluntarily reduced acreage would receive payments that would "restore them to 'parity,' or the same level of purchasing power they had in the golden age" of 1909-1914 for cotton and rice, and 1919-1929 for tobacco. In 1933 farmers faced the problem of producing another bumper cotton crop at a price of near five cents per pound. The program worked temporarily, with prices increasing about eleven cents in July, but decreased to between eight and ten cents as the crop was picked.

In October 1933, Roosevelt created the Commodity Credit Corporation (CCC) under the Reconstruction Finance Corporation. CCC loans put the cotton price at ten cents during 1933 and at twelve cents in 1934. In 1930, tenants operated 55.5 percent of all farms in the South. Few benefits trickled down to them, although in 1935 two out of three tenants were white. Tenant families numbered about five and a half

million whites and more than three million blacks,
approximately one of four southerners.(185)   Michael
Holmes found that the AAA, although discriminatory
against the small farmer and tenants, played a "great
role" in Georgia's recovery program.(186)   Numan
Bartley explained the political implications   of
agricultural relief programs, a factor that primarily
motivated Talmadge: "Planters, who readily accepted
farm price supports, could appreciate" Talmadge's
"efforts to prevent the New Deal from spoiling
sharecroppers and field hands."   After all, "Talmadge
enjoyed the support of many textile mill owners and
other low-wage employers," but turned mainly on the
stump to poor farmers for whom Tom Watson had spoken.(187)

In 1936, as expressed in a speech at Macon to
the "Grass Roots" Convention, Talmadge opposed the
policy of Roosevelt and Russell of destroying crops,
hogs, and cattle to increase demand and prices.(188)
Although somewhat like his own plan, at Royston he
portrayed the New-Deal policy as being an absurd
attempt to bring about a "more abundant life" through
"scarcity."(189)   Talmadge had a way of twisting an
argument until it met his needs. He yelled that
Roosevelt and Russell "won't let us grow on our own
land."(190)   Talmadge complained that Secretary of
Agriculture Wallace would burn wheat, plow up cotton
and corn, and import those products from competing
countries, thereby "stiffling production" and placing
Americans "on relief."(191)   Elect "me to the senate"
if you want to send Secretary Wallace "back to
Iowa."(192)   Talmadge argued that destroying "food-
stuffs" was a "sin."(193)   Talmadge blamed Russell
for not speaking out against Roosevelt's policies of
decreasing farm production.(194)

Talmadge envisioned that the "picnic and fol-
lies" of the federal government would end with his
election.(195)   "Pounding his desk" during an interview, he said the "great fight" would be "Americanism
vs. Communism."   Nothing remained of the New-Deal but
"billions of dollars and patronage."(196)   Talmadge
would return the nation to a free enterprise system
in which efforts of individuals would solve economic
problems.   "Real recovery and prosperity" would come
through private industry and "honest" citizens paying
taxes rather than depending upon government for
"anything but a square deal."   The cost of government
had to be reduced.   Southerners knew best of all, he
insisted, that "you can't borrow yourself out of
debt, make water run uphill, and drink yourself
sober."(197)   Talmadge reminded voters of his "public
record" of cutting taxes and utility rates, and
"paying up debts."(198)   He claimed to have reduced

the state ad valorem tax "from 4 to 3 mills," saving
the citizens $1,000,000.(199)   "Waving 2 clenched
fists," Talmadge assured a Monroe audience that,
"You'll hear from me about these taxes."(200)

Talmadge promised that when elected to the
Senate, he would either cut or abolish particular
taxes. In April 1935, he toured Dixie speaking
against the cotton processing tax under the slogan,
"America Wake Up."(201) A tax of $21.25 had been
placed on each bale of cotton, he continued, at a
total cost to farmers of $21,000,000. The processing
tax must be abolished if cotton farmers and textile
industries were to prosper.(202) Cotton had been
selling at fourteen cents a pound, but now sold for
only twelve.(203) If elected, he maintained, those
conditions would improve. Even the cost of postage
would be lowered from three cents to two. Russell
ridiculed his opponent's ignorance of present policies by reminding an audience at Royston that he and
the Congress had already decreased postage to two
cents. The crowd "whooped in laughter."(204) This
revelation did not deter Talmadge. Because the
decrease in the price of a stamp took some months to
be implemented, Talmadge used that lag as an opportunity to challenge Russell's claim and win the argument. In Macon, he asked "those people who mailed a
letter today" whether they paid "2 cents or 3," and
they shouted, "3 cents"!(205)

To solve Georgia's economic woes, Talmadge would
abolish the federal income tax. He reminded a Rome,
Georgia, crowd that, as governor he vetoed the
old-age pension bill, contending that it was premised
upon "taxing poverty to pay poverty."(206) The
income tax was another form of the government's
meddling in states' rights.(207) Russell was able to
capitalize on Talmadge's mulish attitude toward
federal programs, for under his opponent's leadership
as governor Georgians experienced bureacratic
delaying tactics by offended officials. Because of
Talmadge's unruly behavior, funds earmarked by the
federal government for Georgia were denied or
delayed. Talmadge was less able to have his way with
federal officials, although he used them as he did
blacks, to create dissension for political benefit.
Russell reminded Georgians that state soldiers did
not intimidate the federal government. Talmadge
answered that the income tax was a "racket" by which
to "whip" voters into submission. Talmadge aroused
over 25,000 persons at Moultrie by denouncing the
federal government's "reign of terror" against him.
"Set" Roosevelt's "britches afire, Gene," a member of
the audience yelled. The governor said federal
agents were intimidating "his political friends" with

threats to prosecute them for lack of payment of appropriate income taxes.(208)

Talmadge's stand on abolishing the income tax changed as the campaign progressed. When Russell explained the benefits Georgians would lose if the federal income tax were terminated, Talmadge amended his proposal. By the end of August, he advocated, not abolishing the income tax, but placing it under the jurisdiction of the individual states. Roosevelt and Russell were taking $9,000,000 out of Georgia, he shouted. "Think how well you people could get along with that much tax money." Talmadge ignored the amount of funds Georgians would lose if they depended solely upon their neighbors in the state for public funding of programs. At Arlington, Georgia, he said that shifting the income tax to the states would allow poor Georgians to buy more "school houses, reduce taxes and have better times."(209)

Talmadge generally advocated radically reducing the size, cost, and influence of state and federal governments. But after Russell explained the extent of services Georgians would lose under the governor's recommended federal policy, Talmadge advised Georgians to accept their share of Roosevelt's handouts. Russell accurately noted for a Griffin audience how Talmadge, on the one hand, promised to cut all government programs while, on the other, said he would "increase" the benefits coming to Georgia.(210) Promising voters to cut taxes helped elect him to the offices of Commissioner of Agriculture and Governor, and he was following this strategy to the United States Senate. Although he viewed compromise and change on his part as a sign of political weakness, he recognized that working men and women recovering from a tragic economic depression were desperate for relief. He apparently favored economic relief through private business, but finally succumbed to Russell's argument that with Talmadge in the United States Senate Georgians would lose federal funds to other states. Now trying to bargain for votes, Talmadge declared that Washington had approved five billion dollars, "five dollars for every minute since the birth of Christ," and he hoped to bring $90,000,000 of that vast sum to Georgia. "Get your part" now "because it" would be the last to come from Washington.(211) Talmadge would take the money but not if it meant the state going in debt. He would seek "donations" from Washington, but "not loans."(212) He was proud as governor of having "blocked efforts" made to "borrow public works money."(213) Reeling from the federal government's reciprocation of his own obstinance, Talmadge complained that Washington was delaying payment of

$17,000,000 owed to Georgians for roads. Sending him
to the Senate offered voters "the only chance"
available for getting funds for Georgians being
distributed lavishly throughout the country.(214)
Elect him and "millions of dollars" for soil conservation would "pour" into Georgia. Georgia had paid
processing taxes on cotton at a sum of $40,000,000,
with only $30,000,000 being returned to the State,
Talmadge stated. He would "get back" the lost
$10,000,000.(215) If not, he promised to create a
political turbulence throughout the nation.(216)

     Southern leaders such as Talmadge and Russell
wrestled wryly with the political liabilities and
assets that the New-Deal held for them. As George
Tindall noted, "the low-wage philosophy of Southern
expansionism pulled them one way," and "human need
and the political potential of relief another." The
practice of paying "low wages" was one of the "cherished Southern traditions, the great magnet for
outside capital, the foundation of industrial
growth." Blacks were paid even less than whites.
For example, in 1930 salaries paid to white teachers
in the South exceeded those for blacks by "nearly
three to one."(217) Talmadge complained that Russell's New-Deal would pay blacks the same as whites.
Russell looked beyond the race issue to exploit the
political benefit for his candidacy deriving from the
New-Deal's economic relief of Georgians.

     One familiar with Russell's highly conservative
stance in the 1960s in behalf of a limited role of
government in the lives of citizens and in leading
the southern bloc of congressmen against civil rights
bills, may be surprised by his strong support of
Roosevelt's New-Deal programs. As Numan Bartley
explained, however, in the 1930s "a substantial
majority of southerners thought of themselves as
liberals," though "events of the 1940's eroded this
dedication to a politics of reform." Southerners
favored the "economic liberalism" of the New Deal,
but not the accompanying reforms in civil rights for
minorities. By the 1940s the South had turned
conservative.(218) The southern bloc of support for
the New-Deal was "destroyed" because whites in the
region believed that funds made available to blacks
through federal programs threatened their economic
and political dominance. The South desired relief
but not at the expense of its traditions.(219) In
the 1936 campaign, Talmadge advocated the abolishment
of New-Deal programs.

     In 1936, Russell defended New Deal policies as
the best available means of restoring prosperity to
Georgia. At Kingsland the Senator stated candidly
that he was "for government" helping people in

need.(220) He envisioned for a Fitzgerald audience a
time when the "common man can share in the blessings
of our civilization."(221)   Unlike some state officials in Georgia, Russell alerted, Roosevelt would
not "yield to the demagogues."(222) Russell argued
that Talmadge's claim that Roosevelt was "usurping
powers" was "utterly folly."(223) Russell gave his
allegiance to a President he praised as a "part-time
Georgian" who promised economic recovery for citizens, a rhetorical strategy that enhanced his candidacy enormously.   Russell told voters at Columbus
that Roosevelt had resided periodically in Warm
Springs for treatment of paralysis, and could be
depended upon as reliably as a concerned neighbor.(224) The Roosevelt Administration, he argued at
Marietta, was a "friend" that would help Georgians
"who are hungry and miserable" to "find jobs."
     Russell did not allow voters to forget
Talmadge's ridicule of the President's infirmity. In
the Marietta speech, Russell talked kindly of a
President whose legs "God had touched . . . with
infantile paralysis," a man whom Talmadge "sneering-
ly" scorned.(225) "There may be a little something
wrong with President Roosevelt's legs, as Gene so
tactlessly infers," explained Russell, "but there is
nothing wrong with his heart and brain." The crowd
at Commerce "roared" with "resentment" and became
"almost militant" as Russell alluded to Talmadge's
"slur at" the President's "physical infirmity."(226)
This was the President, reminded Russell at
Homerville, Talmadge refused the "common courtesy" of
a greeting when Roosevelt spoke in Atlanta.(227)
Governors from neighboring states attended the
meeting but not Talmadge. Georgia's Governor did not
show the "decency to shake his hands."(228)
     Russell shrewdly represented Talmadge's indis-
cretions as justification for his own re-election.
In a delicate phrase with potent political implication, Russell advised an Adel audience that, "We need
senators to hold up the hand of the President."(229)
Talmadge seemed to have totally misjudged the high
esteem in which Georgians held Roosevelt. Other
Georgia Democrats joined Russell's chorus for the
President. Senior Senator Walter F. George and
Representative Carl Vinson supported Roosevelt's
re-election.(230) Veteran reporter L. A. Farrell
accurately forecast the importance of New-Deal
programs and the part-time President to Russell's
re-election to the United States Senate when he wrote
that Georgia is "always safe for" Roosevelt.(231)
     At Statesboro Russell argued that creating
agencies for national recovery was not wasting money,
but providing citizens an "opportunity to earn" a

"livelihood."(232)   He promised farmers "lower rates"
and poor persons increased government   aid.(233)
Russell's speech at Eatonton illustrated well   the
studied way that he explained to audiences throughout
Georgia what   had   transpired in   government.   "All
legislation passed" for the New-Deal "was not perfect," but "the house was on fire when President
Roosevelt was elected" and the Administration could
not "take time to look in every cupboard."   Russell
said soberly that he "did not expect to be criticized
for not knifing the President" while "he was trying
to put out the fire."   Russell indicated he voted to
help farmers by providing an increase in funding to
Georgia from $58,000,000 to $107,000,000. He backed
the Citizens Conservation Corps so that "boys of
Georgia" could "learn how to work" and be able to
"send parents some money." Russell supported improvements for schools for children. He would rather
be "a rubber stamp" for the Roosevelt Administration
than, "like Gene," a representative of "the Raskob
and duPont interests and the Liberty League."   The
audience at Eatonton "roared its approval."(234)

     In a speech at Jasper, Russell shamed Talmadge
for insulting young persons who worked for pay in the
Citizens Conservation Corps. "I voted for that bill
and I'm proud of it," declared the Senator.   "Those
boys were as good as Gene Talmadge's boy. . . .   We
rescued them."(235)   Russell answered Talmadge's
contention that he blindly supported New-Deal programs to the detriment of Georgians. Indicating his
opponent's preoccupation with self-interest, Russell
told Moultrie listeners that the "leading handler of
jute in Georgia," an imported crop competing with
cotton, supports Talmadge!(236)   Boasting at Fort
Valley of the productive partnership of "Roosevelt
and Russell" that Talmadge denigrated, he listed
legislation he helped enact to support farmers
producing peanuts, tobacco, and turpentine.(237)   He
introduced an amendment in the Senate to tax jute as
a means of protecting Georgia cotton growers.
Russell was proud that he wrote the federal law
providing farmers' "seed loans." At Colquitt,
Russell said that he voted for the home owner's loan
corporation to "bridle the wolves of Wall
Street."(238)

     Russell maintained at Macon that, because of
government support, farmers were payed twelve cents
for cotton rather than five.(239) Farmers received
"better" prices for tobacco, peanuts, hogs, and
cattle. "We see smiles" on faces, he said at Dublin,
rather than "furrows of despair."(240) Repeatedly on
the stump Russell explained issues that Talmadge had
muddled. The processing tax on cotton that Talmadge

protested so loudly was "on the manufacturer," as Georgia "stands fourth in spindles and mills."(241) There was "no connection between the gin tax and the processing tax."(242) Although the National Recovery Act did help remedy "child labor and sweat shops," the Supreme Court invalidated that program, as it did the processing tax. Those were "dead" issues.(243)

Russell promised that under his leadership, farmers would share in social security benefits.(244) Farms would be "eletrified."(245) The Supreme Court ruled against the Agricultural Adjustment Act (AAA) and the processing tax. The second AAA was passed February 1938, re-establishing the program existing from 1933 to 1936, but without processing taxes. Marketing quotas were made compulsory upon approval by two-thirds of the farmers affected. Cotton farmers voted 92.1 percent for the marketing quotas, a stronger endorsement than in 1934. George Tindall found that by the end of the 1930s, agriculture was "still the chief occupation of the South and still in distress." Income from farms had decreased in 1932 to thirty-seven percent of the 1929 receipts; in 1933 they reached forty-five percent and by 1937, seventy-four, but during 1939 and 1940 they sank back to fifty-eight percent. Receipts from cotton in 1939 were only thirty-nine per cent of those in 1929, the lowest point since 1933.(246)

Russell represented the governor to be a politician with little credibility and few personal convictions. Russell warned audiences that Talmadge's recalcitrant attitude toward the federal government as governor "kept millions of dollars out of Georgia."(247) He portrayed Talmadge to be a candidate who shifted loyalties and stands as needed to win votes. Referring to Talmadge's antics at the farm meeting in 1931, studied in Chapter 4 of this book, Russell reminded listeners that, as Commissioner of Agriculture, Talmadge "attempted to intimidate" him, as governor, to hold a special session of the legislature to forbid farmers from "planting a single row of cotton." But now Talmadge criticized the Administration for decreasing crop production and paying "farmers for the reduction."(248) In 1934, Talmadge boasted that he and Roosevelt were like "ham and eggs." "Either the ham or the eggs spoiled," continued Russell at Eatonton, "and I'll leave it to you which was which."(249) Russell exhibited a picture of Talmadge riding a horse at the head of a parade "celebrating the National Recovery Act," a program he now castigated.(250) About Talmadge's claim to having reduced the ad valorem tax in Georgia, Russell explained that, when he, Russell, was Governor, a law was passed requiring the tax to decrease as tax

receipts go up. "Just like old Gene," someone from
the Royston audience shouted.(251)
       Russell opposed the termination of the federal
income tax by highlighting how Talmadge was willing
to exploit politically powerless persons for votes.
He argued that Talmadge "vented his spleen on the old
folks of Georgia who, he thought, had no one to
defend them."(252)   Usurping Talmadge's "good 'ole
boy" ploy, Russell said that the "boys back at the
fork of the roads didn't approve" of losing benefits
that derived from the federal income tax.(253)
Russell envisioned for Georgians what they would lose
if Talmadge's plan to abolish the federal income tax
and slash government programs was adopted.   Voters
would forfeit farmers' benefit payments, drought
relief, and compensation for disabled soldiers.
Postal service would be crippled, and the army and
navy would be disbanded.(254) In a radio address,
Russell maintained that the government would be
unable to assist states with disasters and combating
the boll weevil and screw worm.(255) Citizens in all
states but Georgia would receive social security
benefits.(256)
       Russell contrasted Talmadge's view that govern-
ment should not be in the business of assisting
citizens with that of Georgia's favorite son from
Thomson. He reminded voters at Fort Valley that "Tom
Watson was the daddy of the rural mail system."   If
he were alive, he would "burn" Gene "so badly it
would take half of the Atlantic ocean to put him
out."(257) As for Talmadge's amended solution to
shift the income tax from the federal government to
the states, Russell explained that citizens of New
York and other nonsouthern states were paying more
than Georgians, with the "surplus" going to Georgia.
The southern states could not survive on their own
tax resources.(258)   Persons with incomes of "less
than $5,000" did not pay the large part of the income
tax. At Moultrie Russell said he favored requiring
the "gang" of "duPonts and their moneyed cohorts,"
backers of Talmadge, to pay taxes "in proportion to
their income," with "some of their money" going to
farmers.(259)
       Russell's rallies were not boring workshops on
government and agricultural economics. On the
campaign trail, he produced political dramas that
were well received by crowds and in the press.   A
tough political campaign was no time for false
modesty. During a speech in Dublin, Georgia, he had
E. L. Hill of Twiggs county stand and testify: "I
was about to lose my farm in 1932. But the New Deal
and Senator Russell helped the farmers. . . . I have
kept my home and bought more land."(260) At Griffin,

a man employed in a mill contrasted for Russell and the audience a "Talmadge and Hoover card." The man indicated how in 1932 he worked sixty hours a week and received $5.40, when in 1936, with a "Roosevelt and Russell card" he worked 40 hours and earned $12.00.(261) At Commerce, Russell poked fun at the "soliloquy" Talmadge performed at Lincoln's tomb. He also entertained the audience with a "document" said to be the "last will and testament of Talmadge's political career."(262) During the conclusion of his speech in Swainesboro, a "group of men" walked to the speaker's stand, "stripped off their red suspenders" and said they had been "converted" to Russell. Russell informed the radio audience gleefully that "it's raining red suspenders."(263)

During the 1936 campaign, individuals and groups criticized Talmadge publicly far more than in earlier years. Critics denounced his public behavior. A Fulton County grand jury found Talmadge to be "cruel and unkind" in ridiculing Roosevelt's physical handicap.(264) The Atlanta City Council passed a resolution condemning his "attacks" upon the Roosevelt Administration.(265) Advising Talmadge to "attend" to his duties" as governor, citizens of Meriwether county, home of Roosevelt while he was in Georgia part-time, in a "mass meeting" expressed "indignation" over Talmadge's "references" to the President's "physical condition."(266) Citizens of Dalton opposed Talmadge's "vicious" assaults upon the President and his threats to abolish cotton benefits for farmers. They suggested he might "move to Russia."(267) E. D. Rivers, Russell's candidate for governor, pledged to end "Talmadgeism," lower "the red galluses" from the "flagpole" over the state capitol, and "hoist the Stars and Stripes."(268) Labor leaders opposed Talmadge as a "destructive pest."(269) George L. Googe told six hundred delegates attending a meeting of the Georgia Federation of Labor that Talmadge was a "mouthpiece of cotton manufacturers" and had "sold out to corporate interests."(270) Farmer W. Bridges indicated that he voted for Talmadge in three elections, but would vote for Russell in 1936 because the Governor opposed Roosevelt, a friend of Georgia farmers.(271)

The opposition to Talmadge's candidacy extended to his political rallies. Talmadge thrived on controversy, but he was most effective creating minimum dissension in crowds that he could orchestrate dramatically and effectively from behind the stump. After encouraging hecklers in the crowd, he had them silenced by the roar of a supportive audience. In 1936, from Talmadge's perspective, dissension at his meetings got out of hand. To Talmadge's disadvantage, his rallies became more democratic, with opposing views being expressed, heard, and reported in the press. Unlike former campaigns, when halls could not hold the crowds, in 1936 he was able to deliver some speeches indoors. In 1932, when running for Governor, audiences followed him to a corner store for a cold drink, leaving opponents to speak to a vacant lot. But in 1936 Russell won more than his share of listeners. There were other signs of the increased hostility Talmadge experienced and the drop in voters' support. During his Canton speech, a banner paid "tribute" to Roosevelt.(272) At the base of the platform where he spoke in Nashville, Georgia, was painted the word, "Russell."(273)

During Talmadge's speech at Rome, Georgians booed and yelled above the noise that, "We want Russell."(274) At Griffin and many other towns, he was "heckled and booed by a part" of the audience.(275) One might guess that individual protesters had difficulty being heard, but Talmadge's performances relied upon audience involvement. When the expected and required pauses and accompanying stump dialogue occurred, opponents also joined in. A reporter observed that a Talmadge rally was not "a one-man speaking." Receiving comments "from the crowds," he responded to "friendly utterances . . . with a grin and an elaboration of his line of thought." When an "unfriendly comment comes forth, he lashes back with barbed words. It's what he calls 'the folks doing the talking'."(276) During the 1936 campaign, critics in his audiences did more talking than Talmadge's rhetorical dramas could absorb.

Just as planted prompters called to Talmadge with substantive topics that he was well prepared to exploit for votes, opponents introduced issues that required him to address subjects less favorable to his candidacy. The nature of the scene, the role of the audience, and the rhetorical parley that Talmadge perfected required that he respond. Even the "yapper" of Telfair county, however, had difficulty matching the mounting flood of overt critical response. During his speech at Rome, Georgia, a "youth" carried a banner reminding the audience that as Governor, Talmadge "Vetoed the Old Age Pension," causing Talmadge to bluster in the genre used in the second debate in 1926 when answering J. J. Brown's more decisive arguments, more bluff than substance: "I'll tell you about that. If you can ask the Governor any question he can't answer, he shouldn't be running for anything."(277)

At Cairo, Georgia, a "young man" asked, "What do you say about your claim that a man in overalls is not worth more than $1 a day?," a charge repeated by

Russell. Talmadge's supporters "massed around the
young man" in an intimidating gesture.   Uncomfortable
being repeatedly placed on the defensive, the governor stated: "I've covered that matter just as plain
as I can talk.   I've never said that."(278)   While
speaking at Macon, Talmadge reprimanded young persons
in the audience wearing "Russell emblems."   Several
fist fights broke out, and motorcycle patrolmen
"hustled" the protesters away.(279)   During a
Swainsboro rally, when heckler H. Marsh of Portal
yelled that Talmadge ridiculed boys working in
government-sponsored programs, Talmadge shouted that
the heckler was "paid to . . . cut the fool."
Posturing for the crowd, Talmadge challenged the
protester to a different kind of fight: "If you said
that I made that reference to the CCC boys, I'll meet
you anywhere you say."(280)

On occasions, Talmadge seemed not to understand
why citizens complained, as if he were surprised that
they took his stump hyperbole seriously.   He wanted
citizens to view him more on a personal than professional level.   If critics would "go out hunting or
fishing with Talmadge," he advised, they would "think
more of him."(281)   Talmadge blamed Russell's supporters for the harassment.   He told a Rome audience
that Robert, Richard Russell's brother, brought
"heckling squads" to his speeches.(282)   At Cedartown
and Columbus Talmadge complained that Russell "paid"
individuals to disturb his talks.(283)   Talmadge
criticized the coverage he received in the Georgia
press.   In the 1936 race, many of the state's newspapers did turn against him.   In an example that
characterized his penchant for perceiving events
martially, he told a Sandersville audience that he
could not force a favorable comment from the Atlanta
Constitution, Augusta Chronicle, or Columbus Enquirer
with a "load of dynamite."(284)

L. A. Farrell, veteran reporter of the Atlanta
Constitution noted the mixed response generated by
Talmadge during the 1936 campaign for United States
Senator.   Whether audiences supported him or not,
Talmadge was "one of the greatest crowd-getters the
state has ever seen."   When addressing "State affairs, his audience was with him . . . generally."
But when talking about "national affairs he received
repeated applause from certain sections of the crowd,
silence from others."   At the close of speeches, when
Talmadge asked persons attending rallies to raise
hands if they planned to vote for him, "there were
many who didn't respond."(285)

A straw vote taken in Carroll county in July
indicated that Russell would win the race for
re-election to the Senate in 1936.   In 1934, when

running for Governor, according to the press,
Talmadge lost only twenty of the 250 votes cast in
that county. (Actually Talmadge received 2,249
popular votes, and all four unit votes, while Claude
Pittman won 1,255, and Ed Gilliam 124.) In July
during the 1936 campaign, in a straw poll, nine-
ty-seven persons cast votes unofficially in a box in
a store, with Russell winning two to one, further
pushing Russell's bandwagon.(286) Final returns
published in Georgia's Official Register, show that,
in Carroll County, Russell received 3,891 votes
(sixty-six percent) and Talmadge 1,961. Russell also
won the four unit votes in that county. Reporter L.
A. Farrell, a close observer of Talmadge's campaigns,
agreed with that straw prediction. No one doubted
that Talmadge was a master political dramatist. For
his LaGrange speech, he entered town "driving 2 mules
wearing harness wrapped in red bunting."(287)
Farrell found, however, that Talmadge's campaign
"show" was attracting fewer persons, while Russell's
stock with audiences increased. Talmadge's dramatic
confrontation with crowds had "been witnessed by"
many persons, and was "losing its lure."

By August 12, sensing that his campaign was in
trouble, the Governor increased the number of speeches from one to at least two per week.(288) By August
27, abandoning the strategy of speaking only as many
times as his "duties at the capitol" would allow,
Governor Talmadge planned a "desperate" speaking tour
of the state, making fourteen speeches in a week. On
some days, he delivered five speeches in the morning,
six in the afternoon, and three at night.(289) As
Russell accelerated his attack, voters shifted to his
camp. For each meeting, Russell supporters "pitched"
large gatherings by organizing attendance of citizens
from four, five, and eight counties. His candidacy
also benefited some from support provided by well
organized followers of Senator Walter George.(290)
(In 1938, George was faced with fighting off
Talmadge's campaign to win his Senate seat!) Early
in the 1936 campaign, for "ordinary" meetings,
Russell drew from 1,500 to 2,000, while now he
attracted from 4,000 to 6,000.(291) On August 16,
Farrell wrote that Russell was "running like a house
afire" and was "forging far out in front."(292)

Russell won re-election to the United States
Senate. On September 6, the Atlanta Constitution
mistakenly predicted the "Death Knell of
Talmadgeism." The editor also said that, of the
515,379 eligible voters, 300,000 Georgians would vote
in the White primary.(293) Of the 390,849 votes
cast, Russell received 256,154 (sixty-five percent),
and Talmadge 134,695. Russell won 378 county unit

votes, and Talmadge 32.   Of the eight counties with
largest populations, each having six unit votes,
Talmadge won in none.   In the thirty counties, each
having four units, he won in none.   In the 121
counties, each having two unit votes, the more rural
areas, Talmadge won in only 16.(294) E. D. Rivers,
Russell's choice for governor, won.   Roosevelt,
Russell's silent partner in the campaign, received a
"tidal wave" of votes in Georgia. Talmadge's candidate for Commissioner of Agriculture, Tom Linder,
lost, as did his appointees running for re-election
to the Public Service Commission.(295)   Eastern
newspapers predicted inaccurately "the happy ending
to a type of campaign that has been too familiar in
the south in the past."(296)

In 1938, Talmadge campaigned against incumbent
Walter F. George for the United States Senate.
Shifting his strategy, Talmadge advocated federal
support for programs for Georgians but within a
policy of tight financial constraints. Instead of
abolishing all government programs, he would now
expand the Civilian Conservation Corps as a means of
teaching "our boys a trade." Having learned in 1936
the appeal that government support had for voters,
Talmadge promised that if elected he would see that
federal relief funds were used for providing free
land for citizens. He was for "honesty, hard work,
and saving."(297) At Buford, he "caustically criticized New-Deal 'boon-doggling'," but explained that
the free land would go to the 10,000,000 unemployed.

Talmadge favored encouraging citizens to return
to the farm. "I want to place people on every farm
in Georgia," he told an Ellijay audience.   "Picture
your county with a good family on each of your
abandoned farms and under conditions fair to the
farmer." "Your community would come to life."   The
Roosevelt Administration programs had lost "billions," been "clumsy," and "done little good."
Farmers paying federal land banks was "just as hard"
as paying the "mortgage company."(298)   He said at
Buford that each needy person would be given $500
worth of land taken from "absentee landlords."(299)
Once the citizen had worked and improved the land and
paid taxes on it for five years, the fifty acres
would be deeded to that person, along with stock and
tools required. No one "would challenge this plank,"
he argued, for "they know I am right."(300)   He
warned that "boondoggling" would continue until the
"federal government is bankrupt." He would fight for
a "sound relief program and end the depression."(301)
If the extravagant federal spending continued, "this
government will be destroyed and Christian civilization destroyed with it."(302) As senator, he would

work for the "same program of economy in the federal
government" he had "carried out" in Georgia.(303)
    Talmadge attacked Senator George for represent-
ing the interests of the wealthy at the expense of
the working class. Although Senator George was
unable to mount the effective defense that Richard
Russell displayed in 1936, the elder statesman of
Georgia politics withstood attacks from both Talmadge
and Franklin Roosevelt and won re-election.
Roosevelt opposed Senator George's bid for
re-election because of what he perceived as a lack of
full support for New-Deal programs. Attempting to
purge the Congress of Senator Millard Tydings of
Maryland, Representative John O'Connor of New York,
and others who were not "avowed New Dealers,"
Roosevelt publicly opposed George's re-election and
supported Lawrence S. Camp.(304) On August 11, 1938,
with George sitting on the same platform in
Barnesville, Georgia, President Roosevelt criticized
the senator for not being of "the liberal school of
thought," and advocated bluntly that he be replaced
in the United States Senate with a Georgian who would
"stand up and fight . . . for federal statutes drawn
to meet actual needs. . . . If I were able to vote .
. . I most assuredly would cast my vote for Lawrence
Camp." As for Talmadge, Roosevelt said "his attitude
toward me . . . concerns me not at all, but . . . his
election would contribute little to practical government."(305)
    The Gallup Poll found that Georgians liked
Roosevelt, but resented his attempt to interfere in
their election of a public official. Seventy-five
percent of respondents said Roosevelt should not have
made the Barnesville speech against George.(306)
George responded to the President's criticism in a
balanced and judicious fashion, indicating that he
supported many of the Administration's New-Deal
programs, but reserved the right to ask for improvements that would benefit Georgians.(307) George
warned too that the United States "would cease to be
a democracy 'when the President selects' members of
Congress."(308) George received 141,235 popular
votes, Talmadge, 103,075, Lawrence S. Camp
(Roosevelt's choice), 76,778, and William G. McRae,
223. George won in eighty-six counties, Talmadge in
sixty-five, Camp in eight, and McRae in none. Of the
eight counties each having six unit votes, Talmadge
won in none. Of the thirty counties each having four
unit votes, Talmadge won in nine. Of the 121
counties each having two unit votes, Talmadge won in
fifty-six. George won 242 county unit votes,
Talmadge 148, Camp 20, and McRae 0.(309) As revealed
in Talmadge's losses of the 1936 and 1938 campaigns

for the United States Senate, Reporter Farrell was accurate in his observation that the governor had difficulty winning support on "national" issues.

NOTES

1. Atlanta Constitution, April 19, 1935.
2. Atlanta Constitution, April 17, 1935.
3. Atlanta Constitution, May 18, 1935.
4. Atlanta Constitution, January 30, 1936.
5. Atlanta Constitution, July 1, 1936.
6. Sarah McCulloch Lemmon, "Public Career of Eugene Talmadge, 1926-1936," Ph.D. dissertation, Univer of North Carolina, 1952, p. 107.
7. Atlanta Constitution, July 5, 1936.
8. Atlanta Constitution, September 4, 1936.
9. Griffin speech, Atlanta Constitution, August 27, 1936; Austell speech, August 30, 1936, Atlanta Constitution.
10. Marietta speech, Atlanta Constitution, September 4, 1936.
11. Atlanta Constitution, September 5, 1936.
12. Atlanta Constitution, August 6, 1936.
13. Atlanta Constitution, August 11, 1936.
14. Atlanta Constitution, August 16, 1936.
15. Lincolntown speech, Atlanta Constitution, July 30, 1936.
16. Cartersville speech, Atlanta Constitution, August 9, 1936.
17. Quoted in Atlanta Constitution, August 15, 1936.
18. Cartersville speech, Atlanta Constitution, July 16, 1936.
19. WSB radio speech, Atlanta Constitution, July 21, 1936; Eatonton speech, Atlanta Constitution, August 22, 1936.
20. Cartersville speech, Atlanta Constitution, July 16, 1936.
21. LaGrange speech, Atlanta Constitution, August 13, 1936.
22. LaFayette speech, Atlanta Constitution, August 19, 1936.
23. Quoted in Atlanta Constitution, April 19, 1935.
24. Gunnar Myrdal, An American Dilemma: The Negro Problem and Modern Democracy (New York: Harper and Brothers Publishers, 1944), p. 468.
25. Interview in New York City, Atlanta Constitution, May 18, 1935.
26. Quoted in Atlanta Constitution, April 19, 1935.
27. Quoted in Atlanta Constitution, April 23, 1935.
28. Dewey W. Grantham, Regional Imagination, The South and Recent American History (Nashville: Vanderbilt Univer Press, 1979), p. 201.
29. George Brown Tindall, Emergence of the New South, 1913-1945 (Baton Rouge: Louisiana State Univer

Press, 1967), pp. 385-386, 389-390, 428.

30. Michael S. Holmes, "The New Deal in Georgia: An Administrative History," Ph.D. dissertation, Univer of Wisconsin, 1969, pp. 52-76, 348-367.

31. Cartersville speech, Atlanta Constitution, July 16, 1936.

32. Quoted in Atlanta Constitution, April 17, 1935.

33. Canton speech, Atlanta Constitution, July 5, 1935.

34. Monroe speech, Atlanta Constitution, August 6, 1936.

35. Quoted in Atlanta Constitution, April 10, 1935.

36. Murphy, North Carolina speech, Atlanta Constitution, April 16, 1935.

37. Quoted in Atlanta Constitution, April 10, 1935.

38. Press conference, Atlanta Constitution, April 6, 1935.

39. Griffin speech, Atlanta Constitution, August 27, 1936.

40. Macon speech, Atlanta Constitution, August 21, 1936; Arlington speech, Atlanta Constitution, August 29, 1936.

41. Griffin speech, Atlanta Constitution, August 27, 1936; Arlington speech, Atlanta Constitution, August 29, 1936.

42. Macon speech, Atlanta Constitution, September 5, 1936.

43. WSB radio speech, Atlanta Constitution, August 9, 1936.

44. Atlanta Constitution, July 26, 1936.

45. Atlanta Constitution, August 13, 1936.

46. Atlanta Constitution, July 21, 1936.

47. Adel speech, Atlanta Constitution, August 1, 1936.

48. Atlanta Constitution, August 15, 1936.

49. Atlanta Constitution, September 3, 1936.

50. Atlanta Constitution, August 11, 1936.

51. Kingsland speech, Atlanta Constitution, July 26, 1936.

52. Commerce speech, Atlanta Constitution, September 3, 1936.

53. Swainsboro speech, Atlanta Constitution, August 19, 1936.

54. Atlanta Constitution, August 23, 1936.

55. Atlanta Constitution, August 27, 1936.

56. Atlanta Constitution, August 19, 1936.

57. Atlanta Constitution, September 1, 1936.

58. Quoted in Atlanta Constitution, August 16, 1936.

59. Atlanta Constitution, September 8, 1936.

60. Atlanta Constitution, August 21, 1936.

61. Atlanta Constitution, August 7 and September 2, 1936.

62. Coverage of Talmadge Dalton speech, Atlanta

Constitution, September 9, 1936.
63. Talmadge Canton speech, Atlanta Constitution, July 4, 1935.
64. Columbus speech, Atlanta Constitution, September 8, 1936.
65. Cartersville speech, Atlanta Constitution, August 9, 1936.
66. Hinesville speech, Atlanta Constitution, August 21, 1936.
67. Eatonton speech, Atlanta Constitution, August 22, 1936.
68. Article in Atlanta Constitution, August 30, 1936.
69. Tindall, Emergence of the New South, p. 331.
70. Bartley, Creation of Modern Georgia, p. 175.
71. Atlanta Constitution, September 9, 1936.
72. Lincolntown speech, Atlanta Constitution, July 30, 1936.
73. Cartersville speech, Atlanta Constitution, July 16, 1936.
74. Atlanta Constitution, September 8, 1936.
75. Atlanta Constitution, August 8 and 16, 1936.
76. Statement to Atlanta Constitution, July 16, 1936.
77. Colquitt speech, Atlanta Constitution, August 29, 1936.
78. Coverage of Talmadge Monroe speech, Atlanta Constitution, August 6, 1936.
79. Atlanta Constitution, September 4, 1936.
80. Atlanta Constitution, July 7, 1936.
81. Cartersville speech, Atlanta Constitution, August 9, 1936.
82. Ralph McGill in Atlanta Constitution, August 15, 1936.
83. Atlanta Constitution, August 28, 1936.
84. Macon speech, Atlanta Constitution, September 5, 1936.
85. Royston speech, Atlanta Constitution, August 28, 1936.
86. WSB radio speech, Atlanta Constitution, July 21, 1936.
87. Fort Valley speech, Atlanta Constitution, July 31, 1936.
88. Griffin speech, Atlanta Constitution, August 27, 1936.
89. Atlanta Constitution, July 24, 1936.
90. Eatonton speech, Atlanta Constitution, August 22, 1936.
91. Fitzgerald speech, Atlanta Constitution, August 13, 1936.
92. Statement to Atlanta Constitution, July 16, 1936.
93. Jasper speech, Atlanta Constitution, August 16,

1936.
94. Swainsboro speech, <u>Atlanta Constitution</u>, August 19, 1936.
95. Douglas speech, <u>Atlanta Constitution</u>, September 1, 1936.
96. Richland speech, <u>Atlanta Constitution</u>, August 20, 1936.
97. Macon speech, <u>Atlanta Constitution</u>, September 5, 1936.
98. Ralph McGill on Royston speech, <u>Atlanta Constitution</u>, August 7, 1936.
99. Omega speech, <u>Atlanta Constitution</u>, July 24, 1936.
100. Richland speech, <u>Atlanta Constitution</u>, August 20, 1936.
101. Milledgeville speech, <u>Atlanta Constitution</u>, August 28, 1936.
102. <u>Atlanta Constitution</u>, August 22, 1936.
103. Cartersville speech, <u>Atlanta Constitution</u>, August 9, 1936.
104. <u>Atlanta Constitution</u>, August 28, 1936.
105. <u>Atlanta Constitution</u>, July 31, 1936.
106. Dublin speech, <u>Atlanta Constitution</u>, September 2, 1936.
107. Coverage of Talmadge Macon speech, <u>Atlanta Constitution</u>, August 21, 1936, and of Russell Moultrie speech, <u>Atlanta Constitution</u>, August 26, 1936.
108. <u>Atlanta Constitution</u>, September 4, 1936.
109. Trion speech, <u>Atlanta Constitution</u>, August 23, 1936.
110. <u>Atlanta Constitution</u>, August 20, 1936.
111. <u>Atlanta Constitution</u>, September 4, 1936.
112. <u>Atlanta Constitution</u>, August 13, 1936.
113. <u>Atlanta Constitution</u>, July 19, 1936.
114. <u>Atlanta Constitution</u>, September 5, 1936.
115. <u>Atlanta Constitution</u>, August 7, 1936.
116. Dublin speech, <u>Atlanta Constitution</u>, September 2, 1936.
117. Dalton speech, <u>Atlanta Constitution</u>, September 4, 1936.
118. Richland speech, <u>Atlanta Constitution</u>, August 20, 1936.
119. Eatonton speech, <u>Atlanta Constitution</u> August 22, 1936.
120. Hinesville speech, <u>Atlanta Constitution</u>, August 21, 1936.
121. <u>Atlanta Constitution</u>, August 30, 1936.
122. <u>Atlanta Constitution</u>, August 28, 1936.
123. See Talmadge's <u>Statesman</u>, January 24, 1933; <u>Atlanta Constitution</u>, August 28, 1936.
124. <u>Macon Telegraph and News</u>, April 13, 1933.
125. Austell speech, <u>Atlanta Constitution</u>, August 30,

1936.
126. Atlanta Constitution, August 27, 1936.
127. Atlanta Constitution, August 13, 1936.
128. Atlanta Constitution, August 6, 1936.
129. Atlanta Constitution, August 27, 1936.
130. Atlanta Constitution, August 28, 1936.
131. Griffin speech, Atlanta Constitution, August 27, 1936.
132. Atlanta Constitution, August 8, 1936.
133. Atlanta Constitution, August 13, 1936.
134. Cornelia speech, Atlanta Constitution, September 1, 1936.
135. Atlanta Constitution, September 2, 1936.
136. Cairo, Georgia speech, Atlanta Constitution, August 26, 1936.
137. LaFayette speech, Atlanta Constitution, August 19, 1936.
138. Austell speech, Atlanta Constitution, August 30, 1936.
139. Griffin speech, Atlanta Constitution, August 27, 1936.
140. LaGrange speech, Atlanta Constitution, August 13, 1936.
141. Atlanta Constitution, September 2, 1936.
142. Atlanta Constitution, August 19, 1936.
143. Atlanta Constitution, September 5, 1936.
144. Griffin speech, Atlanta Constitution, August 27, 1936.
145. LaFayette speech, Atlanta Constitution, August 19, 1936.
146. Statement to Atlanta Constitution, July 16, 1936.
147. Moultrie speech, Atlanta Constitution, July 22, 1936.
148. Atlanta Constitution, September 2, 1936.
149. Atlanta Constitution, August 12, 1936.
150. Atlanta Constitution, July 24, 1936.
151. Atlanta Constitution, July 30, 1936.
152. Griffin speech, Atlanta Constitution, August 27, 1936.
153. Swainsboro speech, Atlanta Constitution, August 8, 1936.
154. Atlanta Constitution, August 29, 1936.
155. Lincolntown speech, Atlanta Constitution, July 30, 1936.
156. Arlington speech, Atlanta Constitution, August 29, 1936.
157. Atlanta Constitution, July 23, 1936.
158. Atlanta Constitution, August 7 and 22, 1936.
159. Atlanta Constitution, August 9, 1936.
160. Atlanta Constitution, September 1, 1936.
161. Dalla, Georgia speech, Atlanta Constitution, August 12, 1936.

162. Atlanta Constitution, August 28, 1936.
163. Atlanta Constitution, April 16, 1935.
164. Atlanta Constitution, July 5, 1934.
165. Atlanta Constitution, August 6, 1936.
166. Statement to Atlanta Constitution, April 20, 1935.
167. Nashville, Georgia, speech, Atlanta Constitution, August 22, 1936.
168. Lincolntown speech, Atlanta Constitution, July 30, 1936.
169. Quoted in Atlanta Constitution, April 23, 1935.
170. Cartersville speech, Atlanta Constitution, July 16, 1936.
171. LaFayette speech, Atlanta Constitution, August 19, 1936.
172. Griffin speech, Atlanta Constitution, August 27, 1936.
173. Atlanta Constitution, August 6, 1936.
174. Swainsboro speech, Atlanta Constitution, August 8, 1936.
175. Murphy, North Carolina, speech, Atlanta Constitution, April 16, 1935.
176. Atlanta Constitution, September 1, 1936.
177. Moultrie speech, Atlanta Constitution, July 22, 1936.
178. Monroe speech, Atlanta Constitution, August 6, 1936.
179. Cartersville speech, Atlanta Constitution, July 16, 1936.
180. Macon speech, Atlanta Constitution, August 21, 1936.
181. Atlanta Constitution, July 16, 1936.
182. Holmes, "New Deal in Georgia," p. 379.
183. Atlanta Constitution, August 8, 1936.
184. Atlanta Constitution, August 30, 1936.
185. Tindall, Emergence of the New South, pp. 393-396, 409.
186. Holmes, "New Deal in Georgia," pp. 439-443.
187. Numan V. Bartley, Creation of Modern Georgia (Athens: University of Georgia Press, 1983), p. 175.
188. Atlanta Constitution, January 30, 1936.
189. Atlanta Constitution, August 28, 1936.
190. Quoted in Atlanta Constitution, April 17, 1935.
191. Atlanta Constitution, April 17, 1935.
192. Cartersville speech, July 16, 1936.
193. Austell speech, Atlanta Constitution, August 30, 1936.
194. Interview in Atlanta Constitution, July 13, 1935.
195. Murphy, North Carolina, speech, Atlanta Constitution, April 16, 1935.
196. Interview in Atlanta Constitution, July 13, 1945.

197. Murphy, North Carolina, speech, <u>Atlanta Constitution</u>, April 16, 1935.
198. Lincolntown speech, <u>Atlanta Constitution</u>,   July 30, 1936.
199. Quoted in <u>Atlanta Constitution</u>, July 15, 1936.
200. <u>Atlanta Constitution</u>, August 6, 1936.
201. Quoted in <u>Atlanta Constitution</u>, April 23, 1955.
202. Murphy, North Carolina, speech, <u>Atlanta Constitution</u>, April 16, 1935.
203. Quoted in <u>Atlanta Constitution</u>, April 28, 1935.
204. <u>Atlanta Constitution</u>, August 7, 1936.
205. <u>Atlanta Constitution</u>, August 21, 1936.
206. <u>Atlanta Constitution</u>, September 9, 1936.
207. Cartersville speech, <u>Atlanta Constitution</u>, July 16, 1936.
208. <u>Atlanta Constitution</u>, July 23, 1936.
209. <u>Atlanta Constitution</u>, August 29, 1936.
210. <u>Atlanta Constitution</u>, August 27, 1936.
211. Murphy, North Carolina, speech, <u>Atlanta Constitution</u>, April 16, 1935.
212. Press conference, <u>Atlanta Conference</u> April 6, 1935.
213. Quoted in <u>Atlanta Constitution</u>, April 10, 1935.
214. <u>Atlanta Constitution</u>, August 13, 1936.
215. Cairo speech, <u>Atlanta Constitution</u>, August 26, 1936.
216. Swainsboro speech, <u>Atlanta Constitution</u>, August 8, 1936.
217. Tindall, <u>Emergence of the New South</u>, pp. 483, 318-319, 272.
218. Numan V. Bartley, <u>Rise of Massive Resistance: Race and Politics in the South during the 1940's</u> (Baton Rouge: Louisiana State Univer Press, 1969), p. 28.
219. Grantham, <u>Regional Imagination</u>, pp. 201-202, 10.
220. <u>Atlanta Constitution</u>, July 26, 1936.
221. <u>Atlanta Constitution</u>, August 13, 1936.
222. <u>Atlanta Constitution</u>, July 5, 1935.
223. Statesboro speech, July 5, 1935.
224. <u>Atlanta Constitution</u>, September 8, 1936.
225.   Marietta speech, <u>Atlanta   Constitution</u>, September 4, 1936.
226. <u>Atlanta Constitution</u>, September 3, 1936.
227. <u>Atlanta Constitution</u>, September 1, 1936.
228. Douglas speech, <u>Atlanta Constitution</u>, September 1, 1936.
229. Adel speech, <u>Atlanta Constitution</u>, August 1, 1936.
230. Editorial in <u>Atlanta Constitution</u>, July 11, 1935.
231. <u>Atlanta Constitution</u>, August 16, 1936.
232. <u>Atlanta Constitution</u>, July 5, 1935.

233. Dallas, Georgia, speech, Atlanta Constitution, August 12, 1936.

234. Atlanta Constitution, August 22, 1936.

235. Atlanta Constitution, August 16, 1936.

236. Atlanta Constitution, August 26, 1936.

237. Atlanta Constitution, July 31, 1936.

238. Colquitt speech, Atlanta Constitution, August 29, 1936.

239. Atlanta Constitution, September 5, 1936.

240. Atlanta Constitution, September 2, 1936.

241. Marietta speech, Atlanta Constitution, September 4, 1936.

242. Dublin speech, Atlanta Constitution, September 2, 1936.

243. Statesboro speech, Atlanta Constitution, July 5, 1935; Fitzgerald speech, Atlanta Constitution, August 13, 1936.

244. Kingslad speech, Atlanta Constitution, July 26, 1936.

245. Swainsboro speech, Atlanta Constitution, August 19, 1936.

246. Tindall, Emergence of the New South, pp. 407-409.

247. Marietta speech, Atlanta Constitution, September 4, 1936.

248. Atlanta Constitution, September 4, 1936.

249. Atlanta Constitution, August 22, 1936.

250. Omega speech, Atlanta Constitution, July 24, 1936; statement to Atlanta Constitution, July 16, 1936.

251. Royston speech, Atlanta Constitution, August 7, 1936.

252. Fort Valley speech, Atlanta Constitution, July 31, 1936.

253. Clarkesville speech, Atlanta Constitution, August 11, 1936.

254. Statement to Atlanta Constitution, July 16, 1936.

255. Atlanta Constitution, July 5, 1936.

256. Dallas, Georgia, speech, Atlanta Constitution, August 12, 1936.

257. Atlanta Constitution, July 31, 1936.

258. Douglas speech, Atlanta Constitution, September 1, 1936.

259. Atlanta Consitution, August 26, 1936.

260. Dublin speech, Atlanta Constitution, September 21, 1936.

261. Atlanta Constitution, August 27, 1936.

262. Atlanta Constitution, September 3, 1936.

263. Swainsboro speech, Atlanta Constitution, August 19, 1936.

264. Atlanta Constitution, May 4, 1935.

265. Atlanta Constitution, May 3, 1935.

266. Atlanta Constitution, May 3, 1935.

267. Quoted in Atlanta Constitution, May 5, 1935.

268. Rivers' Clarkesville speech, Atlanta Constitution, August 11, 1936.

269. Response to Talmadge's Wallburg, North Carolina, speech, Atlanta Contitution, July 7, 1935.

270. Atlanta Constitution, April 18, 1935; see Atlanta Constitution, August 16, 1936.

271. At Russell's Richland speech, Atlanta Constitution, August 20, 1936.

272. Atlanta Constitution, July 5, 1936.

273. Atlanta Constitution, August 22, 1936.

274. Atlanta Constitution, September 9, 1936.

275. Atlanta Constitution, August 27, 1936.

276. Coverage of Canton speech, Atlanta Constitution, July 4, 1935.

277. Atlanta Constitution, September 9, 1936.

278. Atlanta Constitution, August 26, 1936.

279. Atlanta Constitution, August 21, 1936.

280. Atlanta Constitution, August 8, 1936.

281. Quoted in Atlanta Constitution, September 9, 1936.

282. Atlanta Constitution, September 9, 1936.

283. Atlanta Constitution, September 2 and 4, 1936.

284. Atlanta Constitution, September 5, 1936.

285. Atlanta Constitution, July 5, 1935; emphasis added.

286. Lowell, Georgia, Atlanta Constitution July 18, 1936.

287. Atlanta Constitution, August 13, 1936.

288. Atlanta Constitution, August 13, 1936.

289. Editorial in Atlanta Constitution, August 28, 1936.

290. Press report in Atlanta Constitution, August 3, 1936.

291. L. A. Farrell in Atlanta Constitution, August 9, 1936.

292. Atlanta Constitution, August 16, 1936.

293. Atlanta Constitution, September 6 and 9, 1936.

294. Alexander Heard and Donald S. Strong, Southern Primaries and Elections 1920-1949 (Freeport, New York: Books for Libraries Press, 1950), pp. 64-65; Georgia's Official Register, 1933-1935-1937, pp. 536-540.

295. Atlanta Constitution, September 10 and 11, 1936.

296. Quoted in Atlanta Constitution, September 12, 1936.

297. Statement to Atlanta Constitution, May 14, 1938.

298. Ellijay speech, Atlanta Constitution, July 31, 1938.

299. Buford   speech, <u>Atlanta</u>   <u>Constitution</u>, May   20, 1938.

300. Dublin   speech, <u>Atlanta</u>   <u>Constitution</u>, July   5, 1938.

301. Jesup   speech, <u>Atlanta</u>   <u>Constitution</u>, July   28, 1938.

302. Griffin   speech, <u>Atlanta</u>   <u>Constitution</u>, August 16, 1938.

303. Danielsville speech, <u>Atlanta</u> <u>Constitution</u>, July 30, 1938.

304. <u>Atlanta</u> <u>Constitution</u>, August 12 and 17, 1938.

305. Roosevelt's   Barnesville,   Georgia   speech, <u>Atlanta</u> <u>Constitution</u>, August 12, 1938.

306. <u>Atlanta</u> <u>Constitution</u>, August 17, 1938.

307. Baxley speech, <u>Atlanta</u> <u>Constitution</u>, August 17, 1938.

308. Eastman   speech, <u>Atlanta</u>   <u>Constitution</u>, August 18, 1938.

309. <u>Georgia's</u> <u>Official</u> <u>Register</u>, 1939-1941-1943, p. 360; <u>Atlanta</u> <u>Constitution</u>, September 16, 1938.

7

Discrediting and Defending the University System

At the American Legion Park in Albany, Georgia, on July 4, Talmadge began his 1940 campaign for Governor. He reminded voters throughout the state by radio that in his previous two terms in that office he paid school teachers' salaries owed them in the past, placed the Highway Department "on a business basis," and built "more roads and bridges" than "in eight years of any other time." He also reduced rates for light, power, and telephone "from 15 to 40 percent." Coatless, with the red suspenders blazing, wearing a white belt and sleeves buttoned, he promised to "pay the state out of debt" accumulated under the Administration of E. D. Rivers. There were "too many engineers, linemen, supervisors, inspectors and clerks" and too little "results," he shouted. He would "slash overhead expenses to provide funds for old-age pensions" and "common schools."(1)

Effectively employing examples familiar to Georgians, at Valdosta Talmadge complained that "the Highway Department now has five times as much road machinery as they need. Look at it scattered in the roads, the swamps, bogged down in ditches."(2) He claimed to have been the first to provide school books for Georgia children, and "drew a burst of laughter" at Greensboro when he ridiculed Governor Rivers for providing "the first free school teachers."(3) At Royston, Talmadge predicted for Georgia a debt in 1941 of "practically fifty million dollars," all caused by "waste, extravagance and red tape."(4) In a radio address, Talmadge announced that because of surgery he would be unable to "visit every county."(5) However, he managed to speak often and effectively.

"Frequently engaging in repartee" with the

Albany crowd, he envisioned "an agriculture program
for permanent pastures" as a means of making Georgia
"the greatest hog, cattle, sheep, horse and mule
state in the southeast." He would "find out" about
gold in north Georgia and oil in the south.(6)   At
Toccoa, he promoted the development of deer and
trout. He would create in south Georgia a "sports-
man's paradise."(7) At Vidalia he promised to make
available to counties "loans of road machinery and
contracts for improvement of rural and post
roads."(8) With bombs reportedly falling "nightly"
on Great Britain, citizens were concerned about world
war. When questioned by a member of the "throng" at
Greensboro, Talmadge advised that "we must prepare
ourselves in this country to defend the nation
against any and all forces in the world." At home,
the country faced "an economic war." To win that
one, he would "cooperate" with the Roosevelt Administration, but not "worship at the feet of any one
man." When asked from the audience about the national Democratic convention in Chicago, with two losses
of campaigns for the United States Senate in mind,
Talmadge said, "This is a governor's race and let's
let it go that way. I learned years ago not to take
in too much territory."(9)

In July, reporter Luke Greene found that the
politicians were having a "tough time" interesting
farmers in the election. They were "disgruntled"
because sons badly needed as "plow hands" were called
to "military camps." Also, rain fell "night and
day," causing grass to "pop up between . . . cotton
rows," accompanied by the "blitzkriegs" of boll
weevils, all leaving potential voters "in a bad
humor." When a candidate approached a farmer, he
acted "as if he didn't hear you and starts right out
to talking about the war."(10) By August, reporter
Greene observed that candidates could find "a fairly
receptive audience around the courthouse," as farmers
gathered there "to whittle, chew their tobacco and
exchange views on crops, politics and everything."(11) Adding to the description of the ambi-
ence of the courthouse scene, Ralph McGill remarked:
"My own experience in going to vote was that I marked
my ballot standing between a gentleman who was
draining off a pause that refreshes and another who
was having coffee and aspirin."(12)

The candidates searched for a topic that interested voters. Ralph McGill complained of the "same-
ness" in the "speeches by the candidates," concluding
that "all were against use of the military," waste,
and more taxes.(13) The topic of racial integration
was noticeably absent from press reports of the
speeches. One issue dominated the campaign, and that

was the credibility of Gene Talmadge. With his aim upon Talmadge, candidate Columbus Roberts, Commissioner of Agriculture, predicted that voters were "weary of the lies of demagogues."(14) In several towns, the candidates participated in the same speaking, but not in the sense of face-to-face debates. Talmadge strolled through the audience, talking to persons while Abit Nix spoke.

At Warm Springs, because of heckling of the speakers, "blood streamed from bashed noses when a head-knocking spree" broke out between supporters of Talmadge and Nix. From the speaker's stand Talmadge said, "Don't hurt 'em boys."(15) Two days later at Gray, Nix quoted "news dispatches" asserting that at Warm Springs, when Talmadge "got up to speak, he gave the signal for an attack against some of my supporters."(16) On the other hand, the Athens Banner-Herald reported that the "Nix boys" heckled Talmadge first at Toccoa and were "getting ready for him at Warm Springs." Talmadge boasted that the "red-gallused boys went to work" and "the Nix crowd got a good whipping." Talmadge said he "always advised" supporters to "be respectful if they go to a meeting of our opponents." Charging that Talmadge "employed the ruthless methods of Hitler," Nix promised to help "destroy Talmadgeism." Illustrating just how potent Talmadgeism had become in Georgia politics, Nix endorsed the extreme "proposal to outlaw the use of paid hecklers at a political gathering."(17)

Talmadge reflected criticism to fuel his own campaign. Reporter L. A. Farrell observed that the "flash and fire" of his delivery was not "dimmed by the years."(18) At Decatur, he explained that each candidate who "abuses me personally is making a speech for Talmadge--not against me."(19) At Eatonton, he maintained that, although "not a wealthy man" and without "wealthy allies," he had "something a lot more effective, the support of the honest voters of Georgia, their faith in my promise, their trust in my ability and integrity."(20)

Talmadge advised that to restore the economy would require "another reconstruction." It would be "no easy task," requiring a man of his "experience" and "courage to say 'No'."(21) "When anything reaches the governor, it is something like the short-stop on the baseball field," he explained. "It comes to him hot. . . . When it comes back to me, I won't dodge." The working people knew "that Gene was in the play."(22) "Every lick I ever get at a tax bill I cut it."(23) He even planned to "get along with a general assembly that desires to see Georgia return to sanity, economy and efficiency,"(24) a goal

he accomplished on occasions by implementing policies
<u>after</u> that legislative body ended its sessions!

In August, to measure the popularity of candidates, "the Georgia Justice and Constables Association mailed 4,061 questionnaires to justices,
ex-officio justices, past and present, of the militia
districts of every county" where "there is a justice
court." A total of 3,642 answers returned showed
Talmadge leading Columbus Roberts twelve to one, Abit
Nix twelve and one-half to one, and Hugh Howell, who
eventually withdrew from the race, seventy-nine to
one. The <u>Augusta Chronicle</u> editorialized for
Talmadge.(25) In a second study, that paper reported
that more than eighty percent of the "opinions
received in favor" of Talmadge "carried the remarks"
that he "keeps his campaign promises" and can be
"relied upon to do what he says."(26)

Talmadge won the election of 1940, receiving
183,133 votes (over fifty-one percent) to Columbus
Roberts' 127,653 (thirty-six percent), and Abit Nix's
44,282 (over twelve percent). Talmadge won 318 unit
votes, Roberts eighty, and Nix twelve. Talmadge won
in 132 counties, Roberts 23, and Nix 4. In the eight
counties each having six unit votes, the more populated areas, Talmadge won in four. In the thirty
counties, each having four unit votes, Talmadge won
in nineteen. In the 121 counties, each having two
unit votes, Talmadge won in 109.(27)

After he was inaugurated as Governor, Talmadge
so embroiled himself with the management of the
University System of Georgia that his abuses cost him
the campaign for re-election in 1942. In 1931,
Governor Richard B. Russell, Jr., and the General
Assembly approved the "reorganization act," a bill
that united all institutions of higher education in
Georgia under the administration of one Board of
Regents. Before that plan was approved, twenty-three
colleges operated under the control of its own Board
of Trustees with only four sponsoring accredited
programs. By 1941 all institutions in the University
System were accredited. In 1940, the senate of Phi
Beta Kappa composed of educators from throughout the
United States concluded that the states of New York
and Georgia had made the most progress in developing
their systems of higher education.(28)

In the Spring of 1941, Governor Talmadge appointed nine new members to the Board of Regents and
became a member himself. With this newly formed
Board, the decade of improvements in the management
of higher education in Georgia was threatened by
Talmadge's political interference with the administration of the University System, causing the Southern Association of Colleges and Secondary Schools to

drop from its membership ten Georgia colleges.(29)
During his involvement in politics, from 1926 to
1941, there were few areas of government that he had
not politicized for self-interests. At the same
time, many persons opposed his attempt to monopolize
authority. When usurping the authority of the Board
of Regents in 1941, certainly Talmadge would have
recalled the opposition that derived indirectly from
that agency in his losing campaign against Senator
Richard B. Russell, Jr., in 1936. At that time,
Philip Weltner was chancellor of the University
System of Georgia. Weltner resigned that office and
met with other delegates in a state convention in
Macon to plan their opposition to Talmadge's 1936
candidacy.(30)

In this chapter, the author analyzes how Governor Talmadge manhandled the Board of Regents and
attempted to justify that flagrant abuse of political
authority to the citizens of Georgia. Equally
significant, the writer investigates the responses by
citizens and groups in Georgia to Talmadge's actions.
Talmadge's planned turbulence in education was begun
in a meeting of the Board of Regents in Athens,
Georgia, on May 30, 1941, when he asked that Dr.
Walter D. Cocking, Dean of the School of Education at
the University of Georgia, and Dr. Marvin S. Pittman,
President of Georgia Teachers' College, Statesboro,
not be rehired. Ostensibly Talmadge created the
convulsive turmoil to prevent the racial integration
of colleges and schools. Another likely explanation
was his attempt to solidify authority in the state
and win support among voters for his 1942 candidacy
for re-election as Governor. Having lost Senate
races in 1936 and 1938, the governor knew how precarious was one's tenure in elected office; thus, he
turned to the time-tested strategy of warning of the
threat of racial integration of southern society.

Obeying the Governor's request, the Board of
Regents voted on May 30, eight to four not to reappoint Dean Cocking and President Pittman. Later that
same day, after recessing to dedicate a building and
after Harmon Caldwell, president of the University of
Georgia threatened to resign in protest, the Board
recinded its decision in order to provide the two
educators an opportunity to answer charges brought
against them. During this series of events, publicly, faculty members of insititutions of higher
education in Georgia were largely silent, aware that
they too could be fired by the governor. However, on
June 1 fourty-three professors from the University of
Georgia signed a letter urging that Dean Cocking be
rehired. They also sent letters to each member of
the board of Regents.(31)

Although advertised to be a public meeting, on June 16 the board met in executive (secret) session in the governor's office to reconsider the vote taken earlier not to reappoint Dean Cocking. No minutes of the five-hour meeting were published.(32) The regents voted eight to seven to rehire Cocking, determining that the governor's claim that Dean Cocking advocated "inter-racial views" lacked evidence "sufficient" to fire him. President Pittman's hearing was postponed until July 14. To intimidate the regents, Talmadge reminded them that it was his "larger duty" to review "carefully the salaries . . . of employees" in state government. Unless he got his way, he threatened to cut the budget and to slash salaries of employees of the University System.(33)

Prior to the July 14 hearing on Cocking and Pittman, Talmadge demanded that Sandy Beaver, Chair, Miller R. Bell, and E. Ormonde Hunter, persons he had appointed to the Board of Regents, resign, ostensibly because too many regents were graduates of the University of Georgia. A 1937 statute required that no more than seven members may have graduated from the same alma mater, a law Talmadge apparently ignored when making initial appointments. Hunter said he had not attended the University of Georgia.(34) Attorney General Ellis Arnall, who would defeat Talmadge in the 1942 gubernatorial race, ruled the three regents could remain on the Board. Talmadge retorted coercively that he had not asked Arnall for "any opinion," and warned that the Attorney General was "headed in the wrong direction on a one-way street." Shifting to a new enemy alleged to be undermining higher education, the governor promised to "stamp out communism" regardless of what the lawyers and "high-pressure" educators did.(35) Georgia's Official Register indicates that, in the 1932 general election for president in Georgia, only twenty-three persons voted "Communist," while 19,863 voted Republican; 234,118, Democrat; 1,125, Prohibition; and 461, Socialist. In the 1936 general election, no one in Georgia voted Communist.

Sandy Beaver, Chair of the Board of Regents, was founder of the Riverside Academy in Gainesville, Georgia and a former classmate of Talmadge's. Being a close friend, Beaver was in New York City attending the Naval Intelligence Corps graduation of Herman, the son of Governor and Mrs. Talmadge, when he learned that back home the governor had asked for his resignation.(36) To have his way, Talmadge would readily sacrifice friend or foe. As Chair of the Regents, Beaver could have stopped reconsideration of the original vote to fire Cocking by voting and rendering the balloting a tie but he refused to so.

Beaver also declined to resign, insisting courageously that the charge made against Cocking by his friend
the governor was "wholly without foundation."(37)   In
an unusual act of conciliation, perhaps because he
had little choice, Talmadge appeared to "patch up his
differences" with Beaver.(38)   At the same time, the
governor managed to replace three regents with
appointees he said were "strong supporters" of him
who "understand the situation."(39)   Talmadge wanted
these persons on the Board by July 14, the date he
would have both Dean Cocking and President Pittman
found guilty and then tried.

Clark Howell of the _Atlanta_ _Constitution_, who
had supported Talmadge in some political campaigns,
resigned from the Regents, explaining that he had
promised Talmadge he would do so if asked, an arrangement he now "regretted."   Howell said he was
proud that the regents "refused to participate in a
witch hunt."   Talmadge announced that Judge Lucien P.
Goodrich, president of the University of Georgia
Alumni Association, had resigned from the Board of
Regents, but Goodrich insisted that he had not.(40)
Miller R. Bell refused to resign, and the governor
announced that Judge Joe Ben Jackson was replacing
him.(41) Bell complained accurately that to be a
Regent while Talmadge was governor one had to "wear
the badge of stooge."(42)   Certainly to stay on the
Board and speak one's conviction required great
courage.   Bell charged that the date when his term on
the regents would end had been falsified from 1947 to
1941.(43) In addition to Jackson, Talmadge appointed
Scott Candler and James S. Peters to the board.
Peters was sworn in at 10 A.M. and "made prosecutor"
at 11 A.M. the day of the July 14 trials for Dean
Cocking and President Pittman. Prior to the trials,
then, Talmadge had forged the majority support he
needed to endorse his decision to fire the two men.

The governor sought information about Cocking
and Pittman he could exploit rhetorically to give the
appearances to the mass of voters that the two
educators deserved to be terminated.   To assist
Talmadge in fabricating a case that justified his
premature decision to fire Dean Cocking, Robert F.
Wood was busy prying into the private life of the
accused.   Wood symbolized the power and political
abuse inherited in state government from the J. J.
Brown/Eugene Talmadge tenures as commissioners of the
Department of Agriculture. In 1941, the year of the
trial of Cocking and Pittman, Wood was employed as an
oil inspector in the State Motor Fuel Tax Unit.
Looking ahead to July 27, 1942, when Talmadge campaigned for re-election as governor against Ellis
Arnold, one finds Robert Wood at work again for the

Governor. Talmadge was speaking in Statesboro to a tobacco auction crowd, home of Georgia State Teachers' College, whose president, Marvin S. Pittman, along with Dean Cocking, in 1941, Talmadge placed on public trial. Students from that college in the 1942 gubernatorial campaign were heckling Talmadge when someone threw what a reporter called "mustard gas" among them. One person was taken to the hospital with burning eyes. The Bulloch County grand jury returned an assault indictment against Robert F. "Cowboy" Wood for allegedly throwing "some liquid, with a strong mustard odor" among the hecklers.   The gas was in "a small copper can with a long spout." At that time, Wood was operating the sound truck for Talmadge's campaign.   The containers had "bounced away from" the sound truck. Wood denied the charges. Two additional cans of gas were found in the sound truck.(44)

     Cowboy Wood lived in Athens, home of the University of Georgia where Cocking was employed as Dean. The press reported that, at one time Wood had planned to run for governor, but decided instead to support Talmadge. Georgia's Official Register shows that in the gubernatorial race of 1938, Wood came in fourth, behind Hugh Howell, J. J. Mangham, and E. D. Rivers, receiving only 2,220 votes and no county unit votes.(45) In 1941, to help Talmadge prepare for the infamous trials, oil inspector Woods was "beating the bushes" for "something" that would incriminate Dean Cocking. Athens photographer Chester Weatherly swore in an affidavit that Wood offered him $50 to "make a fake picture" by superimposing Cocking in a photograph with a "group of Negroes," thereby stirring up the explosive subject of "social equality" on which the Dean would be terminated at the July 14 meeting of the Board of Regents. Angered by a newsman's reporting of this incident, Talmadge admonished that "I've got that picture" of "white folks and Negroes" in Athens "eating together." The picture was of a draft board meeting to honor blacks who joined the military to serve their country. Later, E. R. Hodgson, Chair of the Clarke County draft board, explained that the picture was of a selective service meeting in December, 1940, a "patriotic occasion." Hodgson complained that Talmadge jeopardized the "co-operation between the races in defense of the country."(46)

     Mr. Tommie Banks, Dean Cocking's black "servant," swore that he was taken to a motel where Mr. Robert F. Wood and others told him he was in the Ku Klux Klan headquarters. Banks swore that Wood and others "sought first by bribery and then by intimidation" to have him find from Cocking's private papers information indicating that the dean advocated racial equality. In an account of the incident he later wrote, Cocking said the bribe to steal papers that tied him to "Negro activities" was $5,100.(47) Banks said the group had him sign a two-page statement that he was not allowed to read. They also asked Banks if Cocking had pictures in which Cocking and blacks were photographed together.(48)

No restrictions were placed upon the reliability of the materials that Wood was to find, for Talmadge knew clearly that he would use the information as recklessly as he often inflamed the mass of voters from the stump. Traditionally in the South and beyond that region, accusations of race mixing fueled rhetoric devoid of substantive arguments. At hundreds of political rallies between 1920 and 1941, Talmadge had perfected the tradition-honored craft in Georgia politics of out-"documenting" opponents, which meant primarily one's ability to wave alleged letters, reports, affidavits, and pictures dramatically to Shanghai voters. Because he believed he possessed the power to dominate the proceedings at the trials for Dean Cocking and President Pittman, the information that Woods dug up would not have to satisfy standards of authenticity or validity.

During the trials, Talmadge personally ensured that no information critical of the two professors would be ruled out of order. Indeed, throughout his career in and out of government, Talmadge employed the loose standards by which political rallies were conducted and the rhetorical overstatement employed there as means of cajoling and bullying audiences of all kinds. The sole criterion Wood was to employ in gathering "evidence" was that it be of an emotional nature that Talmadge could employ hyperbolically to stimulate a signal/racist response from many white voters. Based upon alleged findings from Cowboy Wood's nefarious research, Talmadge maintained that he had "new evidence showing that Cocking attended interracial meetings" and that "several pictures might be introduced." Apparently no picture incriminating Cocking of charges brought by Talmadge was found.(49)

During the July 14 meeting, Cocking and Pittman were given alleged trials in which they were prosecuted by newly appointed Board member, James S. Peters, a "highly esteemed banker" who had been sworn in as a Talmadge appointee that same day. To assure a wider public audience, Talmadge had the infamous trials of Dean Cocking and President Pittman held in the State House of Representatives. He proclaimed that, "In the future, any meeting of the Board of Regents, where I attend as a member, will be a public meeting," a decision a storm of criticism would later force him to recant. This rhetorical choice was comparable to Talmadge's bravery in debating incumbents to his advantage, but refusing when underdog candidates challenged him to public disputations. As long as he controlled the publicity of the trials of Cocking and Pittman for the benefit of his political future, he required that the hearings be open to the press and others. Unlike the farm meeting in Macon in 1931, where judicious enforcement of rules of parliamentary procedure prevented Talmadge from dominating the debate, during the trials for Cocking and Pittman the governor orchestrated the process of decisionmaking and packed the regents with persons he could depend upon to vote his way.

During the trials, a majority of the regents allowed Talmadge's will to be done at the sacrifice of education for the youth of Georgia. At this stage of what was a carefully contrived rhetorical turbulence for self-political gain, Talmadge was completely confident that he would create concern for an alleged threat of racial integration, install himself permanently as Georgia's defender of white rule, and defeat Attorney General Ellis Arnall in a race for governor in 1942.(50) He felt unequivacally that he personally would have his way because he now, as he had prophesied, was beyond the reach of "the law." Most importantly, he felt from personal successes on the stump that he could seduce the white voters into believing that a few sissy professors were plotting to breakfast and bed their sons and daughters next to blacks on college campuses in Georgia.

Prior to the July 14 trials, Talmadge primed the public's perceptions of Dean Cocking and President Pittman by representing those educators' attitudes as being repugnant to traditional southern principles. The governor identified Cocking to be "close to the Julius Rosenwald Fund," a Foundation Talmadge said was purchasing support among Georgia professors through grants for racially integrated schools. Talmadge maintained that Cocking's attitude toward race relations was foreign to southern traditions. In some ways, within the historical context in which the trials took place, Cocking appeared to be more subject to criticism by an abusive governor than was Pittman. Cocking was perceived by some persons to be "brash and tactless"--qualities with which the governor should have identified--sympathetic to blacks, but not an advocate of racial integration.(51) Employing methods of research mastered at the stump, the governor said he "looked up" Cocking's "record" and found that he was educated at the University of Chicago and born in Iowa, "where the

racial question is not the . . . same as it is in
Georgia." Cocking's Ph.D. was from Columbia University. "There are too many professors from without
the state, raised under different environments from
the Georgia people," insisted Talmadge. "We have
enough competent, educated, Christian young teachers
in Georgia without jobs . . . to fill our needs."
Flexing the political clout that enabled him to
create the rhetorical turbulence in the University
System in the first place, the governor promised in
the future to consider the residency of applicants
for positions when reviewing the budget for education
in the state.(52) Residency, however, was not
Talmadge's concern, for President Pittman, the second
scapegoat to be placed on "trial," was born in
Mississippi the grandson of a slave owner. Even the
language of Talmadgeism would have difficulty representing Pittman as a "foreigner"!

Talmadge wanted only persons supporting him
personally in places of authority in education and in
government. By maintaining his followers in positions of influence, he pushed his own powers beyond
the control of persons and institutions. To achieve
those goals, he used all stump appeals available. In
a speech in Birmingham, Alabama, Talmadge alerted the
Masonic Lodge that Communism had "shown its dragon
head" in education in Georgia. He assured the Masons
that "we're not going to have any Communists in" his
system of education. "Four generations of his
family" had been educated at the University of
Georgia. Shifting to a second emotional sabotage, he
planned "to send his son there" and hoped it would
"be with white people." For goodwill Talmadge added
that Georgia had some newspapers that "ought to be in
hell."(53) Regents Chair Sandy Beaver, keenly aware
that three of his colleagues on the board had been
fired by the governor, and trying to hold on to his
own position and protect the integrity of the University System without completely alienating his powerful and obstinate friend Talmadge, answered that, if
leaders put the "interest of youth" first, "Communism
and racial equality will never get a foothold."(54)

Persisting in a highly politicized method of
researching issues that produced only "information"
he could exploit for self-interest, Talmadge "ordered" state Auditor B. E. Thrasher, Jr., to make a
list of "all of those foreign professors," that is,
persons holding views different from the governor's.
Anticipating how he would propogandize the trials for
Dean Cocking and President Pittman in the same manner
that he helped orchestrate the 1926 debates with
Commissioner J. J. Brown, Talmadge promised Georgians
that when the necessary information was in hand, "we

are going to have a little fun." Indeed, to Talmadge the flagrant abuse of seemingly defenseless persons and institutions was great entertainment for voters, whether he was challenging H. Marsh of Portal, Georgia, to a fight during a political rally in Swainsboro,(55) employing the National Guard to back his "will at the point of bayonets,"(56) creating a martial setting in which supporters felt secure in gasing and fighting opponents,(57) sacrificing the pensions of the elderly in a campaign for the United States Senate, or attempting to fire a university dean and president without giving them an opportunity to answer vaguely stated and unsupported charges.

Speaking sarcastically of Cocking, Talmadge advised: "If some of those professors can get more money and bigger jobs somewhere else, then we ought to do all we can to help them get those fine jobs." Attempting to add valid reasoning to the discussion Talmadge was conducting prematurely in the press, and sidestepping the primary motivation of the Governor, Regent Chair Beaver insisted that Georgians were "given preference for jobs," but there were occasions when the "exact" employee needed was not available in the state.(58) Less than a week before the trial, the governor boasted that Cocking "ain't agoin' to be any pfessor'."(59)

On July 14, 1941, Talmadge had Dean Cocking and President Pittman tried by the Board of Regents. The governor exercised personal control over every aspect of the so-called trials of Cocking and Pittman, hearings that became recognized locally and national- ly as a mockery of justice, the cause of ten colleges in Georgia losing their academic accreditation, and the primary reason that the governor was defeated by Ellis Arnall in the gubernatorial election of 1942. When two of his newly hand-picked regents, banker James S. Peters and Judge Joe Ben Jackson entered the hall of the House of Representatives for the trials, Talmadge "saw to it" that they "had chairs up on a rostrum just below the one" occupied by Beaver. From this vantage point, they made and seconded the motions for dismissing Cocking and Pittman. Reporter Frank Drake concluded that the governor put his two "trained seals," Peters and Jackson, through the motions of a trial whose verdict had been rehearsed and decided in an earlier executive session. Meeting in the governor's private office prior to the trials, the Regents had voted nine to five to reconsider the board's June 16 decision to re-employ Cocking. The script that Talmadge required Peters to follow in the trials had been carefully planned and typed, to the point of instructing "when each bit of evidence was to be introduced." Prosecutor Peters reportedly was

allowed to introduce evidence used before, while
Hatton Lovejoy, attorney for Cocking, was not.(60)
S. V. Sanford, Chancellor of the University System
did not attend the trials, claiming prophetically but
faintly that "there wasn't any use."(61) Sanford had
recommended that the two educators be reappointed.

The governor produced and directed the trials.
Throughout the hearings, when Peters faltered,
Talmadge advised him on selection of words, physical
expressions, and verbal delivery he knew from stump
experience could flimflam enough white Georgians to
re-elect him governor in 1942. Once more, he was
taking his case rhetorically to the people, this time
by sacrificing two competent and respected educators
at the judicial stump. Talmadge sat "sprawled" in a
chair near prosecutor Peters, wearing a white coat,
with "cigar clamped in an iron jaw." When the Chair
of the Regents ruled on a procedure that Talmadge did
not like, the governor "jumped to his feet and
flashed his cigar at Beaver, shouting, 'You can't
rule until you hear from'" prosecutor Peters. When
Peters "faltered or forgot to bring out some point,"
the governor "prompted" him. "Frequently" Talmadge
called Peters "to him" and told "him what to do
next." Reporter Drake described how, when Peters
"hestitated" in developing the case against Cocking,
and Talmadge "noted that the audience was" becoming
"restive," the governor gave the prosecutor
"oratorical-instructions: 'Hit the chair and hol-
ler'." Talmadge had memorized the stump theorem that
shouting was inverse to the substance of arguments, a
strategy in his arsenal second only to calling one a
race mixer.

Because he was so experienced and effective
making sweeping charges against opponents, Talmadge
was impatient with banker Peters' tentativeness in
pursuing Cocking's contrived guilt. Talmadge was
itching to replace Peters at the podium. When Peters
"paused for a moment" to gather his thoughts, the
governor directed, "Go ahead, keep it going."
Another time, Talmadge admonished, "They're listening
to you; don't stop." Once when Peters read from a
college textbook that he said proved that the two
educators "advocated Negroes and white people sitting
together," Talmadge "wanted it emphasized" more.
Following the tutoring in stump rhetoric, Peters then
"put more 'oomph' in his delivery." Prosecutor
Peters also emulated a rhetorical strategy long a
mainstay in the governor's coercive persuasion,
directing his emphasis "more to the audience" in the
hall than the regents.(62) The Regents had voted
Talmadge's will in private before the trials began;
now, in the public hearings, Talmadge sought votes

for his 1942 candidacy. Ultimately Talmadge wanted
his "people" to render this verdict, not any community of educators or opposing journalists.

Although Walter D. Cocking, Dean of the School
of Education at the University of Georgia was tried
first, the procedure became somewhat confusing as
cross-charges against Cocking and Pittman were made
as prosecutor Peters and Talmadge deemed advantageous
for their cause. Governor Talmadge had Peters
attempt to demonstrate that Cocking intended to
establish a racially integrated school. In a statement to the press prior to the trials, Talmadge said
that Ms. Sylla W. Hamilton, "a high-toned, intelli-
gent Christian lady," charged that Cocking "advocated" establishing a "new campus" thirty minutes from
Athens for "whites and blacks," to be staffed by
professors in the Department of Education at the
University of Georgia. Hamilton charged that the
students would "practice [teach] together and study
educational, social, economic, financial and health
problems."(63) Hamilton had been fired from an
instructorship in a public high school sponsored by
the College of Education of which Cocking was Dean.
Her family was influential in state politics. She
was fired because she allegedly lacked the "temperament" needed for teaching.(64) Hamilton was not
taken off the pay roll, but reassigned secretary to
the Institute for the Study of Georgia Problems under
Dean R. Preston Brooks.(65) Harmon Caldwell, president of the University of Georgia, defended Cocking's
record at the trial, and insisted that the charges
brought against the Dean were not true. He reminded
the regents that thirty-five or forty faculty had
attended the faculty meeting described by Hamilton,
and that they "did not interpret what was said as"
she had.

In his research, Ramsey found that some persons
believed that Dean Cocking and Edwin R. Embree,
president of the Rosenwald Fund, were leading a
"movement to promote racial equality in Georgia."
Apparently Talmadge was told some years earlier that
"Cocking . . . revealed" what the source perceived to
be "plans 'for the co-education of the races'" to a
University Council meeting in Statesboro in 1935.
Talmadge, unable to run for re-election in 1936,
campaigned for the United States Senate against
Richard B. Russell; thus, Cocking continued as dean
under the administration of Governor E. D. Rivers.
In 1938, Dean Cocking sponsored a meeting at the
University of Georgia "on the higher education of
blacks," attended by "a small group of segregated
black delegates," an event that caused some "controversy" in the press.(66) Under his direction, the

College of Education at the University of Georgia, in January 1939, published "The Present Program of Teacher Education of the University of Georgia and Its Future Development," in which white and black schools were compared and the creation of the demonstration school outside of Athens in which black and white teachers would be trained was recommended.(67) During the trial, one of the three newly appointed Regents, Scott Candler, asked President Caldwell if he did "not think" Dr. Cocking's "usefulness . . . had been impaired by these charges." Caldwell, who had threatened to resign as president if Cocking and Pittman were fired without a hearing, replied wisely that "the usefulness of the University of Georgia and many of us over there has been impaired by these charges."(68)

A number of books and pamphlets were introduced by prosecutor Peters to attempt to identify Cocking with the racial integration of education. Peters displayed the book, Brown America: The Story of a New Race, by Edwin Rogers Embree of the Rosenwald Fund, a foundation Talmadge claimed was using its considerable financial resources to bring about the racial integration of southern schools. Dean Cocking denied any connection with the book. Upon hearing the persistent criticism of the Rosenwald Fund, Regent E. Ormonde Hunter, the most out-spoken supporter of Cocking and Pittman during the "trials," said sarcastically that, if money from the Rosenwald Fund were so corrupting, the Board of Regents should "return all" the payments made to higher education in Georgia by that foundation, a motion ruled out of order because it had not been submitted in writing.(69) That Talmadge and Peters would ignore Hunter's recommendation was understandable for the Julius Rosenwald Fund had awarded a minimum of $325,000 to Georgia for education over the previous five years.(70) Rosenwald foundation funds were used to build a school at Warm Springs, at whose dedication Franklin D. Roosevelt spoke.(71)

Attorney Hatton Lovejoy, representing Dean Cocking, insisted that neither his client nor President Pittman advocated integration of the races, reminding the Regents cunningly that all the books cited by Peters were written and published outside of Georgia, a favorite decision-making criterion of the governor. Upon hearing Lovejoy's defense, Talmadge prompted Peters: "Tell'em about the niggers from Tuskegee [Institute] visiting" Georgia Teachers' College in Statesboro, a late charge brought against Pittman, president of that institution. Following instructions Peters asserted that "Negro teachers" had "eaten on" the Statesboro campus "with white people." Demonstrating how peculiar had become the conventions that dictated interactions between blacks and whites in the South, Professor R. J. DeLoach, member of the faculty at Statesboro, explained surgically how he "saw the Negroes eating something on the campus," but refused to say that blacks and whites "were sitting around tables . . . eating together," a distinction many whites in 1941 and beyond considered important and Talmadge was masterful in exploiting.(72)

As so often happened on the occasions when Talmadge performed his turbulent acts, during the first trial a fight broke out in the House of Representatives when an opponent of the governor attempted to express a minority view. Judge Joe Ben Jackson, newly appointed regent, arguing against the reappointment of Cocking and Pittman, had proclaimed that "the most uneducated white man is better than the best Negro," a claim a New Hampshire member of the audience challenged. For expressing an opinion quite foreign to those shouted historically in this hall, the New Hampshire guest was "slugged," learning firsthand an important lesson in the southern hospitality of Talmadgeism. The governor had "at least" four state highway patrolmen in plain clothes "constantly moving around." Increasingly, during his public appearances, as illustrated in Chapter 6 on his campaign against Richard B. Russell, Jr., the governor took with him armed national guardsmen and others of a more personal loyalty and persuasion. As was true at political rallies, persons in the House of Representatives attending the trial who called out in support of Talmadge's charges were treated favorably. When John Anderson McDuff, an Atlanta lawyer, yelled to Hatton Lovejoy, attorney for Dean Cocking, "Who is paying you," Talmadge and Beaver instructed a guard not to remove him from the audience.(73)

Dean Cocking called the charges a "nightmare," and stated that the press had "disclosed almost unbelievable things" concerning how the investigation took place "that make the blood of the believer in any sort of justice and fair play run cold." With the investigating tactics of oil inspector Cowboy Wood apparently in mind, Dean Cocking denied that he had advocated racial equality, maintaining that evidence "of the filthiest sort" had been "concocted" against him. Cocking also denied claims by I. M. "Bull" Bray that allegations had been made that Cocking stayed with his black cook after taking her home and that he was a homosexual, assertions for which there was no evidence. Bull Bray, like Cowboy Wood, worked in Talmadge's campaigns. He was the individual who at times, in one of the canned gestures by which Talmadge seduced crowds and the press, lifted Talmadge on his arms after the governor finished speaking at political rallies throughout the state, and carried him from the crowd. Some of the personal accusations against Cocking apparently were not brought up at the trials.(74) When Cocking defended his innocence, from the audience attorney John Anderson McDuff again "cat-called, 'Yankee talk'." The only Regents who defended Cocking and Pittman at the trials were the highly courageous E. Ormonde Hunter and George Woodruff. "Hunter frequently tried to bring out the shallowness of Peters' investigation . . . but was unable to get very far."(75)

Later Talmadge offered a peculiar assessment of the nature of the testimony given in support of the defendent. He agreed that "A great many witnesses were called on behalf of Dr. Cocking." Although "all swore" they had "never heard" him advocate "mixing" the races "in schools," that "was negative evidence. He could have advocated it and they not have heard it." Whereas Hamilton "swore that she heard him offer the plan."(76) As noted above, however, President Caldwell testified that thirty-five or forty other faculty members present at the faculty meeting did hear their dean's presentation, but rejected Hamilton's claim.

When the so-called trial of Dean Cocking ended, Chair Beaver suggested that the board recess, but Talmadge "voiced strenuous objections," opposing any "break" between the two trials, further effort by the governor to steamroll guilty verdicts. At the meeting of the Board of Regents on May 30, 1941, when Talmadge first recommended that Cocking and Pittman be terminated, the regents initially supported his motion. But during a recess, when regents contemplated the decision away from the intimidation of the governor, a majority voted to reconsider the cases. During these trials Talmadge was determined to exercise more control over the procedure and the decisions. Without recessing, Peters began the prosecution of Pittman, President of Georgia Teachers' College of Statesboro. W. G. Nevill was Pittman's legal counsel.

Attempting to demonstrate wrongs done by President Pittman was difficult because there was less emotional information that Talmadge could exploit rhetorically. Consequently, for several weeks prior to the July 14 trial, as accusations introduced against Pittman were refuted, the governor changed the charges, all this after having already asked the Board of Regents to fire the man. Because the governor could be so reckless in discussing issues and personalities on the stump, it did not shake his confidence or change his strategy that even he had some difficulty keeping straight the charges made against Pittman and Cocking. In this kangaroo court the Governor needed no license to preach.

During his trial, President Pittman reminded the regents that originally two charges were brought against him, that he was too active in partisan politics and that he did not fit into the community of Statesboro. Two weeks before the trial Talmadge said that Pittman was taking "too enthusiastic an interest in politics."(77) When Talmadge's oil inspector Robert F. "Cowboy" Wood left Athens, having finished looking for incriminating evidence about Dean Cocking, he traveled to Statesboro where he sought materials that would justify the governor's earlier recommendaton that President Pittman be fired. Arno Bennet, college electrician, said that Pittman did not allow former students and college laborers to attend a Talmadge rally. In an account he later wrote of the charges, President Pittman stated that during a political campaign he had "banners" supporting Talmadge's candidacy removed. Pittman also wrote that Philip Morgan indicated that word went out that if the Statesboro district failed to vote for Talmadge in the next election, the governor might make changes in the faculty and even move the college.(78) Georgia's Official Register shows that in Bulloch County, locale of Statesboro, Talmadge won in 1926, 1928, 1930, 1932, and 1940, but lost in 1936 and 1938.

The charge that Pittman did not "fit in" at Statesboro was a shear stroke of stupidity, probably deduced by oil inspector Cowboy Wood from his pene- trating study at the scene of the College. Pittman had been president of Georgia Teachers' College for seven years, and was immensely popular with citizens, civic groups, and ministers, many of whom documented that support in writing when the false accusations were made. Even Talmadge had difficulty accusing Pittman of being under the influence of persons from outside the South. Pittman did not fit Talmadge's original representation of a "foreigner." In a later speech, Pittman explained that he was "a southerner by birth and rearing. I am the grandson of a slave owner, the son of a Confederate soldier."(79) Pittman was born in Mississippi, and held a Ph.D. from Columbia University. At this time, few southern universities sponsored doctoral programs comparable to well established universities outside the region. Apparently Pittman had worked in politics in Louisi- ana and Michigan, but not in Georgia. Unlike the outspoken Dean Cocking, personally Pittman was less a target, "quiet and discreet." But he was able to "inspire others," providing competition for loyalties that Talmadge disliked.(80)

To bolster an obviously weak case, Talmadge shifted to the charge that Pittman employed labor and materials from Georgia Teachers' College on his thirty-acre farm for personal gain. Prosecutor Peters produced an affidavit in which Ernest Cannon, ex-foreman of the college farm charged that machinery, seed, and fertilizer belonging to the college had been used on Pittman's personal farm for two years. It was also reported that employees of the college had been employed on Pittman's farm to clear fence rows, till the land, and plant pine trees at a total cost of $3,000. Pittman reminded the regents that he had informed them two years before that he was allowing the college to use his land. Pittman claimed that all proceeds from the farm went to the college, that over a two-year period the state had realized $535.32, and he had not received "one penny." He had bought such materials as fence posts. Regent Hunter argued that "if anybody has erred it's the board of regents."(81) Before the trial, Talmadge stated that the charges that Pittman was too involved in politics and used college resources for personal benefit were "not of as serious a nature" as those made against Cocking.(82)

In a later speech, Regent E. Ormonde Hunter explained how inconsistent were the charges brought against President Pittman. Although initially blamed for "undue political activity and not fitting into his community," during the trial in Atlanta of Pittman, insisted Hunter, "not one word was said" about either of those counts. Then, when a "belated charge" of employing college resources for his own profit "began . . . to backfire," prosecutor Peters turned to the recurring theme of race. Regent Hunter ridiculed: "I honestly thought that the prosecution was going to acquit Pittman."[83]

When the other accusations deteriorated, like Dean Cocking, Pittman was charged with favoring racial integration. Charges of integration of the races could lose one an election in the South or one's life. Talmadge believed he could make this vague and emotional accusation effectively against Pittman or any other person. Prosecutor Peters maintained that the "same sentiment" for integrating the races that existed at the University of Georgia "has slipped into Statesboro" where Pittman served as President of Georgia Teachers' College. Having learned from Talmadge during the trial of Dean Cocking how to cover over a weak argument by increasing one's volume, Peters "cried, 'You've got to kill this thing while it's a little serpent'." Peters claimed that the book, <u>Calling</u> <u>America</u>: <u>The</u> <u>Challenge</u> <u>of</u> <u>Democracy</u> <u>Reaches</u> <u>Over</u> <u>Here</u>, originally published as a special issue of <u>Survey</u> <u>Graphic</u> by Harper and Brothers in 1939, had been "used in Statesboro with Pittman's approval."(84) Peters complained that the book "showed a Negro naked and in shackles," apparently concerned more with the former condition than the latter. Pittman said he knew nothing about the book, only that it was recommended by the Social Science Committee of the University System, under the direction of the Board of Regents, and presumed to be found in other colleges in Georgia. Pittman was also accused of having whites and blacks eat together on the campus in Statesboro.(85)

Pittman denied the newly conceived indictments that he favored racial integration and allowed "un-American books" to be used in classes at Georgia Teachers' College. Dr. William A. Sutton, Atlanta city school superintendent, gave a "stirring speech" during the trial that surprisingly "drew thunderous applause"; apparently a number of persons opposed to Talmadge attended the trials but were able to testify only under very difficult conditions. Sutton said he was "not pleading for Dr. Pittman" but for "Georgia and her boys and girls. We have an opportunity to train young men and women in the state so that they won't hate anybody," an important step he said was being "taken by Dr. Pittman." "Turning to Dr. Pittman," Sutton concluded courageously and wisely that "if Georgia doesn't want that kind of people, God have mercy on Georgia."(86) No longer willing to just sit on the sideline and prompt Peters, Talmadge asked School Superintendent Sutton if he believed black and white teachers should receive the same pay,(87) a line of reasoning the governor attempted unsuccessfully when opposing President Roosevelt, the New-Deal, and Richard Russell in the 1936 campaign for the United States Senate. (Under the guise of preventing the racial integration of public schools, Talmadge later threatened to have himself made chair of the State Board of Education.)(88)

When the infamous trials ended under Governor Talmadge's watchful eye, a majority of the Board of Regents voted to fire Cocking and Pittman; the recently appointed Regents forged a new majority for Talmadgeism.(89) When the decision "was announced, Governor Talmadge turned and smiled to the throng sitting and standing in the house of representatives." With the audacity of a person confident that his powers were immune from any threat by others, the governor assured the public that the two educators received "a fair hearing" because he "appointed men

that would give them a fair hearing."(90)   Regent   L.
W. "Chip" Robert, former .assistant secretary of   the
United States Treasury, introduced a   resolution
praising Talmadge and denying that the governor   had
injected politics into the   University System.   The
resolution thanked Talmadge for assistance   rendered
to the University of Georgia, the people of the
state, and to generations to follow, particularly his
defense of "fundamental principles . . . of the
southland" and his upholding of the "welfare of both"
blacks and whites. Although the resolution was   protested vigorously by Regents E. Ormonde Hunter   and
George C. Woodruff, after considerable argument,   it
was approved.(91)

Regents supporting Talmadge and voting to fire
Dean Cocking and President Pittman were John J.
Cummings, L. W. "Chip" Robert, K. S. Varn, Susie T.
Moore, Julian Strickland, Jr., James S. Peters, Scott
Candler, Joe Ben Jackson, and Joe Jenkins.   Regents
supporting the rehiring of Cocking and Pittman were
E. Ormonde Hunter, T. Jack Lance, George C. Woodruff,
R. D. Harvey, and W. S. Morris. Lance, president of
Young Harris College, resigned soon after the infa-
mous trials.(92) More confident of its newly sanc-
tioned powers, in an executive meeting following the
"trials," the regents terminated J. Curtis Dixon,
Vice Chancellor of the Board of Regents, R. E. Davis,
Beef Cattle and Sheep Specialist with the Agricultural Extension Service, and P. D. Bush, Professor at
North Georgia College. Eventually several others
were fired.

Because the governor had rendered the   two
educators guilty in public statements prior to the
"trials," and because Dean Cocking, President
Pittman, and their supporters found it difficult to
present their sides of the story in those hearings,
Cocking, Pittman, Vice Chancellor Curtis Dixon, and
others gave their cases later in public speeches.   To
their credit, the Kiwanis Club of Griffin, the Lions
and Rotary clubs of Atlanta, the Rotary Club of
Decatur, the Kiwanis Club of Savannah, and WSB Radio
of Atlanta provided forums in which opponents of the
governor could defend themselves. Supporters of
Talmadge were also given an opportunity to defend
their positions.

On July 16, 1941, fired President Marvin Pittman
spoke to an audience at Georgia Teachers' College and
asked that "teachers 'live and defend truth'.   Many
of the teachers wept."(93) On July 31, Pittman spoke
to Georgians by way of WSB radio in Atlanta.   In this
address, Pittman accused Governor Talmadge of being
"unfair" by assuming that he "knows so much" that his
judgment should "prevail over that of all the good

and the wise people," by the manner in which he produced trials of "sham and shame," and because he brought "baseless dishonest" charges.   Pittman scorned Talmadge for fabricating "reasons" for terminating employees that he "cannot even remember." Talmadge fired persons "to satisfy some grudge and to put the fear of the big stick" into employees, continued Pittman.   Pittman told how Talmadge's oil investigator, Robert F. Wood, tried to "dig up evidence" against Cocking and himself.

Pittman revealed that prior to the trials, Talmadge sent a member of the Board of Regents to persuade him and Cocking to resign.   He said they were told that if they agreed to resign the governor would "deal generously with us."   If he did not step down, the governor "would use any means, however ruthless, in order to fire" him and "smear" his reputation.   Pittman refused to resign, telling Talmadge's messenger that he had "done no conscious wrong."   He said Cocking agreed to resign if the Governor would promise to "make certain fundamental changes in the administration of the University System."   As for accusations that five teachers from Tuskegee Institute visited his college in Statesboro, they were there for "a half day observing the opera-tion of our practice schools."   In a statesman-like stand that was quite rare for the period, Pittman said publicly that it was "un-American . . . to raise again the old race issue of the south, the cause of so much pain . . . and for the cure of which all men of good will have striven so earnestly."(94)

In a speech on July 23, 1941, to a large crowd of the Griffin Kiwanis Club and their guests, the Exchange and Rotary clubs, fired Dean Walter D. Cocking warned that "agents of despotism are on the move."   Program chairman Otis Weaver invited Cocking to speak. B. C. Oliff, principal of Spalding High School, introduced Cocking.   Cocking declared that Georgians had to determine whether "ruthless and unprincipled men making use of the twin threats of ignorance and prejudice" would be permitted to "destine the Empire State to a permanent place of decadence."   Cocking explained the persuasive method by which Talmadge abused those he opposed.   Talmadge relied upon character assasination, presenting his false charges in a "dramatic fashion" to impress "the popular but uneducated mind."   Dictators like Talmadge cultivated "hatred toward class, race, or religion."   This "greed for power" by "ruthless" leaders threatened democracy.   The despot always "sought to control peoples by controlling schools."(95)

In a speech to the Atlanta Lions Club on August

9, J. Curtis Dixon, fired as vice chancellor of the
University System for ties to the Rosenwald Fund,
stated that he had never "advocated" racial equality.
He explained how the Rosenwald Fund had supported
substantial improvements in education in Georgia with
no requirement that schools be racially integrated.
He did "believe in and advocate better educational
advantages for Negro children." He advised that if
Talmadge and the Board of Regents served the "governed rather than for those who govern" Georgians
would "enjoy the full values . . . of democracy."
Comparing Talmadge's take-over with acts of Nazis and
Fascists, and defining the essence of the tragic
events, Dixon concluded that "the colleges in this
state are no longer yours. They belong to the
Governor."(96)

A number of other highly respected observers
spoke out against Talmadge's convulsive assault upon
the University System. In a speech to the Atlanta
Rotary Club on July 21, Marion Smith, an Atlanta
attorney and former Chair of the Board of Regents,
called Talmadge "a dictator comparable in a small way
with Hitler." He noted that "all dictators, and we
have a minor one in Georgia," go "into a frenzy
whenever they are crossed." Talmadge was attempting
to "dominate the educational system" and to "use" it
for "political purposes." Smith maintained that "no
man of intelligence would believe" the "false"
charges brought against Cocking and Pittman. Smith
predicted that the accreditation of Georgia's colleges was "imperiled" by Talmadge's interference in the
administration of higher education.

Smith explained how vital funds from foundations
had been for improving higher education in Georgia,
including those received from the Rockefeller Foundation's General Education Board, Julius Rosenwald
Fund, American Church Institute, and Carnegie Foundation. Speaking from personal experience as former
chair of the regents, Smith stated that, when accepting funds, the regents had not made "commitments to
educate white and Negroes in the same schools."
Claims that regents sanctioned "social equality" were
"nonsense." In a strong indictment of Talmadge's
political motives, Smith admonished: "I have nothing
but contempt for the politician who, to advance his
own selfish interest, seeks to disturb race relations
in the south . . . by spreading statements which he
himself must know to be false." Smith explained how
Talmadge would be snared in his own recurring plot of
seeking the people to rescue him from self-destruc-
tion. "Under our system of government," noted Smith,
"every temporary dictator must come back to the
people . . . to be voted on again." Then Smith

reminded citizens of their responsibility: "Eternal
vigilance is the price not only of liberty but of
decency in government as well."(97)

In a speech to the Decatur Rotary Club on July
30, J. R. McCain, president of Agnes Scott College,
in his thirty-seventh year of residence in Georgia,
said that the Board of Regents were now under the
"control of a person whose chief qualification is
that of ability to 'get the votes'." Comparing the
present predicament with the loss of accreditation of
colleges in Mississippi that resulted from the acts
of Theodore Bilbo, and in Louisiana, because of the
interference by Huey Long, McCain forecast the
hardships to be experienced by students, faculty, and
administrators in Georgia's institutions of higher
education, fears that in 1942 cost Talmadge the
campaign for re-election as Governor. McCain explained to his civic-minded audience the role of free
citizens in preserving a precarious freedom. "We
must realize the place that our colleges hold in
preserving freedom and democracy, and the dangers
that come from dictatorships and prejudices."(98)
Upon reading about President McCain's charges,
Talmadge "attacked" him by means of statements to the
press.(99)

From the very beginning, Regent E. Ormonde
Hunter courageously opposed Talmadge's abuse of
authority. The day after the trials he was "so
incensed" that he "wanted several days 'cooling off'
time before issuing a statement."(100) In a speech
to the Savannah Kiwanis Club on July 26, Regent
Hunter provided insightful background into the
mystery, scope, and motivation of Talmadge's exploitation of political power. Hunter told how, when
Talmadge appointed him a regent, the members of the
board were a "friendly" group. No one was trying to
"undermine the Governor's program." The regents were
willing to "support any proposal the Governor might
make." But the facts of what happened and the
charges brought against Dean Cocking and President
Pittman "shriek out loud." Talmadge "intended to
personally undertake the prosecution of these two
men, for what reason I really have no idea." Hunter
concluded that Talmadge "sacrificed" Cocking and
Pittman "on the political altar." "I am ashamed to
be on a board which deliberately crucified the
reputation and future of two apparently honorable
gentlemen."(101)

Many newspaper editors reproved Talmadge's
dismal leadership. The day after the "trials," with
Clark Howell having resigned from the regents and now
commenting from the sidelines, he editorialized in
the <u>Atlanta</u> <u>Constitution</u> that "dictatorship" ruled

Georgia, a condition that stirred "racial hatreds for
the purpose of political appeal to the unthink-
ing."(102) The editor quoted from a New York speech
by Burgess Meredith, acting president of the Actors'
Equity Association. Meredith could have justifiably
had in mind the performances at the "trials" of
Talmadge's hand-picked prosecutor James S. Peters and
Regent Judge Joe Ben Jackson when he explained that
"nobody knows better than an actor what it means to
speak only what has been given him to speak."   A
"stooge" has mere "parts rather than lives to play."
"Democracy," Meredith continued, "was written by the
hearts of all men. Democracy is our show."(103)   The
Atlanta Constitution's Ralph McGill labeled   the
trials "farcical." McGill had witnessed a number of
Talmadge's stump speeches, in and out of office, and
knew the governor's dictatorial strategies better
than most. McGill predicted accurately that the
so-called trials would provide the platform upon
which Talmadge would campaign for public office in
1942. McGill explained correctly that   Talmadge
attacked Cocking and Pittman as a means of uniting
the "Talmadge factions" and attracting a "flood of
publicity." McGill said that it was "sickening" and
"frightening" that faculties of the University System
could be terrorized by "scurrilous and untruthful
affidavits obtained largely by purchase or by intimidation."(104)

     Reacting to the accelerating criticism of his
abuse of authority, Governor Talmadge blamed the
"Atlanta newspapers" for stirring "up something that
is not to the best interest of Georgia."(105)
Talmadge criticized the press for "becloud[ing] the
real issue," which he said was the "intermingling of
the races."(106) The governor warned he would "withhold" information from the two Atlanta newspapers "if
they don't correct their attitude." Attorney General
Ellis Arnall reassured that all state records were
open to the press.(107) Talmadge accused McGill of
accepting a Rosenwald Fund grant to travel "abroad"
so that he could write falsely about education in
Georgia. (Upon his return, McGill and Thomas C.
David's Two Georgians Explore Scandinavia was published by the Georgia State Department of Education.)
The governor also chided McGill for being paid $100 a
month from public funds to head the state athletic
commission. Talmadge claimed that University of
Georgia President Harmon Caldwell received support
from the Rosenwald Fund, ignoring the fact that the
educator did not accept the grant.(108)

     Civic clubs in Georgia played a significantly
constructive role during this difficult   period.
Unlike government agencies and colleges, civic clubs

were largely beyond the reach and control of the
power-hungry governor. The Atlanta Civitan Club
unamimously approved a resolution "deploring and
condemning 'any effort to use and control the educational system . . . to advance the political aims of
any individual' and 'the incitement of race against
race'."(109) Devereaux McClatchey, chair of the
club's Public Affairs Committee, recommended that
resolution. The Graduate Education Club, whose
members were graduates of the University of Georgia's
College of Education, praised Dean Cocking as "a
brilliant scholar." They condemned Talmadge for
"meddling with the University System" and refusing to
"admit he was wrong." The club warned that the "boys
and girls of Georgia will be the losers." Many in
the club said they had been supported with scholarships from the Rosenwald Fund, but none had been
asked to endorse racial integration of the
schools.(110) In a rare if not the only publicly
initiated protest from a faculty group, albeit from a
regional body, the Southern Political Science Association condemned Talmadge for "interfering" in the
administration of the University System and maintained that the governor's unwise acts were
"detrimental to democracy itself."(111)

A number of persons and organizations from
outside the South joined in the chorus of condemna-
tion. In a speech celebrating the fiftieth anniver-
sary of Stanford University, Dr. Raymond B. Fosdick,
President of the Rockefeller Foundation that sponsored the General Education Fund, one of the organizations Talmadge blamed, said "We all . . . have
been the sad spectators of a drama played at the
University of Georgia." Fosdick lamented that
Talmadge had struck "a blow" at the "integrity of
American University standards everywhere. . . . The
search for truth is suspended in a section of the
United States."(112) Local branches of the American
Federation of Teachers in New York City and Philadel-
phia opposed "the Governor Talmadges of this country"
who made "charges of communistic activity." The
governor answered that it was the "finest compliment"
ever "paid me."(113)

Sensing that he was losing control of the
rhetorical turbulence that he had created as a means
of solidifying his political authority and winning
votes in the 1942 gubernatorial election, Talmadge
forecast that "at the proper time" the Board of
Regents would return to "secret" sessions. Regent W.
S. Morris, Augusta publisher who had voted not to
fire Cocking and Pittman, opposed secret sessions but
would "exclude" reporters who failed to "interpret
the proceedings correctly."(114) As criticism of his

interference in the administration of higher education increased, Talmadge's public responses ranged in kind from glib denials of concern to contentious defenses of his actions. In answer to reporters' inquiries about his political intervention in educational affairs, he replied: "Today's Sunday, and I have been reading my Bible."(115) Even with the power he had accumulated as governor, however, he was unable to ignore the great concern expressed from all segments of society, in and out of Georgia. In the most ironic statement imaginable, the Governor complained that critics were employing against him "every time dishonored appeal to race prejudice and passion that has been invented" since the Civil War.(116)

The governor defended his actions as being in the best interest of Georgians. At the occasion of the dedication of Amicalola Rural Electrification on July 26, Talmadge "reviewed his attack" upon Cocking and Pittman and promised to "rid the state of any signs of social equality." Sharing the speaker's platform, Senator Richard B. Russell, Jr., and Attorney General Ellis Arnold warned of the "dangers" confronted "from abroad" and, with eyes on Talmadge, from "within," and called "for an end to despotism."(117) To "document" his harangues, Talmadge ordered 500 "personal copies" of Brown America and 500 of Calling America, "evidence" used by the governor to show that Cocking and Pittman favored integrating blacks and whites in the colleges.(118) In a press conference, he displayed a copy of Marion Cuthbert's We Sing America as an example of a work that advocated the doctrine of "racial equality and co-education." The governor promised to ask the legislature to "pass a resolution to burn" that genre of book. Talmadge "chuckled frequently as he read passages" that described "Negro and white children attending school together."(119)

The Governor had Ms. S. C. Patterson, chair of the Library Textbook Committee of the State School Board, screen publications for content unacceptable to him and others. Patterson reported the following "objectionable teachings" in books: "discrimination of the south against Negroes, criticism of democratic form of government, and teachings that the Bible was a myth and that man and monkeys descended from the same animal." Eventually twenty-three books were banned by the State School Board, including Howard Odum's Southern Regions. For its infamous research, Talmadge "commended the committee warmly."(120) Talmadge had Al Henson, Assistant Attorney General in the Labor Department, examine "books used" in colleges so that "those that advocated Communism or anything else except Americanism"--and Talmadgeism-- could be ferreted out. The result, the Governor warned, could be a "mass purge of professors and textbooks."(121)

In a speech over WSB radio in Atlanta on July 25, 1946, Talmadge found it necessary to defend his decision to have Georgia educators terminated at will. "Such men as Embree, Cocking, and Pittman are smart," claimed Talmadge; they knew better than to "boldly" advocate racial integration. Using "a subtle channel," they picked "canny speakers" who could "teach the young this theory of social equality in America. As long as I am your Governor, there won't be any co-education or co-mingling of the races in Georgia."(122)

Scott Candler, DeKalb County Commissioner and Talmadge appointee to the Board of Regents who voted to fire Dean Cocking and President Pittman, in a speech to the Decatur Rotary Club, supported the governor's actions. Speaking "from pencilled notes" to seventy-five persons, the "largest" audience "in weeks," Candler complained that "there is a movement . . . to bring the races together in southern schools and colleges." Georgians would have to "choose between" education and "the foundations." J. R. McCain, President of Agnes Scott College and a critic of the governor's actions, was in the Rotary audience. After the speech, McCain shook Candler's hand but said he "disagreed" with his assessment.(123) Regent Judge Joe Ben Jackson continued to parrot the wishes of Talmadge. In a regents' meeting on September 8, Talmadge "leaned over and whispered" instructions to the judge, and Jackson "got up and launched into an oration in which he warmly praised the Governor."(124)

Two separate but related accrediting agencies investigated Talmadge's involvement in the administration of the University System. They were the Southern University Conference and the Southern Association of Colleges and Secondary Schools. On October 13, the Southern University Conference dropped the University of Georgia from its accredited list of institutions because of "a clear case of political interference" by Governor Talmadge. Firing Dean Cocking "without due" notice on "charges" that were "not substantiated," the Southern Conference concluded, was "a contradiction of the ideals of education and a threat to democracy in America."(125)

Accustomed to over-powering persons who opposed him, Talmadge appeared quite shocked that an organization existed beyond his control. In public statements, he "bitterly attacked" the conference's decision, insisting that "no out-of-state agency has

Talmadge reads speech to a state-wide radio audience. (Photograph reprinted from the Atlanta Constitution by permission of that paper.)

the authority . . . to dictate to the Board of Regents." Increasingly strident, and with his mind on the 1942 campaign for Governor, he claimed that most of the persons in the Southern University Conference favored "co-education of blacks and whites." Disregarding the devastating damage he brought upon the University System, Talmadge boasted that Georgia would not remain in an association that "tolerates . . . social equality."(126) In a speech at the Southeast Georgia Fair in Waycross, Talmadge blamed the "unpleasantness" in the University System upon professors who "advocated co-education of the races." As Governor, he would not allow "a self-appointed agency from outside the state" and the "Rosenwald fund" to "prescribe to Georgians what they shall do with their own university."(127) He charged that blacks from outside the state and the Communist party were "slurring" Georgia. The governor launched a new offensive in the form of a campaign bribe. To counter the criticism resulting from his abuse of the colleges, in what he called a "sequel to the $3 tag," he promised a "college education for every able bodied man and woman who wants one."(128)

On December 4, the second accrediting agency, the Southern Association of Colleges and Secondary Schools, removed ten state colleges in Georgia from its list of accredited institutions because of "unprecedented and unjustifiable political interference." Loss of accreditation would begin on September 1, 1942. Talmadge responded to the decision by saying: "I hope that the" Atlanta newspapers "are satisfied." "I am proud," he claimed, "that the degrees of the University students are not affected by the ruling and will not be."(129) Assuming he would run rough-shod over this accrediting organization, as he had done with the Board of Regents and other state agencies, Talmadge scorned: "That ain't in Georgia. We credit our own schools down here."(130) Talmadge had boasted that "there ain't no danger" Georgia's colleges would lose their accreditation. And if they do, that's fine for "the state would save some money." If Georgia's colleges were removed from the accredited list, he would "cut the salaries of the professors in the college in half" because "they wouldn't be worth as much" as before. He wanted professors with his brand of southern "character," rather than mere academic "degrees."(131)

Before and after the colleges lost their accreditation, criticism of Talmadge increased. Many students enrolled in Georgia's public and private colleges protested Talmadge's political interference with higher education. Before the trials of Dean Cocking and President Pittman, three hundred students at Georgia Teachers' College sent a "strongly worded petition" to Talmadge demanding that Marvin S. Pittman be retained as their president.(132) They paraded behind the College's band through the business section of Statesboro with banners, one which read: "Keep Politics Out of the School."(133) On July 4, Willis Johnson, managing editor of the _Red and Black_, the student newspaper at the University of Georgia, spoke over WSB radio in Atlanta. A representative of the Student Political League, Johnson pledged that organization's "uncompromising opposition" to Talmadge. He maintained that Georgians must see that Talmadge "shall never again occupy any position of responsibility in our state government."(134)

Students "paraded" through Athens "hooting and howling." They hung the governor in effigy in "front of the historical old arch." They burned pictures of the governor.(135) There was talk on campus about "Dictator Talmadge." Students were heard to say they would transfer to other schools. Dick Kenyon, President of the Panhellenic Council at the University

of Georgia, stated they would oppose Talmadge in the
1942 election. Publicly the faculty "had little or
nothing to say about" the situation. William Tate,
assistant to President Harmon W. Caldwell, reported
that the "excitment . . . has momentarily demoralized
the entire university." Harley Bowers, editor of the
student newspaper, planned to mail throughout the
state 16,000 copies of the <u>Red</u> <u>and</u> <u>Black</u> in which
he editorialized against Talmadge's abusive ac-
tions.(136)   During half-time ceremonies of the
Georgia-Dartmouth football game in Athens, students
produced a drama in which a person dressed in the
role of the recently fired Dean Cocking chased
"Governor Talmadge" off the field to the "resounding
applause" of 18,000 fans.(137) Using a strategy that
threatened Talmadge's political future, and one that
confronted the governor in an arena that he always
strived to control, Mary Ann Adair urged fellow
students to "write letters to their parents," and
"influence men in their hometowns, representatives,
[and] newspapers." The Biftad Club declared that
Talmadge was no longer an alumnus of the University.
The Georgia Tech Student Council protested the
Governor's "political interference."(138)

Students and businessmen planned a motorcade
from Athens to Atlanta to oppose the "political hand"
of Talmadge. A petition would be taken to Atlanta
that said "no racial equality has been taught . . .
or practiced." More than two thousand students voted
to go to Atlanta. Students were advised that professors would "be lenient" to persons missing classes.
When Alpha Fowler, Jr., student leader, announced
that female students could "go if they get permission" from parents, women "rushed to the telegraph
offices to wire home." Mary Ann Adair, president of
the Woman's Panhellenic Council, said the trip was
"as important to the girls . . . as the boys. I urge
all the girls to participate." The protesters would
"demand" that the governor and regents he recently
appointed resign.

When the motorcade reached Atlanta, ironically
students "hoisted a bust of the red-suspendered"
Talmadge to "the top of Tom Watson's statue." One
hundred cars "draped with ribbons and placards and
bulging" with students made the trip to protest the
governor's political interference with their education. There were "about as many women as men students."(139) Cheerleader Bill Malone "directed the
throng." "Are we scared of Talmadge," Malone "bellowed." "Hell no," answered the students. They sang
the University's alma mater and yelled, "Yea Georgia
Bulldogs . . . Glory to Ole Georgia." Dick Kenyon
read the petition. B. C. Gardner inspired fellow

students with the observation that football player "Frankie Sinkwich has never been known to give up when it looked as if the Bulldogs were about to be beaten," and there was "no reason to believe the rest of us cannot stick in there" and protect the University's "scholastic standing."(140)   Other students from Mercer University,(141) Georgia State College for Women,(142) Agnes Scott College,(143) and University of Florida protested Talmadge's actions.(144) With stories of the Confederacy in mind, Atlanta Junior College students held a "mass meeting" where one placard read: "OURS IS NOT A LOST CAUSE."(145)

Many others attempted to restore the colleges' credibility. Judge Lucien P. Goodrich, President of the University of Georgia Alumni Society and fired member of the Board of Regents, said that he could not support Talmadge, for "a great injustice" had been done to the "children of Georgia." Goodrich expressed concern for his daughter and other students enrolled at the University of Georgia.(146) The Board of Managers and officers of the University of Georgia's Alumni Society praised the students' protests.(147) In a three-hour "long fight," members of the University's Alumni Association rejected a resolution praising the governor. Instead they courageously condemned the governor's "political interference" with their "beloved university."(148) The grand jury in Clarke County, home of the University of Georgia, called upon the General Assembly to remove the university from the "political dominance" of the governor.(149) The Atlanta branch of the American Association of University Women criticized Talmadge's "unscrupulous" acts.(150) Howard A. Dawson, Director of rural education for the National Education Association, explained that Georgia was among the minority of states that permitted the governor to allocate funds "largely at his own will," allowing Talmadge to "invoke his personal will in education matters."(151) Edwin Mims, Professor of English at Vanderbilt University, and a teacher of Ralph McGill, spoke publicly "against demagogues . . . who crave despotic authority."(152)

Some legislators called for a special session to strip the governor of his authority to appoint regents, but most opposed that action. Legislators were as intimidated by the impulsive governor as were a majority of the Board of Regents and faculty members. Talmadge dismissed the efforts to convene legislators as merely a movement being "stirred up by" the press of Atlanta.(153) Dr. John Temple Graves II, of the <u>Birmingham</u> <u>Age-Herald</u>, in a speech at Nashville, was pleased that many southerners opposed Talmadge's demagogic actions. He said that the "southwide outcries against Eugene Talmadge for his compounded felonies" were "a sign . . . of new hope."(154)

While Talmadge deemphasized the impact that loss of accreditation would have on students and the state, word spread of the devastation that could occurr. J. R. McCain, President of Agnes Scott, and Harvey W. Cox, president of Emory University, advised that being dropped from the Southern University Conference would adversely affect the "morale" of high school students, for many of them were "working with the University of Georgia as their objective."(155) Because of their institutions' loss of accreditation, Georgia students might lose the opportunity to train in the Army and Navy to be pilots.(156) Students expressed concern that the medical school, law school, and teachers training program could lose their accreditation. The chapter of Phi Beta Kappa at the University might be suspended. Civil service jobs could be closed to students at a time when eighty-six percent of graduates in agriculture worked for the government. The University could even lose prospective football players.(157)

Once Talmadge realized that many Georgia colleges would lose their accredited status, he made an adjustment in his public argument. To save face, however, he distinguished between what he personally would do and what the Board of Regents now might do on its own. When the storm was strongest, the governor abandoned the ship that he scuttled. Talmadge only debated publicly when he knew it was to his political advantage! Talmadge said he "won't back down in his fight, but if a majority of Board of Regents decide it was time to rally behind the University he would be helpless to prevent the members from making concessions to the" Southern Association's investigating committee.(158)

Talmadge stated that the "few changes" he attempted to make, that is, the firing of Cocking and Pittman, had been blown into a "verbal cyclone," the exact kind of turbulence he personally created for his political benefit, whether at a political debate in McRae in 1926 or a farm meeting in Macon in 1931. But the conflict over the University System he began for self-interests now engulfed him. This time he wondered out loud "just what has happened and how such a cyclone could have been developed." To repair damage brought upon his credibility, Talmadge charged the regents to "make whatever changes to my suggestions and actions" were needed to remove higher education from the "purely political quagmire." Increasingly concerned about what the voters thought and about his coming campaign for re-election in

1942, Talmadge asked that "the parents, old graduates, and . . . students" be assured "their Governor"
would not "let them down."(159)

As of the end of September, 1941, the number of
applications to the University of Georgia were down
from 3,204 to 2,778, and to the Georgia Teachers'
College in Statesboro from 506 to 339.(160) The
General Education Board of the Rockefeller Foundation
cut $25,000 from the University of Georgia budget, a
decision that caused seven members of the library
staff to be terminated.(161) M. L. Brittain, President of Georgia Tech, reported that his institution
had been dropped by the Association of American
Universities because of "unjustified political
interference."(162) Dr. Pittman accepted a position
as director of instruction at Louisiana State Teachers' College, but later, when invited back by the
Board of Regents, returned to the presidency of
Georgia Teachers' College in Statesboro where he
served until 1947.(163) Dean Cocking took a job with
the Federal Security Agency in Washington.(164) E.
Ormonde Hunter, the regent who opposed Talmadge's
domination of the board and defended Dean Cocking and
President Pittman at the tragic trials, remarked
wisely that there had been "no chance" of "remedying"
the problem as long as Talmadge "thought that he had
half a chance of gaining his point."(165) Hunter
reported that he would soon ask for a leave of
absence from the regents and enter the army.(166)
Carey G. Arnett replaced Hunter on the Board in
January 1942.(167)

Talmadge's attempt to exploit the University
System and the topic of racial integration to win
votes in the 1942 gubernatorial election failed.
Campaigning against the beleaguered Talmadge, Attorney General Ellis Arnall criticized his "undemocratic
policies." Arnall told a radio audience that he "had
received more than 16,000 letters and hundreds of
financial contributions."(168) Arnall defeated
Talmadge, and restored accreditation of the colleges,
retroactive September 1, 1942.

On December 7, 1941, prior to the 1942 election,
the Japanese bombed Pearl Harbor. Hoping that world
war could cover his mistakes, one week later Governor
Talmadge announced that he was casting aside "all
personal, political, sectional or group interest" and
going to Washington to help Franklin D. Roosevelt,
the man whose infirmity he had so callously ridiculed
during his 1936 campaign for the United States
Senate.(169) But the impulsive governor was unable
to hold his fire. In Washington he "attacked the
educational groups, but revised his statement several
times" to accommodate the harsh discovery that "you

have to be careful when you're dealing with the
intelligentsia." He threatened to send complaining
professors to war in "the Philippines and let them
wear their caps over there." Just wait, he warned,
that accrediting organization would "come to Georgia
some time. We'll catch 'em."(170)

NOTES

1. Atlanta Constitution, July 5, 1940.
2. Atlanta Constitution, September 1, 1940.
3. Atlanta Constitution, July 25, 1940.
4. Augusta Chronicle, September 5, 1940.
5. Atlanta Constitution, July 20, 1940.
6. Augusta Chronicle, July 5, 1940.
7. Atlanta Constitution, July 24, 1940.
8. Atlanta Constitution, August 11, 1940.
9. Atlanta Constitution, July 24, 1940.
10. Atlanta Constitution, July 16, 1940.
11. Atlanta Constitution, August 18, 1940.
12. Atlanta Constitution, September 4, 1940.
13. Atlanta Constitution, July 6, 1940.
14. Augusta Chronicle, September 8, 1940.
15. Augusta Chronicle, July 28, 1940.
16. Atlanta Constitution, July 31, 1940.
17. Quoted in Atlanta Constitution, July 31,
1940; Augusta Chronicle, August 2, 1940.
18. Atlanta Constitution, July 5, 1940.
19. Augusta Chronicle, August 4, 1940.
20. Augusta Chronicle, August 22, 1940.
21. Dalton speech, Atlanta Constitution, August 25,
1940.
22. Atlanta Constitution, July 5, 1940.
23. Danville speech, Atlanta Constitution, July 12,
1940.
24. Carrollton speech, Augusta Chronicle, August
23, 1940.
25. Augusta Chronicle, September 1, 1940.
26. Augusta Chronicle, September 2, 1940.
27. Georgia's Official Register, 1939-1941-1943,
pp. 498-501.
28. Speech by Marion Smith to Atlanta Rotary Club,
Atlanta Constitution, July 22, 1941.
29. Findings of the Southern Association, Atlanta
Constitution, December 5, 1941.
30. V. O. Key, Jr., Southern Politics in State and
Nation (New York: Vintage Books, 1949), p. 125.
31. James F. Cook, Jr., "Politics and Education in
the Talmadge Era: The Controversy Over the University
System of Georgia, 1941-42," Ph.D. dissertation,
Univer of Georgia, 1972, pp. 66-69, p. 92.
32. Atlanta Constitution, December 5, 1941.
33. Atlanta Constitution, June 19, 1941.
34. Atlanta Constitution, June 22 and 26, 1941.

35. _Atlanta Constitution_, June 27, 1941.
36. _Atlanta Constitution_, June 21, 1941.
37. _Atlanta Constitution_, June 27, 1941.
38. _Atlanta Constitution_, July 12, 1941.
39. _Atlanta Constitution_, June 21, 1941.
40. _Atlanta Constitution_, June 27, 1941.
41. _Atlanta Constitution_, July 12, 1941.
42. _Atlanta Constitution_, July 20, 1941.
43. M. C. Huntley, "Report on Charges of Political Interference in the University System of Georgia, 1941," p. 24, in University of Georgia Library, Athens.
44. _Augusta Chronicle_, July 29, 1941.
45. _Georgia's Official Register_, 1939-1941-1943, pp. 357-360.
46. _Atlanta Constitution_, September 9, 1941.
47. "Report on Charges of Political Interference," p. 55.
48. _Atlanta Constitution_, July 14, 1941.
49. _Atlanta Constitution_, July 13, 1941.
50. _Atlanta Constitution_, June 19, 1941.
51. Cook, "Politics and Education in the Talmadge Era," pp. 42-47.
52. _Atlanta Constitution_, June 19, 1941.
53. _Atlanta Constitution_, July 5, 1941.
54. _Atlanta Constitution_, June 27, 1941.
55. _Atlanta Constitution_, August 8, 1936.
56. _Atlanta Constitution_, August 30, 1936.
57. _Augusta Chronicle_, July 29, 1942; _Atlanta Constitution_, August 21, 1936.
58. _Atlanta Constitution_, June 20, 1941.
59. _Atlanta Constitution_, July 12, 1941.
60. _Atlanta Constitution_, July 15, 1941.
61. _Atlanta Constitution_, July 15, 1941.
62. _Atlanta Constitution_, July 15, 1941.
63. _Atlanta Constitution_, June 19, 1941.
64. Cook, "Politics and Education in the Talmadge Era," p. 56.
65. Sue Bailes, "Eugene Talmadge and the Board of Regents Controversy," _Georgia Historical Quarterly_, 53 (December 1969), 410.
66. B. Carlyle Ramsey, "The University System Reexamined: The Talmadge-Holley Connection," _Georgia Historical Quarterly_, 61 (Summer 1980), 192-193.
67. James F. Cook, "The Eugene Talmadge-Walter Cocking Con- troversey," _Phylon_, 35 (Summer 1974), 184.
68. _Atlanta Constitution_, July 15, 1941.
69. _Atlanta Constitution_, July 15, 1941.
70. M. C. Huntley, "Report on Charges of Political Interference in the University System of Georgia, 1941," p. 5.

71. Atlanta Constitution, July 18, 1941.
72. Atlanta Constitution, July 15, 1941.
73. Atlanta Constitution, July 15, 1941.
74. Cook, "Politics and Education in the Talmadge Era," pp. 57-58.
75. Atlanta Constitution, July 15, 1941.
76. Atlanta Constitution, June 19, 1941; emphasis added.
77. Atlanta Constitution, June 1, 1941.
78. Huntley, "Report on Charges of Political Interference," pp. 63-64.
79. WSB radio speech, Atlanta Constitution, August 1, 1941.
80. Cook, "Politics and Education in the Talmadge Era," pp. 80-88.
81. Atlanta Constitution, July 15, 1941.
82. Atlanta Constitution, June 19, 1941.
83. E. Ormonde Hunter speech to Savannah Kiwanis Club, Georgia, Atlanta Constitution, July 27, 1941.
84. [No author], Calling America: The Challenge of Democracy Reaches Over Here (New York: Harper and Brothers, 1939).
85. Atlanta Constitution, July 14, and 15, 1941.
86. Atlanta Constitution, July 15, 1941.
87. Atlanta Constitution, July 19, 1941.
88. Atlanta Constitution, July 18, 1941.
89. "Minutes of the Meeting of the Board of Regents of the University System of Georgia," July 14, Atlanta, Georgia, p. 13.
90. Atlanta Constitution, July 15, 1941.
91. Atlanta Constitution, July 15, 1941.
92. Atlanta Constitution, August 8, 1941.
93. Atlanta Constitution, July 17, 1941.
94. Atlanta Constitution, August 1, 1941.
95. Atlanta Constitution, July 24, 1941.
96. Atlanta Constitution, August 10, 1941.
97. Atlanta Constitution, July 22, 1941.
98. Atlanta Constitution, July 31, 1941.
99. Atlanta Constitution, August 7, 1941.
100. Atlanta Constitution, July 16, 1941.
101. Atlanta Constitution, July 27, 1941.
102. Atlanta Constitution, July 15, 1941.
103. Atlanta Constitution, September 2, 1941.
104. Ralph McGill, Atlanta Constitution, July 15, 1941.
105. Atlanta Constitution, September 21, 1941.
106. Atlanta Constitution, July 21, 1941.
107. Atlanta Constitution, July 22, 1941.
108. Atlanta Constitution, July 16, 1941.
109. Atlanta Constitution, July 24, 1941.
110. Atlanta Constitution, August 1, 1941.
111. Atlanta Constitution, November 27, 1941.

112. Atlanta Constitution, October 2, 1941.
113. Atlanta Constitution, August 21, 1941.
114. Atlanta Constitution, September 9, 1941.
115. Atlanta Constitution, July 21, 1941.
116. Atlanta Constitution, October 10, 1941.
117. Atlanta Constitution, July 27, 1941.
118. Atlanta Constitution, August 31, 1941.
119. Atlanta Constitution, August 2, 1941.
120. Atlanta Constitution, September 11, 1941.
121. Atlanta Constitution, June 20 and July 18, 1941.
122. Atlanta Constitution, July 27, 1942; see Ramsey, "The University System Reexamined," pp. 190-203.
123. Atlanta Constitution, August 21, 1941.
124. Atlanta Constitution, September 9, 1941.
125. Atlanta Constitution, October 15, 1941.
126. Atlanta Constitution, October 14 and 15, 1941.
127. Atlanta Constitution, October 16, 1941.
128. Atlanta Constitution, October 23, 1941.
129. Atlanta Constitution, December 5, 1941.
130. Atlanta Constitution, July 17, 1941.
131. Atlanta Constitution, August 21, 1941.
132. Atlanta Constitution, June 1, 1941.
133. Atlanta Constitution, June 3, 1941.
134. Atlanta Journal, July 5, 1941.
135. Atlanta Constitution, October 14 and 15, 1941.
136. Atlanta Constitution, October 25, 1941.
137. Atlanta Constitution, November 23, 1941.
138. Atlanta Constitution, October 21 and 22, 1941.
139. Atlanta Constitution, October 16, 1941.
140. Atlanta Constitution, December 5 and October 16, 1941.
141. Atlanta Constitution, October 23, 1941.
142. Atlanta Constitution, October 25, 1941.
143. Atlanta Constitution, October 31, 1941.
144. Atlanta Constitution, November 9, 1941.
145. Atlanta Constitution, October 28, 1941.
146. Atlanta Constitution, October 17, 1941.
147. Atlanta Constitution, November 2, 1941.
148. Atlanta Constitution, November 2, 1941.
149. Atlanta Constitution, October 17 and November 2, 1941.
150. Atlanta Constitution, October 16, 1941.
151. Atlanta Constitution, October 19, 1941.
152. Atlanta Constitution, December 5, 1941.
153. Atlanta Constitution, October 19, 1941.
154. Atlanta Constitution, October 31, 1941.
155. Atlanta Constitution, October 17, 1941.
156. Atlanta Constitution, October 16, 1941.
157. Atlanta Constitution, October 14, 1941.
158. Atlanta Constitution, October 28, 1941.
159. "Minutes of the Meeting of the Board of

Regents of the University System of Georgia," November 1, 1941, Atlanta, Georgia, pp. 73-75.

160. Atlanta Constitution, September 30, 1941.
161. Atlanta Constitution, July 19, 1941.
162. Atlanta Constitution, November 2, 1955.
163. Atlanta Constitution, January 31, 1942; Cook, "Politics and Education in the Talmadge Era," p. 289.
164. Atlanta Constitution, September 19, 1941.
165. Atlanta Constitution, December 6, 1941.
166. Atlanta Constitution, October 30, 1941.
167. Atlanta Constitution, January 8, 1941.
168. Atlanta Constitution, December 7, 1941.
169. Atlanta Constitution, December 13, 1941.
170. Atlanta Constitution, December 30, 1941.

8

Resurging Talmadgeism and Response

From 1920 until his death in 1946, Eugene Talmadge employed a virulent mode of persuasion to increase his political authority over all competitors in and out of government. Responding on audio tape to questions submitted by the author, Herman Talmadge, manager of his father's 1938, 1940, and 1946 campaigns, recalled that Eugene Talmadge's primary motivation "was to get elected." By emulating the style of the elderly Tom Watson, Talmadge felt that he could control the mass of voters, the means by which he was elected Commissioner of Agriculture and Governor and to which he returned in times of trouble. Herman Talmadge said his father "was a natural orator," with an "uncanny ability to get complete empathy with his audience immediately," the "greatest master with a mass audience I ever saw." He "dealt direct with every issue, right to the point, without evasion, and that was his style of speaking." If speaking on television today, continued Herman Talmadge, his father would be "outstanding," addressing "an issue brutally and frankly," getting "to the point immediately in a very convincing way."

To appeal to the working class, Talmadge and supporters created a rhetorical turbulence that aroused interests in his candidacy and in his causes through hundreds of personal appearances, in the press, and by means of regularly scheduled time purchased over WSB radio out of Atlanta at a cost of between $300 and $400 per speech. In his autobiography, Herman Talmadge emphasized the extent to which his father depended upon the support of working men and women. He maintained that, while persons chauffeured in limousines underestimated his father, that "didn't make any difference" for "the common people

loved" and voted for him.(1)   Herman Talmadge reported to the author that his father "projected the
issues that the people, as a rule, supported, with
rare exceptions. And he was an extremely convincing
speaker. He knew how to carry his campaign direct to
the people. Now we live in a mass-media type political situation, and that was not true in that time.
Speakers would go from county to county, hopefully
gettin' a good crowd and sell their program to the
audience. He always had much larger crowds than any
of his opponents."

In the communities where Talmadge was to speak,
he and campaign helpers created a scene that brought
people from fields, town, and cities. In several
campaigns, Talmadge baited citizens with barbecue and
watermelon. At Bainbridge, supporters served "nine
tons of beef," "hundreds of gallons of sauce," and
"thousands of loaves of bread." In Louisville, when
the twelve thousand plates ran out, "several hundred"
participants used "newspapers or anything else they
had to hold their lunch." At Moultrie, "J. W.
Toney's farm hands fired the big black syrup kettles
at dawn," and "all day long the pungent aroma of
frying fish was wafted through the pine land" attracting people. "Piled high on makeshift wooden
tables were stacks of mullet. 'We got 15,000 pounds
from the Gulf Coast,' Mr. Toney said. He figured one
pound would feed two folks." Also on the stump menu
were "5,000 pounds of potato chips, 100 gallons of
pickles, and 2,000 loaves of bread." During the 1946
campaign, the well established Talmadge changed his
strategy, providing "no barbecue for the rank and
file" on occasions but for "a chosen few" who "ate
very well at a local roadhouse."(2)

To hear him speak, citizens came from several
surrounding counties and Atlanta and other cities in
trucks, buses, cars, wagons, train, school buses,
old-fashioned buggies, "farm conveyances of every
description," mules, and on foot. Vehicles "fanned
out beyond the crowd." Motorcades brought hundreds,
with flags flying from fenders of the lead car, and
groups carrying posters proclaiming their home
counties. Attendance varied with the density of the
population, but Talmadge often attracted relatively
large audiences, including 700 at Fort Valley, 1,000
at Danielsville, 1,200 at Toccoa, 3,500 at Elberton,
11,000 at Thomson, 19,000 at Griffin, and 25,000 at
Bainbridge. "Fiddling John Carson" and the Cartersville string band "amused vast" crowds throughout the
state. Carson sang about "Talmadge and his $3 Auto-
mobile Tag."(3) Although a "holiday mood" prevail-
ed, Talmadge and followers planned these raucous
speakings to entertain supporters, intimidate

opponents, and build a reputation as a fighting
warrior, a strategy that worked well on many occasions, but translated into fewer votes in the 1936
and 1942 campaigns.(4)

There was a sharp contrast between the people's
anticipation to hear Talmadge and his attitude in
preparation for speaking. When asked if his father
ever doubted his ability to satisfy the great expectation of the crowds, Herman Talmadge judged that,
"He never had any doubt whatever. In fact an overwhelmingly large audience would not impress him or
deter him in the least. Sometimes he would sleep
right until we got to the city limits of the town
where he was scheduled to make a speech. He would
speak completely without notes. Whoever was driving
the vehicle would wake him up about the time they got
to the platform. He would awake immediately and
completely alert. It was amazing the way he could
sleep. He could sleep sittin' on a stool."

The order of events immediately preceding his
speeches were carefully scheduled to condition the
crowd to participate supportively in a speak-along
led by Talmadge. Repeatedly there was a "sea" of
"rustic and vociferous" faces "close-packed" around
the speaker's stand, waiting for Talmadge to appear,
hardly a forum for a democratic debate. The audience
called, "we want Talmadge" and, on time or thirty
minutes late, he walked heroically onto the newly
constructed stand amidst "wild cheering, whistling,
and applause." The throng became silent, as a
partisan sheriff, editor, doctor, mayor, colonel,
veteran with one leg, woman superintendent of education, or blind minister gazed seriously about before
announcing the "official" attendance as the "largest
crowd ever assembled" in that county! On cue, the
"chorus" of potential voters interrupted the intro-
ducer, and the candidate stepped to the microphone
set up by Cowboy Wood (working out of the sound
truck). The applause became "deafening" as "auto
horns" honked their approval, and excitement "spread
from throat to throat." A reporter concluded that
the effect was that of a "Roman holiday, and no scene
in the Circus Maximus ever surpassed the fire of its
enthusiasm, the intensity of the fervor of the
greeting."(5)

The scene was comparable to a "rock concert" of
the 1960s and beyond. Many persons over the age of
fifty ask of a rock concert, "how can they hear the
words over the loud music?" With a Talmadge speech
as well, the crowd came to participate in the wild
man's performance, for they already knew the words of
his stump message. Talmadge incorporated specific
responses of audience members within his speech.

Listening to an audio recording of his July 13, 1946, speech in Columbus, Georgia, reprinted at the end of this book, one hears one or more "rebel" calls from the crowd, within easy reach of the microphone, possessing a remarkably piercing quality, like a veteran handler calling the dogs in from a deer hunt, echoing across the audience and leading them in a variety of vocal responses. Thomas F. Coffey, Jr., Editor of the Savannah Morning News, described for the author the involvement of audience members he observed in a Talmadge rally in 1946: "Talmadge . . . commanded attention, and then some. . . . Our old Municipal Auditorium, capacity about 1,200 was packed to the rafters, and the rebel yells rang out with . . . choreographed regularity. . . . In the audience at strategic locations were various men who, at certain points in his speech, would rise and extend their right hands in a cheering gesture which would set off the yells." A reporter described the response of the 25,000 to his speech at Bainbridge on July 4, 1934:

> Time and again, although his crowd was with him
> wholeheartedly, the governor had to appeal for
> permission to continue, so warmly was his ad-
> dress received. The great throng, which defied
> all efforts of the police to keep it within
> bounds, surged about the speaker's stand, pushing
> women and children and making it impossible for
> authorities to maintain any semblances of order.
> From the way Governor Talmadge's address was
> received it was impossible to determine which,
> if any, portion of it received wider approval
> than the others. It all brought satisfaction
> to the immense throng.

At Sardis Church in Hart County that same year, the audience "surged upon the speaker's platform and caused it to collapse just after" Talmadge "finished his speech."(6) (For some indication of the frenzied nature of a Talmadge rally, see the stenographic text of his attempt in a July 4, 1936, McRae speech, re-printed at end of this book, to control overt crowd response enough to be heard.)

Proud of his father's accomplishments, Herman Talmadge described the man's persuasive effective-ness. Eugene Talmadge spoke in "a very clear, resonant and distinctive voice" that "people would recognize." "Sometimes" he "would speak for an hour or more in the boiling hot sun with the temperature over a hundred degrees." During that period, "some-times women with babes in arms would stand in the hot sun and listen. It was amazing how he could capti-vate an audience and hold them. You never saw any

Talmadge Prepares to Speak to "the People" (Photograph reprinted from the Atlanta Constitution by permission of that paper.)

people leave one of his speeches. They always stayed through the entire speech." Has father was "always entertaining," and "never boring" or "dull." He was a "master with a mass audience," actually becoming "part of the audience. He could sense immediately what they were interested in. I've seen him," continued Herman Talmadge, "when he was speaking and was covering an issue that apparently he felt the audience was not interested in, and he'd just wheel like a skilled backfield football player into another issue. And it was so imperceptable you couldn't notice a change unless you studied it carefully."

Empathizing with the audience, Talmadge became "a complete part of his speech." When "he said something humorous, he'd laugh with the crowd," continued his son. "If he said something that provoked the crowd, he could scowl with the crowd. And all of his gestures were completely natural. None of 'em were artificial. Sometimes he would pace on the stage back and forth." He would "wave his arms" and "ball his fists." "His stump speeches were really a dialogue with the audience." "The audience would shout back and forth to him, and he would answer the questions." "If he was making a gradua-tion speech at the University of Georgia," Talmadge used "good English" and spoke "on subjects that would be of interest to them." He "used a complete manu-script on his inaugural addresses" and on "formal occasions," although films of excerpts of two of his inaugural speeches seem to indicate that he rarely referred to the written text. Herman Talmadge said that, when presenting the Confederate Memorial Address in Atlanta, a very important occasion in that day, his father followed a text "prepared for him by Judge Luther P. Goodrich."

"If he was speaking to a group of farmers," stated Herman Talmadge, he spoke "in simple English where they could understand every word. He never used three syllables if two syllables would do the job, never used two syllables if one syllable would do the job." "He'd use their language and their idioms." It was "part of his makeup to understand his audience and his audience would understand him." At public rallies, Talmadge's "political speeches were wholly extemporaneous. He spoke completely off the cuff without notes of any kind."

Talmadge inspired working Georgians by publicly recognizing their suffering, and envisioning for them a better future, creating stump images with which farmers and others identified, appreciated, and applauded. In the small town of Homer, Georgia in the 1932 campaign, Talmadge captured the suffering and sacrifices of the working class, ending with the

clear notion that only he could remedy those problems: "What I am preaching to you today is not all
fun and pleasure, for there is sorrow and pathos
behind what I am ɛ ying. There are aching backs and
blistered hands, discouraged souls and broken hearts,
hungry women and crying children; there are men able
and willing to work walking our streets trying to get
work with which to obtain food for their loved ones,
and yet waste, extravagance and graft still exist at
our capitol."(7) Defending what critics called his
exploitative behavior, Talmadge argued that to see
"hundreds and hundreds of homes and farms being sold
each month for taxes, and know that our people, on
account of high taxes, are unable to pay the taxes on
their homes, it is enough to make a man wild. If you
could go over the state as I have during the past
summer, and see in the fields of Georgia the ragged
women working in the fields, with a suckling babe
underneath the trees, and knowing that that woman is
hungry, and has a hungry family, it is enough to make
me wild."(8)

Although capable of expressing the needs and
dreams of working men and women in words that lifted
the human spirit, often Talmadge employed hyperbole
for its immediate impact at the stump, imagining for
"farmers . . . irrigation pumps and lakes" in their
"back yards" so that "when the men come to call on
the young ladies, they can go out on the lake and sit
in the moonlight in a beautiful gondola." When
elected, he would "fill up those four or five acres"
around the governor's house "with hound dogs, cows
and chickens. I want you all to come see us there
and bring me a ham."(9)

Audiences so came to expect exaggerated acts
from Talmadge that he left himself little latitude in
which to adjust for changing times and issues. He
was simply too obstinate personally to adapt rhetorically and politically. He persisted in making
extravagant and often indefensible claims no matter
what the criticism or the cost. For example, although attacked from all sides for interfering
politically with the management of personnel of the
University System, and advised by his son that he had
misjudged that situation, Talmadge refused to
change.(10) When the author inquired of Herman
Talmadge if this example was typical of the way his
father made decisions, he answered: "Oh sure. He was
the most determined man I ever saw. He would listen
to advice, consider it, but once he made a decision
it was planted in concrete and no one could change
it." His father knew nothing "about a flanking
attack. Every attack was a frontal assault. And
he'd approach the issue direct, abruptly, and in a

very determined manner."

Sensing that Talmadge was weakened by the mess
he created for himself in causing ten Georgia colleges to lose their accreditation, on November 1, 1941,
Ellis Arnall announced his candidacy for Governor on
the premise that "dictatorship" must be uprooted and
"democratic administration of public affairs" restored to Georgia.(11)   On July 4, 1942, a politically wounded Talmadge announced for a fourth term as
governor, promising to manage finances prudently and
provide a college education for every "able-bodied
boy and girl." Primarly he warned of racial integration, claiming that only he could save the state from
a society of "social equality." When prodded from
the audience, Talmadge cried that, "Before God,
friends, the 'niggers' will never go to a school
which is white while I am governor."(12)

The issue was joined. Because of his own
political arrogance in bullying the University
System, Talmadge had severely undermined his candidacy for the 1942 race and placed himself in a defensive position comparable to the one occupied by J. J.
Brown in 1926. Candidate Ellis Arnold seized the
political advantage. At Chatsworth, Arnold criticized Talmadge for trying to "incite race riots,"
referring to him as that "pee-wee dictator" who was
"willing to shed blood to further his political
ambitions."(13) Unwilling to alter the stance that
imperiled his candidacy, in a WSB radio speech on
August 14, 1942, Talmadge assaulted the poorly
departed Dean Walter D. Cocking.(14) Talmadge
persisted that Edwin R. Embree and the Rosenwald Fund
wanted America to be a "mulatto" nation.(15)

When the returns were counted, Ellis Arnold won
the election in 1942 for governor, receiving 174,757
popular votes (over fifty-seven percent) to
Talmadge's 128,394. Arnall also won in county unit
votes, receiving 261 to Talmadge's 149. Arnall won
in 89 1/2 counties, and Talmadge in 69 1/2. In the
eight counties with largest population, each having
six unit votes, Arnall won in all of them. In the
thirty counties, each having four unit votes, Arnall
won in twenty-five; thus, he received strong support
in the more populated areas. In the 121 counties,
each having two unit votes, Arnall won in fifty-six
and split two unit votes in an additional county,
with Talmadge winning in sixty-four of those rural
counties.(16)

Young Arnall won the race for Governor, but not
because he professed unusually moderate views on race
relations. Arnall promised a Ringgold audience that,
upon his "word as a white man, that a Negro," while
he was governor, "never will be a white man's boss in

a cotton mill." Arnold assured white voters that he
would "defend with" his "blood" the "separation of
the races."(17) Talmadge lost the election by his
demagogic usurpation of the administration of the
Board of Regents of Georgia. A poll conducted by the
University of Georgia's student newspaper, the Red
and Black, in July of the 1942 campaign, found that
94.7 percent of students were for Arnall,(18) as were
most of their parents. While conceding that he lost
the race, Talmadge claimed that on the issue of
"co-education of the races" he was victorious because
it would be "a great many years before any of our
college professors will attempt to carry our white
girls around visiting Negro colleges." Reporter
Ralph McGill made a different prediction, that
Talmadge and the Board of Regents "would lynch no
more professors."(19)

In 1942, his efforts to artificially manufacture a "threat" to Georgia's racially segregated
colleges failed. In his campaign for a fourth term
as Governor in 1946, Supreme Court decisions provided
Talmadge an issue ready-made for his turbulent mode
of rhetoric. The Court ruled that holding primaries
for whites only was unconstitutional.(20) This was a
campaign theme that Talmadge was well equipped to
exploit rhetorically for votes. Although few persons
spoke publicly for the civil rights of blacks, there
were other signs of racial moderation that Talmadge
could exploit. By 1944, the anti-New Deal attitude
in the South had become "a more distinctly racial
reaction."(21) Researcher Dewey W. Grantham recognized a strain of southern progressivism surfacing in
the form of the Commission on Interracial Cooperation
in which Ralph McGill participated.(22) While
continuing in 1946 to write that "separation of the
races" is the "best and only workable system,"(23)
McGill criticized the South's leadership for failing
"to give the Negro equal justice in our courts,"
education, and civic facilities.(24) Governor Ellis
Arnall, prevented by law from running for reelection,
offered the minority recommendation that white Georgians accept blacks' right to vote.(25)

In the 1946 campaign, many blacks spoke for
their own interests, an involvement with which
Talmadge frightened white voters. Blacks organized
to register additional black voters. In a meeting at
the Wheat Street Baptist Church in Atlanta, blacks
made plans for registering 25,000 blacks to vote.(26)
Meeting in Brunswick, black Democrats set a goal of
100,000 additional registered black voters.(27)
Candidate James V. "Jimmie" Carmichael encouraged
blacks to register because he knew they would support
him over Talmadge. The Talmadge camp "challenged the

registration" of blacks and, where possible, purged "some thousands from the rolls." V. O. Key estimated that, in 1946 the number of black registrants was about 110,000 after the purge, out of a total adult black population in Georgia of 580,000, with approximately 85,000 voting in the primary.(28)

Thus, in 1946, some public discussion and actions in state and nation concerning an improved political, economic, and rhetorical status of blacks in the South enabled Talmadge to re-crank a prototype of turbulent persuasion. Blacks were asserting a higher <u>rhetorical status</u>, a practice Talmadge emphasized. Certainly there was little opportunity for blacks to suddenly dominate at Georgia's polls, but Talmadge was confident he could convince enough whites of the "threat," and he was correct. George Tindall noted that "in 1940 the South was on the threshold of its greatest economic growth yet, amid the tragedy of another world war,"(29) perhaps another reason Talmadge shifted his emphasis from economic abuse of the working class to the topic of racial desegregation.

In addition to numerous appearances around the state, Talmadge and son, Herman Talmadge, campaign manager, planned for the candidate to speak numerous times over WSB, a station that made available as a "commercial feature" radio time for "all candidates." In introducing his father to the radio audience on May 4, 1946, Herman Talmadge announced they had purchased "radio time on WSB each Monday afternoon at 6:30 P.M. and each Saturday afternoon at 4:00 P.M. . . . until the election is over." Herman Talmadge asked the radio listeners to "go to your telephone and call some of your neighbors and tell 'em that Eugene Talmadge will be on the air in just about five minutes on this station." He urged them to create "G.I. Clubs for Talmadge" in each of the counties.

On that same audio recording, one hears Eugene Talmadge tell the voters that he and the other candidates agreed on the need for improved educational opportunities for youth and for programs for veterans returning from World War II. He said the one issue that separated him from the challengers was his promise to restore the "white Democratic primary." "When my opponents go around speaking," Talmadge urged, "ask 'em how they stand on the white primary. It's the silence that thunders my opponents on this proposition." He predicted that opponents would not provide "many stickers" for vehicles because they were "afraid that too many of those stickers would be on cars and trucks driven by Negroes." But "Talmadge stickers" were available for "the white people" of Georgia.(30) In an audio

recording of his July 13, 1946, speech at Columbus,
Georgia, presented during a powerful thunder storm
and reprinted in this book, Talmadge defied the
Supreme Court, and promised that as Governor he would
require that only whites "vote in our white primary
the next four years (cheers from audience)."(31)

On April 4, 1946, Talmadge formally announced
his candidacy on a platform to preserve the "Democratic 'white' primary."(32) Because it was "too wet
to plow," three thousand persons gathered in Lyons to
hear Talmadge indict "Yankee influences" for trying
to "break down Jim Crow laws." He berated "Henry
Wallace, Red Russia, Harlem, carpetbaggers and the
FEPC [Fair Employment Practices Committee]."
Talmadge's audience cheered "lustily" when he urged
them to "let the white people of this world know that
Georgia is still a white man's state." He warned
that because blacks would vote in a bloc, whites
should avoid splitting their votes, and coalesce
around his candidacy. Hoping to heal the wounds kept
open by the University System debacle, he admonished
"white people" to "lay aside the petty differences
and let's have a solid march of white people" for
Talmadge.(33) He boasted at Dublin that he was the
"only candidate against nigger voting."(34)

Throughout the campaign, Talmadge kept the
subject of race before the voters, attempting to
apply it to every personality and issue to his
advantage. He predicted at Thomasville that Jimmie
Carmichael "would be out of the race if the Negroes
weren't allowed to vote."(35) He promised a Rochelle
audience that under his administration there would be
a white primary and that "the nigger" would "come to
the back door with his hat in his hand."(36)
Talmadge spoke at Douglas of "sorry white folks who
make sorry Negroes."(37) Talmadge said he would
allow no person or law to stand in his way. He
promised at Swainsboro to "repeal the county-unit
system law and all laws against election frauds in an
effort to" restrict the white Democratic primary to
whites.(38) He would "abolish all election laws" in
Georgia to prevent blacks from voting.(39) "Elect
the right man," Talmadge insisted at Cartersville,
and even "the Supreme Court will get in line."(40)

In June 1946, the Supreme Court handed Talmadge
a second plank for his platform of racial exploitation. The Court ruled that a state could not segre-
gate white and black passengers when they crossed
state lines in public transportation.(41) The
prospect of blacks and whites sitting next to each
other on a bus traveling across Georgia was a theme
Talmadge relished on the stump. This was a subject
he could embellish to show voters they must elect him

if race mixing in Georgia were to be prevented. In a speech at Moultrie, Talmadge promised to erect a magnolia wall around the state. He would "put little depots within 50 feet of the State line on all highways to enforce segregation."(42)

Talmadgeism was back! Improvising policies at the stump, Talmadge devised novel ways to defy implementation of the Court's ruling. He would require passengers to purchase a "new ticket each time a bus crosses the State line."(43) "Elect me Governor and I'll put inspectors in at the State line to look into every sleeping car and see that there's no mixing of the races in Georgia."(44) In the audio recording of the Columbus speech, one hears Talmadge describe how he would have the Public Service Commission of Georgia . . . license buses" only for _intra_-state travel. "If you want to take a trip to Montgomery, Alabama, you'll have to buy a ticket just this side of the Alabama line, and then get you one to go on further." Talmadge's rhetoric of deception was reving to full capacity now. From long experience with the topic, he recognized clearly that, when dramatized in the turmoil of a political rally, racial integration was a subject that many white Georgians would not scrutinize closely and a lure that a significant percentage could not resist. The wilder the claims about social equality the more favorably many whites responded, and Talmadge was the master of that mode of political exhibitionism.

At the same time, as the distribution of popular votes in the 1946 election would indicate, a majority of Georgians opposed Talmadge's candidacy. His abuse of the University System of higher education angered and frightened many citizens. Over half of the voters had become immuned to Talmadgeism. A reporter noted that in 1946 the shouts of "Tell 'em about it, Gene" and "That's right Gene," upon which his mode of stump speaking depended, were "few and far between."(45) As in 1936 and 1942, Talmadge found opposition at his rallies. For example, he experienced a "hectic time" when speaking in the Fine Arts building at the University of Georgia. Students hung him "in effigy" and "nearly laughed, booed and heckled" him "off the stage." Talmadge's scorn of blacks voting "drew both cheers and boos." At Athens someone asked if he would prevent black veterans from voting, and he replied "'yes,' and many veterans" returned from World War II "booed."(46)

Upon hearing Talmadge promise to abolish laws, the _Atlanta_ _Daily_ _World_, published by blacks, editorialized that Talmadge campaigned for votes "upon the premise that in some fashion the governor of the state will be the one person above the law and the

Constitution."(47) The editor advised blacks that
they would "never win their full liberty" by "supporting candidates who endorse violence and preach
hate."(48) The records of Talmadge and E. D. Rivers
were "repugnant" to the interests of "well thinking"
blacks, the editor continued, and warranted "our
support of James V. Carmichael."(49)   Journalist
Ralph McGill, stating that he had "always opposed
so-called social equality or mixing of the races,"
argued that Talmadge "by his historic emotional
instability" demonstrated "that he is not fitted for
an important public office."   McGill warned that
Talmadge's claim that southern society was about to
be suddenly racially integrated was "entirely false"
and that the candidate "deliberately seeks to fright-
en and deceive the people."(50) The regional director of the Congress of Industrial Organizations (CIO)
announced its opposition to Talmadge.(51) At Winder,
determining that race was a stronger appeal than
union of workers for economic interests, Talmadge
answered that he "was the white man's candidate, CIO
or no CIO."(52) Talmadge predicted that he would
receive "90 percent of the CIO" members' votes
because the Political Action Committee of that labor
union used "Negro votes as a tool to put across the
FEPC."(53)
     Opponents of Talmadge tried to keep alive the
charges brought against him successfully by Ellis
Arnall in the 1942 campaign.   Explaining that a
candidate with Talmadge's potent political personality could only be defeated when opponents united
around one person, V. O. Key found that in the 1946
Democratic primary, "Arnall followers, 'good government' people, Talmadge enemies, many labor and civic
groups, and certain newspapers" cooperated in an
attempt to elect James V. Carmichael. E. D. Rivers,
who depleted the state treasury when he was governor,
ran an ineffective race but divided Talmadge's
opposi-
tion.(54)
     In the 1946 campaign, Rivers called for the
defeat of "forces of 'prejudice' and . . . 'demagoguery'."(55) Rivers said Talmadge was "an obstruction-
ist who gets power drunk and like a mad bull just
charges all over the place not caring what he
wrecks."(56) At Moultrie, Jimmy Carmichael lashed
out at "ranting dictators in red suspenders" who
"wasted Georgia's money and disgraced the State."(57)
In a speech at Tifton, Carmichael told a "laughing
audience" that, "Ever since I was 10 years old,"
Talmadge had "played the role of a modern Paul
Revere, hollering 'Wake up, wake up, the nigger is
coming'."(58)
     Persons in Talmadge's camp improvised numerous

ways by which to disrupt opponents' rallies, as did
supporters for other candidates. Carmichael complained at Hinesville that during his speech in
Savannah "henchmen from the opposition stood in front
of the auditorium and offered Negroes 10 dollars if
they would sit on the main floor with the white
people rather than go to the balcony customarily used
by Negroes." In this manner, Carmichael argued,
Talmadge attempted to "buy a race riot."(59) As for
his own credentials as a segregationist, Carmichael
reminded voters at Franklin that he "helped write
into the State Constitution a provision that separate
schools be maintained for white children and Negroes."(60)

Carmichael, Rivers, and other critics underestimated the vitality of Talmadgeism. Assuring voters
at Baxter that when elected he would not "establish a
dictatorship," Talmadge argued that "in the past he
had been 'forced to use strong legal measures' to
brush aside 'chronic obstructionists who have attempted to prevent me from carrying out the clear
mandates of the people'"--his ultimate excuse for
acts of demagoguery.(61) At Camilla, Talmadge stated
that critics claimed he put forth the racial issue as
merely a "smoke screen." He warned voters to "look
beneath the smoke and you will see a raging holocaust
burning away at the very foundation of our Southern
traditions and segregation laws."(62) At Waycross,
Talmadge maintained that a "failure to prohibit Negro
voting in the primaries would result in social
equality."(63)

He asked "all white Georgians to work for
Talmadge. I want Catholics, the Ku Klux Klan and
Jews." He was the "only candidate," he claimed,
making "an issue of not wanting Negroes to vote."(64)
Give them a "right to vote," Talmadge envisioned, and
"Negro candidates for public office will be thick as
flies around a jug of molasses." About character
qualities with which he was intimately familiar, he
said at Statesboro that blacks "will become arrogant
and drunk with their own power."(65) Talmadge
maintained that a "black minority voting in a bloc
can elect any state candidate they wish over a
divided majority of white people."(66) He told a
Greensboro audience that, "with the white primary out
of the way . . . negroes will vote in numbers and
repeal our laws requiring" segregation "in schools,
hotels, and on trains--even those which prohibit
intermarriage."(67) The former commissioner of
Agriculture alerted a Thomaston audience of the
"danger" of black foremen in mills "being placed over
white women workers if he is not elected governor."(68)

Talmadge tried to frighten blacks not to vote.
In a Swainsboro speech, he told blacks to "stay away
from the white folks' ballot boxes." Whites would be
the "true friends of Negroes . . . as long as they
stay in the definite place we have provided for
them." Talmadge warned blacks that "it would be
extremely wise for" them "to stay away from the white
folks' ballot boxes" because "neither the United
States Attorneys nor" candidate "Jimmie Carmichael
will have a corporal guard to back them up."(69)
Characteristically displaying an arrogant disdain for
legal processes, the former governor predicted at
Kingsland that few blacks would be able to vote if
"registrars do their duty."(70) In his research,
Joseph L. Bernd found that the "conspiracy" by
Talmadge and supporters to deny blacks an opportunity
to cast ballots enabled Gene to win unit votes of key
counties that he otherwise probably would have lost.
This also allowed him to invest "money, time, and
effort" for votes in counties less under his control.(71)

To assure victory, Talmadge abandoned any
caution he displayed in previous elections when
making campaign vows, and supplemented the alleged
threat of racial integration with promises of the
following benefits for persons voting for him:
"largest road-building program ever," increased
pensions for the elderly, special license privileges
for veterans, every Sheriff placed on the rolls of
the Georgia Bureau of Investigation,(72) increased
funding for vocational education,(73) "hospitals in
every county," improved farm-to-market roads, rural
electrification, expanded and improved farmers'
markets,(74) and better labor conditions.(75) In the
audio recording of the May 4, 1946, radio address, to
help returning veterans and others who "could not go
to college," one hears Talmadge promise to provide
one million dollars to fund "vocational programs in
every school in the state." When citizens were
provided with "real practical training," "the farm
lands and the farm homes of this country could be
made to blossom and bloom like the rose."

In the recorded May 4 address, to veterans
returning from World War II Talmadge promised those
"fellows of the flag" exemption from ad valorem taxes
for five years and free business and drivers licens-
es. In addition, if he inherited a debt-free budget,
he would "put on the largest road program the state
ever saw." Declaring that "the horse and buggy day
is over," he stressed the critical need for paved
roads. "Around Atlanta, when you get off a paved
road . . . after a slight rain, it'll be so slick
you'll slide in a ditch, and in the summer in a

drouth, if the young ladies have on a pretty white
dress, it'll be covered in red dust and they won't
feel like goin' anywhere so dirty." Speaking stump
poetry at his best, he regretted that, because of bad
roads, homes away from jobs in the towns and cities
had been "deserted and are standing idle in the
county, a lots of 'em with the roof fallin' in, the
<u>chimley</u> broken down, the yard goin' up in bushes and
weeds, and the once beautiful fence around the yard
not kept up. With good roads, where we can make the
trip to the centers of trade . . . this property can
be built back and it'll be a much more desirable home
than living in close little apartment trying to raise
a family." Talmadge would make all those improvements without citizens having "to pay more taxes to
get them." He would "get the money through proper
administration of state funds and by firing off the
state payrolls a horde of free riders."(76)

His speech to a Cleveland, Georgia, audience
illustrated the inflated style in which he bartered
promises for votes in 1946: "This mountain section
will blossom like a rose when more roads are opened
up, roads that will permit your children to get to
school even in bad weather, farmers to get their
produce to market and tourists to reach some of the
most beautiful spots in the world."(77) As for the
southern section of the state, he assured Savannah
residents that if elected he would make their port
"equal" to "any harbor on the East Coast."(78)

Talmadge won the campaign for Governor in 1946,
although a majority of Georgians cast their ballots
for Jimmie Carmichael and against the reinstallment
of Talmadgeism. Carmichael received 313,389 votes
(fifty-one percent), Talmadge 297,245, E. D. Rivers
69,489, and Hoke O'Kelley 11,758. Talmadge won 242
county unit votes, Carmichael 146, Rivers 22, and
O'Kelley 0. He won in 105 counties, Carmmichael in
44, Rivers in 10, and O'Kelley in 0. Talmadge's
claim that southern society would be racially integrated unless he was elected particularly appealed to
voters in rural counties. In the 121 counties, each
having only two unit votes, Talmadge won in ninety.
In the thirty counties, each having four unit votes,
he won in fourteen. In the eight counties, each
having six unit votes, Talmadge won in only one.(79)
The press reported that more than eighty percent of
the registered black voters ignored Talmadge's
threats and voted.(80) But the Bernd study refer-
enced above demonstrats that blacks in key counties
were intimidated not to vote. Had the county unit
system not rescued his candidacy, Talmadge would have
needed votes of blacks, although during the campaign
he told a Lawrenceville audience that, "If I get a

Negro vote, it will be an accident."(81)
    Talmadge died in 1946 before taking office, but
the political turbulence he founded in 1926 and
perfected in 1946 continued beyond his funeral, with
his son, Herman, Ellis Arnall, M. E. Thompson, and
others, in the mold of Talmadgeism, literally bolting
and knocking down doors in their frenzy to get to the
governor's office to replace the deceased.   Herman
Talmadge told the author that Eugene Talmadge's voice
and his "were almost identical. People would
frequenlty confuse us on the telephone." The same
was true of their message.   In a recording on WSB
radio on May 4, 1946, Herman Talmadge spoke for his
father, helping also to launch his own intermittently
turbulent political career.   Within the conventions
of Talmadgeism, Herman Talmadge's comparison of
veterans' sacrifices in World War II with the efforts
he challenged them to make for his father's campaign
for governor was not considered profane. "I know
that the veterans" hold "in their hearts the same
patriotism now that they carried with them on the
battle field," Herman Talmadge stated.   In this
campaign, "we must determine whether or not we will
fight to preserve" the "Jim Crow laws" as "we fought
on our ships at sea and as we fought on foreign
soil."
    The Atlanta Daily World editorialized its
"surprise" and "disappointment" in Talmadge's victory, since "'white supremacy' was the principal issue"
in his "platform." The black editor viewed the
"result" of the "primary" to be "a setback to the
cause of democratic government. It reveals clearly
to what extent the passion of racial prejudice can be
inflamed." The editor offered advice that all
citizens of a democracy should heed, that "the Negro
in Georgia and the South . . . must adopt more real
and practical methods of exercising his political
strength." The editor predicted optimistically that,
with the election of Eugene Talmadge governor in
1946, "Democracy" had "suffered only a temporary
setback."(82)

NOTES

    1. Herman E. Talmadge with Mark Royden Winchell,
Talmadge, A Political Legacy, A Politician's Life
(Atlanta: Peachtree Publishers, Ltd., 1987), pp.
16-17.
    2. Atlanta Constitution, July 1, 1934, May 19,
1946; Atlanta Journal, July 5, 1942; see Cal M.
Logue, "The Coercive Campaign Prophecy of Gene
Talmadge," in Logue and Howard Dorgan, eds., Oratory
of Southern Demagogues (Baton Rouge: Louisiana State
Univer Press, 1981), p. 107.

3. _Atlanta Constitution_, July 13, May 23, June 23, and August 5, 1934; _Atlanta Journal_, July 10, 1942; Logue, "Coercive Campaign," pp. 204-209.

4. _Atlanta Constitution_, July 5, 1940; July 20, 27, and 31, and August 2, 6, 23, and 28, and September 2, 12, 13, and 16, 1932; July 1, 5, and 13, and August 9, 16, and 19, and September 1, 1934; _Augusta Chronicle_, July 28 and August 8, 1940, and July 25, 1942; _Macon Telegraph and News_, July 5, 1942; _Marietta Journal_, July 21, 1932.

5. _Macon Telegraph and News_, August 20, 1932, and July 5, 1942; _Atlanta Constitution_, August 6, 14, 24, and 28, September 1, 4, 6, and 12, 1932, July 5, 13, and 26, August 16, 19, 21, and 28, September 1, 5, 6, and 9, 1934, June 2 and 23, 1946; _Savannah Morning News_, June 14, 1946.

6. _Atlanta Constitution_, July 5 and 26, 1934.

7. _Atlanta Constitution_, September 2, 1932.

8. _Atlanta Constitution_, September 9, 1932.

9. _Atlanta Constitution_, July 15, 1932, July 29, 1942, and May 24 and June 1, 1946.

10. Talmadge, _Talmadge_, pp. 62-63.

11. _Atlanta Constitution_, November 2, 1941.

12. Moultrie speech, _Atlanta Journal_, July 5, 1942.

13. _Augusta Chronicle_, August 11, 1942.

14. _Augusta Chronicle_, August 15, 1942.

15. Dalton speech, _Augusta Chronicle_, August 16, 1942.

16. _Georgia's Official Register_, 1939-1941-1943, p. 656.

17. _Augusta Chronicle_, August 25, 1942.

18. _Atlanta Journal_, July 18, 1942.

19. _Augusta Chronicle_, September 14, 1942; _Atlanta Constitution_, August 12, 1941.

20. _Atlanta Constitution_, April 2, 1946.

21. Numan V. Bartley, _Rise of Massive Resistance Race and Politics in the South During the 1950's_ (Baton Rouge: Louisiana State Univer Press, 1969), p. 29.

22. Dewey W. Grantham, _Southern Progressivism: The Reconciliation of Progress and Tradition_ (Knoxville: Univer of Tennessee Press, 1983), p. 413.

23. _Atlanta Constitution_, June 12, 1946.

24. _Atlanta Constitution_, March 20, 1946.

25. _Atlanta Constitution_, April 5, 1946.

26. _Atlanta Daily World_, May 10, 1946.

27. _Atlanta Daily World_, May 14, 1946.

28. V. O. Key, Jr., _Southern Politics in State and Nation_ (New York: Vintage Books, 1949), p. 520.

29. George Brown Tindall, _Emergence of the New South, 1913-1945_ (Baton Rouge: Louisiana State Univer Press, 1967), pp. 471-472.

30. Audio recording of May 4, 1946, WSB radio

speech, in Special Collections Department, Georgia State University, Atlanta, Georgia.

31. Audio recording of July 13, 1946, WSB radio speech, in Special Collections Department, Georgia State University, Atlanta, Georgia.

32. Atlanta Constitution, April 5, 1946.

33. Atlanta Constitution, May 19, 1946.

34. Atlanta Constitution, May 30, 1946.

35. Atlanta Constitution, May 24, 1946.

36. Atlanta Constitution, June 1, 1946.

37. Atlanta Constitution, May 23, 1946.

38. Atlanta Constitution, July 12, 1946.

39. Atlanta Constitution, July 14, 1946.

40. Atlanta Constitution, June 5, 1946.

41. Atlanta Constitution, June 4, 1946.

42. Atlanta Constitution, June 2, 1946.

43. Atlanta Constitution, June 5, 1946.

44. Atlanta Constitution, June 2, 1946.

45. Douglas speech, Atlanta Constitution, May 23, 1946.

46. Atlanta Constitution, May 17, 1946.

47. Atlanta Daily World, May 22, 1946.

48. Atlanta Daily World, May 28, 1946.

49. Atlanta Daily World, June 30, 1946.

50. Atlanta Constitution, May 31, 1946.

51. Atlanta Constitution, June 10, 1946.

52. Winder speech, Atlanta Constitution, June 11, 1946.

53. Atlanta Constitution, June 23, 1946.

54. Key, Southern Politics, p. 415.

55. Atlanta Constitution, May 12, 1946.

56. Savannah Morning News, June 26, 1946.

57. Atlanta Constitution, May 12, 1946.

58. Tifton speech, Atlanta Constitution, June 5, 1946.

59. Atlanta Constitution, July 7, 1946.

60. Atlanta Constitution, June 20, 1946.

61. Atlanta Constitution, July 12, 1946.

62. Atlanta Constitution, June 27, 1946.

63. Atlanta Constitution, June 14, 1946.

64. Atlanta Daily World, May 14, 1946.

65. Atlanta Constitution, June 28, 1946.

66. Statesboro speech, Atlanta Constitution, June 28, 1946.

67. Savannah Morning News, June 4, 1946.

68. Atlanta Constitution, May 26, 1946.

69. Atlanta Constitution, July 12, 1946.

70. Atlanta Constitution, June 7, 1946.

71. Jospeh L. Bernd, "White Supremacy and the Disfranchisement of Blacks in Georgia, 1946," Georgia Historical Quarterly, 66 (Winter 1982), 492-501.

72. Douglas speech, Atlanta Constitution, May 23, 1946.

73. Thomasville speech, _Atlanta Constitution_, May 24, 1946.

74. Thomaston speech, _Atlanta Constitution_, May 26, 1946.

75. Dublin speech, _Atlanta Constitution_, May 30, 1946.

76. Blackshear speech, _Savannah Morning News_, June 8, 1946.

77. _Atlanta Constitution_, June 19, 1946.

78. _Savannah Morning News_, June 21, 1946.

79. _Georgia's Official Register_, 1945-1950, pp. 486, 493.

80. Editorial in _Atlanta Constitution_, July 18, 1946.

81. _Atlanta Constitution_, June 23, 1946.

82. _Atlanta Daily World_, July 19, 1946.

II

MAJOR SPEECHES

Debate with John J. Brown during Campaign for Commissioner of Agriculture

August 3, 1926, McRae, Georgia

Under a broiling south Georgia sun, Eugene Talmadge, candidate for Commissioner of Agriculture and J. J. Brown, incumbent, locked horns for supremacy in their race.[1] When they had finished, two and a half hours later, the two thousand people in the audience from twenty south Georgia counties, gave Talmadge an endorsement by acclamation.

As he finished speaking, Talmadge asked that all those who believed he should get out of the race, raise their hands.

"Come on," Mr. Talmadge called. "Come on, all you fertilizer inspectors and everybody else." Not a hand was raised. "Now," said Mr. Talmadge, "all of you who believe that Mr. Brown should get out of this race, raise your hands." Every hand in the crowd went up and there was a great whooping and yelling. When the debate was over, Talmadge was lifted to the shoulders of the crowd and carried in a triumphal procession.

During the rebuttal by Mr. Brown, he revealed for the first time what he said to be real facts in the break in his department with Fred Bridges, assistant commissioner and Lem B. Jackson of the Bureau of Markets. According to Mr. Brown, he discovered that Mr. Bridges had been collecting money from the various oil and fertilizer inspectors over the State without his knowledge.

"What this money was to be used for," Mr. Brown said, "God only knows. I don't. There was also some dissension as to my son being employed. I didn't intend to tell this, but this is the truth."

During the debate Mr. Brown attacked Mr. Talmadge's record as county attorney in Telfair County and charged that "he was not a dirt farmer."

Mr. Talmadge, in his address, charged that several relatives of Mr. Brown were employed in the department; that money had been collected from various inspectors as a campaign fund for Mr. Brown and also to "fix the Legislature"; that the Georgia law only provided for ten oil inspectors but a clause gave Mr. Brown power to appoint as many more "in his discretion."

The debate began shortly after 11 o'clock with Mr. Brown speaking first, being allowed an hour.

"I have been in office for nine years," Mr. Brown began. "I ran many times and for the first six years of my candidacy not a daily paper supported me. Only four weeklies were behind me. Then, when I was given a plurality of 10,000 votes by Gilmore County switching in the Macon convention, I was defeated. I was urged by my friends at this time to run as an independent but I was loyal to my party and waited until the next election to run again. I charge that Mr. Talmadge was not always loyal to his party. He ran as an independent once."

"Mr. Talmadge was then named county attorney. While in this position he recommended that the county commissioners purchase a tract of land. They bought this land from Mr. Talmadge at $30 per acre." Mr. Brown then said that grand jury of Telfair County later recommended that the sale be revoked, holding that ground was worth not more than $10 an acre. Mr. Brown said if Mr. Talmadge had handled the affairs of the county in that manner that he was no man to be entrusted with direction of the department of agriculture.

It was charged by Mr. Brown that Mr. Talmadge drew $150 of the county's money to go to Atlanta to defeat a local bill. He said that Mr. Talmadge went at the instigation of the county commissioners. "Yet Mr. Talmadge has taken me to task for going before the senate and house committees in interest of legislation for the farmers," Mr. Brown said. "They have charged me with having a powerful political machine. Before I was elected, they had no fear of a plain practical farmer. The people that howl about the machine are those that fail to court the favor of the Agriculture Department. There is an ex-governor of the state who was later elected to the Senate and he had the favor of the Agriculture Department."

Mr. Brown here launched into an attack of the Macon Telegraph and directed his remarks to W. T. Anderson, editor of the paper, whom he observed seated on the speaker's platform. "This same man," Mr. Brown continued, "was being fought by The Macon Telegraph and supporting Cliff Walker. This paper charged that this man threw a bomb into his own home.

The <u>Telegraph</u> was forced to make an apology after being faced with a $100,000 law suit. "This same man ran again and <u>The Telegraph</u> saw fit to support that man, whom they had charged with throwing a bomb into his own camp. The editor of <u>The Telegraph</u> had changed his mind."

"At this time I was forced to withdraw my support from this man because of the falsehoods about me that were coming from his office. I made 40 political appointments at his own request. But the shoe was on the other foot at this time. I supported good old Cliff Walker and, thank God, he won." "The <u>Macon Telegraph</u>," Mr. Brown shouted at Mr. Anderson, "has never elected a governor to my knowledge. It has never supported me and I don't want it." "You can't get it," Mr. Anderson called back. This brought cries of "Hurrah for Talmadge" from the crowd and Mr. Brown had to cease speaking until quiet reigned once more.

"The press of this State will have to be fair," Mr. Brown continued. "On Sept. 8 they will see how the people feel. I cite <u>The Telegraph</u> as an instance of what I have to contend with. I have nothing personal against the editor of <u>The Telegraph</u> or any person connected with it that may be here today. <u>The Telegraph</u> is a good paper. Its news columns are the best in the State, but, gentlemen, when you read the editorials you have to take them with a grain of salt."

Mr. Brown then referred to the administrations of Tom Hudson and Obadiah Stephenson and said that the question of oil inspectors had been the bone of contention at that time.
"They used to call Tom Hudson 'Oily Tom'" Mr. Brown said. "I made the appointments as the law requires. I have nothing to fear."

Mr. Brown then went into details as to service the Bureau of Markets had rendered the farmers. He cited Telfair County farmers who, he said, had been aided by that department. At this point he accused Mr. Talmadge of acting as the middlemen for Shippey Brothers of Atlanta in the sale of hogs.

Mr. Brown went into details as to the money expended by the department each year and told of the money derived from the gasoline tax. He said that his department turned in a clear profit each year of $600,000 derived from the various inspection fees. "In my first race," Mr. Brown said, "I stood for the fair distribution of co-ops. I have kept faith, gentlemen, and I wish to show you the <u>Market Bulletin</u> issue in which the farmers sell hundreds of dollars worth of stuff. In spite of the politicians we have been able to publish this great bulletin and thanks to the Legislature. Praise God for such men."

"I now turn to the investigation they conducted into the affairs of the departments three years ago. Here gentlemen are the minutes of that body and they proved all the charges against the department worthless. In this record are statements from Hugh Dorsey, former governor, saying that funds of the department are properly disbursed. I also have in here the testimony of George Carswell, who is now running for governor and Cecil Neill, speaker of the House, that they never conferred with me relative to the appointment of the committee to investigate."

"They charge me with controlling the Senate and House but, gentlemen, let me tell you they did elect a president of the Senate without consulting me," Mr. Brown said. "Marvelous," came the cry from many in the crowd. As Mr. Brown was discussing the records of the investigating and going at length into the testimony of those favorable to him, some one called from the crowd. "Have you the testimony of Lawson Stapleton, of Americus?" "I haven't that with me," Mr. Brown replied. "Oh, you didn't bring that with you?" "No, I haven't got his testimony and his was just like some of the poppycock that The Macon Telegraph puts out. But Mr. Stapleton was on the payrolls of the Department of Agriculture for six years and he was kicked off." "O. R. Bennett, who was on the investigating committee, was offered $2,000 to make a minority report against the Department of Agriculture. But he was an honest man and he refused."

Mr. Brown then declared that the fertilizer inspectors were like police in any city and protected the interest of the farmers. He then turned to Judge Max L. McRae who presided, and inquired if he hadn't received a rebate on fertilizer through the Department of Agriculture. Judge McRae said that he had. Mr. Brown then reviewed the heads of the different departments and cited their capability of holding such jobs. "They have been attacking me," Mr. Brown said. "But truth crushed to earth will rise again."

"Colonel Talmadge is not a dirt farmer. Take any of these books here listing Georgia people and you will see that he is given as a lawyer. You know how out of place I would be as a lawyer and that is just the position Mr. Talmadge would be in if I were in his place."

Mr. Brown then flashed a paper with a statement by Mr. Jackson, chief of the Bureau of Markets and leaning over the table and flourishing the paper under Mr. Talmadge's face said: "Here is a statement from L. B. Jackson. Would you believe him under oath?" "You know him better than I do," Mr.

Talmadge replied. "You had him in your employ for
ten years." This brought cheers for Talmadge from
the crowd.   Mr. Brown then attacked the <u>Southern
Ruralist</u> for its stand against him.
     In concluding his address, Mr. Brown praised the
work of the market bulletin and said that he had only
followed the law as it provided. "I can show you
where nine-tenths of the men running for office have
asked for the support of the Department of Agriculture," he concluded.
     Mr. Talmadge walked calmly to the center of the
stage as Mr. Brown concluded and was greeted by
cheering from the crowd. "Boys," Mr. Talmadge began,
"Mr. Brown has charged that I am not a lawyer of good
repute. I ask any lawyer that has ever practiced law
with me at the bar to hold up their hands."   Several
hands went up.   "Haven't I always conducted myself as
a lawyer should and have I ever violated the ethics
of the profession?"   This brought forth answers in
favor of Mr. Talmadge and cheers from the crowd.
     "Mr. Brown says I am not a dirt firmer.   How
many of you people here have ever seen me farming?"
Hundreds of hands went up in all parts of the crowd.
"How many of you have ever seen me plowing? How many
of you have ever seen me putting out fertilizer? How
many of you have ever farmed with me?" Cries of "I
have" came from all parts of the crowd while many
called, "Go to it, Talmadge." Mr. Brown sat calmly
in his chair, his expression never changing.
     "When Mr. Brown first ran for commissioner of
agriculture," Mr. Talmadge said, as he launched into
his address, "he was running a store and selling
fertilizer for Armour and Company. Yet he says I am
not a dirt farmer. I invite you, Mr. Brown, and all
of these newspaper men out to see my crops and you
can take away as many watermelons as you wish."
     Here Mr. Talmadge called on the lawyers, judges
and his clients in the crowd to back up his assertion
that he had never violated the ethics of the law
profession.
     "Is the charge that I am not a dirt farmer
false, boys?" Mr. Talmadge said.   The crowd yelled
yes. "Is the charge that I am not a good lawyer
false?" "You bet it is" came the cry from the crowd.
Cheering continued for some time at this point and
many shouted, "Go to it Talmadge."
     "Mr. Brown tried to hit me with that land deal,"
Mr. Talmadge said. "He came down here and tried to
scare up an argument that we had forgotten.   There
wasn't anything illegal about that deal. The judges
of the courts have held that. The county commissioners wanted to buy some land out where I happened to

own some.   I   sold it   to   them for $30   an   acre."
"Judge McRae had some right about where mine is and a
lady had some on the other side.   They both wanted to
sell to the county commissioners also."   "You   wanted
$40   an   acre   for   yours   didn't   you   Judge?,"   Mr.
Talmadge said, turning to Judge McRae.   "I did,"   was
the reply.   "When   the   new   commissioners came   in
office and said they didn't want the land I bought it
back from them at $30 an acre,   the same price   that
they paid me."

"Have I   ever   been   short or   done   anything   I
shouldn't in that deal?," Mr. Talmadge asked a member
of the commission who was   in the crowd at the   time.
"No," he   replied.   "You   are   for me,   aren't   you?"
"You bet I   am," was   the answer.   "So   you see,   Mr.
Brown," Mr.   Talmadge said,   "they are   with me   just
like the majority of Georgia happens to be.   You came
down here to   kick up   a family row,   but you   didn't
have anything to start on about."

"Now as to the State auditor's report and   about
your oil inspectors.   I am   going to show you   people
that through the inspection system he is conducting a
banking department at   the expense of   the State   and
with your   money.   The   law provides   that   the   oil
inspectors collect the   fees, deduct   their fees   and
then forward the rest to the commissioner of agriculture."   Here Mr. Brown interrupted to say it was   the
State treasurer.   "You have got   to admit that it   is
credited to your   department," Mr. Talmadge   replied.
"Here in the   auditor's report   of 1925   I find   that
$62,000 has not been paid in by the inspectors by the
first of   the year."   "Take Fulton   County, for   instance.   Here   I   find   that Mr.   C.   E.   Gregory,   a
reporter for   The   Atlanta   Journal,   was   short   over
$2,000 in his   inspection fees."   Mr. Talmadge   then
read the names of   other inspectors in Fulton   County
and the   amounts   they were   short   at the   time   the
report was compiled.

"No, gentlemen, this man has to appoint only ten
oil inspectors, under   the law, but   still he has   an
army of 191.   And I   tell you, Mr. Brown, that   these
people all   over the   State don't   work six   hours   a
day."   "Mr. Brown can talk about the market   bulletin
but I say this,   that ads come out   in the paper   all
messed up.   I promise you, gentlemen, if I am   elected, I will give it   my personal supervision and   will
not be out over the State running around campaigning.
Mr. Brown   says   that   this   is   the   most   important
department in the   State, yet he   leaves it and   runs
around the State campaigning."

"Who is in charge of the Bureau of Markets   now,
Mr. Brown?," Mr. Talmadge asked.   "The assistant has
been placed in charge," Mr. Brown replied.   Mr.

Talmadge then said that the law did not provide for an assistant commissioner of agriculture and that Mr. Brown had appointed one. "I was following a precedent," Mr. Brown said. "Oh yes, the others made an error and you just followed it up," was Mr. Talmadge's reply. "Yet Mr. Brown is out campaigning and he doesn't even put an assistant in charge," Mr. Talmadge said. "He is filled up with promises and right today he is leading 200 jackasses around the country by promises."

"Oh I have met men over the State who said you were good at promising but when the time came to make good you couldn't do it. No, you would tell them with tears in your eyes how sorry you were that you couldn't fulfill your promises." "Up in Elbert County, you got Mr. Lunsford to circulate a petition in your behalf and you promised him a long term fertilizer inspector's job. Then you didn't give it to him and cried when you told him that you couldn't." "Who did you appoint, Mr. Brown?," Mr. Talmadge asked. "Pope Brown," was the reply. "Who is Pope Brown?" "My son." "All of you people had better look out for his promises," Mr. Talmadge continued. "He is scared this time. He has never had anyone up his collar but I am up there to stay this time and I will be there until after September 8." The crowd cheered Mr. Talmadge for several minutes at this point and he was forced to discontinue speaking.

"Don't let those oily boys outwork you at the polls," Mr. Talmadge warned. "They beat him up in Elbert County before and he moved down to Baxley. If he gets beat this time he will move out into the ocean."

At this point Mr. Talmadge addressed several questions to Mr. Brown. "Would you mind telling the crowd who is Walter Brown?," Mr. Talmadge asked. "He is my son," was the reply. "What does he do?" "He is my secretary." "Who is Marion Brown?," Mr. Talmadge asked. "He is my half brother," Mr. Brown replied. "He is a long term fertilizer inspector." "Isn't it a fact, Mr. Brown," Mr. Talmadge asked, "that Walter Brown was a clerk in the Bureau of Markets making about $30 a month and you put him in your office at over $200 per month?" "He worked in the Bureau of Markets," Mr. Brown replied. "Wasn't Marion Brown employed to help him?," was another question. "Who is W. L. Neice?," Mr. Brown was asked. "I don't know," was the quick reply. "Isn't it true he got up your campaign fund in 1924?," Mr. Talmadge asked again.

Mr. Brown [was] then asked as to who was W. Greenway, whose salary was said to be $1,250; H. L.

Grimm, another distant relative, who is employed in chemical laboratory, salary, $1,250; H. W. Meubourne, brother-in-law to Pope Brown, salary $2,400; and P. B. Rice, statistician, Bureau of Markets, $2,750. "Who is Vester Brown?," Mr. Talmadge asked again. "He is my son," was the reply. "What position does he hold?" "He is an apiary inspector," Mr. Brown replied.
"Apiary inspector," shouted Mr. Talmadge. "Why don't you say bee inspector?" "Who held the position before he had it?" "No one," Mr. Brown replied. "Then you created a job for him," Mr. Talmadge said.

"He talks about Jackson betraying him and calling him Judas," Mr. Talmadge said, "yet when he needs Jackson, he calls on him. When he was elected, he was selling fertilizer for Jackson and then he took him with him when he was elected." "Yes, this is the man that boasts that he makes and unmakes men. He boasts that he controls the legislature. Senator Morgan of the first district said that Mr. Brown told the Senate committee last year to kill the distillation test bill. He has made Georgia the dumping ground for all the bad gasoline of the world. That is the kind of gas that he gives you and it is the kind that chokes up your car with carbon and forces you to use more oil. But when he opposes the distillation test he threw the monkey wrench in his own machine."

"I call on you now, Mr. Brown, to name a date at Elberton when we are to meet in a joint debate and name the date and place in every congressional district of the State. Get all of your oils and other kind of inspectors that have expense accounts and bring them along. I will meet the entire bunch."

"No, gentlemen, a truthful man is the best thing in the world and when he tells the truth he means it. But when a man takes the truth and uses it to an unfair advantage to deceive the people it is mighty low. Yet Mr. Brown, through W. C. Holland, a one-legged World War veteran of Forsyth, used Mr. Holland's statement to deceive the people. Last July a year ago, when the legislature was in session, Fred Bridges went down to Forsyth to see Mr. Holland to collect $40, which he said was to be used in 'fixing the legislature'. Mr. Holland was in the hospital at the time and Bridges saw his father, T. S. Holland. I have affidavits here that Mr. Holland made the statement that Bridges came and asked for $40 to fix the legislature to keep the bill to reduce the number of oil inspectors from passing. Mr. Holland said that he started to give Mr. Bridges a check but that Mr. Bridges didn't want the check. He said he gave two $20 bills instead. Mr. Holland, the war veteran,

the other day when he saw the piece in the papers
that he had made the statement, sent a denial to Mr.
Brown. Mr. Brown took that and paraded over the
state, misleading the people." Mr. Holland, the war
veteran, was on the platform during the time Mr.
Talmadge was relating this incident and vouched for
it. "It is inexcusable for Mr. Brown to deceive the
people by such methods," Mr. Talmadge shouted. "He
ought to be hung," someone yelled from the crowd.

"Mr. Brown says he always stuck to Tom Watson
and he did while Mr. Watson was living but just as
soon as he died he forgot all about him. Over in
Helena, Mr. Davenport, who was a good friend of Mr.
Watson's, was appointed oil inspector at the late
senator's request. He told Mr. Brown that he wanted
Mr. Davenport to remain in office just as long as he
lived. But as soon as Mr. Watson died Mr. Brown
displaced Mr. Davenport. Just as sure as Tom Watson
elected you," Mr. Talmadge shouted, turning to Mr.
Brown, "his spirit will defeat you."

"You say you never ran as an independent, but
what about the time you let the hair grow down over
your shoulders and you went off over the county as a
Bull Moose?" Mr. Brown denied this charge.

Tom Linder, representative from Jeff Davis, was
called to the platform by Mr. Talmadge to tell of Mr.
Brown opposing a bill to provide for better fertilizer inspection laws. "There ought to be a penalty for
a fertilizer company to have to give a rebate," Mr.
Talmadge said. "When there was whisky in the country
it was inspected at the distilleries as all oil and
fertilizer should be."

"I call on you people to go to the polls Sept. 8
and repudiate Mr. Brown. I now want to ask you if
you think I should withdraw from this race, now that
I have presented my side. If anyone here thinks that
I should, raise your hands." Not a hand was raised.
"If you think that Mr. Brown should retire, raise
your hands." Hundreds of hands went up amid the
shouting of the crowd.

In rebuttal, Mr. Brown said that the statements
about the oil inspectors being short was a misinter-
pretation of the auditor's report; that such a report
was false. In defending the system of oil and
kerosene inspection, Mr. Brown said that it was the
only way to keep the gasoline pure and kept gasoline
out of kerosene. "As I stand here today, gentlemen,"
Mr. Brown said, "I say before the Almighty God that
if money has ever been solicited from any of the
employes [sic], it has been without my knowledge and
consent."

Yielding to questions from Mr. Talmadge, Mr.
Brown again repeated that he knew nothing of the

collections. "Then you are the blankest man on this earth," Mr. Talmadge shouted. Mr. Brown then reviewed the departments under his supervision and praised the various heads. Mr. Brown then made an assertion once more that Mr. Talmadge was not a "dirt farmer." Mr. Talmadge leaped to his feet instantly and demanded recognition. "Ask Judge McRae if I am not a farmer and a good one," Mr. Talmadge said. "Yes sir, you are a farmer and a pretty good one," Judge McRae said.

Mr. Brown then accused Mr. Linder, the representative from Jeff Davis County, of having sent the tax collector of that county to him seeking his support. This was denied by Mr. Linder. Mr. Jackson at this point related the break between with [sic] Mr. Bridges and Mr. Jackson.

In reply to questions as to future debates, Mr. Brown said that he would meet Mr. Talmadge in Elberton and Atlanta and would name the dates as soon as he could confer with his campaign headquarters. "I will be elected by the biggest majority ever given a candidate," Mr. Brown said in conclusion.

The speakers were limited to one hour each, with 20 minutes for rebuttal. Mr. Brown had the opening and closing.

Before the exercises started, Judge Alex Stephens of the Court of Appeals made a short appeal to the voters in his behalf. Judge Stephens is opposed by Judge J. P. Highsmith of Baxley. The speaking was held in the opening in Windsor Park. The crowd was massed around the stand.

NOTE

1. This is the first of three debates that helped Talmadge defeat incumbent John J. Brown for the position of Commissioner of the State Department of Agriculture in Georgia, analyzed in Chapters 2 and 3 of this book. Text of speech from Macon Telegraph, August 4, 1926; for second account of this debate see Atlanta Constitution, August 4, 1926. For articles by journalist on the debates see, W. T. Anderson, Macon Telegraph, August 5, 1926, and Lovelace Eve, Americus Times-Recorder, August 4, 1926.

Supporting the Abolition of Cotton

August 27, 1931, Cordele, Georgia

Farmers and citizens of Crisp and adjoining counties in mass meeting this morning at the local courthouse voted unanimously at the conclusion of the speech of Commissioner of Agriculture Eugene Talmadge and talks by Representatives Cain, of Crisp county, Wall, of Putnam county, and Holt, of Wilcox county, to forward resolutions to Governor Russell requesting an extraordinary session of the Georgia legislature for the purpose of putting into effect and enacting laws for the discontinuance of cotton cultivation for the year 1932 and declaring a three months moratorium this year.[1]

The resolutions were drawn up and signed by the greater part of the 500 or more citizens who jammed the courthouse room. Private telegrams and letters favoring the plan of Governor Huey Long of Louisiana were pouring out of this city to Atlanta today and Governor Russell will be deluged in the morning with communications from this section.

Commissioner Talmadge was greeted with applause as he was introduced by J. A. Griffin, of Cordele. Mr. Talmadge quickly proceeded to unfold the details of the Long Plan and to explain why it alone was the one practical and feasible proposition for the cotton farmer to adopt.

Commenting on the future of the Farm Board to handle the situation, Talmadge then proceeded to give side lights on the huge meeting held in New Orleans which he attended. Talmadge was one of the thirty-five men who were chosen at that meeting to select the best plan for handling the cotton crisis. As everyone now knows, the Long Plan was adopted.

The George Plan was rejected because it could not, in the opinion of the committee, be carried into execution. The Tax Plan was refused since it cut directly at the farmer instead of siding him.   The Limited Acreage Proposal was turned down as it was not believed it could be enacted into a law and was not feasible.   Other ideas were discussed but all were thrown aside and the plan as presented by Talmadge today was adopted at New Orleans.

The Long Plan as finally adopted by the committee said:

"Resolved, That this committee go on record in calling on governors of cotton growing states of the South to immediately assemble their legislatures in extraordinary session to pass laws prohibiting the planting of one seed of cotton for the year 1932 and providing further that these laws become effective when 75 percent of the legislatures of the South pass the act."

Talmadge, in discussing the plan, declared it was constitutional as a "quarantine measure" and that similar legislation had been enacted in Florida and Louisiana on citrus fruit and cotton.

He pointed out that of the foreign countries producing cotton, largely Russia, India, China and Egypt, only Russia would grow more if the law passed and that Russia knew mighty little about growing cotton, essentially a crop of the South.

An immediate rise in price was predicted if the proposition was made a law. The possibilities of twenty-five cent cotton are not beyond reason.

The psychological effect would be tremendous in that it would cause the people to think and thereby aid in their own salvation.

Mr. Talmadge thoroughly approved the three months moratorium suggested by Representative Wall, of Putnam county, leader of the Farm Bloc in the house.

Concluding, the Commissioner urged immediate action and the signing of the resolutions of the Governor followed.

The resolutions, which were unanimously voted, and which will be forwarded to the Governor by Representative Cain, declared:

"Whereas a mass meeting of Farmers and Business Men of Five Hundred or more was held in Crisp county courthouse today for the purpose of considering the Governor Huey Long Plan of discontinuing cultivation of cotton for the year 1932 and

"Whereas the mass meeting discussed the advisability of the three months moratorium be declared by the laws of the General Assembly, and

"Whereas the mass meeting voted unanimously for these two propositions, then resolved that the Governor call an extraordinary session of the Georgia

legislature immediately for the purpose of putting
into effect and enacting laws to carry out in effect
these resolutions."

After his address Mr. Talmadge and Representative Wall had lunch with Mr. and Mrs. J. E. Baynard
and then left for an engagement this afternoon in
Douglas.

NOTE

1. In 1931, as explained in Chapter 4, Eugene
Talmadge attempted to have the Huey Long Plan of
helping the farmers by stopping the planting of
cotton during 1932 adopted in Georgia. He strategy
was to stump the state to have voters pressure
Governor Richard B. Russell, Jr., to call a special
session of legislature to adopt the Long/Talmadge
plan. This Cordele speech was one of those he
delivered in favor of ending the picking of cotton in
1931 and stopping the planting of that staple crop in
1932. Text of speech from Cordele Dispatch, August
28, 1931.

Campaigning for Governor
August 24, 1932, Bainbridge, Georgia

Eugene Talmadge, candidate for governor, was greeted
here today by a large audience.[1] Every seat in the
Decatur county courthouse was filled and all standing
room on the main floor and the balcony was taken. He
was introduced by Lucien Bower, prominent businessman
of Decatur county. Bower said Talmadge "has struck
the shackles from the office that he now holds
[Commissioner of Department of Agriculture], and has
made it non-political," adding that the commissioner
of agriculture is a "pioneer in doing things." He
presented Talmadge to the audience as the "next
governor of Georgia," stating that there was little
doubt that he would be nominated on September 14.
John E. Drake, former state senator and prominent
attorney, preceded Bower in an introductory speech in
which he said: "There is not a farmer in Georgia
that has not been benefited in some way by the man
who is our guest here today."

Stating that his opposition was now trying to
center on a compromise candidate, Talmadge said:
"Whenever you go into the highway business, or into
any other public business where graft is being
practiced, and where the prices of materials are
being raised in order for private individuals to get
a rake-off; whenever you undertake to uncover this
graft and corruption; whenever you undertake to
discharge unnecessary employes [sic] and to cut
salaries that are too high, and to eliminate unnecessary expense, you are not going to run things smoothly, but will have a fight on your hands. Of course,
a man who represents special interests like power
companies and other great corporations, believes in
running things smoothly because it is his job to get
special concessions from the municipalities, from the

legislature, which will give these special interests the right to rob the people of the state."

"He could not go into Athens, or Atlanta, or Tifton, or any other town in Georgia and get these special concessions by raising a row. The only way that they can be obtained is to work smoothly and put a 'blind' over the eyes of the people, and get franchises granted before the people find out that they are going to be robbed under these franchises. Consequently, a man whose life is devoted to this kind of service must learn to run things smoothly. The trouble with this state now is that its business has been run too smoothly."

"John [N. Holder] ran the highway department so smoothly that they got away with thousands and thousands of dollars of the taxpayers' money before anybody found it out. When smart railroad attorneys go to work to get freight rates raised they know how to work things smoothly, and let not a ripple appear on the surface of the water. When the packers combine to rob the farmers out of their hogs they are very careful to work things smoothly and not let it appear what they are trying to do."

"Whenever anything is undertaken by anybody with the object of robbing the people who have to live by the sweat of their brow, it is always worked so smoothly that such nefarious schemes are put over before the people find out what is being done. Probably some of you have noticed numbers of paid workers traveling quietly and smoothly through this state, preaching the gospel that you should vote for a man who can run things smoothly. That is a smooth piece of business being conducted by people who know how to run things smoothly. In fact they hope to work this so smoothly as to make their candidate who has no chance on earth of being elected governor, a factor if there should be a run-over [runoff] primary."

"This smooth crowd wants to have a stalking horse on which to trade because the interests need a bridle on the man in the governor's chair. When the Georgia Power Company--in making rates which you must pay for your lights and power--they claim that their property in Georgia is worth $288,000,000. But, when they go across the hall to pay their taxes, they claim that all of their property in this state is worth $45,542,813."

"When I called atten[t]ion in the Market Bulletin to the unreasonably high freight rates and to the fact that the farmers were being robbed by combinations of the packers, and when I called attention to the fact that the farmers of this state were being robbed by the Georgia Cotton Growers' Co-operative

Association, things did not run smoothly. The steel began to strike the flint, and the sparks began to fly. My countrymen, you will never get the graft and rottenness out of the state government; you will never get taxes cut down; you will never get the expenses of government cut down; you will never get rid of useless offices and useless expenses by running things smoothly, but it will take some one who is not afraid to fight to get relief from these things."

"When you see paid workers running about in the different counties of the state telling you to vote for some certain man because he is having nothing to do with anybody's row, because no one has said anything about him, and because he will run things smoothly, you can rest assured that there is 'a nigger [sic] in the woodpile' somewhere."

NOTE

1. Speech given by Talmadge at the end of his third term as Commissioner of Agriculture, when he stumped the state in 1932 as part of his campaign for governor. The speech shows that by this time in his career in politics, because of controversial acts performed while in office, he was having to justify the "rows" in which he became involved; as he often claimed, he behaved "wildly" for the good of "the people." For analysis of his 1932 campaign for governor, see Chapter 5 in this book. Text of speech from Atlanta Constitution, August 25, 1932.

Speech to "Grass Roots" Convention

January 29, 1936, Macon, Georgia

The south has been the champion and the defender of
democratic principles for three-quarters of a century.[1] The south has fought for states' rights.
That great conflict is over. We are back to the
Union, and back to stay. The south wishes to share
her part of the burdens and responsibilities of the
national government. States' rights are in the
balance today more than they were in the days of
1861. At that time, states' rights were obliterated
by humanitarian pleas for the freedom of slaves.
Today, in every capital of the various states, and in
every county site in America, the federal government
is working consistently to tear down states' rights.

If the present program is continued for four
more years, the lines between the states will be only
a shadow on paper, and the government of the separate
states will be subservient to the will of a central
power at Washington. This time, there is nothing to
becloud the issues of sovereignty of states and local
self-government. Our brothers in the east, and
north, and west are with us to see that local
self-government and the sovereignty of our separate
states is not obliterated by the whims of bureaucrats.

Every true democrat hangs his head in shame when
he realizes that under a democratic administration
are boards, and boards, and boards--and that the
President in Washington [Franklin D. Roosevelt] has
had enacted laws where they could tell the manufacturers, store keepers, hotels and shops what to pay
their labor, and how many hours they could work. And
the present administration crowned this challenge to
states' rights with the NIRA [National Industrial
Recovery Act], taking for its emblem a blue eagle.

The originator of the thought must have been inspired, because during the reign of the NIRA, the American eagle (emblem of our great country) was certainly blue and sad. But let's not say any more about the NIRA. It is gone. And nine months after the supreme court said that it was gone, the President said so. He then announced that he was stopping the pay of thousands of workers who were being paid millions of dollars per month out of the taxpayers' money to carry on an organization that the supreme court had ruled unconstitutional.

Again every true democrat hangs his head in shame, when he realizes that under the name of a democratic administration, boards and bureaus, and the President himself, say [sic] that the way to bring back prosperity in this country is through scarcity--have less to eat, and less to wear. To carry out this crazy, infamous plan, they ordered millions of hogs and cattle killed, and thrown into the rivers or buried. Millions more of little sucking pigs were shipped off to Chicago. On top of this, they paid a premium to get to cut a good brood sow's throat. It took a little time for this travesty but when they struck the sheep and goats, they drove them on top of the mountains, forcing them to jump off the cliffs and kill themselves in the valleys below. And when the starving people went there to retrieve some of these carcasses that were not too badly mangled by the rocks, the trained welfare workers ran them off, leaving them as food only for the coyotes and wolves. They burned up wheat and oats, and plowed under cotton here in the south.

Yet, in Washington, with their faces wreathed in smiles, they were telling the people that they were bringing back "the abundant life." And something else happened too, while all this was going on! What next do we see? Importation in greater numbers than ever before of these same products that had been destroyed here in America. And they are announcing that they want to keep it up!

When the supreme court again saved America by saying that the AAA [Agricultural Adjustment Act] was unconstitutional, announcements came from Washington that [Rexford G.] Tugwell, [Felix] Frankfurter, [Henry] Wallace and even the President himself were studying and looking for plans to devise a law that would get around the supreme court, and continue their policy of scarcity here in America. They do all of this under the name of a democratic administration.

What else do they do? They have cabinet officers who try to intimidate governors, and

and legislatures to pass their New Deal legislation in order to centralize government in Washington.

I am sad to say that some of the governors in these United States have "goose-stepped" into line and saddled on their states and counties taxes that it will take a century to pay, giving over the freedom and the sovereignty of their states to boards and bureaucrats in Washington. Georgia did not "goose-step" on the New Deal bills which they sent down to Atlanta to me to be crammed through the legislature, providing for thousands of federal jobs in the state of Georgia at the expense of the state. And when the Governor of Georgia [Talmadge] did not "goose-step" he was labeled by a member of the cabinet as "his chain gang excellency, whose word is no good."

The only one of the New Deal bills that passed was one to defraud the bounties of the state out of the highway scrip, where they had a bonded indebtedness for roads. Secretary [of the Interior Harold L.] Ickes had accepted these highway certificates, contrary to law, and wanted to make the Governor of Georgia a party to his illegal contract.

This explains the wrath of Ickes when he tries to make the people of America believe that the word of the Governor of Georgia is not good. I hope that he is listening in at this talk, as I want to tell him something now. The people of Georgia can answer this for him, and the people of the United States are going to answer it in November of this year by driving him and all of his cohorts from Washington, and never allowing them to return.

Trying to help the farmer! Telling him what to plant on his land, and how little, and then telling him that taxing it over 50 per cent of its worth will help him! And those who were hired and given jobs with the government pretend to believe it. Before their crazy dream of "prosperity from scarcity" will ever work in this world, they will have to invent some ointment to take the place of sweat.

The democrats of the south owe it to the nation to rally to the principles of Thomas Jefferson, the founder of this party. You owe it to the north, and the east and the west to help in this fight to see that no communist or socialist steals the democratic nomination, and mocks you with smiles and jeers by telling you that the south is always solidly democratic. Yes, the south is democratic, true to the faith and true to the principles of Thomas Jefferson: "Sovereignty of state's rights"; "The least governed are the best governed"; "Local self-government." The south is going to remain true to these fundamentals of democracy.

What is the fight for the democratic party in 1936? What is the fight for all true Americans in 1936? Here it is: Shall we cling to our present form of government, or abolish it? Shall we barter away Americanism for communism?

Shall we continue to borrow and spend, or settle down and settle up? Shall we substitute lunacy for sanity? Shall we convert democrats into bureaucrats? Shall we share our wealth through charity, or lose it through taxation? Shall we replace impartial Uncle Sam with old Mother Hubbard playing favorites? Shall we remain idle and import food, or work and produce it? Shall we starve the litter of 12 to feed the thirteenth pig, or give them all a break? Shall we pamper or punish enemies without gates? Shall we march under the Stars and Stripes, or under a crazy quilt?

You Americans, good and true, cannot be bought and bribed. In self-defense, you have had to take parity checks, bicycles, skates, rat traps or any other thing that Washington thought they could buy your souls with. Washington has not been paying for these things. The government is not paying for them. The government never pays for anything. It collects the money from the people--and has made every man, woman and child in America a taxpayer a thousand-fold more than they ever dreamed.

The supreme court has come to our rescue. Let's hold up their hands. Let's don't allow a bunch of communists to have four more years to appoint the successors to such stalwart men as Chief Justice Hughes and Associate Justices Butler, McReynolds, Sutherland and Van Devanter. If the New Dealers can pick their own supreme court, the wheels of our democracy would catch fire and burn down our freedom.

The New Dealers have tried by billions of dollars to hold back a natural recovery due this country. They are determined that the bonus checks will be paid in June, so that there will be a flush of money to go on through until election time in November. But the play is too plain. No such joker can come from under the table and fool the soldiers of America who defended this country, and ask only for the payment of an acknowledged debt.

What else is the job of democrats and all other true Americans this year? Rewrite the platform of 1932! Nominate men on this platform whose word is so good that the best test of it is to have the New Dealers call him a "liar." Then America will know that his word is good. Cut taxes! Stop nine-tenths of the federal activities in America! Stop all competition of the government with private industry! Cut down the expense of the federal government by

tearing down seven-eighths of the buildings in
Washington, and cover the grounds with beautiful
parks! Pay up the national debt!

Go back to the doctrine (not in a $50 a plate
mockery celebration) of the stalwart man, Andrew
Jackson, who celebrated the victory of the Battle of
New Orleans by announcing to America that within one
year he had kept his platform pledge, and paid up all
the debts of America. Go back to the doctrine of
George Washington and Thomas Jefferson, who warned us
that autocrats would rise up in the name of emergency
to tear down our form of government. And that sturdy
soldier, George Washington, said that whenever this
happens, to rise up and smite them. Nineteen hundred
and thirty-six will go down in history equal in
importance with July 4, 1776.

> How sure the bolt that Justice
>   wings;
> How weak the arm a traitor
>   brings;
> How mighty they, who steadfast
>   stand
> For freedom's flag, and free-
>   dom's land.

NOTE

1. As discussed in Chapter 6 of this book, in
1935-1936 Talmadge toyed with running for president
of the United States. A number of wealthy persons
sponsored the "Grass Roots" convention in Macon for
the posssibility of nominating Talmadge for that
office. At the convention, he continued his attack
upon President Franklin Roosevelt and New Deal
programs. Text of speech from Atlanta Constitution,
January 30, 1936. For responses to "Grass Roots"
convention, see Ben F. Meyer, Atlanta Constitution,
January 30, 1936, and J. J. Brown (Talmadge's opponent in the 1926 campaign for Commissioner of Agriculture), Atlanta Constitution, January 30, 1936.

Campaigning for the United States Senate

July 4, 1936, McRae, Georgia

Mr. Chairman and My Fellow Countrymen:[1] I wish to thank my friends here in my home county of Telfair and surrounding counties and the friends all over the state who have made this meeting possible. The first time I talked to the state of Georgia from McRae was in 1926. At that time I was a candidate for commissioner of agriculture, and let's go back there for just a moment. At that time I told you there were about two campaign promises in that race. One was if you would elect me commissioner of agriculture that we would make the sun melt the oil inspectors out of Georgia and we would take the sand out of the fertilizer. I did not realize it to be hard to do, but when we got up there I found that whenever you go to reducing patronage, when you go to taking somebody off the pay roll of the state, that pretty soon you are a bad boy, and when we tried to correct the fertilizer laws of Georgia to protect the farmers, we gathered a lobby in Atlanta, from Maine to Florida, and they defeated us for two years, but finally we got it across and protected us.

And, then, my countrymen, when I went on a little further and tried to enforce the bureau of market laws that regulate markets, tried to enforce those laws to protect the people in the sale of their hogs, when I ran into a packers' trust and tried to buck them and succeeded in raising the price of hogs to 6 1/2 cents a pound, I had to face impeachment charges before the general assembly, and let me tell you this -- if it had not been for the people in the country that rallied to my cause, and crowded the capitol building, and walked in the corridors, and talked to the members of the legislature and sent them letters, I would have got there.

And, let me tell you something I found right there (and this WSB I am talking on right now, is being listened at in Washington, D.C.), my efforts against business in government, when I acted to regulate the price of hogs, I found that business in government cannot help the people. If you try to work it to help the people, the special interest you are trying to straighten out will bring any charge on earth against you. That was the lesson I found out there. Well, after we got through with that little trouble up there--wait a minute -- get through with the pictures now take all you want and then get through. Go to it! Come on and take them and get through. Now, give the people a chance. Wait a minute, boys--After that five years and a half in the commissioner of agriculture's office, when we had gone through the fight, the farmers of this state called on me to get a little bigger job, to get a job where they thought they could not law me, where the law would protect you, and four years ago I answered that call here in this park and announced for governor.

Judge Graham has just outlined to you the campaign pledges made four years ago. Now, let me see them. Let's go back over them and see how we stood on them. For years ago I told you here in this park--where is H. B. Edwards? Get up here. He is a good one boys, let me tell you. Here was the platform four years ago right here. I told you that we had to have lower utility rates, that we had to have lower freight rates; lower bus rates; lower passenger rates; lower telephone, and lower power rates. That was the first one. I told you to stop extravagance in the Highway Department and put the money to building roads, paving and bridges. I told you a $3 tag and I told you this--pay the state out of debt and not raise the taxes one dime. There you are! All right. Let's see what we did, and you boys watch my time now. Let's see what we did?

The first thing, we tackled the utility rates. We had five men elected by the people up there that had been there for years that said: "You ought to pay just as much for hauling 5-cent cotton on the freight trains as you did when it was 40 cents a pound." They said that you ought to double the rates on watermelons to Chicago and New York. They said you ought to raise power rates and telephone rates although the price of everything else was going down.

Here I talked to those people about that and plead with them, and they said: "The rates are reasonable, we cannot cut them," and when they gave me that "song and dance," after the legislature had been up there and I called on them to appoint an investigating committee, and the legislature went home, then we had a little hearing, and we put in five men there. And, what did they do? They cut the telephone rates in McRae, Ga.; they cut them in Atlanta. They cut the power and light, and they cut the freight rates, and they cut the bus rates, and when we talked about 2-cent passenger rates, everybody said I was crazy. Yes sir! And, let me tell you something else, we put that 2-cent rate on. And, what did it do? The railroad men, the conductors, and the firemen and engineers knew I was right. They knew it because it filled up the trains and depots again, and after we put it on in Georgia it was adopted by several other states in this Union. Those utility rates that we cut in the past three years have benefited the people of this state over $10,000,000 a year.

What else [did] we strike after that? Well, we struck the Highway Department. We struck the Highway Department! And, listen, when I acted there, when we struck the Highway Department and acted there to put in men to put that money to building roads, what did they do in Washington? Up there in Washington, D.C., they said: "No! We are going to name who is head of your Highway Department." But, they did this--wait a minute boys, now, listen a while--they did not do that but here is what they did do--they held up the money that was coming to Georgia five long months. It was Georgia money, raised here in Georgia, and they held it up! And, listen, we had ten congressmen there in Washington, and two United States senators, and with the exception--listen, quiet now, listen closely--while Georgia was being punished--you see, they had already collected the money out of Georgia, that tax money they were just simply paying back--while Georgia was being punished, that congressional delegation of ten congressmen and two senators, with the exception of three congressmen--there were three that were not in it--but with that exception everyone of them said: "I will sit by," and abetted that in punishing Georgia. Oh! yes, they wanted us to bow. Why, in South Carolina, and you know it, they made the governor there take Sawyer back. He got rid of him but Washington made him take him back. But, they did not do it in Georgia! When for five months they kept us out of the money.

Now let's talk about it. Oh! the $3 tags. That is easy. Here is the point on that. You men find out from your candidate for Governor and all your representatives now, and your senators that are running--now is running time, and every cow needs his tail in fly time. Don't you forget it. You good people ask them: "Are they going to keep that tag for $3?" You do that. Oh! . . . And let's see what happened. When we put on the $3 tag we had an increase of 108,751 motor vehicles on the road and we had an increase in the gasoline taxes up to $15,901,000, or nearly $4,000,000 increase a year. We more than made the revenue back. That is all.

Now, what is next? The next was this--and some of my friends that write big newspapers--where is my friend W.T. Anderson? Is he here? I wish he was here--some of my good friends told me, said: "Why, Talmadge, you have got to get some more revenue to pay the debts." I said: "I don't think so." I says: "I used to make cotton when it was 40 cents a pound. I had to make it when it was 5 cents and I learned how to take them cuts." I told them, I says: "If you will cut out useless jobs, if you will make the money give a dollar's worth, you can pay the state out of debt." So, let's see what I did. I cut the ad valorem taxes in Georgia 25 per cent. I cut it from 5 mills to 4, and I called on the counties of the state to follow suit and some of them did. We cut that outside of cutting the tag tax. Give me the auditor's report and I will read it. When I went in as Governor of Georgia, according to the auditor's report of 1932, we were in debt $7,524,724.88. That is the debt we owed. All right, let's see the last auditor's report. Here is the auditor's report for 1934. "In debt, not a dime." Not a dime! All right. Auditor's report of 1935, instead of 1934. Make that correction for me. All right. What else? I told you I would reduce that ad valorem tax from 5 mills to 4 mills, didn't I? All right.

In July of each year, the Governor has to assess the ad valorem rate for state purposes. In July, this month, I am telling you--he has to assess it--5 mills is the limit, and every other governor kept it at 5 mills until I hit it. What am I going to do? I am going to reduce it from 4 mills to 3. Now, take that word home! Now, let me tell you something else. Let me tell you something else! There has been a lot of talk in Georgia about free books, ain't there? Now, listen at this. Listen at this, now! Your schools are going to start the last of August and September. We have got in the state treasury over $400,000 to buy school books with, and the Board of Education, at 9 o'clock--where are you? Stand up out there. There is one member. She has already got her notice to be in Atlanta Tuesday, and I am going to submit a motion to that board to give free school books to each grade through the sixth grade, from the first to the sixth. Now, listen, and I think the most important thing for any school chillun to know is the three R's--"readin', ritin' and rithmetic."

Now, let me tell you something else. We are not only out of debt, but I want to give you a report of the money we have got on hand. Let's see it. Listen quiet now. We have on hand, up to June 1, this year, in the banks and vaults, $3,636,842.14. All right, that is it, but, now listen, that last platform that I told you about, that last platform of paying the state out of debt, had to be this. We had to have an appropriation bill within the anticipated revenue of the state. If the legislature was to go up there and pass a greater appropriation bill beyond our revenue, I would either have to raise the taxes or we would be in debt. Anybody with a second-grade education knows that. So, you people voted on that pledge, and you elected representatives and senators to go up to Atlanta to carry it out. So, what happened? Here is what happened. We met up there, and they carried out in law every other pledge I had made to you until they struck the appropriation bill, and when they struck the appropriation bill they would not agree on it.

The senate passed an appropriation bill within the anticipated revenue of the state and put the grandfather clause on every item. So, if the revenue did not come up to what you thought it was there would not be any debt. You would have to cut it off, but when they sent it back to the house they would not take it, and right here, in justice to the members of the house and senate I want to tell you this, the great majority of the members of the house and senate was in favor of an appropriation bill that would carry out the pledge that I made to you. Who defeated it? I will tell you who defeated it! Ed Rivers and Roy Harris. That is who defeated it! And, let me tell you how they did it. He was speaker of the house. They had been up there 70 days. Roy was chairman of the rules committee. They have parliamentary tactics up there, you know. So, they decided if they would not pass an appropriation bill they would force old Talmadge to call the legislature back and they would be up there for months and months, where they could write letters on state stationery and use state stamps, and they could go out and make Rotarian and Kiwanis speeches, campaign for governor on the state's money and on the state's time. Now listen! I am not giving you any idle talk.

At nine o'clock on Saturday night before the legislature adjourned at 12, the speaker of the house told Dr. Sanford, chancellor of the university, that they were going to have an extra session to pass the appropriation bill, and after that time they appointed three conference committees not to agree on it.

Now, that is it. Now, what did they do? All right;
they went ahead and when they did not get called back
before Christmas they got busy and they said: "Well,
old Talmadge has enough money to run on there a month
and a half. They saved that up." Yes, sir, Talmadge
stole enough to run on for a month and a half.   "So,
during this month and a half we will get busy and we
will starve him into submission."   Calling me a
dictator, and they are going to dictate. Catch the
difference? Beware of him who first calls names!

Did you ever think about a nigger's way of
getting into court? Just let two niggers have a
fight and the one that can get to the courthouse
first he thinks he is clear if he goes there and
prosecutes the other, regardless of how it is, if he
beats the other man there.   What did they do?   They
talked with the treasurer and the comptroller general
and they said: "If you go through this plan, Talmadge
has a lot of money in the Atlanta banks, laying up
there, yes, sir, and we will talk to the Atlanta
lawyers and we will get them not to cash any checks
for anybody except the treasurer that is in there."

And, they got the comptroller general to agree
to it because he has to okeh the checks before they
get to the treasurer, and after they did that, they
thought of the bonds the law requires to be kept in
the vaults in the capitol--you have to deposit the
bonds to guarantee the state's money deposited in the
banks in the state's name--and they got this treasurer and said: "Now, if you will slip them bonds out,
take them out of that vault, and trot them over to
the banks who have the state's money, why old Gene
will have a rope around his neck and we can break
it." So, my countrymen--what is that?--I don't think
it is broke yet. Now, my countrymen, that is what I
run into.   Wait a minute, boys, I have to speak
against time and it is costing me over $400--let me
talk. On February 18 was when those bonds were
slipped out of the vault. On February 24--give me
that check--on February 24, they needed some money
over there at Milledgeville to feed the people shut
up in the asylum that God had touched; they needed
money for those little blind children in Macon, and
they needed money for the deaf and dumb at Gracewood
and Cave Spring. Mrs. Hill--she is secretary of the
board of control--drew a requisition for $139,704.11.
All right.

Under the proclamation the attorney general had
given me the old appropriation bill still stands,
and it does. Under the constitution it is the only
way you can run a state. The legislature cannot
abolish a state, so if it cannot abolish it, it
cannot break it down by refusing to pass an amended

appropriation bill. Our forefathers thought of that, and wisely. So, under my duty, I drew that requisition for that $139,000 to go to those people. What happened? It went over to the comptroller general and he sent it back, but let me tell you that treasurer--keep quiet now--that treasurer, you know, come from a cold climate, way off up yonder where they are fast. Yes, he run around to the comptroller general even before it got to him, and he said: "If it had come to me I would not have paid it."

Now, listen, was it up to me to let those people dictate to me? Was it up to me to refuse to see that the convicts and guards were fed and paid? Was it up to me to refuse for the judges of this state to get their money? Was it up to me to see that every school closed down? Well, listen, I either had to do that or I had to let them dictate to the state of Georgia. That was all.

And, listen, if I had a' let those few men dictate an extra session, I would have established a precedent that would have been going on for the next century in this state. Well, now, my countrymen, I did not do it. There is the check, there is the picture of the check right there. We put men in there that paid it. It is okehed there and it went through and got paid and they got the money. And, let me tell you something else. At the end of this year when I report to the next general assembly, we are going to be out of debt, and I am going to have some cash money to turn over to them.

So, now, where are we? You people know whether I have kept the faith. You know. Let me tell you. I forgot to tell you this a while ago. Not only did Washington stop the money for road work, but after that, they said: "We are going to see what you pay your own engineers out of Georgia taxes; what you are going to pay your own bookkeepers and stenographers; we are going to dictate," and they also said this: "We are going to see where you put bridges and where you put roads," and you remember about that time a certain little bridge by the name of "Ball's Ferry" fame got into history and poetry. Well, listen, they wanted to make me bow to Mikado. I went up there and they told me about that; they said: "The money is hung on a hook." They said: "It is hung on a hook."

I come back to Atlanta and I told the attorney general's office, I said: "We have done started one suit up there in the supreme court of the United States, and we had just as well start another one.". . . I said: "You get ready to bring a mandamus in the United States supreme court in the name of the state of Georgia for that money," and she come. Well, let's leave that out. I will tell you later about that. You all know about it. You all know. You all know! Whenever the attorney general makes a ruling, he ought to stick to it, I will tell you that much. All right. Now, listen! That was the second time within eight months of holding up those funds on the highways. That was not all. This year, you know, the fall election is coming. They thought: "Well, if we will stop road building again we will stop old Gene," and this year again they held up the funds and said: "We have got a right to say who is treasurer of Georgia." They even took that position! I answered them back: "You have nothing to do with the internal affairs of Georgia.". . . Wait a minute, boys! There were two more little campaign pledges I had two years ago when we met here. You know, I said something about a lieutenant governor. The reason I did that, the lieutenant governor is president of the senate, and why not the people name him in place of the special interests? That is one of the reasons we need a lieutenant governor.

I said something about a four-year term for governor and I said: "The reason you need a four-year term is because most politicians are under a two-year term and before they get the chair warm some smart folks start talking about opposition," and when they start talking about that, haven't you seen how docile most politicians get? They are timid. . . . Now, listen closely! Wait a minute, let me tell you something else! . . . I have received letters and messages from thousands of people over the state of Georgia wanting me to run for governor again. Now, wait a minute, keep quiet, let me get this out of my system. I am talking from the bottom of my heart. Now, listen! I appreciate their request and it is the highest monument on this earth, wanting me to go on and stay there awhile. It is in the heart of the people, it reaches to the skies, but, listen, you good Christian men and women, if you love me, why do you love me? You love me because you think I keep my word. That is why! You have never seen me any place where I had to back and trim. You never have and I will never get there! But, listen, I am interested in what we started in Georgia; I want to see it driven through to protect the workingmen, women and children in this state, and I did not forget you. I have got you a man that will make you a good governor. . . .

And, listen. I am a candidate for the United States senate from Georgia. Boys, give me a little time; I have to talk against time. Where is that crowd from Barrow county? Where are you? Yes, sir. My boys, listen at this now. Listen! Let's see, now, where abouts is it? Where do I start? Listen

at this! I told you that for 13 longs [sic] months
the state of Georgia's money was held up. It was not
federal money. It was money levied on you by taxes
of every kind. . . . They forgot that principle of
the constitution of the United States, and if I go to
the senate, regardless--wait a minute, now--if I go
to the United States senate, regardless of who is
elected governor, and we have several in the race,
regardless of whether I favor him or not, if I am in
the senate and any money is held up that is coming to
Georgia, I will rock the old nation from Maine to
California.

Now, listen again! Do you know what has protected Georgia and has kept us from owing billions
and billions to punish babies unborn? Do you know
what done it? No, it was not Gene Talmadge! It was
way back yonder that give me the power to do it. At
the last constitutional convention, Bob Toombs wrote
in the platform of the state that you cannot cast a
debt against the state beyond the calendar year
except in time of war and to repel invasion, and all
those other debts I found there were illegal and
contrary to the constitution. If I am in the senate,
I propose that we will write into our national
platform of the United States the same provision that
Georgia started and now is in 17 state platforms,
that we will have in the platform, in the constitution of the United States, that you cannot--let me
read it--we will have written into our national law
the same provision of our state law, which reads as
follows: "Creating no debt against the nation beyond
the fiscal or calendar year, except in time of war,
and to repel invasion.". . .

If I am in the senate, here is something else
that I am going to put across, stop the issuance of
any tax-exempt government bonds, stop the issuance of
any federal bonds of any kind, unless adopted by the
several states of this Union, and voted on by the
people. That is it. That will put money in McRae,
Ga. That will put it on Sugar creek. That will give
jobs to people that will take them off of relief, and
you know it. And, right here, my heart goes out, I
see a lot of them that I know--good men and women--on
relief. They ain't going to get that 15-mill limita-
tion in Georgia. Vote that and you will just about
stop it.

Let me tell you something else. When I see
those people drawing their dole for work at
Passamaquoddie, which is in Maine, I believe it is,
going to stop the waves of the ocean in Maine, to cut
a big ditch across Florida and building a dog hospital in Mempis, Tenn., and building monkey cages in
Atlanta and elephant pools in California, why the

people that do that work know that the government is
leading them off. Let the money get where they know
they are doing work to produce and it elevates your
heart. Now, let's see what else. . . . Well, now,
here. Here is what I am going to do to them if you
send me to Washington. I am going to cut this annual
budget to under $1,000,000,000, and when I do, these
little surveyors and these snoopers and these federal
fellows that are growing by leaps and bounds will
fade out of Georgia and the rest of the states of
this union, just about like your oil inspectors did
in 1926. What next? What
next? . . .
    Here is the fourth pledge I make to
you--recognize the constitution of the United States
and remember my oath of office to uphold the constitution of the United States in every vote cast. All
right. Now, let's go a little further. Now, here is
the fifth one, and listen close to this--remove every
cabinet officer who endeavors to change our form of
government. I will talk to you about that in a
minute.
    Now, what is the last one? Now, here is the
last one--no, here is the sixth one--I will get to
that in a minute under the fifth one. Here is the
sixth--allow no taxes to be collected from the people
by any ruling of any board or bureau at Washington.
No taxes by any board or bureau. Keep to congress
the sole power of levying all taxes and not delegate
it to the President or anyone else, and in levying
taxes my course will be the same as it has been in
Georgia, that every time they give me a lick at them
I will cut them.
    All right, now the seventh. Here is a sort of a
$3 tag that has hit the nation. Here it is. Listen
at it! Reduce the postage stamp from 3 cents back to
2 cents.
    All right, let's see what else. Eighth--now
listen at this. You know I told you when I got mixed
up in that hog field I found out that the government
in business could not serve the people? It cannot do
it. Now, here is the eighth. Take government out of
competition with private industry and let it act only
as a referee and an umpire.
    All right, now, here is the last one, and here I
want every candidate in Georgia that is running for
governor to listen at this. Regardless of who is
elected governor of Georgia, Georgia is going to get
her share of federal money for road-building purposes
or any other purpose, and this here is to be computed
by the constitution of the United States, which says
that the money must be distributed equally among the
several states according to the population. That is

it.

Now, my countrymen, when you vote for a lawmaker, do you want to vote for a rubber stamp? . . .

Now, let's come to it again. Talking about boards and bureaus levying taxes. One of the greatest board and bureaus to levy them up there is the Department of Agriculture. They have got it up there that covers a whole lot of great skyscraping buildings, that take up parks with acres and acres of halls and offices; yes sir, you send me up there to the senate and I am going to trim that United States Department of Agriculture down to where it can go to work. . . . I like to have forgot something a while ago. I will get back to this in a minute. Listen, you know [Henry] Wallace has been telling us, "Shoot down cows, cut our brood sow's throats and throw her in the river, plow up wheat, plow up cotton and then bring the same things from abroad." And, listen at this, organized labor and unorganized labor, whenever you do that you are the greatest enemy to American labor on the face of the earth.

Listen at this. In North Georgia this year we are having a terrible drouth. It is on down here. But there it will make your heart bleed to see it. Yes, sir. The Old Master looked on that wanton waste that happened a few years ago. He looked on it. What does the Bible say? I hasten to this. From the 28th chapter of Proverbs, 19th verse: "He that tilleth his land shall have plenty of bread, but he that followeth after vain pleasure shall have poverty enough until it hurts.". . .

I have eight minutes [of radio time]. Now you folks, you just keep writing because I am going to be running Georgia until the 9th day of September, and I am going to make them think that hades is a cool place compared to down here, and we want to get it awfully dry, too. You know every time they put a dollar in Iowa, a state with about the same farm population as Georgia, about the same number of farmers--they have been putting $8 in Iowa to the farmer to $1 down here--but my announcement for the senate this year will help you farmers. You wait and see if it don't.

But listen, here is my advice to you. Take the money and keep your mouth shut and on the 9th day of September vote as your conscience dictates. . . .

Where are all of you from? Let's see. How many are here? I have seven minutes. All right, anybody here from Appling? The Bs, Barrow? Is Barrow here? Quiet boys, I have not got but seven minutes. Let's hear from you. Is Bartow county around here? Yes. Is anybody here from the Tennessee line? What about the Florida line? Yes. What about over on the

ocean? Anybody here on the Alabama line? Yes. This
is the biggest crowd that has ever been gathered in
the south. All right, my countrymen, it is my duty
to stand for the state of Georgia. It is my duty to
see that a governor is backed up when he is trying to
do the right thing. If you have got a man in the
United States senate that will do that for Georgia,
it will help every other state in the nation, and it
will end up by helping the nation. Now listen, in
1776 the men that wrote the Declaration of Independence, and later wrote our constitution, were
white men. They leveled these Tories, and cleared
our fields, and built our churches and schoolhouses,
and our towns.

     And listen! This is a white man's country not
only in the south, but I have heard from up in the
north the white people there know it and Georgia
don't want any dictation from any federal bureaus and
boards of a mixed race, and by the eternal God we
won't have it. Now it is time to write the Declaration of Independence on that, and when some of them
get caught between third and home base it is time to
open up, Brother Gelders. It is time to open up.
Oh! my countrymen, yes sir, as long as they are
giving away money, yes, you bet your boots we have
got to pay it back! But listen, we are going to stop
that "gimme" business and we are going to stop crooks
too, and we are going to give every man and woman a
chance to work and see that some great interest don't
rob them of their pay. You put a tax on people of
over half they make and you will see the grass grow
in the streets, and, my countrymen, the principles of
democracy, the principles of the democratic party
demands [sic] that someone goes from Georgia that
will stand on those principles to save our Union.

NOTE

1. After winning state-wide elections in 1926, 1928,
1930, and 1932, Talmadge was confident he could
defeat incumbent United States Senator Richard B.
Russell, Jr., Georgians waited anxiously for this
speech, in which Talmadge would announce his plans
for running for office. Text of speech from "stenographic report" to Atlanta Constitution, July 5,
1936, providing a reliable version of the sometimes
frantic nature of Talmadge's delivery before a lively
crowd. Because of the considerable length of the
speech, some of Talmadge's amplification of points
has been deleted.

Radio Speech on University System Controversy

July 25, 1941, Atlanta, Georgia

My Fellow Countrymen:[1]

I want to take this opportunity to express my sincere thanks to WSB for their courtesy in extending to me this time, free, to talk to you. On January 1, 1941, the total obligations of the state of Georgia were $29,759,642.18. On June 30, 1941, the total obligations of the state were $16,542,136.87. In other words, within six months we were able to pay on the paid indebtedness of the state $13,217,505.31. This was done without any increase in taxes.

The departments of the state are operating efficiently, with some major increases in certain departments.

In the State Department of Public Welfare the number of individuals receiving old-age assistance has increased from July 1, 1940, to June 30, 1941, from [?]6,261 to 52,163; aid to blind from 1,113 to 1,583, and aid to dependent children from 9,694 to 11, 858.

At the Training School for Mental Defectives in Gracewood the number has increased from 318 on July 1, 1940, to 413 on July 1, 1941. At the Training School for Boys the number has increased from 135 on July 1, 1940, to 228 on July 1, 1941. At the Milledgeville State Hospital the number of inmates has increased from 7,334 on July 1, 1940, to 7,750 on July 1, 1941. Patients at the State Tuberculosis Sanatorium here increased from 269 on July 1, 1940, to 440 on July 1, 1941. And, there is an anticipated increase at all of these state institutions.

Of course, the increase on the pension rolls calls for more money.

The increase at our sanatarium and training schools calls for more money. I want to explain to you here how this indebtedness has been paid, and also the current bills of the state paid. All departments of the state, with the exception of the University System, voluntarily made a cut in their personnel, and in their salaries. This included the heads of the various departments, who voluntarily consented for the legislature to reduce their salaries.

There was a considerable saving in the State Department of Education, headed by Dr. M. D. Collins, superintendent, and he was one of the heads of the departments who voluntarily took a reduction in salary. They have co-operated with the general assembly and the present administration in bringing about this paying off the debts of the state, and are to be commended and given proper credit.

I wish to thank The Atlanta Journal for carrying the extra's that I have just read, under Mr. Gregory's column on the second editorial page. I was of the opinion that it was such an item of news interest in the state that all of the papers would carry it on the front page--but, of course, the papers know better than I. We have some great newspapers in Georgia, and we cannot do without them. And, I sometimes think that newspapers could not do without me. Especially during the past month when we almost pushed the war news off the front page [with controversy over University System]. And why? And for what? I am going to tell you the story in full:

At the first meeting of the Board of Regents at Athens, Ga., on May 30, we met to consider the re-employment of over 1,500 teachers for the next school term, beginning this fall.
Out of the over 1,500 names submitted, I objected to only two--Dr. Walter D. Cocking and Dr. Marvin S. Pittman. I read a very short statement to the Board of Regents from Mrs. Sylla B. Hamilton on Dr. Walter D. Cocking's racial attitude, and the Board of Regents voted not to re-employ these two men.

We proceeded with other business. Within about 30 minutes there came an invitation for us to recess and go over to the Arts building to dedicate its formal opening, and hear some music. Most of the members of the Board of Regents objected to taking the recess, but on the insistence of Dr. S. V. Sanford, chancellor, we decided to go over. During this recess was when the Julius Rosenwald Fund, with its millions of dollars, got under way. When we came back to the session, the chairman very excitedly stated that Harmon Caldwell, president of the University of Georgia, had offered his resignation if we did not give Dr. Cocking a hearing on the charges.

I argued against it, on the ground that the re-employment of a professor was not such a position

as to have a hearing. It was only for the consideration by the Board of Regents--that they were trustees
and directors, and re-employing people was not
breaking a contract nor terminating an office--and
that it was the duty of the Board of Regents which
must be done every year. Should they give everyone
whom they had on their list a hearing as to why they
are dropped, are not re-employed, they would not have
time to do anything else, except to hold hearings for
every day in the year--a hearing a day for 300 days
in the year. A majority of the board voted for the
hearing, and we decided to have the hearing in
executive session on the 16th day of June in the
Governor's office. At that hearing, an affidavit was
read, signed by Mrs. Sylla B. Hamilton. I will read
it to you: ". . . In the spring of 1930 I attended a
faculty meeting in the Peabody College of Education
of the University of Georgia, over which Dr. Walter
D. Cocking, dean, presided. He . . . said that he
wished to build a training school . . . for both
blacks and whites--in order to uplift the state of
Georgia. . . ." (Signed) "Sylla B. Hamilton."

I will also read you an affidavit signed by
Constance Scott, the stenographer who made notations
of the meeting that Mrs. Hamilton swore to. . . . In
these notations, Mrs. Hamilton was the only member of
the faculty of the College of Education who objected
to Dr. Walter D. Cocking's plan to have a campus
within 30 minutes' drive of Athens, for both blacks
and whites to study together, practice
together--social, economical, religious and health
problems.

There were several professors from the University of Georgia who appeared at the hearing, in behalf
of Dr. Cocking, and swore that they never heard of
him advocating any co-mingling of the races in our
schools. Of course, this was negative evidence. Two
other professors who appeared in behalf of Dr.
Cocking are heads of colleges here in Georgia, not
connected with the State University System. I will
not call their names for fear it might damage their
schools. But these two professors have allowed the
young Georgia white girls to go to mixed meeting of
Negroes and whites. One of the institutions sent
white Georgia girls over to Tuskegee, Ala., to a
Negro college, and they stayed there on the campus
for about three days. This institution receives a
large endowment from the Rosenwald Foundation fund.

I can understand why some Georgians rather doubt
these statements. I did myself, when they were
first brought to my attention. They were so foreign
to our teachings until I did not dream that any
college professor in the southland would want an

intermingling of the races in our schools. But money does its work. Back in the days of Judas, the disciple who took 30 pieces of silver to betray Christ--we are taught how money would do evil things. They called it "bribery" then. Today, in some of our higher educated, misguided circles, they call these same 30 pieces or more of silver "scholarships and fellowships."

"Brown America"--a book written by Edwin R. Embree, president of the Rosenwald Foundation fund, advocates the co-mingling of the races, using the same parks, the same hotels, the same golf courses, the same restaurants, the same libraries, and the same schools. In other words, the hope and the dream of this Edwin R. Embree is for an amalgamation of the two races in America, to make a brown America! We revolt at the thought! It is hard for us to believe that any white man, north or south, would preach such a doctrine. You would say that he could not get anywhere with it. But, you forget that the Rosenwald Fund has the power to give away $40,000,000!

What do they do with it? They give scholarships and fellowships to newspaper editors [Ralph McGill] here in Atlanta. They also give these scholarships and fellowships to white teachers in the University System of Georgia, and to other teachers in various colleges in Georgia. The University of Georgia paid Dr. Cocking a salary of $5,200 a year, and the Rosenwald Fund added more to his salary, and to the salaries of other professors at the university. For what? To try to persuade them, or blind their vision and get them to believing that we should have coeducation of the races in Georgia. Thanks for the quotation in the <u>Atlanta</u> <u>Journal</u> of today, July 25, under Shakespeare Says.

> Oh what a world of vile ill-
> favored faults,
> Looks handsome in 300 pound
> a year!

Remember this. Such men as Embree, Cocking and Pittman are smart. They knew that they could not come boldly into the front door in Georgia with a plan like this. They knew that they had to come in in a subtle channel, and, using their own words, "pick out canny speakers" to teach the young this theory of social equality in America.

All right--the vote was taken. Dr. Cocking was retained by a vote of 8 to 7. Then, new evidence was offered. Books were found in the library at the college at Statesboro, and in the University System in general, advocating co-education of the races.

These books were used in the course for parallel readings, which were necessary before the students could obtain their diplomas. One of these books, "Calling America," was complimenting the Communist party of America for its efforts in behalf of abolishing all casts and race lines in a democracy.

Now, with a Board of Regents composed of the following gentlemen: John J. Cummings, L. W. Robert, Jr., T. Jack Lance, W. S. Morris, K. S. Varn, E. Ormonde Hunter, Honorable Susie T. Moore, George C. Woodruff, James S. Peters, Scott Candler, Judge Joe Ben Jackson, R. D. Harvey, Julian Strickland, Jr., General Sandy Beaver and Dr. Joe L. Jenkins, the case was heard with the evidence above outlined, and the following affidavit from a young man by the name of Connell, who was in charge of the farm at Statesboro, Ga., was read. This affidavit swore positively that Dr. Pittman bought a farm adjoining the state's property, had it worked, and improvements and repairs made with the state's machinery, the state's employees and the NYA students, used fertilizer and seed from the state's supplies.

Dr. Marvin S. Pittman, who was president of the college at Statesboro answered this by saying that he wrote the agricultural teacher at Statesboro that he was going to operate this farm at the expense of the state and turn over the proceeds to the college there. Dr. Pittman swore that he mailed a copy of this letter to the members of the Board of Regents from his district, and also to the chancellor of the University System. There was no evidence from either the Board of Regents or the chancellor that they ever received the letter.

Dr. Pittman's answer of justification did not satisfy 10 members of the Board of Regents, and the reason is obvious. If Dr. Pittman had a right to have the state operate his farm, clear the land, and improve it, every private citizen who had property adjoining that farm had the same right. If Dr. Pittman had this right, then every head of a state institution in the state of Georgia could have bought them a farm and had it cleared and improved at the expense of the state, and given the same statement--"that they would turn over the proceeds of the farm to the state." Dr. Pittman's action was clearly against the law.

After considering the evidence, the Board of Regents voted 10 to 5 not to re-elect Dr. Cocking or Dr. Marvin S. Pittman. Immediately a howl went up over the state that these men who voted not to re-elect these two professors were stooges, trained seals, idiots, men without character, and men who had committed a public lynching in the state capitol.

Hard words, aren't they? But, remember the ramifica-
tions of   the $40,000,000,   and think   of   the
"Tweedle-dum" and "Tweedle-dee"'

At first, the press tried to convey the impression that there was no evidence against the two
professors. Some of the northern papers readily
admitted that there was evidence, and an issue,
joined on the subject of co-education of the races,
and that Georgia had crucified the Negroes, and made
martyrs of Dr. Marvin s. Pittman and Dr. Walter D.
Cocking by not allowing them to have Negroes in the
same schools with the whites in our state.   However,
I will say this in the credit of the press of Georgia. Within the last week they too have finally
admitted that there was evidence, and an issue of
racial equality in the re-employment of these two
professors. News items in both of the Atlanta papers
of July 24 quoted Dr. Embree, president of the
Rosenwald Fund, as saying that the purposes of this
fund is to work towards the elimination of the Jim
Crow laws in the south, and for co-education of the
races in the south.   At last the papers told the
story, and the facts and the issues in this
much-talked-of case.

Also, on July 24, page 24 of The _Atlanta_ Consti-
tution, there was a news item relative to a statement
made by the "Atlanta Civic and Political League"
composed of   Negroes and   whites--principally
Negroes--protesting the action of the Board of
Regents in denying equality of opportunity in education to the Negro race in Georgia, which they said
composed one-third of our population, and makes "our
laws a farce and our preachments about a democracy
the quintescence of hypocrisy itself. . . ."

It would be interesting to note the names of
some of our newspapermen who belong to these
inter-racial societies here in Atlanta and in the
state of Georgia. But I look on these white men with
charity. They think it does not amount to anything
much. They think that it is all right to get these
scholarships and fellowships and go ahead and do the
work and write a big, blowing editorial in a newspaper about it. They underrate their work. More
people read the newspapers than they dream. A free
and a true press is the most important foundation
stone of a Christian democracy.

I was born and raised in Georgia. Four generations of my ancestors sleep beneath Georgia's sod. I
am a graduate of the University of Georgia. My
father and my grandfather also were students at the
University of Georgia, and walked those paths, and in
those halls where the dearest memories and the
grandest traditions of Georgia were molded. I love

the University of Georgia. I showed it. I sent my
only son there. And I love the University enough to
put up a fight for it when I think that any foreign
element is trying to destroy the great traditions of
that grand institution.

And, did you notice that I used the word "foreign"? What did I mean by that? I did not mean that
just because someone was born across the line from
Georgia that he was a "furriner" and would not make a
good Georgian. No! There are some native-born
Georgians who have been taking this Rosenwald Fund.
I mean by the term "foreigner" someone with training
and teaching who believes that things are eternally
right--that Georgians have been taught and trained to
believe are eternally wrong.

We welcome people to come into our state.   But,
we don't want them to come here to try and change our
ideas of democracy, our ideals of humanity, our
ideals of education. We don't want them to come here
to try to make us believe that Alexander Stephens,
Bob Toombs, Henry W. Grady, Thomas E. Watson, and a
long list of others that I could name, were ignorant,
prejudiced, Negro-haters.

The south, and Georgia, the Empire State, knows
exactly how to get along with the Negro race. The
south started out after the days of 1886 with a
scorched earth, smokehouses burned down, stock run
off, railroads torn up, and seven million slaves
emancipated and given the rights as free citizens.
The south and Georgia solved this problem without any
outside help. She has built back and is the pride of
America today, the fountain seat of democracy, and
will take the lead in defending this great country of
ours in its hour of peril.

The Negro in Georgia--what is his status here?
What does your Governor think of him? I am going to
give you my answer in a statement by an old Negro,
over 70 years old. His hair was white. He is the
leader of his race in Georgia. He is the president
of the Negro college at Albany, Ga.--a branch of the
University of Georgia:

"Address to the general council of the University System at Statesboro, Ga., in 1935, by J. W.
Holley:

It is a great privilege, Mr. Chancellor, to
address this council on the important subject of What
Should Be the Place of the Negro Units in the University System. This question might more correctly be
put in this form; namely, Have the Negro Units Any
Place in the University System? I make bold to say,
in the outset, they have not.

The background of the Negro is vastly different
from that of the white man; his environment is unlike

that of the white man, and his future outlook so
different, that it will be impossible to orientate or
fuse both races in one educational system. . . . The
great mass of our people need to be trained in
agriculture, mechanic arts, the trades and industries, and the art of homemaking. . . . We are proud
of the achievements of our people, and we want a
separate little university of our own. A university
made of two or three branches or units, with courses
of study based upon the needs of our people. . . .
Give us this and we'll take our stand in Dixie Land,
and live and die for Dixie."

NOTE

1. As covered in Chapter 7, in 1941 Governor
Talmadge had two Georgia educators fired from their
positions, causing two accrediting agencies to remove
a number of Georgia's colleges from their lists of
accredited institutions of higher education. Because
individuals and organizations criticized the Governor
for "interfering politically" into the administration
of higher education in the state, the Governor was
placed on the defensive, and lost his bid for
re-election in 1942. In this speech he defends his
action of having the professors fired. Text of
speech from Atlanta Constitution, July 27, 1941.

Campaigning for Governor

July 13, 1946, Columbus, Georgia

[When WSB radio began taping the speech, Talmadge was already speaking; he was defending his action during an earlier term as governor to veto pensions for the elderly.] . . . at every paragraph, and if it's a trick and a fraud, it's up to the governor to deal fairly with the people. Well that's what they put onto my desk.[1] And when I read that, I knew that it was a trick and a fraud to fool the old people of the state of Georgia that was expectin' an old age pension. And the only way I could deal fairly with 'em was to veto it, and let 'em know if they wanted to pass an old age pension bill it had to be one that could be worked. [Thunder heard on audio recording, off in distance, and some vocal response from crowd.] All right, it went back, and they passed an old age pension law.

And my last term in there, let me tell you about it. I raised a number of pensioners. I struck one coming on the stand today--and everybody in Georgia--and raised the amounts of some. The man I struck got it, and when I got out it was cut off. Since I've gone out of the governor's office, instead of an increase in the number to receive the old age pension, they've reduced it--and in a great many instances, the amount. But they are still getin' old age pension money more than ever befo'.

But I want to tell you what's becomin' of it. They are givein' it to young people. The head of it, Judge Hartley, had his salary raised out of old age pension money, from five thousand a year to seven thousand, and then a travelin' expense account, an extra two thouand a year. Think of how many old age pensions that would paaay.

And now while we are on the subject of Judge

Hartley--Judge Hartley was the one that wrote that poll--that you saw in the Sunday paper, here in Columbus and everywhere else. He says he has a committee of Justices of the Peace that he writes to and obtains his poll. How many JPs here have heard from Judge Hartley? Throw up your hands; let's see 'em. Well I struck a few over the state--one I see, yeah, I found one.

And the JPs that I have heard from say to me that Judge Hartley didn't print that poll like they wrote it. In other words, Judge Hartley had to plant a poll like the present Administration wants it, because they have a handpicked candidate, and he has a job under the present Administration.

So Judge Hartley with his poll raised his salary two thousand a year out of old age pension money, when he's in his thirties. There is one poll though that Judge Hartley hasn't thought about, and that's that poll that I'm gonna' ride him out of that capitol on the second week in January. [Cheers, yells, "Tell 'em Gene."]

Now, the government--the federal guv'ment makes the boast that they will match state funds up to a certain amount in payin' old age pensions. Well now my friends did it ever occur to you that the federal guv'ment to obtain any money first has to collect it out of the people of the state by 'a tax? Every time you send a long distance telephone call or telegram, or buy a gallon of gas or cee'gars or tobacco or chewing tobacco or cigarette or jewelry or furs or a thousand articles, you pay a tax to the federal guv'ment.

And then the federal guv'ment says the only way you can get it back is to match it with so much mo' state tax. [Yell from audience.] Well it's our money anyhow and I think it's a wise thing to get it back in Georgia, and I've made up my mind that I'm gonna' match those federal funds as high as they'll go and bring 'em back to Georgia and give it to the old people in the state of Georgia. [Rebel-like yells and applause.]

Now the next question that you're interested in--and I know what it is--you're interested in the proper care, the proper respect, the proper honor, and the proper remuneration of our G.I. boys. I want'a know how many of 'em are listenin' at me. Raise your hands you G.I. boys--al'right, all of you, G.I.--Listen at this. You G.I. boys are my campaign managers. You're the ones that I'm countin' on next Wednesday to match that solid block of Nigra votes that I know's gonna' vote a'ginst me. [Applause and cheers; "Tell 'em Gene."] And I think you can do it.

Now listen. You G.I. men were carried away from

home, some of you away from ya' families and ya'
children. Some of ya' homes have broken up. All of
you were carried away from your business. Your
business went to nothin'. You lost years from it,
and you know--while you men were carried out on the
seas, and some of you under the seas, in foxholes--a
lot of us people here at home made more money on
account of the war, a lots of us. [Yell from audience.]

And I have--I have one opponent in this race
that says I'm goin' around offerin' to you boys
handouts, and that particular opponent of mine
certainly got his part while the war was goin' on.
[Yells, cheers.] And, you know, I don't think that
opponent of mine would have made that remark if one
of his sons or some of his family had'a been carried
off to the war and kept there for years where he'd 'a
been afraid to open a telegram, expectin' the
worse--I don't believe he'd 'a done it. But sometimes you know sudden riches produces arrogance, and
it might 'a been in a spirit of arrogance that he
made that remark saying I's offering handouts to men
that had given their all. [Soft thunder.]

Now listen my friends, your main help comes from
the federal law, the G.I. Bill of Rights that was
passed by Congress before the surrender. Under that
Bill, it provides for educational and a trainin'
course, and to pay you from 65 to 90 a month while
you're takin' it. Now our colleges are full of G.I.
boys. I'm proud they're there. I wish there was
room for more, but there's not. And Congress recognized that, and provided in that Bill that those
courses could be taken at home in your counties, and
you'd get your pay while it was goin' on. And our
state legislature in '45 created a state agency to
help the G.I. boys [thunder] familiarize themselves
with the workin' of that Bill, because they knew that
the average citizen wouldn't know the benefits of a
federal law. But they have not been functionin' for
the G.I. boys. And I'll tell you why. I'll tell ya'
why. They've been up there drawin' the salaries, but
they haven't been helpin' our G.I. boys. I haven't
seen a one that's got the loan, not a one.

And here's the reason they--[loud thunder]
here's the reason they haven't been helpin' our G.I.
boys. Our present Governor has been [thunder] too
busy talkin' about "good governmentment," and has a
candidate runnin on good government--to think about
the G.I. boys. And what does this spread eagle,
Mother Hubbard platform of good government mean?
You've heard about Mother Hubbard before--covers all
and touches nothin'! [Yells.] And when you see a
Mother Hubbard platform like that, there's somethin'

always they're trying to hide. And here's what they're tryin' to hide, and what they hate to hear me talk about in every speech I make, and that's restorin' the Democratic white primary in Georgia. [Loud cheers accompanied by thunder.]

Now to the G.I. boys--the state can be some help. Some states have given five hundred dollars bonus. I wish that Georgia was able, but with over three hundred thousand G.I. boys [thunder], at five hundred a piece, it's over a hundred and fifty million in one year, and our present taxes can't bare that. [Thunder.] But there are other things that we can offer which in a run of years will amount to that much and more. And--makin' it short--here is what they are: exemption to G.I. boys from ad valorem tax for a period of five years [thunder, cheers], a business license to every G.I. man, both of World War I and II [thunder], free of charge to fellows of the flag. [Loud thunder. Reacting to thunder, Talmadge said to himself, "Boy'ee".]

And the third, which won't amount to much in dollars and cents, but I think the G.I. boys will appreciate it--and I know the state's able to do it [thunder]--the G.I. boys that left this country, and went over across the seas, drove airplanes and automobiles and motorcycles and trucks on enemy soil--they didn't have to buy a license from the country. [Two loud claps of thunder.] They drove those vehicles facing death and shot and shells, and what were they doin'? They were defending the roads and bridges here of Georgia. And if I am your governor, I want to see every G.I. boy given an honorary driver's license as a badge of honor, free of charge, the balance of his life.

[Prolonged thunder, as a frightening storm passed over. Voice softly to Talmadge: "The radio folks say they can't take it [the thunder]; Talmadge answered, "can't take it?" Reply: "nope."] Well, I'll go ahead--naa. The radio people say they can't take it, but I'll go on. Now listen. Now I've come--[loud thunder; "ooo'eee"] now I've come to the one issue on which all of my opponents and I vitally disagree. And at this point, I want to thank the Atlanta Journal for comin' out about two months ago and statin' plainly that Talmadge was the only candidate for governor in this race that was champion[ing] the restoration of a Democratic white primary in Georgia. [Cheers and yells.]

My countrymen, when they said that--[loud burst of thunder] they told the truth and the whole truth. Now what do my opponents say? They say that it's the law, and Nigras will vote in the primary--this year, next Wednesday--[loud thunder] and it stops right there!

What do I say?   I say it's the law this year,
and some of the Nigras will vote, the fewer the
better, but I add to it this: if I'm your governor,
they won't vote in our white primary the next four
years. [Cheers and very loud thunder. Talmadge
responding to himself about the thunder: "Gosh!" A
voice to crowd: "If the Governor has to stop talking
on account of the storm and the radio's inability to
take it, come into the courtroom and we'll here 'em
through there."]

I'll go ahead. Now wait a minute--stay still,
stay still--hold on, wait--ain't got to go yet--I'll
finish in a minute.

Listen, you read the bus decision where the
Supreme Court held that Nigras could pick [a seat]
beside of any people on your buses. Did you read it?
[From audience: "yeah".] It was decided about four
weeks ago.   Listen, that's based on innerstate
commerce-- [immense thunder]--that was based on
innerstate commerce. If I'm your governor, the
Public Service Commission of Georgia will only
license buses for intrastate, and if you want to take
a trip to Montgomery, Alabama, you'll have to buy a
ticket just this side of the Alabama line [thunder],
and then get you one to go on further. [Crowd
noise.]

Now, in conclusion, let's--let us put one more
question to you. [Soft rolling thunder.] The FEPC
[Federal Employees Practices Commission] is what
they're trying to pass. That's to put foremans in
your mills of any race or color.   [Soft rolling
thunder; Talmadge said privately: "looks like it's
gonna' rain."] You know that won't work in Georgia,
and if you boys'll get out next Wednesday [loud
thunder]--next Wednesday in that election, and join
hands--awe it's great enough for all white men and
white women to join hands. And what's breakin' the
opposition's heart--they know the majority of the
white people in Muscogee County are for Talmadge.
Let's get the great majority [cheers], and then come
on to the convention in Macon.   And there won't be
anybody in that convention but white women and white
men if I am your governor. [Cheers] Good-bye.   I'm
glad to see you.

NOTE

1. After losing a gubernatorial campaign in 1942,
Talmadge resolved for the election of 1946 that he
would win white votes by warning of racial integration, courting veterans' votes, and promising to
build more roads and to improve education. As shown
in the text, Talmage was reluctant to even be

interrupted by the powerful forces of nature!
Typescript of this speech from Atlanta WSB radio
audio recording housed in Special Collections Department, Georgia State University, Atlanta.   Talmadge
delivered the "address" on the courthouse lawn.   The
announcer for the radio station introduced the speech
by indicating that WSB was providing "a commercial
service to all gubernatorial candidates." The author
and Andrew Logue transcribed the text of the speech
verbatim from the audio recording.

Selected Bibliography

Allen, John E. "Eugene Talmadge and the Great
    Textile Strike in Georgia, September 1934." In
    Gary M. Fink and Merl E. Reed, eds., Essays in
    Southern Labor History: Selected Papers.
    Westport, Connecticut, 1977.
Analyses of Talmadge 1932 Campaign. Marietta Jour-
    nal, July 21, 1932; Savannah Evening Press,
    September 10, 1932; Dalton Citizen, September 14,
    1932.
Analyses of Talmadge 1934 Campaign. Atlanta Consti-
    tution, July 5, 1934, and September 9, 1934.
Analyses of Talmadge 1936 Campaign. Atlanta Consti-
    tution, July 5, 1935, August 13 and 28, 1936,
    September 6 and 9, 1936.
Analyses of Talmadge 1946 Campaign. Atlanta Daily
    World, July 5, 16, and 19, 1946; Atlanta
    Constitution, June 1 and 14, July 14, 1946;
    Savannah Morning News, July 17, 1946.
Anderson, William. The Wild Man from Sugar Creek:
    The Political Career of Eugene Talmadge. Baton
    Rouge: Louisiana State University Press, 1975.
Anderson, W. T. On the Talmadge-Brown McRae Debate.
    Macon Telegraph and News, August 5, 1926.
_____. Analyses of Talmadge Campaigns. Atlanta
    Constitution, September 5, 1936; Macon Telegraph
    and News, July 5, 1942.
Bailes, Sue. "Eugene Talmadge and the Board of
    Regents Controversy." Georgia Historical
    Quarterly 55 (1969), 409-423.
Belvin, William L. Jr. "Georgia Gubernatorial
    Primary of 1946," Georgia Historical Quarterly 50
    (March 1966), 37-53.
Bernd, Joseph. "White Supremacy and the Disfran-
    chisement of Blacks in Georgia, 1946." Georgia

Historical Quarterly 66 (1982), 492-513.
Bouton, Michael Wickham. "Depression Era Extremists:
    A Study of Three Demagogues and Their Tactics."
    Ph.D. dissertation, Illinois State University,
    1978.
Brown, John J. Criticism of "Grass Roots" Conven-
    tion. Atlanta Constitution, January 30, 1936.
Caldwell, Harmon W. Statement on University System
    Controversy. Augusta Chronicle, August 3, 1941.
Candler, Scott. Speech on University Controversy to
    Decatur Rotary Club, Atlanta Constitution, August
    21, 1941.
Chadwick, John. On Talmadge Speaking and Rally.
    Macon Telegraph and News, July 5, 1942.
Cocking, Walter Dewey. "Report of the Study on
    Higher Education of Negroes in Georgia." Special
    Collections, University of Georgia, 1938.
_____. Speech on University System Controversey
    to Griffin Kiwanis Club, Atlanta Constitution,
    July 24, 1941.
Cobb, James C. "Not Gone, But Forgotten: Eugene
    Talmadge and the 1938 Purge Campaign." Georgia
    Historical Quarterly 59 (1975), 197-209.
Cook, James F. "The Eugene Talmadge-Walter Cocking
    Controversey." Phylon, Atlanta University Review
    of Race and Culture 35 (1974), 181-192.
_____. "Politics and Education in the Talmadge
    Era: The Controversy Over the University System of
    Georgia, 1941-1942." M.A. thesis, University of
    Georgia, Athens, 1972.
Couric, John. Analysis of Talmadge Campaign.
    Atlanta Constitution, May 23, 1946.
Cox, Eugene. Response to Eugene Talmadge. Atlanta
    Constitution, May 9, 1935.
Crooks, Mary Glass. "The Platform Pledges of Gover-
    nor Eugene Talmadge and Resulting Statutes." M.A.
    thesis, University of Georgia, Athens, 1953.
DeLoach, Bennett. Analysis of Talmadge Campaign.
    Savannah Morning News, June 16, 18, and 26, 1946.
Dixon, J. Curtis. Speech on University System
    Controversy to Atlanta Lions Club. Atlanta
    Constitution, August 10, 1941.
Dykeman, Wilma. "The Southern Demagogue." Virginia
    Quarterly Review 33 (1957), 558-568.
Eve, Lovelace. On Talmadge-Brown Debate. Americus
    Times-Recorder August 4 and 5, 1926.
Farrell, L. A. Analyses of Talmadge Campaigns.
    Atlanta Constitution, August 5 and September 9,
    1934; May 14 and September 11, 1938; July 5,
    1940.
"Findings of the Southern Association" on the Univer-
    sity System Controversy, Atlanta Constitution,
    December 5, 1941.

Fossett, Roy E.   "Impact of the New Deal on Georgia
    Politics, 1933-1941."   Ph.D. dissertation,
    University of Florida, Gainesville, 1960.
Furnis, Jim.   Analysis of Talmadge Campaign.   Atlanta
    Constitution, May 22, 1946.
Gibson, Chester.   "Eugene Talmadge's Use of Identifi-
    cation During the 1934 Gubernatorial Campaign in
    Georgia."   M.A. thesis, University of Georgia,
    1967.
Gilbert, G. M.   "Dictators and Demagogues."   Journal
    of Social Issues 11 (1955), 51-53.
Green, Luke.   Analyses of Talmadge's campaigns.
    Atlanta Constitution, August 18, 25, 28, 29, and
    31, 1940.
_____.   Article on Eugene Talmadge's 1941 Inaugu-
    ral Address.   Atlanta Constitution, January 15,
    1941.
Hardy, J. B.   Assessment of Talmadge's Persuasive
    Appeals and State of Politics in Georgia.
    Thomaston Times, August 14, 1931.
Hearn, Guy.   Breaks with Talmadge.   Atlanta Constitu-
    tion, July 10, 1946.
Henson, Allen Lumpkin.   Red Galluses: A Story of
    Georgia Politics.   Boston: Edinboro Publishers,
    1945.
Howell, Hugh.   Statement against Talmadge.   Atlanta
    Constitution, August 23, 1942.
Hunter, E. Ormonde.   Speech on University System
    Controversy to Kiwanis Club, Savannah, Georgia,
    Atlanta Constitution, July 27, 1941.
Huntley, M. C.   "Report on Charges of Political
    Interference in the University System of Georgia,
    1941."   University of Georgia Library, Athens.
Hoffman, Abraham.   The Bosses.   New York: Macmillan,
    1972.
Holmes, Michael Stephan.   "The New Deal in Georgia:
    An Administrative History."   Ph.D. dissertation,
    University of Wisconsin, 1969.
Huntly, M. C.   "Report on Charges of Political
    Interference in the University System of Georgia."
    Special Collections, University of Georgia
    Library, 1941.
Knox, Frank.   Speech Supporting Eugene Talmadge
    Doctrines.   Atlanta Constitution, January 17,
    1935.
Larson, Allan Louis.   Southern Demagogues: A Study in
    Charismatic Leadership.   Ann Arbor: University
    Microfilms, 1964.
Lemmon, Sarah McCulloh.   "Governor Eugene Talmadge
    and the New Deal," in Joseph Carlyle Sitterson,
    ed., Studies in Southern History.   Chapel Hill:
    University of North Carolina Press, 1957.
_____.   "The Ideology of Eugene Talmadge."

Georgia _Historical_ _Quarterly_ 38 (1954), 226-248.
_____. "The Public Career of Eugene Talmadge:
1926-1936." Ph.D. dissertation, University of
North Carolina, Chapel Hill, 1952.
Logue, Calvin M. "The Coercive Campaign Prophecy of
Gene Talmadge." In Calvin M. Logue and Howard
Dorgan, eds., _Oratory_ _of_ _Southern_ _Demagogues_.
Baton Rouge: Louisiana State University Press,
1981.
_____. "Eugene Talmadge (1884-1946), Four-Time
Governor of Georgia," in Bernard K. Duffy and
Halford R. Ryan, eds., _American_ _Orators_ _of_ _the_
Twentieth _Century_: _Critical_ _Studies_ _and_ _Sources_.
Westport, Connecticut: Greenwood Press, 1987.
Luthin, Reinhard H. "Eugene Talmadge: 'The Wild Man'
of Sugar Creek, Georgia." _American_ _Demagogues_
Twentieth _Century_. Boston: Beacon Press, 1954.
McCain, J. R. Speech on University System Controver-
sy to Decatur Rotary Club, _Atlanta_ _Constitution_,
July 31, 1941.
McGill, Dan. Analysis of Talmadge campaign, _Macon_
Telegraph _and_ _News_, August 21, 1932.
McGill, Ralph. On Talmadge. _Atlanta_ _Constitution_,
July 6 and 31, 1940, October 13, 1941, May 31,
July 6, 12, and 13, 1946.
Mead, Howard N. "Russell vs. Talmadge: Southern
Politics and the New Deal." _Georgia_ _Historical_
Quarterly 65 (1981), 28-45.
Meyer, Ben F. On the "Grass Roots" Macon Convention.
Atlanta _Constitution_, January 30, 1936.
Middle _Georgian_ critique of Eugene Talmadge's speak-
ing, in _Elberton_ _Star_, August 10, 1926.
"Minutes of the Board of Regents of the University
System of Georgia, 1941," University of Georgia
Library, Athens.
Morris, William S. Statement on Talmadge and Univer-
sity System Controversy. _Augusta_ _Chronicle_, July
24, 1932.
Pittman, Marvin S. "Political Interference of
Governor Eugene Talmadge with the Georgia Teachers
College." Typescript in Special Collections,
1941, University of Georgia Library, Athens.
_____. Speech on University System Controversy to
Georgia Teachers' College, _Atlanta_ _Constitution_,
July 17 and August 1, 1941.
Ramsey, B. Carlyle. "The University System Contro-
versy Reexamined: The Talmadge-Holley Connection."
Georgia _Historical_ _Quarterly_ 64 (1980), 190-203.
Rhodes, W. K. Interview with W. D. Thurmond in
Atlanta _Constitution_, September 12, 1926.
Rodabaugh, Karl. "'Farmer Gene' Talmadge and the
Rural Style in Georgia Politics." _Southern_
Studies 21 (1982), 83-96.

Southern Association of Colleges and Schools.
    "Investigation by the Committee Appointed by the
    Southern Association of Colleges and Secondary
    Schools." Atlanta, Georgia, 1941.
    In University of Georgia Library, Athens.
Smith, Marion. Speech on University System
    controversey to Atlanta Rotary Club, Atlanta
    Constitution, July 22, 1941.
Spalding, Jack. Article on Eugene Talmadge 1941
    Inaugural Address. Atlanta Constitution, January
    15, 1941.
St. John, M. L. Analyses of Talmadge Campaign.
    Atlanta Constitution, April 28, and May 21, 1946.
Steinberg, Alfred. "Gene Talmadge: Wild Man in Red
    Galluses." The Bosses. New York: Macmillan
    Company, 1972.
Sutton, Willis A., Jr. "The Talmadge Campaigns: A
    Sociological Analysis of Political Power." Ph.D.
    dissertation, University of North Carolina, Chapel
    Hill, 1952.
Talmadge, Eugene. Answers John J. Brown in Americus
    Times-Recorder, August 16, 1926.
_____. Interviews in Atlanta Constitution, July
    13 and 25, 1932.
_____. Interview in New York City, Atlanta
    Constitution, May 18, 1935.
_____. Letter in Athens Banner-Herald, July 27,
    1926.
_____. Participation in farmers' meeting, Macon,
    Georgia. Macon Telegraph and News, August 28,
    1931.
_____. Performance during trials of Walter
    Cocking and Marvin Pittman. Atlanta Constitution,
    July 15, 1941.
_____. Platform Statement for 1946 Campaign.
    Atlanta Constitution, April 7, 1946.
_____. Press Conference. Atlanta Constitution,
    April 6, 1935.
_____. Written address on State of Agriculture in
    Georgia. Atlanta Constitution, June 14, 1928.
_____. Statement on campaign. Atlanta
    Constitution, July 31, 1940.
_____. Statement on campaign. Augusta Chronicle,
    September 15, 1942.
_____. Warning in his Statesman to Blacks to Stay
    Away from the Polls, in Augusta Chronicle, August
    24, 1942.
Talmadge, Herman. Speech at Rebecca, Georgia, for
    Eugene Talmadge candidacy ("the first political
    speech of his life") Atlanta Constitution,
    September 8, 1934.
_____. Speech introducing Eugene Talmadge. WSB

radio audio recording, May 4, 1946. Special
Collections Department, Georgia State University,
Atlanta, Georgia.
_____. Response on audio tape to Calvin M.
Logue's questions concerning Eugene Talmadge's
public speaking, June 1988.
_____. With Mark Royden Winchell. Talmadge: a
Political Legacy, a Politician's Life, a Memoir.
Atlanta: Peachtree Publishers, 1987.
Tarver, Jack. Analyses of Talmadge Campaign.
Atlanta Constitution, May 18, 19, and 30, June 2,
1946.
Tate, William. "Memo on Cocking." Special
Collections, University of Georgia Library, 1970.
Williams, Gladstone. Article on Eugene Talmadge and
New Deal. Atlanta Constitution, May 7, 1935.
_____. Article on "Grass Roots" Convention.
Atlanta Constitution, January 30, 1936.

ARTICLES AND EDITORIALS ON TALMADGE
Article on Eugene Talmadge's 1935 Inaugural Address.
Atlanta Constitution, January 17, 1935.
Article on Eugene Talmadge speech against the New
Deal. Atlanta Constitution, May 8, 1935.
Editorials on Talmadge. Atlanta Constitution, August
23 and 28, 1936, and July 15, 1941.
Editorials on Talmadge and politics. Atlanta Daily
World, September 12, 13, and 15, 1940, May 9, 22,
and 28, June 25 and 30, 1946.
Editorial on Talmadge. Atlanta Journal, July 12,
1942.
Editorials on Talmadge. Augusta Chronicle, July 25
and 29, August 2, September 1 and 11, 1940.
Editorial on Talmadge. Gainesville News, in Atlanta
Constitution, June 10, 1946.
Editorials on Talmadge. Macon Telegraph and News,
July 16 and August 21, 1932.
Editorial on Talmadge. Savannah Morning News, July
6, 1946.
Editorial on Talmadge. Walton Tribune, in Atlanta
Constitution, August 6, 1936.

NEWSPAPERS

Americus Times-Recorder, 1922.
Athens Banner-Herald, 1926-1946.
Atlanta Constitution, 1926-1946.
Atlanta Journal, 1926-1946.
Augusta Chronicle, 1940-1942.
Cordele Dispatch, 1926.
Covington News, 1926.
Dalton Citizen, 1926.
Dawson News, 1926-1931.
Eastman Times-Journal, 1920.

Elberton Star, 1926.
Lyons Progress, 1926.
Macon Telegraph and News, 1926.
Marietta Journal, 1932
Middle Georgian, 1926.
Monroe Advertiser, 1926.
Rome News-Tribune, 1926.
Sandersville Progress, 1926.
Savannah Morning News, 1946.
Telfair Enterprise, 1920-1928.
Thomaston Times, 1931.

SELECTED SPEECHES BY EUGENE TALMADGE

        Campaigning for Commissioner of Agriculture
Sandersville, Georgia, Atlanta Constitution, June 25,
    1926; Sandersville Progress, June 30, 1926.
Rome, Georgia, Atlanta Constitution, July 17, 1926.
Newnan, Georgia, Atlanta Constitution, July 23, 1926.
League of Women Voters, Athens, Georgia, Athens
    Banner-Herald, July 30, 1926.
Tifton, Georgia, Atlanta Constitution, August 1,
    1926.
Debate with J. J. Brown, McRae, Georgia, Macon
    Telegraph and News, August 4, 1926.
Debate with J. J. Brown, Dawson, Georgia, Americus
    Times-Recorder, August 5, 1926.
Debate with J. J. Brown, Elberton, Georgia, Elberton
    Star, August 13, 1926; Atlanta Constitution,
    August 13, 1926; Macon Telegraph and News, August
    13, 1926.
Winder, Georgia, Atlanta Constitution, August 19,
    1926.
Americus, Georgia, Americus Times-Recorder, August
    23, 1926; Atlanta Constitution, August 22, 1926.

        As Commissioner of Agriculture
Athens, Georgia, Telfair Enterprise, January 27,
    1928.
Covington, Georgia, Americus Times-Recorder, August
    27, 1928.
Thomaston, Georgia, Thomaston Times, August 28, 1931.
Cordele, Georgia, Cordele Dispatch, August 28, 1931.

        Gubernatorial Campaign of 1932 and Inaugural
        Address
McRae, Georgia, Atlanta Constitution, July 5, 1932.
Statesboro, Georgia, Macon Telegraph and News, July
    10, 1932.
Cairo, Georgia, Atlanta Constitution, July 13, 1932.
Tifton, Georgia, Atlanta Constitution, July 13, 1932.
Talbotton, Georgia, Atlanta Constitution, July 15,
    1932.
Blairsville, Georgia, Atlanta Constitution, July 16,
    1932.

Dalton, Georgia, <u>Atlanta Constitution</u>, July 16, 1932.
Franklin, Georgia, <u>Atlanta Constitution</u>, July 17,
    1932.
LaGrange, Georgia, <u>Atlanta Constitution</u>, July 17,
    1932.
Fort Valley, Georgia, <u>Atlanta Constitution</u>, July 19,
    1932.
Washington, Georgia, <u>Atlanta Constitution</u>, July 21,
    1932.
Griffin, Georgia, <u>Marietta Journal</u>, July 21, 1932.
Thomson, Georgia, <u>Atlanta Constitution</u>, July 22,
    1932.
Sparta, Georgia, <u>Atlanta Constitution</u>, July 22, 1932.
Swainsboro, Georgia, <u>Atlanta Constitution</u>, July 23,
    1932.
Sandersville, Georgia, <u>Atlanta Constitution</u>, July 23,
    1932.
Lyons, Georgia, <u>Atlanta Constitution</u>, July 27, 1932.
Barnesville, Georgia, <u>Atlanta Constitution</u>, July 27,
    1932.
Greensboro, Georgia, <u>Atlanta Constitution</u>, July 28,
    1932.
Douglas, Georgia, <u>Atlanta Constitution</u>, July 29,
    1932.
Lakeland, Georgia, <u>Atlanta Constitution</u>, July 30,
    1932.
Cumming, Georgia, <u>Atlanta Constitution</u>, August 3,
    1932.
Toccoa, Georgia, <u>Atlanta Constitution</u>, August 5,
    1932.
Gainesville, Georgia, <u>Atlanta Constitution</u>, August 7,
    1932.
Conyers, Georgia, <u>Atlanta Constitution</u>, August 9,
    1932.
Dallas, Georgia, <u>Atlanta Constitution</u>, August 10,
    1932.
Sylvester, Georgia, <u>Atlanta Constitution</u>, August 12,
    1932.
Thomasville, Georgia, <u>Atlanta Constitution</u>, August
    13, 1932.
Macon, Georgia, <u>Atlanta Constitution</u>, August 20,
    1932.
Bainbridge, Georgia, <u>Atlanta Constitution</u>, August 25,
    1932.
Macon, Georgia, <u>Macon Telegraph and News</u>, August 28,
    1932.
Elberton, Georgia, <u>Atlanta Constitution</u>, August 28,
    1932.
Hartwell, Georgia, <u>Atlanta Constitution</u>, September 3,
    1932.
Nahunta, Georgia, <u>Atlanta Constitution</u>, September 6,
    1932.
Crawfordville, Georgia, <u>Atlanta Constitution</u>, Septem-

ber 8, 1932.
Atlanta, Georgia, Atlanta Constitution, September 9,
    1932.
Madison, Georgia, Atlanta Constitution, September 13,
    1932.
McRae, Georgia, Atlanta Constitution, September 16,
    1932.
Gubernatorial Inaugural Address, Atlanta, Georgia;
    Atlanta Constitution, January 11, 1933.

    Gubernatorial Campaign of 1934 and Inaugural
    Address
Bainbridge, Georgia, Atlanta Constitution, July 5,
    1934.
Albany, Georgia, Atlanta Constitution, July 6, 1934.
Louisville, Georgia, Atlanta Constitution, July 13,
    1934.
Sardis Church, Hart County, Georgia, Atlanta Consti-
    tution, July 26, 1934.
North Georgia, Atlanta Constitution, August 5, 1934.
Atlanta, Georgia, Atlanta Constitution, August 8,
    1934.
Thomson, Georgia, Atlanta Constitution, August 9,
    1934.
Griffin, Georgia, Atlanta Constitution, August 16,
    1934.
Gainesville, Georgia, Atlanta Constitution, August
    19, 1934.
Decatur, Georgia, Atlanta Constitution, August 21,
    1934.
Manchester, Georgia, Atlanta Constitution, August 24,
    1934.
Rockmart, Georgia, Atlanta Constitution, August 26,
    1934.
Atlanta, Georgia radio, Atlanta Constitution, August
    29, 1934.
Waycross, Georgia, Atlanta Constitution, August 31,
    1934.
Darien, Georgia, Atlanta Constitution, September 1,
    1934.
Savannah, Georgia, Atlanta Constitution, September 1,
    1934.
Macon, Georgia, Atlanta Constitution, September 4,
    1934.
Albany, Georgia, Atlanta Constitution, September 5,
    1934.
Ashburn, Georgia, Atlanta Constitution, September 5,
    1934.
Columbus, Georgia, Atlanta Constitution, September 6,
    1934.
Newnan, Georgia, Atlanta Constitution, September 7,
    1934.
Rome, Georgia, Atlanta Constitution, September 9,

294   Selected Bibliography

1934.
Athens, Georgia, _Atlanta Constitution_, September 10,
    1934.
Atlanta, Georgia, _Atlanta Constitution_, September 12,
    1934.
Gubernatorial Inaugural Address, Atlanta, Georgia;
    Atlanta Constitution, January 17, 1935.

    Campaign for United States Senate in 1935-1936
Murphy, North Carolina, _Atlanta Constitution_, April
    16, 1935.
Washington, D.C., _Atlanta Constitution_, May 8, 1935.
New York City, NBC radio, _Atlanta Constitution_, May
    19, 1935.
University of Chicago, Illinois, _Atlanta Constitu-
    tion_, May 21, 1935.
Providence, Rhode Island Rotary Club, _Atlanta Consti-
    tution_, May 22, 1935.
Speaking Tour of "North and Middle West," _Atlanta
    Constitution_, May 23, 1935.
Canton, Georgia, _Atlanta Constitution_, July 5, 1935.
Macon, Georgia, _Atlanta Constitution_, January 30,
    1936.
McRae, Georgia, _Atlanta Constitution_, July 5, 1936.
Cartersville, Georgia, _Atlanta Constitution_, July 16,
    1936.
Moultrie, Georgia, _Atlanta Constitution_, July 22,
    1936.
Lincolntown, Georgia, _Atlanta Constitution_, July 30,
    1936.
Monroe, Georgia, _Atlanta Constitution_, August 6,
    1936.
Swainsboro, Georgia, _Atlanta Constitution_, August 8,
    1936.
LaGrange, Georgia, _Atlanta Constitution_, August 13,
    1936.
LaFayette, Georgia, _Atlanta Constitution_, August 19,
    1936.
Macon, Georgia, _Atlanta Constitution_, August 21,
    1936.
Nashville, Georgia, _Atlanta Constitution_, August 22,
    1936.
Cairo, Georgia, _Atlanta Constitution_, August 26,
    1936.
Griffin, Georgia, _Atlanta Constitution_, August 27,
    1936.
Royston, Georgia, _Atlanta Constitution_, August 28,
    1936.
Arlington, Georgia, _Atlanta Constitution_, August 29,
    1936.
Austell, Georgia, _Atlanta Constitution_, August 30,
    1936.
Carrollton, Georgia, _Atlanta Constitution_, September

2, 1936.
Savannah, _Atlanta Constitution_, September 5, 1936.
Rome, Georgia, _Atlanta Constitution_, September 9, 1936.

Campaign for United States Senate in 1938
Buford, Georgia, _Atlanta Constitution_, May 20, 1938.
Atlanta, Georgia radio, _Atlanta Constitution_, May 29, 1938.
Dublin, Georgia, _Atlanta Constitution_, July 5, 1938.
Dallas, Georgia, _Atlanta Constitution_, July 21, 1938.
Winder, Georgia, _Atlanta Constitution_, July 22, 1938.
Swainsboro, Georgia, _Atlanta Constitution_, July 24, 1938.
Jesup, Georgia, _Atlanta Constitution_, July 28, 1938.
Danielsville, Georgia, _Atlanta Constitution_, July 30, 1938.
Ellijay, Georgia, _Atlanta Constitution_, July 31, 1938.
Franklin, Georgia, _Atlanta Constitution_, August 3, 1938.
Tifton, Georgia, _Atlanta Constitution_, August 11, 1938.
Griffin, Georgia, _Atlanta Constitution_, August 16, 1938.
Blackshear, Georgia, _Atlanta Constitution_, August 17, 1938.
Quitman, Georgia, _Atlanta Constitution_, August 17, 1938.
Cartersville, Georgia, _Atlanta Constitution_, August 20, 1938.
Jackson, Georgia, _Atlanta Constitution_, August 23, 1938.
Moultrie, Georgia, _Atlanta Constitution_, August 24, 1938.
LaGrange, Georgia, _Atlanta Constitution_, August 25, 1938.
Louisville, Georgia, _Atlanta Constitution_, August 26, 1938.
Jasper, Georgia, _Atlanta Constitution_, August 27, 1938.
Dalton, Georgia, _Atlanta Constitution_, August 27, 1938.
East Point, Georgia, _Atlanta Constitution_, August 28, 1938.
Irwinton, Georgia, _Atlanta Constitution_, August 30, 1938.
Waycross, Georgia, _Atlanta Constitution_, August 31, 1938.
Midway, Georgia, _Atlanta Constitution_, September 2, 1938.
Fort Valley, Georgia, _Atlanta Constitution_, September 3, 1938.

Clarkesville, Georgia, Atlanta Constitution, September 4, 1938.
Columbus, Georgia, Atlanta Constitution, September 7, 1938.
Mt. Vernon, Georgia, Atlanta Constitution, September 8, 1938.
Bainbridge, Georgia, Atlanta Constitution, September 9, 1938.
Commerce, Georgia, Atlanta Constitution, September 10, 1938.
Dublin, Georgia, Atlanta Constitution, September 11, 1938.
Clayton, Georgia, Atlanta Constitution, September 13, 1938.
Forsyth, Georgia, Atlanta Constitution, September 14, 1938.

Gubernatorial Campaign of 1940 and Inaugural Address
Albany, Georgia, Atlanta Constitution, July 5, 1940; Augusta Chronicle, July 5, 1940.
Danville, Georgia, Atlanta Constitution, July 12, 1940.
Atlanta, Georgia radio, Atlanta Constitution, July 20, 1940.
Toccoa, Georgia, Augusta Chronicle, July 24, 1940.
Greensboro, Georgia, Augusta Chronicle, July 24, 1940.
Macon, Georgia, Augusta Chronicle, July 26, 1940.
Warm Springs, Georgia, Augusta Chronicle, July 28, 1940.
Decatur, Georgia, Augusta Chronicle, August 4, 1940.
Gainesville, Georgia, Augusta Chronicle, August 5, 1940.
Vidalia, Georgia, Augusta Chronicle, August 11, 1940.
Georgia Women's Democratic Club, Atlanta [?], Georgia, Atlanta Constitution, August 7, 1940.
Barnesville, Georgia, Augusta Chronicle, August 16, 1940.
Atlanta, Georgia radio, Atlanta Constitution, August 17, 1940.
Eatonton, Georgia, Augusta Chronicle, August 22, 1940.
Carrollton, Georgia, Augusta Chronicle, August 23, 1940.
Atlanta, Georgia, Augusta Chronicle, August 24, 1940.
Fayetteville, Georgia, Augusta Chronicle, August 24, 1940.
Dalton, Georgia, Augusta Chronicle, August 25, 1940.
Jefferson, Georgia, Atlanta Constitution, August 28, 1940.
Atlanta, Georgia, Atlanta Constitution, August 29, 1940; Augusta Chronicle, August 29, 1940.

Swainsboro, Georgia, Atlanta Constitution, August 30,
    1940; Augusta Chronicle, August 30, 1940.
Atlanta, Georgia radio, Augusta Chronicle, August 31,
    1940.
Waycross and Valdosta, Georgia, Atlanta Constitution,
    September 1, 1940.
Eastman, Georgia, Atlanta Constitution, September 4,
    1940.
Fitzgerald and Hawkinsville, Georgia, Atlanta Consti-
    tution, September 8, 1940; Augusta Chronicle,
    September 8, 1940.
Royston, Georgia, Augusta Chronicle, September 5,
    1940.
Moultrie, Georgia, Augusta Chronicle, September 6,
    1940.
Atlanta, Georgia radio, Augusta Chronicle, September
    7, 1940.
Brunswick, Darien, Woodbine, Kingsland, Nahunta, and
    Folkston, Georgia, a "wide swing into southeast
    Georgia," Atlanta Constitution, September 10,
    1940.
Gubernatorial Inaugural Address, Atlanta, Georgia;
    Atlanta Constitution, January 15, 1941.

        As Governor in 1941
Birmingham, Alabama, Atlanta Constitution, on Univer-
    sity System of Georgia Controversy, Atlanta
    Constitution, July 5, 1941.
Atlanta, Georgia radio, on University System of
    Georgia Controversy, Atlanta Constitution, July
    27, 1941.

        Gubernatorial Campaign of 1942
Moultrie, Georgia, Atlanta Journal, July 5, 1942;
    Macon Telegraph and News, July 5, 1942; Augusta
    Chronicle, July 5, 1942.
Atlanta, Georgia radio, Atlanta Journal, July 10,
    1942; Augusta Chronicle, July 11, 1942.
Atlanta, Georgia radio, Atlanta Journal, July 18,
    1942.
Gainesville, Georgia, Macon Telegraph and News, July
    19, 1942; Augusta Chronicle, July 19, 1942.
Statesboro, Georgia, Macon Telegraph and News, July
    29, 1942; Augusta Chronicle, July 28, 1942.
Atlanta, Georgia radio, Macon Telegraph and News,
    August 1, 1942.
Cedartown, Georgia, Macon Telegraph and News, August
    2, 1942.
Greensboro, Georgia, Augusta Chronicle, August 7,
    1942.
Atlanta, Georgia radio, Augusta Chronicle, August 15,
    1942.
Dalton, Georgia, Augusta Chronicle, August 16, 1942.

Marietta, Georgia, <u>Augusta Chronicle</u>, August 23,
    1942.
Jasper, Georgia, <u>Augusta Chronicle</u>, August 25, 1942.
Arlington, Georgia, <u>Augusta Chronicle</u>, August 28,
    1942.
Waycross, Georgia, <u>Macon Telegraph and News</u>, August
    30, 1942.
Columbus, Georgia, <u>Augusta Chronicle</u>, September 6,
    1942.

        Gubernatorial Campaign of 1946
Atlanta, Georgia radio, <u>Atlanta Constitution</u>, May 14,
    1946.
Athens, Georgia, <u>Atlanta Constitution</u>, May 17, 1946.
Lyons, Georgia, <u>Atlanta Constitution</u>, May 19, 1946;
    <u>Atlanta Daily World</u>, May 22, 1946.
Atlanta, Georgia, <u>Atlanta Constitution</u>, May 21, 1946.
Douglas, Georgia, <u>Atlanta Constitution</u>, May 23, 1946.
Thomasville, Georgia, <u>Atlanta Constitution</u>, May 24,
    1946.
Thomaston, Georgia, <u>Atlanta Constitution</u>, May 26,
    1946.
Dublin, Georgia, <u>Atlanta Constitution</u>, May 30, 1946.
Rochelle, Georgia, <u>Atlanta Constitution</u>, June 1,
    1946.
Moultrie, Georgia, <u>Atlanta Constitution</u>, June 2,
    1946.
Greensboro, Georgia, <u>Savannah Morning News</u>,
    June 4, 1946.
Cartersville, Georgia, <u>Atlanta Constitution</u>, June 5,
    1946.
Kingsland, Georgia, <u>Atlanta Constitution</u>, June 7,
    1946.
"Handshaking Tour of Three Rural Counties in South-
    east, Georgia," <u>Atlanta Constitution</u>, June 7,
    1946.
Blackshear, Georgia, <u>Savannah Morning News</u>, June 8,
    1946.
Winder, Georgia, <u>Atlanta Constitution</u>, June 11, 1946.
Elberton and Clarkesville, Georgia, <u>Atlanta Constitu-
    tion</u>, June 12, 1946.
Eatonton and Indian Springs, Georgia, <u>Savannah
    Morning News</u>, June 13, 1946.
Waycross, Georgia, <u>Savannah Morning News</u>, June 14,
    1946.
Summerville, Georgia, <u>Savannah Morning News</u>, June 14,
    1946; <u>Atlanta Constitution</u>, June 16, 1946.
Douglasville, Georgia, <u>Savannah Morning News</u>, June
    18, 1946.
Cleveland, Georgia, <u>Atlanta Constitution</u>, June 19,
    1946.
Savannah, Georgia, <u>Savannah Morning News</u>, June 21,
    1946.

Lawrenceville, Georgia, <u>Atlanta</u> <u>Constitution</u>, June
    23, 1946.
Canton, Georgia, <u>Atlanta</u> <u>Constitution</u>, June 25, 1946;
    <u>Savannah</u> <u>Morning</u> <u>News</u>, June 24, 1946.
Fitzgerald, Georgia, <u>Atlanta</u> <u>Constitution</u>, June 26,
    1946.
Camilla, Georgia, <u>Atlanta</u> <u>Constitution</u>, June 27,
    1946.
Donalsonville, <u>Atlanta</u> <u>Constitution</u>, June 27, 1946.
Statesboro, Georgia, <u>Atlanta</u> <u>Constitution</u>, June 28,
    1946.
Monroe, Georgia, <u>Savannah</u> <u>Morning</u> <u>News</u>, June 29,
    1946.
Rome and Cedartown, Georgia, <u>Atlanta</u> <u>Constitution</u>,
    June 30, 1946; <u>Savannah</u> <u>Morning</u> <u>News</u>, June 30,
    1946.
Gainesville, Georgia, <u>Atlanta</u> <u>Constitution</u>, July 5,
    1946.
Dalton, Georgia, <u>Atlanta</u> <u>Daily</u> <u>World</u>, July 5, 1946.
Griffin, Georgia, <u>Savannah</u> <u>Morning</u> <u>News</u>, July 6,
    1946.
Carrollton, Georgia, <u>Atlanta</u> <u>Constitution</u>, July 7,
    1946; <u>Savannah</u> <u>Morning</u> <u>News</u>, July 7, 1946.
Nashville, Georgia, <u>Savannah</u> <u>Morning</u> <u>News</u>, July 9,
    1946.
LaFayette, Georgia, <u>Savannah</u> <u>Morning</u> <u>News</u>, July 10,
    1946.
Fort Valley, Georgia, <u>Savannah</u> <u>Morning</u> <u>News</u>, July 11,
    1946.
Swainsboro, Georgia, <u>Atlanta</u> <u>Constitution</u>, July 12,
    1946; <u>Savannah</u> <u>Morning</u> <u>News</u>, July 12, 1946.
Baxley, Georgia, <u>Atlanta</u> <u>Constitution</u>, July 12, 1946;
    <u>Savannah</u> <u>Morning</u> <u>News</u>, July 12, 1946.
Cochran, Georgia, <u>Savannah</u> <u>Morning</u> <u>News</u>, July 13,
    1946; <u>Atlanta</u> <u>Constitution</u>, July 13, 1946.
Columbus, Georgia, <u>Savannah</u> <u>Morning</u> <u>News</u>, July 14,
    1946.
Atlanta, Georgia radio addresses, <u>Savannah</u> <u>Morning</u>
    <u>News</u>, July 17, 1946.

Recordings of Talmadge's Speeches
Excerpts on film of inaugural address for governor,
    January 11, 1933, Atlanta, Georgia. WSB
    television collection in Instructional Resources
    Center, University of Georgia, Athens. Record
    40353, Tape Reel 0854.
Excerpts on film of inaugugral address for governor,
    January 17, 1935, Atlanta, Georgia. WSB
    television collection in Instructional Resources
    Center, University of Georgia, Athens. Record
    41261, Tape Reel 0888.
Silent film of speech at outdoor rally; date and
    locale of speech unknown, but models of cars in

film indicate the speech was delivered after 1939.

Campaigning for governor, audio recording of WSB radio speech, Atlanta, Georgia, May 4, 1946. Special Collections Department, Georgia State University, Atlanta, Georgia.

Campaigning for governor, audio recording of WSB radio speech, Columbus, Georgia, July 13, 1946. Special Collections Department, Georgia State University, Atlanta, Georgia.

Index

About the Author

CALVIN M. LOGUE is a professor at the University of Georgia who specializes in the history and criticism of southern discourse. He published essays on southern rhetoric in *Communication Monographs* and *Quarterly Journal of Speech.* He wrote one of the essays in *Oratory in the New South,* and coedited *Oratory of Southern Demagogues* and *A New Diversity in Contemporary Southern Rhetoric.* He contributed essays to *American Orators Before 1900: Critical Studies and Sources* and *American Orators of the Twentieth Century: Critical Studies and Sources.* The Research Foundation of the University of Georgia awarded Logue the Creative Research Medal for published analysis of southern discourse.

Great American Orators

Defender of the Union: The Oratory of Daniel Webster
Craig R. Smith

Harry Emerson Fosdick: Persuasive Preacher
Halford R. Ryan